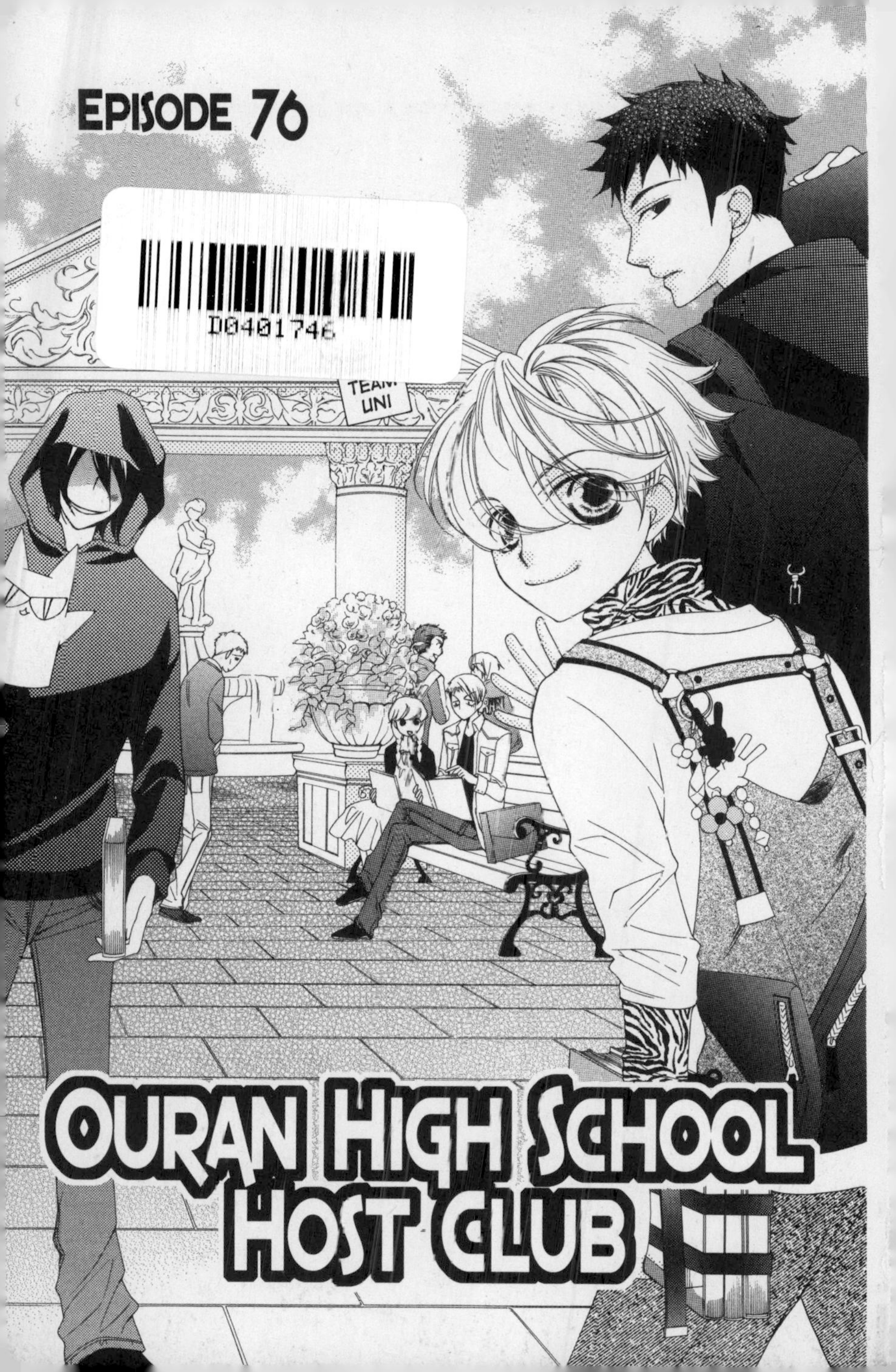
EPISODE 76
TEAM UNI
OURAN HIGH SCHOOL HOST CLUB

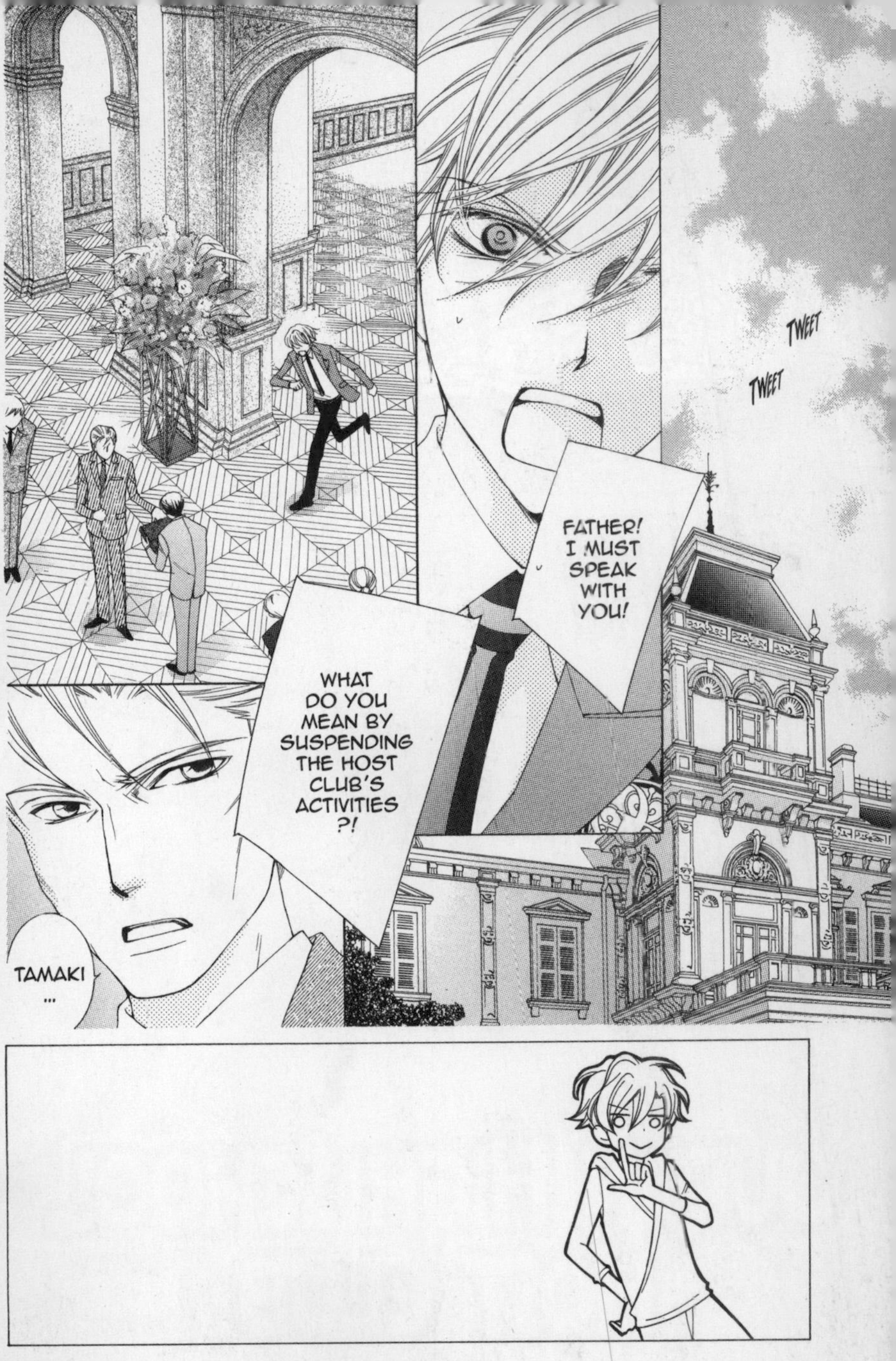
TWEET
TWEET
FATHER! I MUST SPEAK WITH YOU!
WHAT DO YOU MEAN BY SUSPENDING THE HOST CLUB'S ACTIVITIES?!
TAMAKI ...

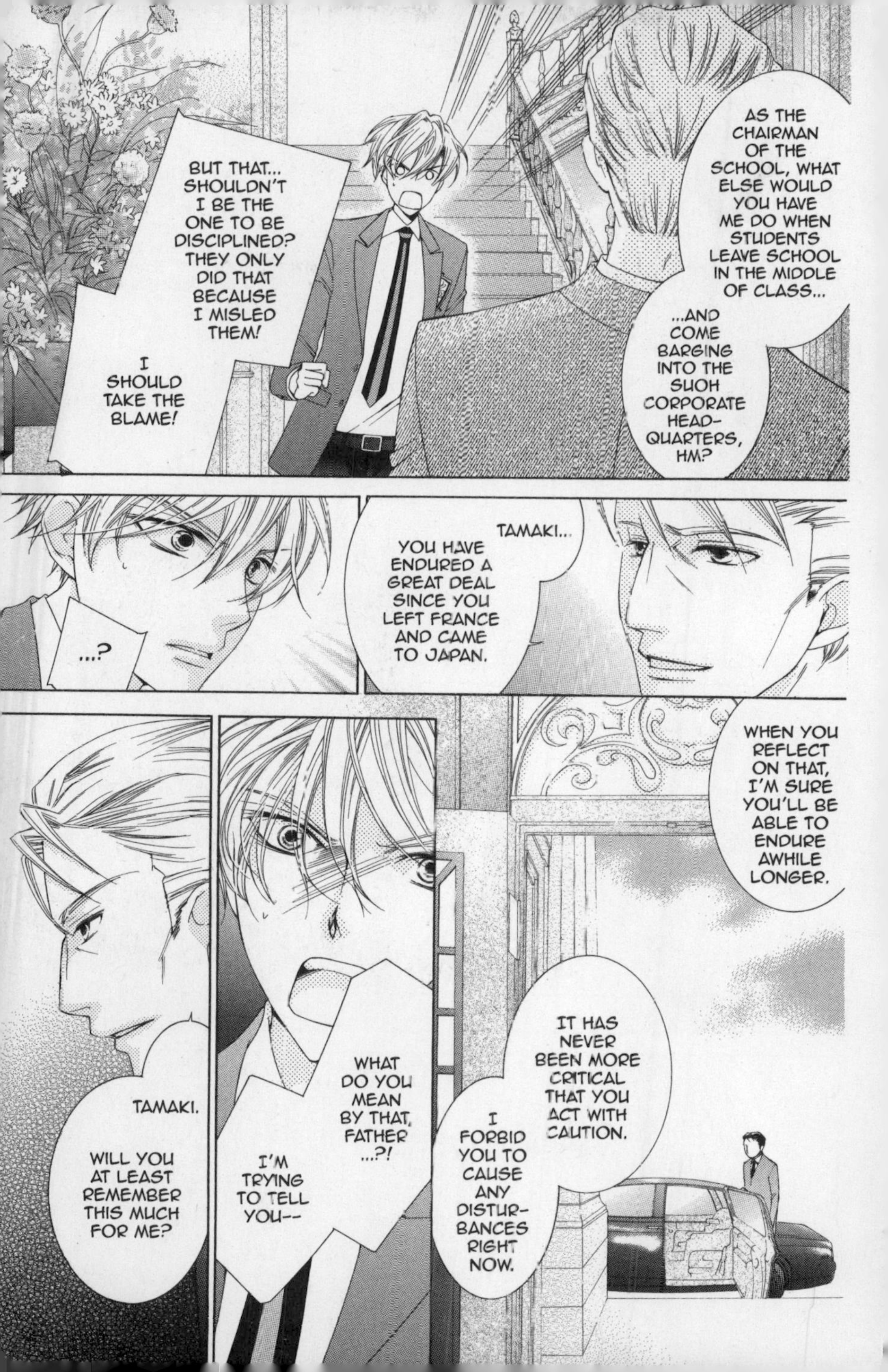
AS THE CHAIRMAN OF THE SCHOOL, WHAT ELSE WOULD YOU HAVE ME DO WHEN STUDENTS LEAVE SCHOOL IN THE MIDDLE OF CLASS...
...AND COME BARGING INTO THE SUOH CORPORATE HEAD-QUARTERS, HM?
BUT THAT... SHOULDN'T I BE THE ONE TO BE DISCIPLINED? THEY ONLY DID THAT BECAUSE I MISLED THEM!
I SHOULD TAKE THE BLAME!
TAMAKI...
YOU HAVE ENDURED A GREAT DEAL SINCE YOU LEFT FRANCE AND CAME TO JAPAN.
...?
WHEN YOU REFLECT ON THAT, I'M SURE YOU'LL BE ABLE TO ENDURE AWHILE LONGER.
IT HAS NEVER BEEN MORE CRITICAL THAT YOU ACT WITH CAUTION.
I FORBID YOU TO CAUSE ANY DISTUR-BANCES RIGHT NOW.
WHAT DO YOU MEAN BY THAT, FATHER ...?!
I'M TRYING TO TELL YOU--
TAMAKI.
WILL YOU AT LEAST REMEMBER THIS MUCH FOR ME?

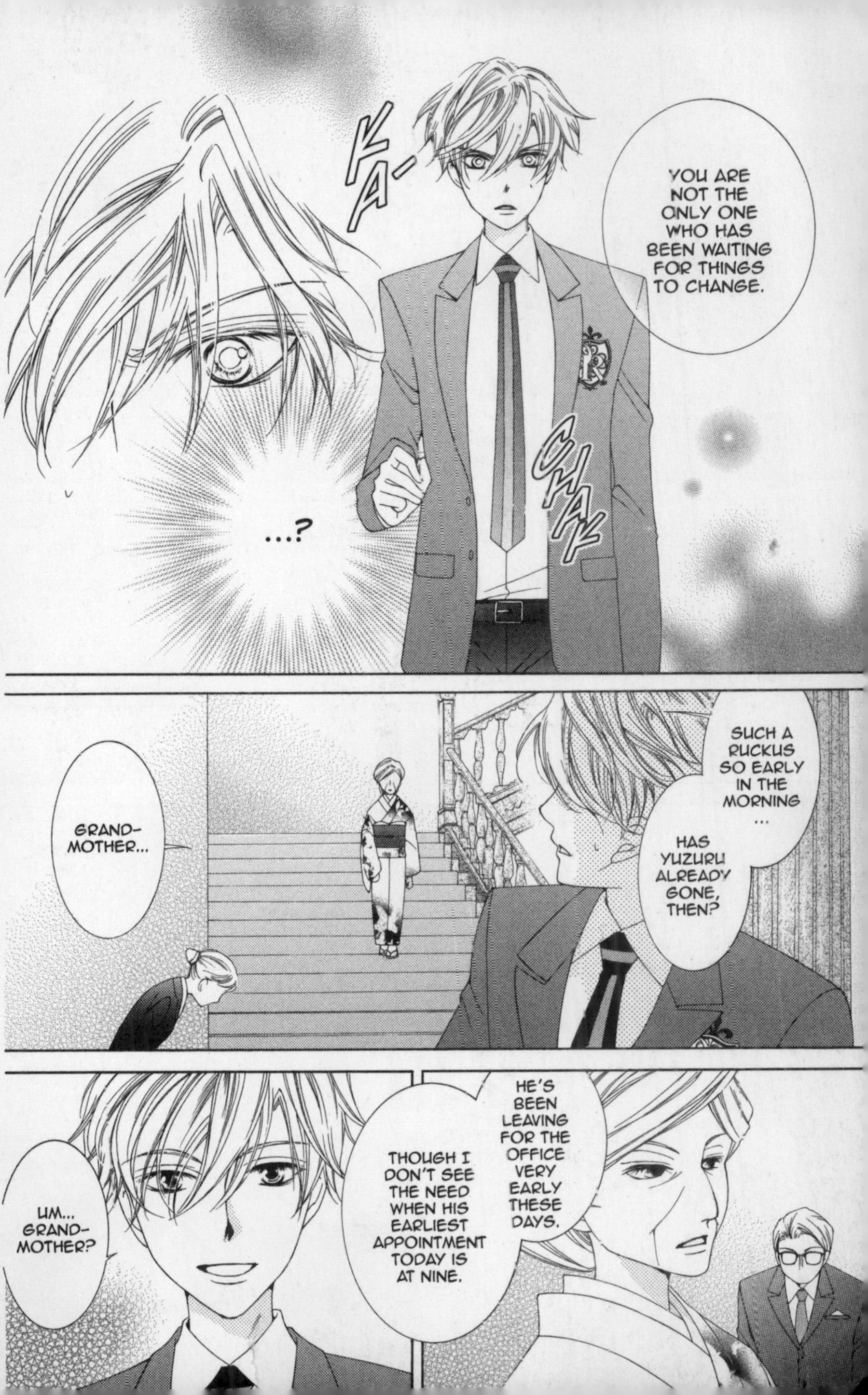
YOU ARE NOT THE ONLY ONE WHO HAS BEEN WAITING FOR THINGS TO CHANGE.
KA-
CHAK
...?
SUCH A RUCKUS SO EARLY IN THE MORNING ...
HAS YUZURU ALREADY GONE, THEN?
GRAND-MOTHER...
HE'S BEEN LEAVING FOR THE OFFICE VERY EARLY THESE DAYS.
THOUGH I DON'T SEE THE NEED WHEN HIS EARLIEST APPOINTMENT TODAY IS AT NINE.
UM... GRAND-MOTHER?

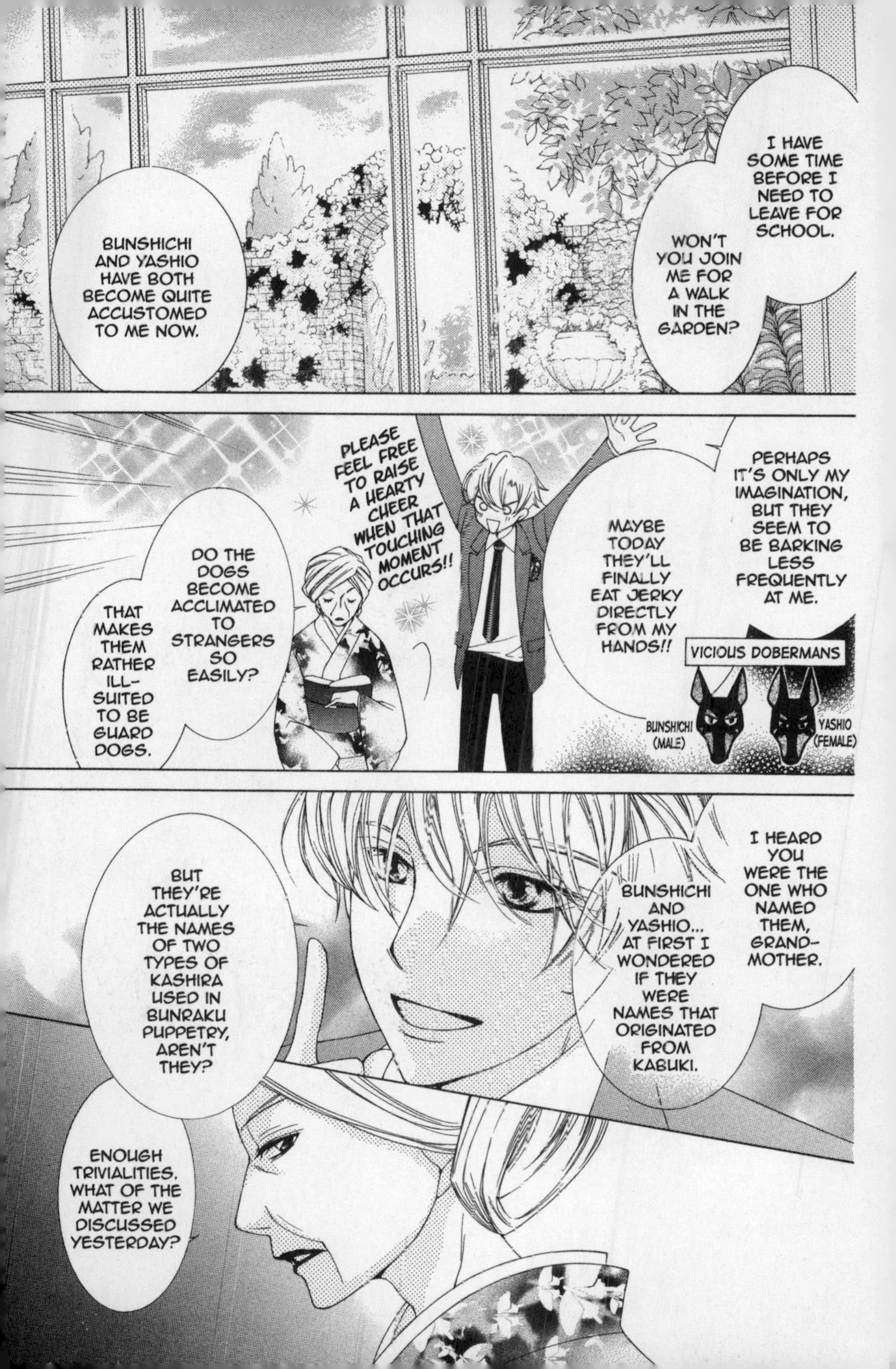
I HAVE SOME TIME BEFORE I NEED TO LEAVE FOR SCHOOL.
WON'T YOU JOIN ME FOR A WALK IN THE GARDEN?
BUNSHICHI AND YASHIO HAVE BOTH BECOME QUITE ACCUSTOMED TO ME NOW.
PERHAPS IT'S ONLY MY IMAGINATION, BUT THEY SEEM TO BE BARKING LESS FREQUENTLY AT ME.
MAYBE TODAY THEY'LL FINALLY EAT JERKY DIRECTLY FROM MY HANDS!!
VICIOUS DOBERMANS
BUNSHICHI (MALE)
YASHIO (FEMALE)
PLEASE FEEL FREE TO RAISE A HEARTY CHEER WHEN THAT TOUCHING MOMENT OCCURS!!
DO THE DOGS BECOME ACCLIMATED TO STRANGERS SO EASILY?
THAT MAKES THEM RATHER ILL-SUITED TO BE GUARD DOGS.
I HEARD YOU WERE THE ONE WHO NAMED THEM, GRANDMOTHER.
BUNSHICHI AND YASHIO... AT FIRST I WONDERED IF THEY WERE NAMES THAT ORIGINATED FROM KABUKI.
BUT THEY'RE ACTUALLY THE NAMES OF TWO TYPES OF KASHIRA USED IN BUNRAKU PUPPETRY, AREN'T THEY?
ENOUGH TRIVIALITIES. WHAT OF THE MATTER WE DISCUSSED YESTERDAY?

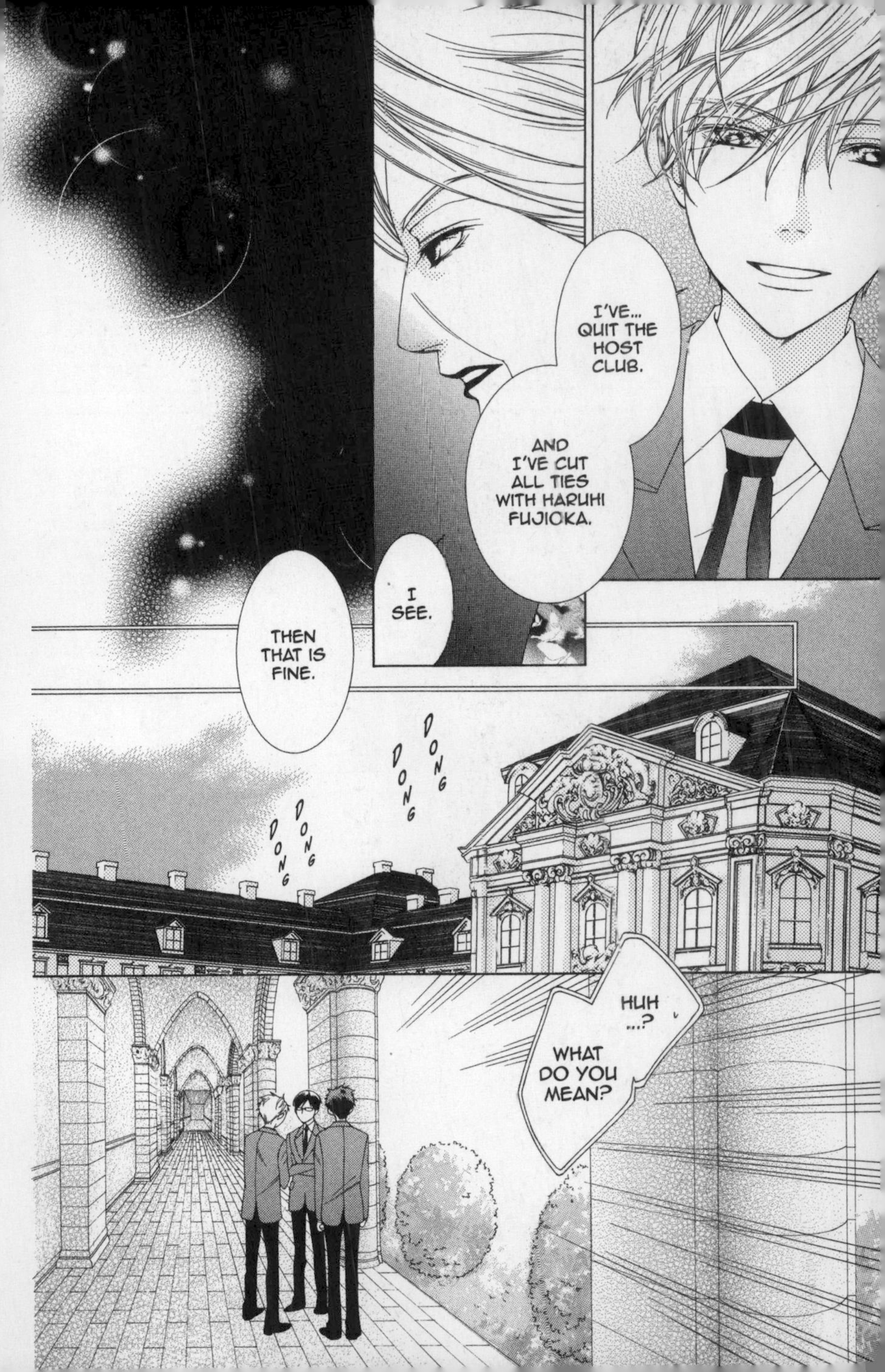
I'VE... QUIT THE HOST CLUB.
AND I'VE CUT ALL TIES WITH HARUHI FUJIOKA.
I SEE.
THEN THAT IS FINE.
DONG DONG
DONG DONG
HUH ...? WHAT DO YOU MEAN?

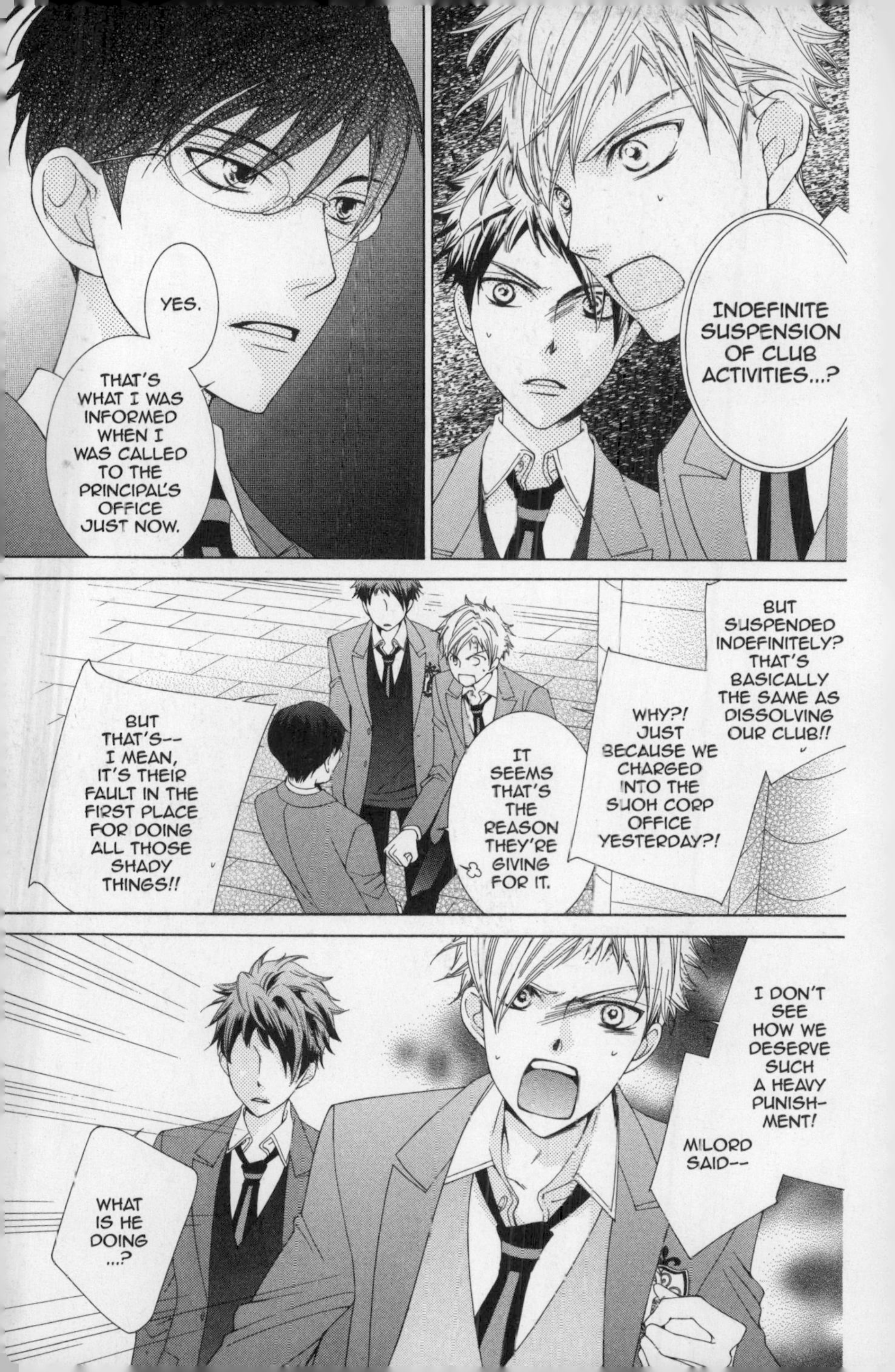
INDEFINITE SUSPENSION OF CLUB ACTIVITIES...?
YES.
THAT'S WHAT I WAS INFORMED WHEN I WAS CALLED TO THE PRINCIPAL'S OFFICE JUST NOW.
BUT SUSPENDED INDEFINITELY? THAT'S BASICALLY THE SAME AS DISSOLVING OUR CLUB!!
WHY?! JUST BECAUSE WE CHARGED INTO THE SUOH CORP OFFICE YESTERDAY?!
IT SEEMS THAT'S THE REASON THEY'RE GIVING FOR IT.
BUT THAT'S-- I MEAN, IT'S THEIR FAULT IN THE FIRST PLACE FOR DOING ALL THOSE SHADY THINGS!!
I DON'T SEE HOW WE DESERVE SUCH A HEAVY PUNISH-MENT!
MILORD SAID--
WHAT IS HE DOING ...?

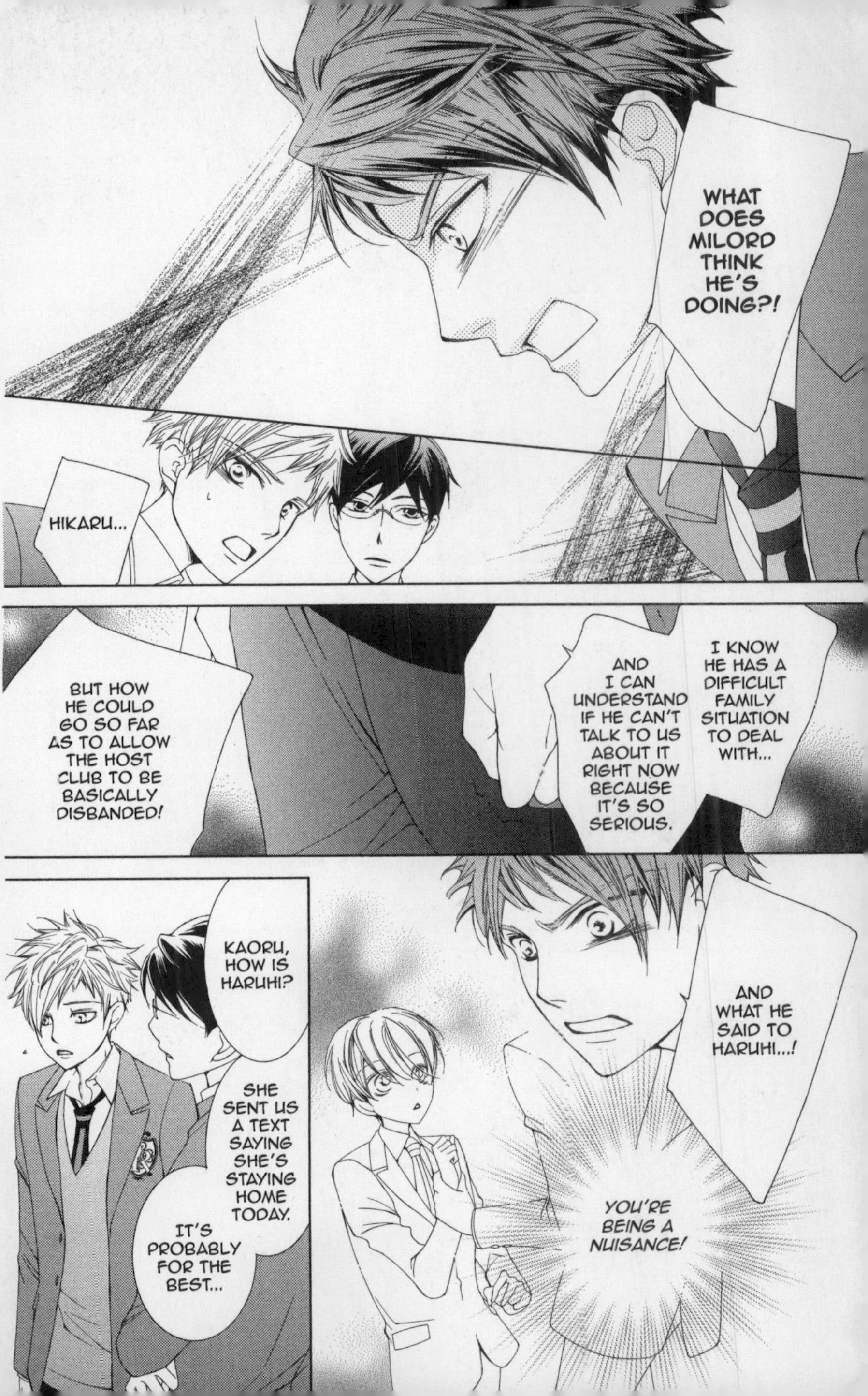
WHAT DOES MILORD THINK HE'S DOING?!
HIKARU...
I KNOW HE HAS A DIFFICULT FAMILY SITUATION TO DEAL WITH...
AND I CAN UNDERSTAND IF HE CAN'T TALK TO US ABOUT IT RIGHT NOW BECAUSE IT'S SO SERIOUS.
BUT HOW HE COULD GO SO FAR AS TO ALLOW THE HOST CLUB TO BE BASICALLY DISBANDED!
AND WHAT HE SAID TO HARUHI...!
YOU'RE BEING A NUISANCE!
KAORU, HOW IS HARUHI?
SHE SENT US A TEXT SAYING SHE'S STAYING HOME TODAY.
IT'S PROBABLY FOR THE BEST...

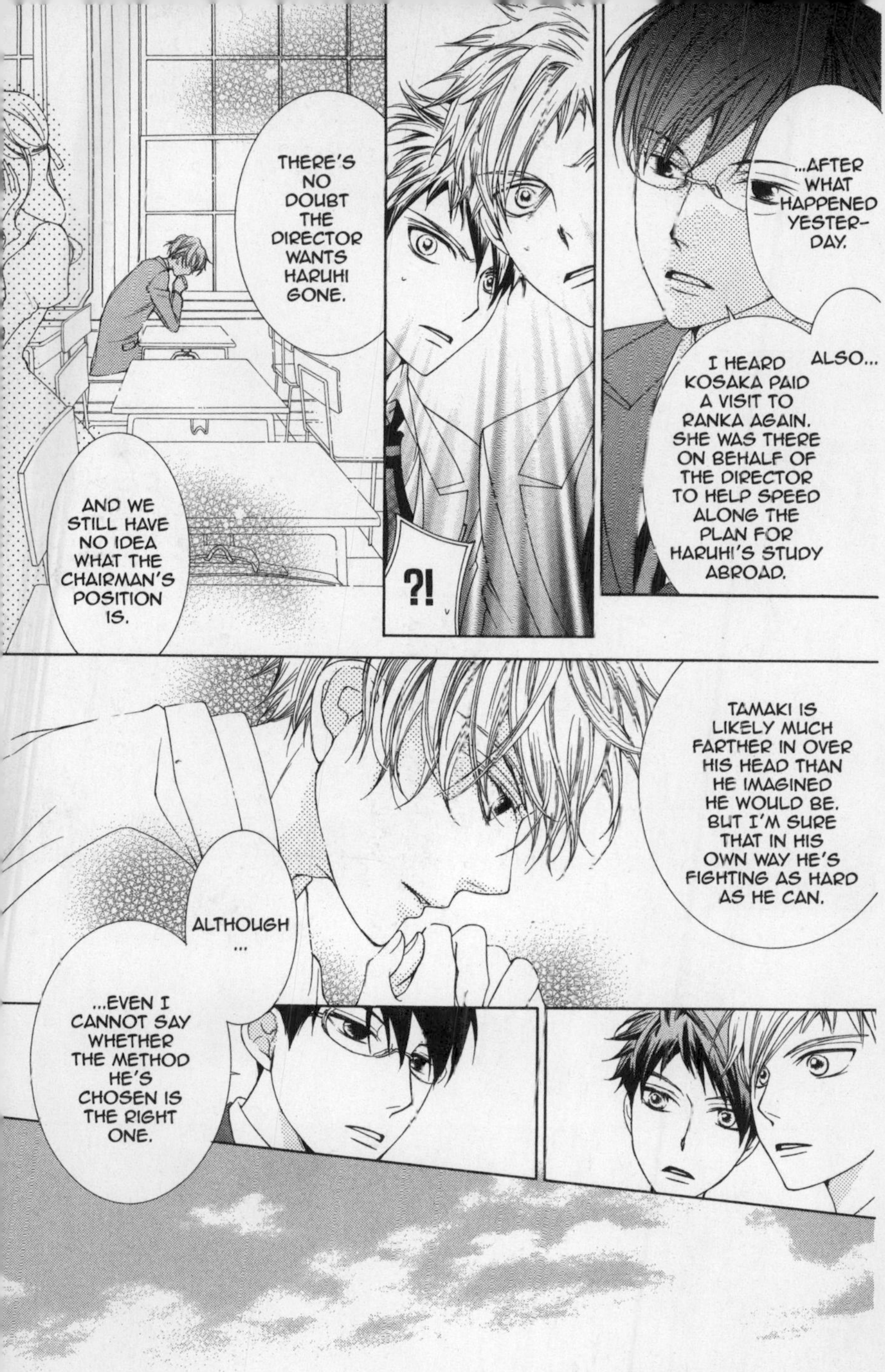
...AFTER WHAT HAPPENED YESTER-DAY.
ALSO...
I HEARD KOSAKA PAID A VISIT TO RANKA AGAIN. SHE WAS THERE ON BEHALF OF THE DIRECTOR TO HELP SPEED ALONG THE PLAN FOR HARUHI'S STUDY ABROAD.
?!
THERE'S NO DOUBT THE DIRECTOR WANTS HARUHI GONE.
AND WE STILL HAVE NO IDEA WHAT THE CHAIRMAN'S POSITION IS.
TAMAKI IS LIKELY MUCH FARTHER IN OVER HIS HEAD THAN HE IMAGINED HE WOULD BE. BUT I'M SURE THAT IN HIS OWN WAY HE'S FIGHTING AS HARD AS HE CAN.
ALTHOUGH...
...EVEN I CANNOT SAY WHETHER THE METHOD HE'S CHOSEN IS THE RIGHT ONE.

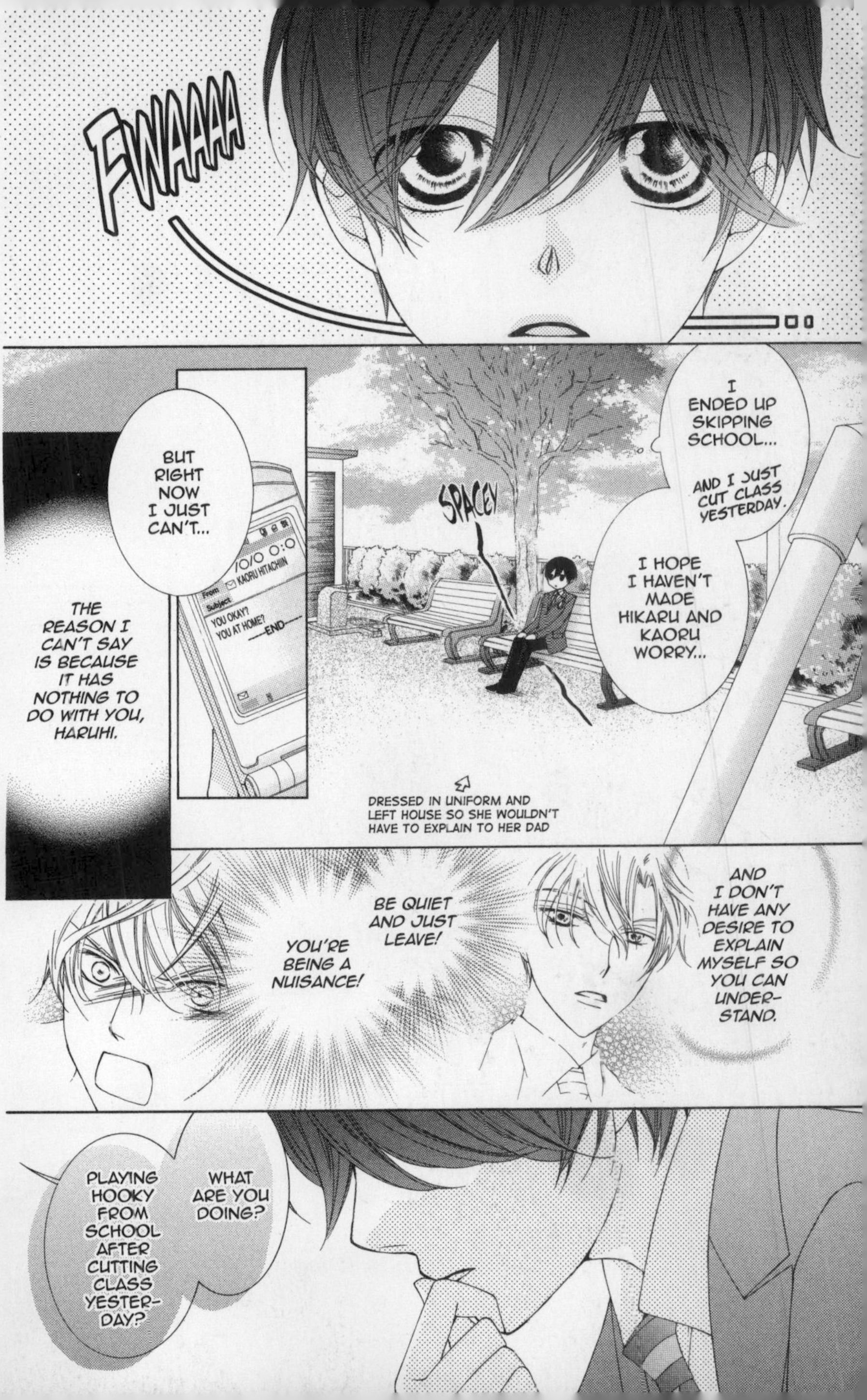
FWAAAA
I ENDED UP SKIPPING SCHOOL...
AND I JUST CUT CLASS YESTERDAY.
I HOPE I HAVEN'T MADE HIKARU AND KAORU WORRY...
SPACEY
DRESSED IN UNIFORM AND LEFT HOUSE SO SHE WOULDN'T HAVE TO EXPLAIN TO HER DAD
BUT RIGHT NOW I JUST CAN'T...
From KAORU HITACHIIN
Subject
YOU OKAY? YOU AT HOME? ——END
THE REASON I CAN'T SAY IS BECAUSE IT HAS NOTHING TO DO WITH YOU, HARUHI.
AND I DON'T HAVE ANY DESIRE TO EXPLAIN MYSELF SO YOU CAN UNDER-STAND.
BE QUIET AND JUST LEAVE!
YOU'RE BEING A NUISANCE!
WHAT ARE YOU DOING?
PLAYING HOOKY FROM SCHOOL AFTER CUTTING CLASS YESTER-DAY?

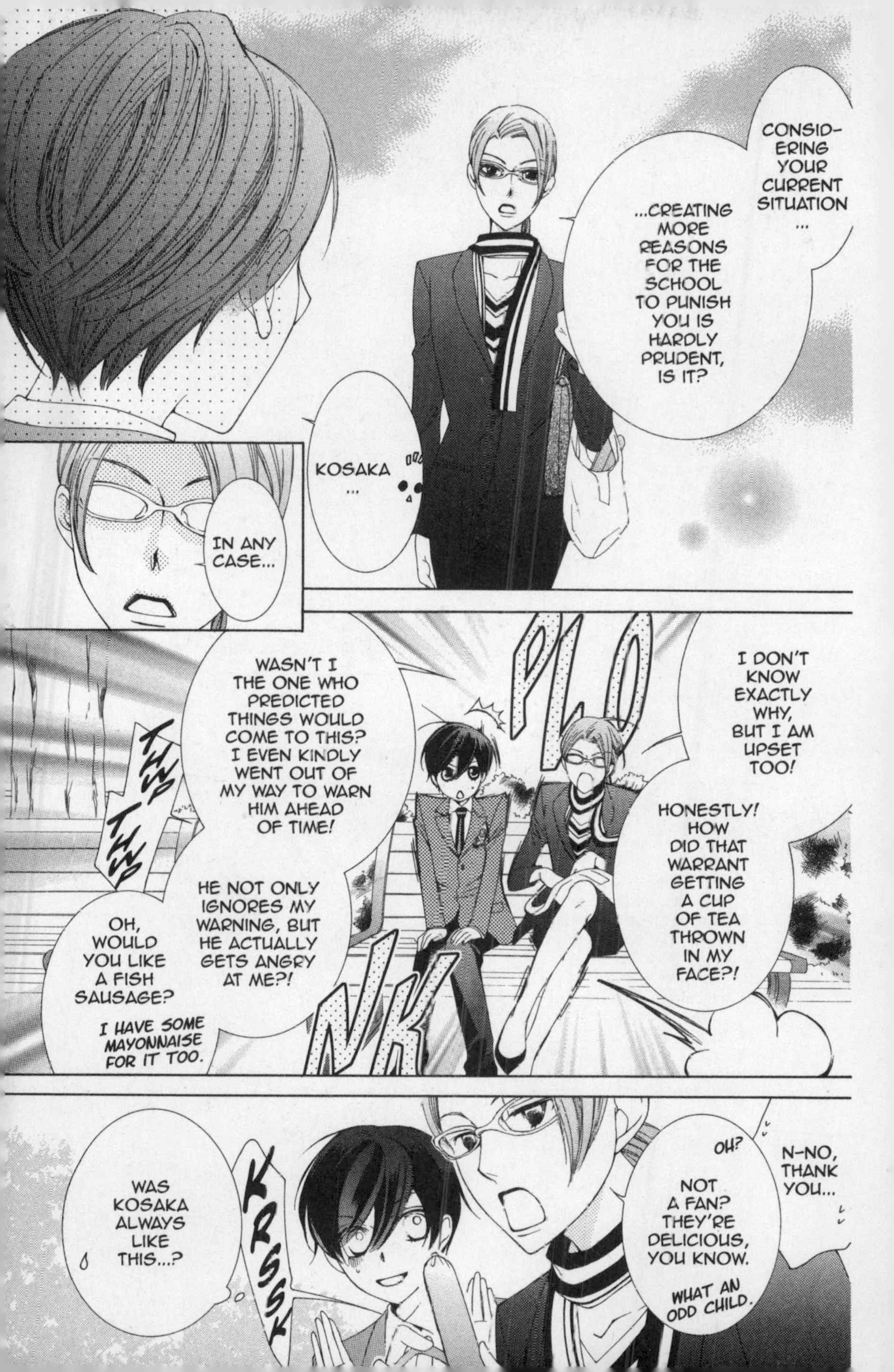
CONSIDERING YOUR CURRENT SITUATION...
...CREATING MORE REASONS FOR THE SCHOOL TO PUNISH YOU IS HARDLY PRUDENT, IS IT?
KOSAKA...
IN ANY CASE...
I DON'T KNOW EXACTLY WHY, BUT I AM UPSET TOO!
HONESTLY! HOW DID THAT WARRANT GETTING A CUP OF TEA THROWN IN MY FACE?!
PLONK
WASN'T I THE ONE WHO PREDICTED THINGS WOULD COME TO THIS? I EVEN KINDLY WENT OUT OF MY WAY TO WARN HIM AHEAD OF TIME!
HE NOT ONLY IGNORES MY WARNING, BUT HE ACTUALLY GETS ANGRY AT ME?!
THWP THWP
OH, WOULD YOU LIKE A FISH SAUSAGE?
I HAVE SOME MAYONNAISE FOR IT TOO.
N-NO, THANK YOU...
OH?
NOT A FAN? THEY'RE DELICIOUS, YOU KNOW.
WHAT AN ODD CHILD.
KRSSK
WAS KOSAKA ALWAYS LIKE THIS...?

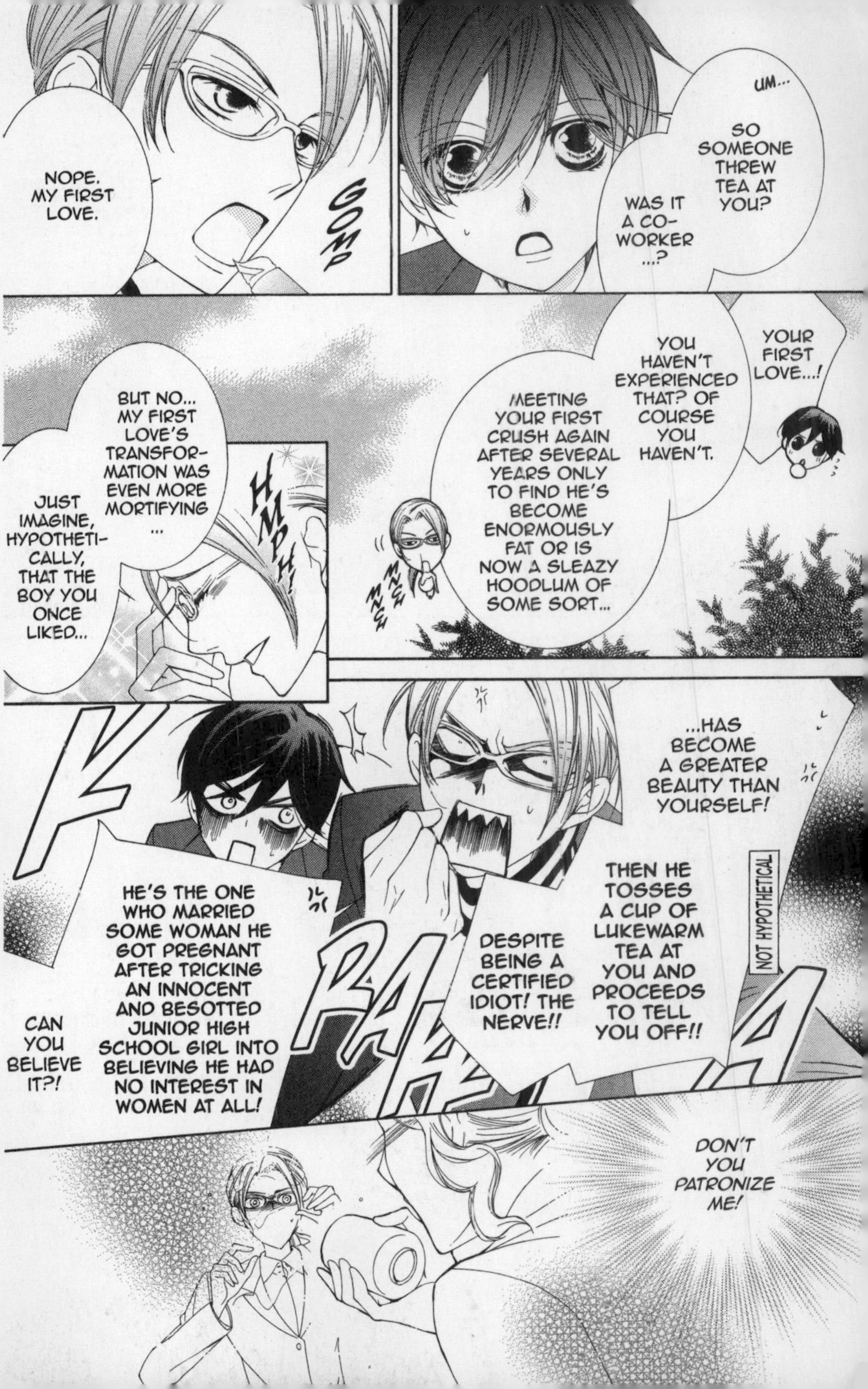
UM...
SO SOMEONE THREW TEA AT YOU?
WAS IT A CO-WORKER ...?
GOMP
NOPE. MY FIRST LOVE.
YOUR FIRST LOVE...!
YOU HAVEN'T EXPERIENCED THAT? OF COURSE YOU HAVEN'T.
MEETING YOUR FIRST CRUSH AGAIN AFTER SEVERAL YEARS ONLY TO FIND HE'S BECOME ENORMOUSLY FAT OR IS NOW A SLEAZY HOODLUM OF SOME SORT...
MNCH MNCH
BUT NO... MY FIRST LOVE'S TRANSFORMATION WAS EVEN MORE MORTIFYING...
HMPH!
JUST IMAGINE, HYPOTHETICALLY, THAT THE BOY YOU ONCE LIKED...
...HAS BECOME A GREATER BEAUTY THAN YOURSELF!
NOT HYPOTHETICAL
THEN HE TOSSES A CUP OF LUKEWARM TEA AT YOU AND PROCEEDS TO TELL YOU OFF!!
DESPITE BEING A CERTIFIED IDIOT! THE NERVE!!
HE'S THE ONE WHO MARRIED SOME WOMAN HE GOT PREGNANT AFTER TRICKING AN INNOCENT AND BESOTTED JUNIOR HIGH SCHOOL GIRL INTO BELIEVING HE HAD NO INTEREST IN WOMEN AT ALL!
CAN YOU BELIEVE IT?!
DON'T YOU PATRONIZE ME!

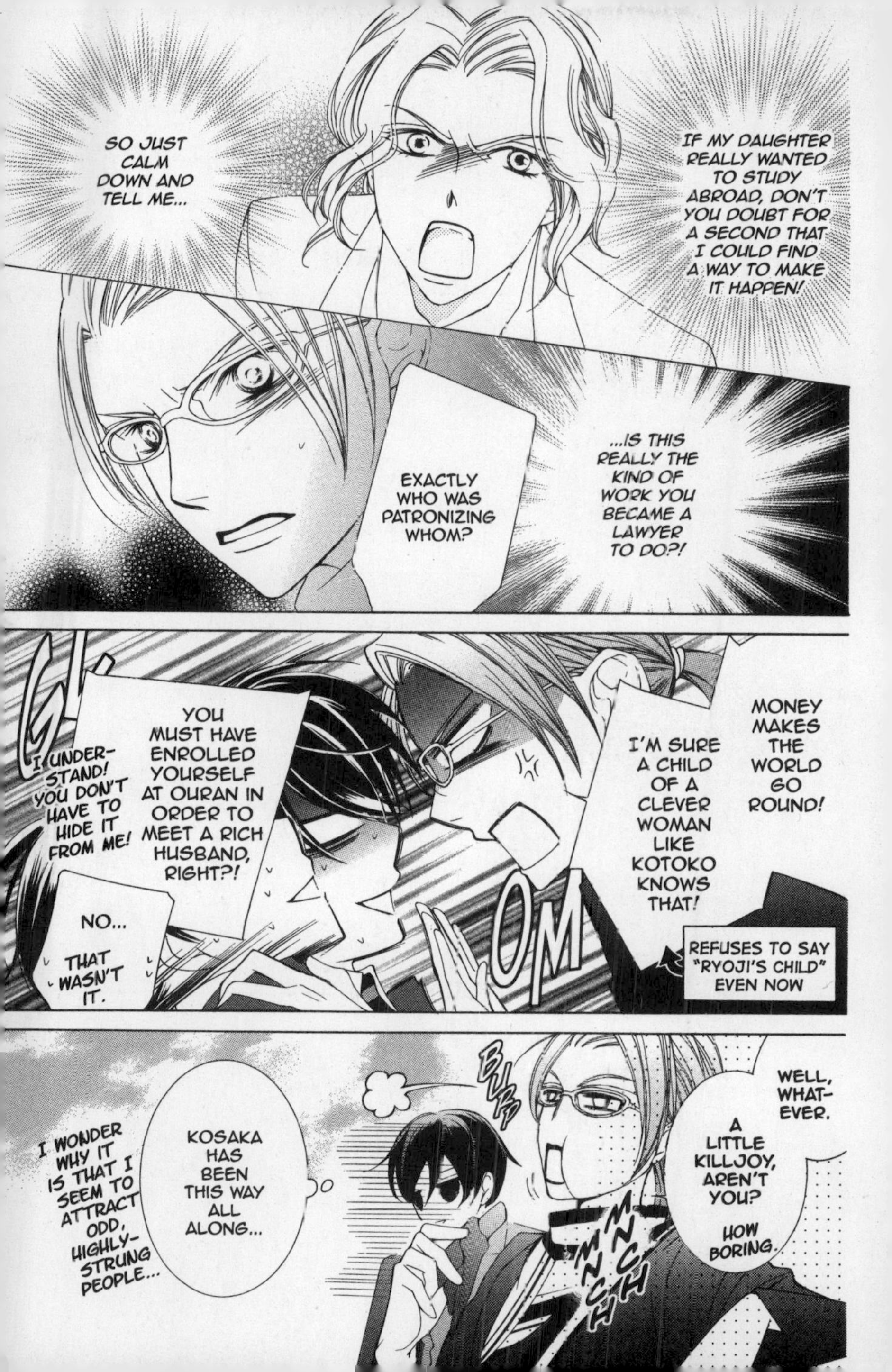
IF MY DAUGHTER REALLY WANTED TO STUDY ABROAD, DON'T YOU DOUBT FOR A SECOND THAT I COULD FIND A WAY TO MAKE IT HAPPEN!
SO JUST CALM DOWN AND TELL ME...
...IS THIS REALLY THE KIND OF WORK YOU BECAME A LAWYER TO DO?!
EXACTLY WHO WAS PATRONIZING WHOM?
MONEY MAKES THE WORLD GO ROUND!
I'M SURE A CHILD OF A CLEVER WOMAN LIKE KOTOKO KNOWS THAT!
REFUSES TO SAY "RYOJI'S CHILD" EVEN NOW
OM
YOU MUST HAVE ENROLLED YOURSELF AT OURAN IN ORDER TO MEET A RICH HUSBAND, RIGHT?!
I UNDERSTAND! YOU DON'T HAVE TO HIDE IT FROM ME!
GL
NO...
THAT WASN'T IT.
WELL, WHATEVER.
A LITTLE KILLJOY, AREN'T YOU?
HOW BORING.
MNCH MNCH
BURP
KOSAKA HAS BEEN THIS WAY ALL ALONG...
I WONDER WHY IT IS THAT I SEEM TO ATTRACT ODD, HIGHLY-STRUNG PEOPLE...

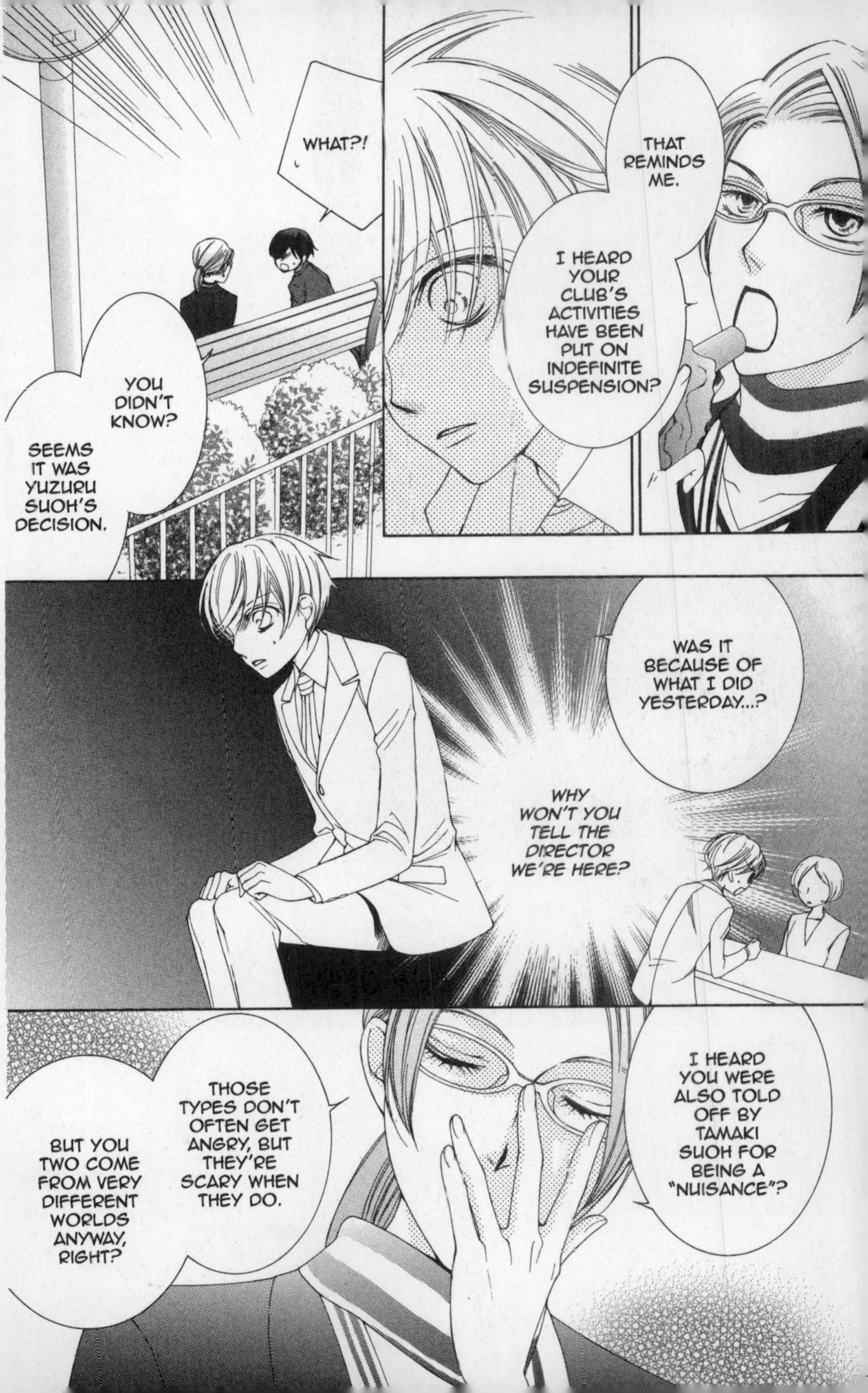
THAT REMINDS ME.
I HEARD YOUR CLUB'S ACTIVITIES HAVE BEEN PUT ON INDEFINITE SUSPENSION?
WHAT?!
YOU DIDN'T KNOW?
SEEMS IT WAS YUZURU SUOH'S DECISION.
WAS IT BECAUSE OF WHAT I DID YESTERDAY...?
WHY WON'T YOU TELL THE DIRECTOR WE'RE HERE?
I HEARD YOU WERE ALSO TOLD OFF BY TAMAKI SUOH FOR BEING A "NUISANCE"?
THOSE TYPES DON'T OFTEN GET ANGRY, BUT THEY'RE SCARY WHEN THEY DO.
BUT YOU TWO COME FROM VERY DIFFERENT WORLDS ANYWAY, RIGHT?

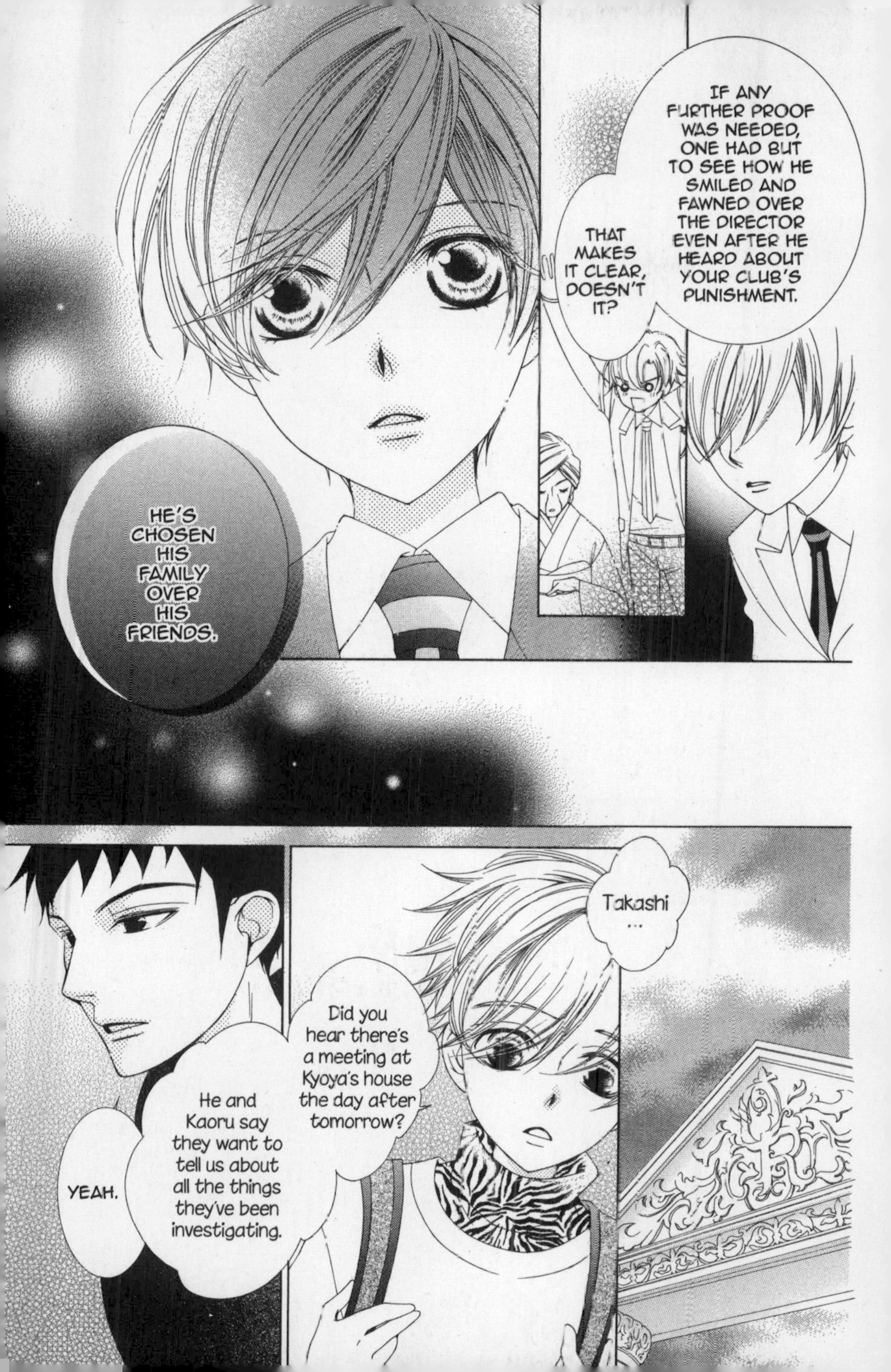
IF ANY FURTHER PROOF WAS NEEDED, ONE HAD BUT TO SEE HOW HE SMILED AND FAWNED OVER THE DIRECTOR EVEN AFTER HE HEARD ABOUT YOUR CLUB'S PUNISHMENT.
THAT MAKES IT CLEAR, DOESN'T IT?
HE'S CHOSEN HIS FAMILY OVER HIS FRIENDS.
Takashi...
Did you hear there's a meeting at Kyoya's house the day after tomorrow?
He and Kaoru say they want to tell us about all the things they've been investigating.
YEAH.

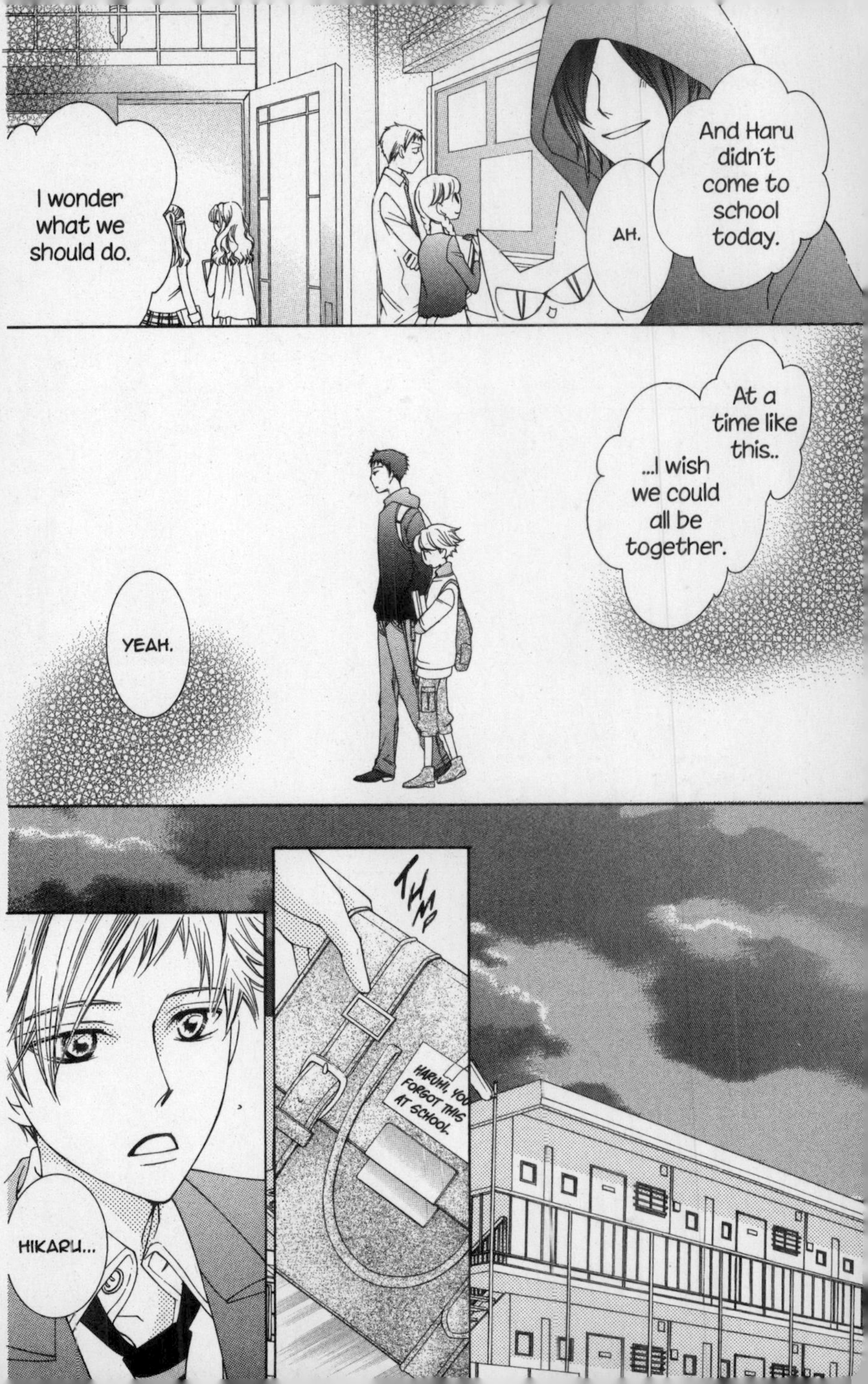

And Haru didn't come to school today.
AH.
I wonder what we should do.
At a time like this..
...I wish we could all be together.
YEAH.
THMP
HARUHI, YOU FORGOT THIS AT SCHOOL.
HIKARU...

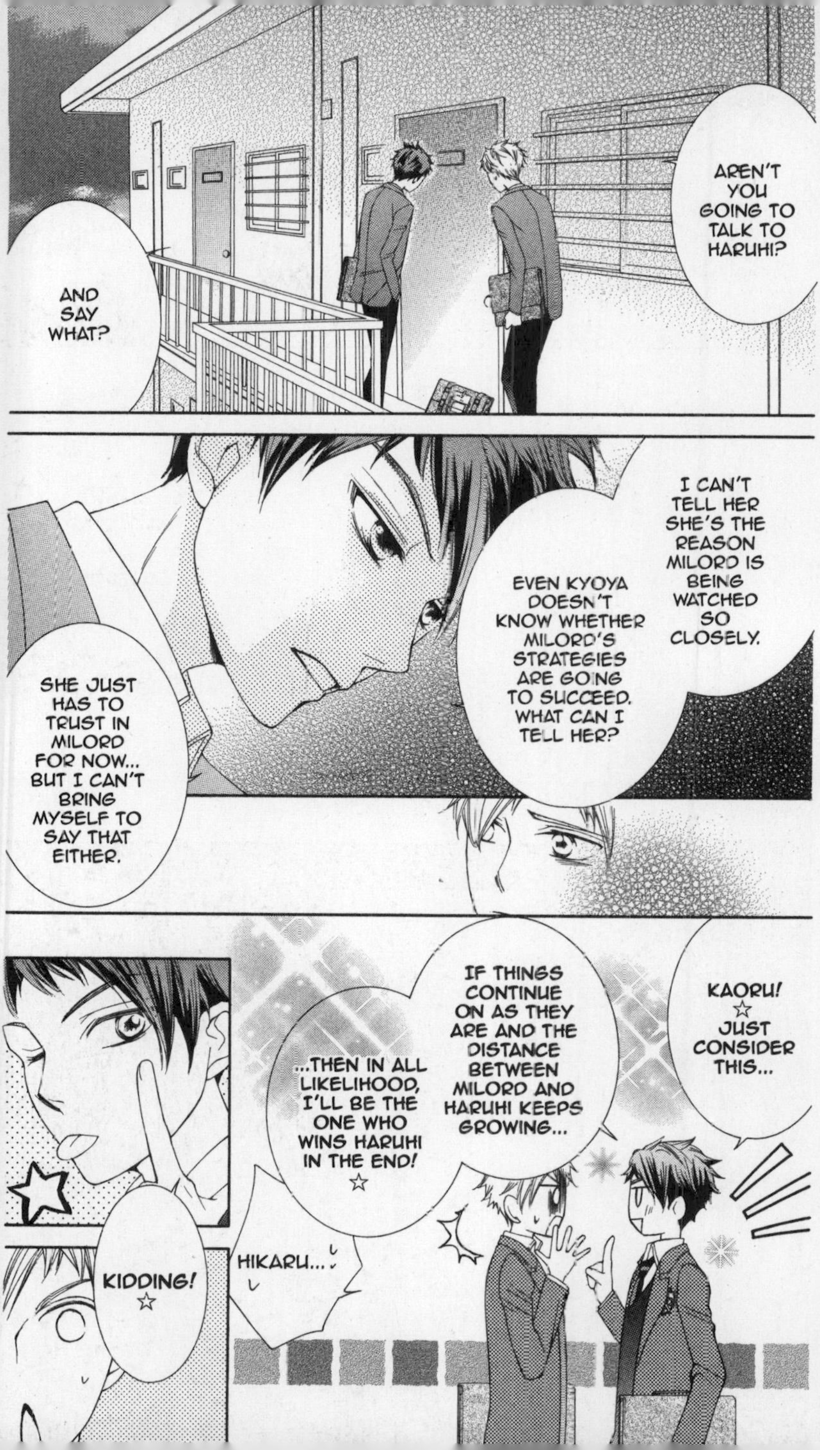
AREN'T YOU GOING TO TALK TO HARUHI?
AND SAY WHAT?
I CAN'T TELL HER SHE'S THE REASON MILORD IS BEING WATCHED SO CLOSELY.
EVEN KYOYA DOESN'T KNOW WHETHER MILORD'S STRATEGIES ARE GOING TO SUCCEED. WHAT CAN I TELL HER?
SHE JUST HAS TO TRUST IN MILORD FOR NOW... BUT I CAN'T BRING MYSELF TO SAY THAT EITHER.
KAORU! ☆ JUST CONSIDER THIS...
IF THINGS CONTINUE ON AS THEY ARE AND THE DISTANCE BETWEEN MILORD AND HARUHI KEEPS GROWING...
...THEN IN ALL LIKELIHOOD, I'LL BE THE ONE WHO WINS HARUHI IN THE END! ☆
KIDDING! ☆
HIKARU...

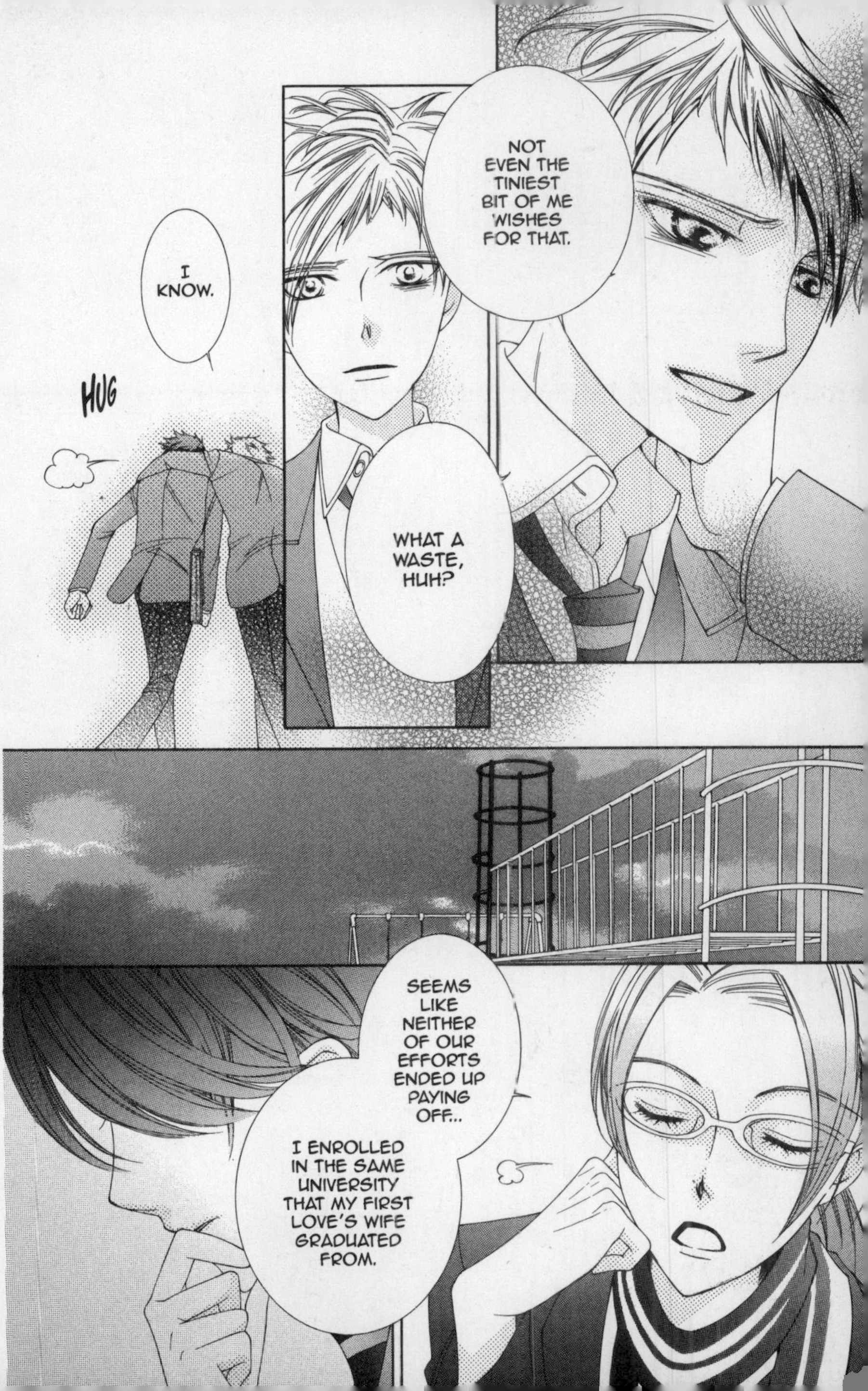
NOT EVEN THE TINIEST BIT OF ME WISHES FOR THAT.
WHAT A WASTE, HUH?
I KNOW.
HUG
SEEMS LIKE NEITHER OF OUR EFFORTS ENDED UP PAYING OFF...
I ENROLLED IN THE SAME UNIVERSITY THAT MY FIRST LOVE'S WIFE GRADUATED FROM.

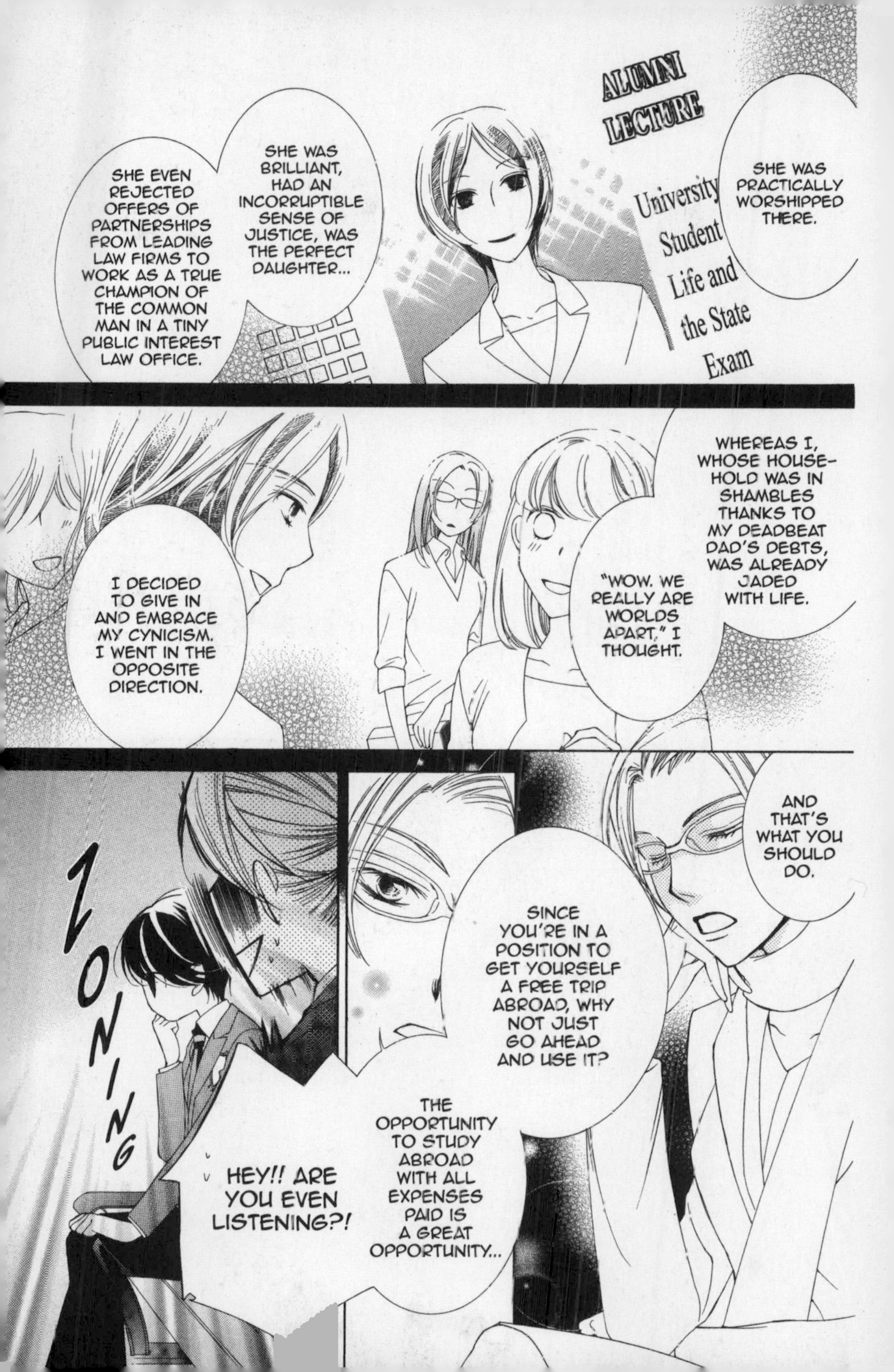
ALUMNI LECTURE
University Student Life and the State Exam
SHE WAS PRACTICALLY WORSHIPPED THERE.
SHE WAS BRILLIANT, HAD AN INCORRUPTIBLE SENSE OF JUSTICE, WAS THE PERFECT DAUGHTER...
SHE EVEN REJECTED OFFERS OF PARTNERSHIPS FROM LEADING LAW FIRMS TO WORK AS A TRUE CHAMPION OF THE COMMON MAN IN A TINY PUBLIC INTEREST LAW OFFICE.
WHEREAS I, WHOSE HOUSE-HOLD WAS IN SHAMBLES THANKS TO MY DEADBEAT DAD'S DEBTS, WAS ALREADY JADED WITH LIFE.
"WOW. WE REALLY ARE WORLDS APART," I THOUGHT.
I DECIDED TO GIVE IN AND EMBRACE MY CYNICISM. I WENT IN THE OPPOSITE DIRECTION.
AND THAT'S WHAT YOU SHOULD DO.
SINCE YOU'RE IN A POSITION TO GET YOURSELF A FREE TRIP ABROAD, WHY NOT JUST GO AHEAD AND USE IT?
THE OPPORTUNITY TO STUDY ABROAD WITH ALL EXPENSES PAID IS A GREAT OPPORTUNITY...
ZONING
HEY!! ARE YOU EVEN LISTENING?!

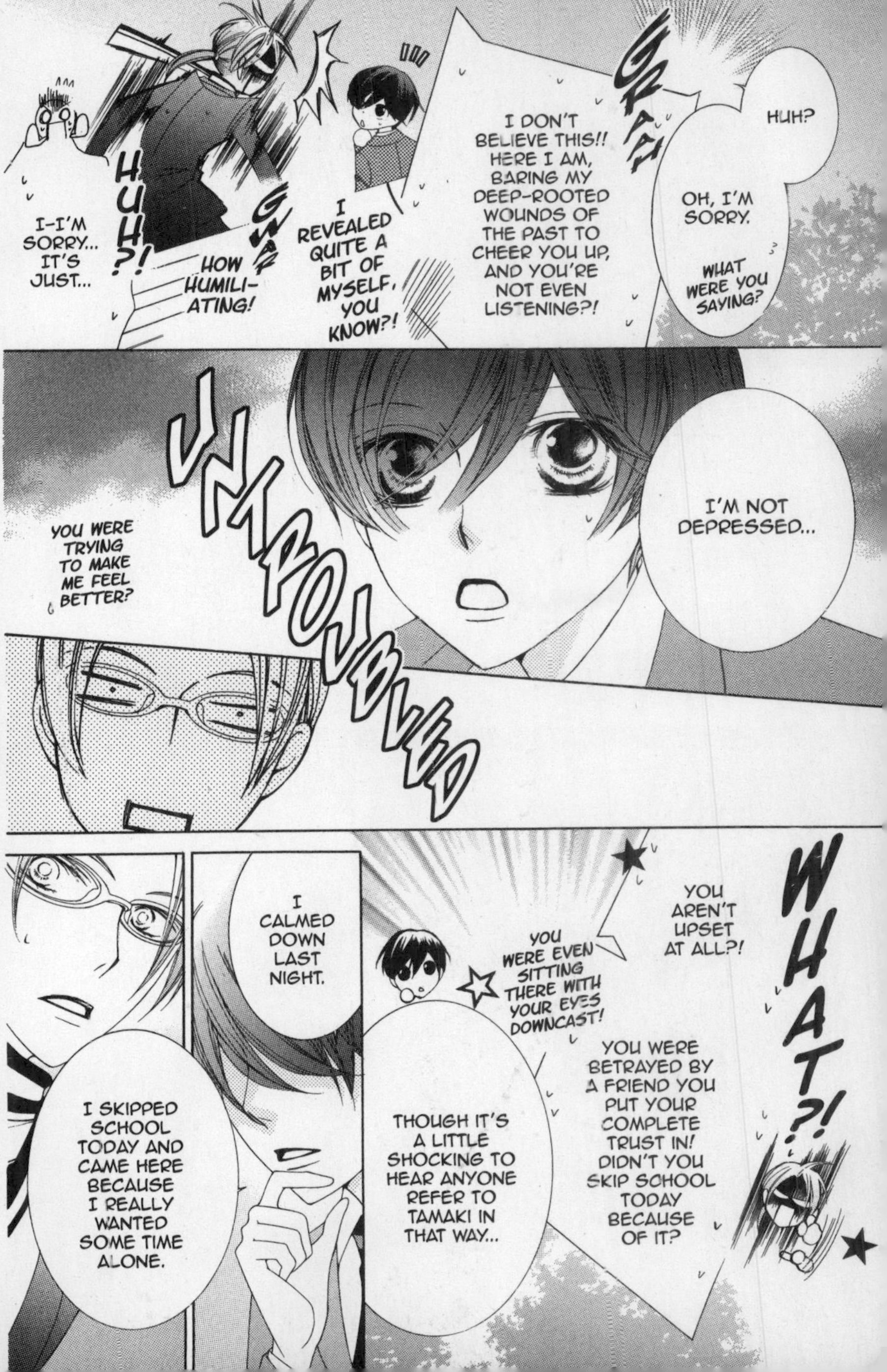
HUH?
OH, I'M SORRY.
WHAT WERE YOU SAYING?
I DON'T BELIEVE THIS!! HERE I AM, BARING MY DEEP-ROOTED WOUNDS OF THE PAST TO CHEER YOU UP, AND YOU'RE NOT EVEN LISTENING?!
I REVEALED QUITE A BIT OF MYSELF, YOU KNOW?!
HOW HUMILIATING!
HUH?!
I-I'M SORRY... IT'S JUST...
I'M NOT DEPRESSED...
YOU WERE TRYING TO MAKE ME FEEL BETTER?
WHAT?!
YOU AREN'T UPSET AT ALL?!
YOU WERE EVEN SITTING THERE WITH YOUR EYES DOWNCAST!
YOU WERE BETRAYED BY A FRIEND YOU PUT YOUR COMPLETE TRUST IN! DIDN'T YOU SKIP SCHOOL TODAY BECAUSE OF IT?
THOUGH IT'S A LITTLE SHOCKING TO HEAR ANYONE REFER TO TAMAKI IN THAT WAY...
I CALMED DOWN LAST NIGHT.
I SKIPPED SCHOOL TODAY AND CAME HERE BECAUSE I REALLY WANTED SOME TIME ALONE.

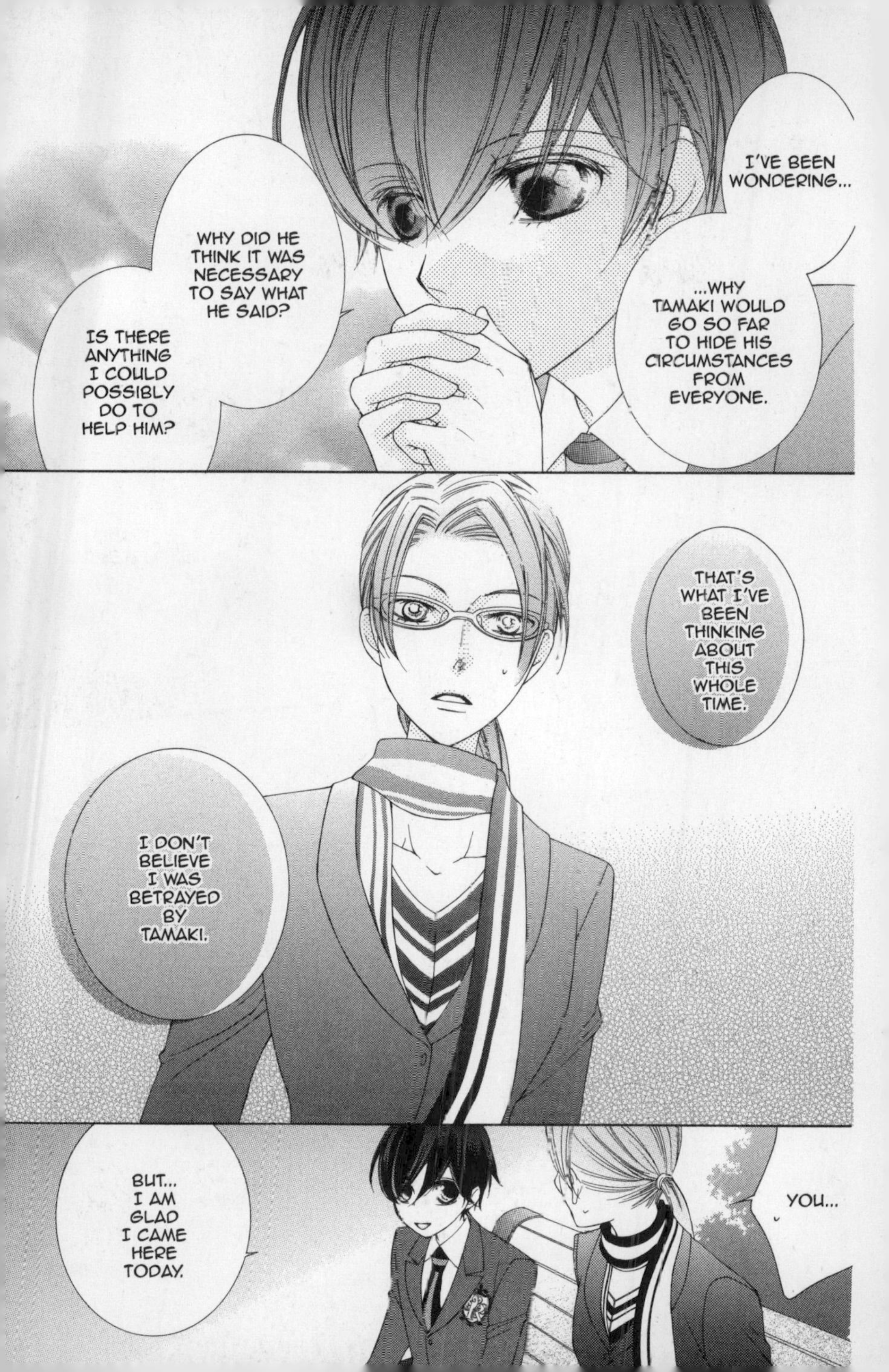
I'VE BEEN WONDERING...
...WHY TAMAKI WOULD GO SO FAR TO HIDE HIS CIRCUMSTANCES FROM EVERYONE.
WHY DID HE THINK IT WAS NECESSARY TO SAY WHAT HE SAID?
IS THERE ANYTHING I COULD POSSIBLY DO TO HELP HIM?
THAT'S WHAT I'VE BEEN THINKING ABOUT THIS WHOLE TIME.
I DON'T BELIEVE I WAS BETRAYED BY TAMAKI.
YOU...
BUT... I AM GLAD I CAME HERE TODAY.

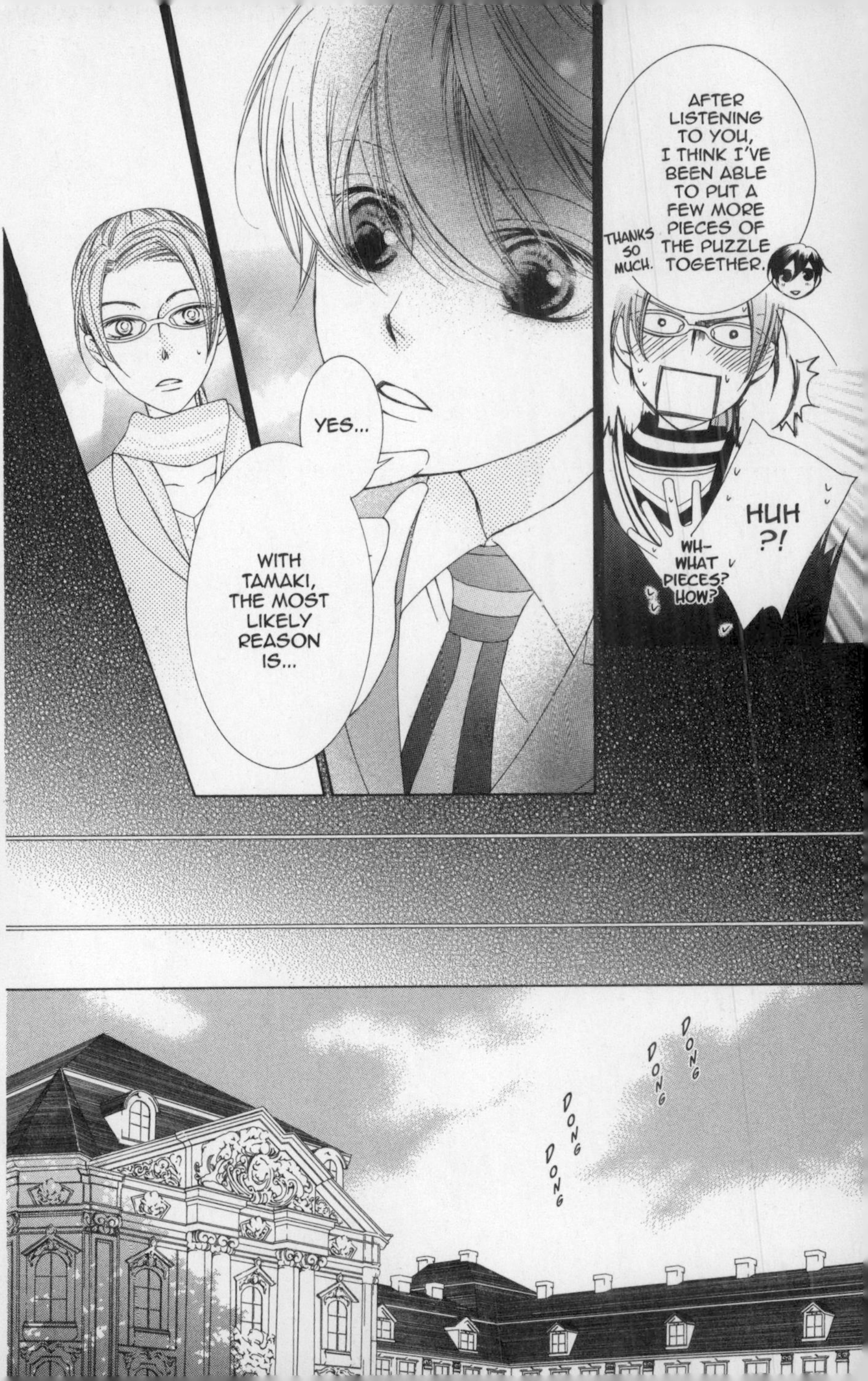
AFTER LISTENING TO YOU, I THINK I'VE BEEN ABLE TO PUT A FEW MORE PIECES OF THE PUZZLE TOGETHER.
THANKS SO MUCH.
HUH?!
WH-WHAT PIECES? HOW?
YES...
WITH TAMAKI, THE MOST LIKELY REASON IS...
DONG DONG
DONG DONG

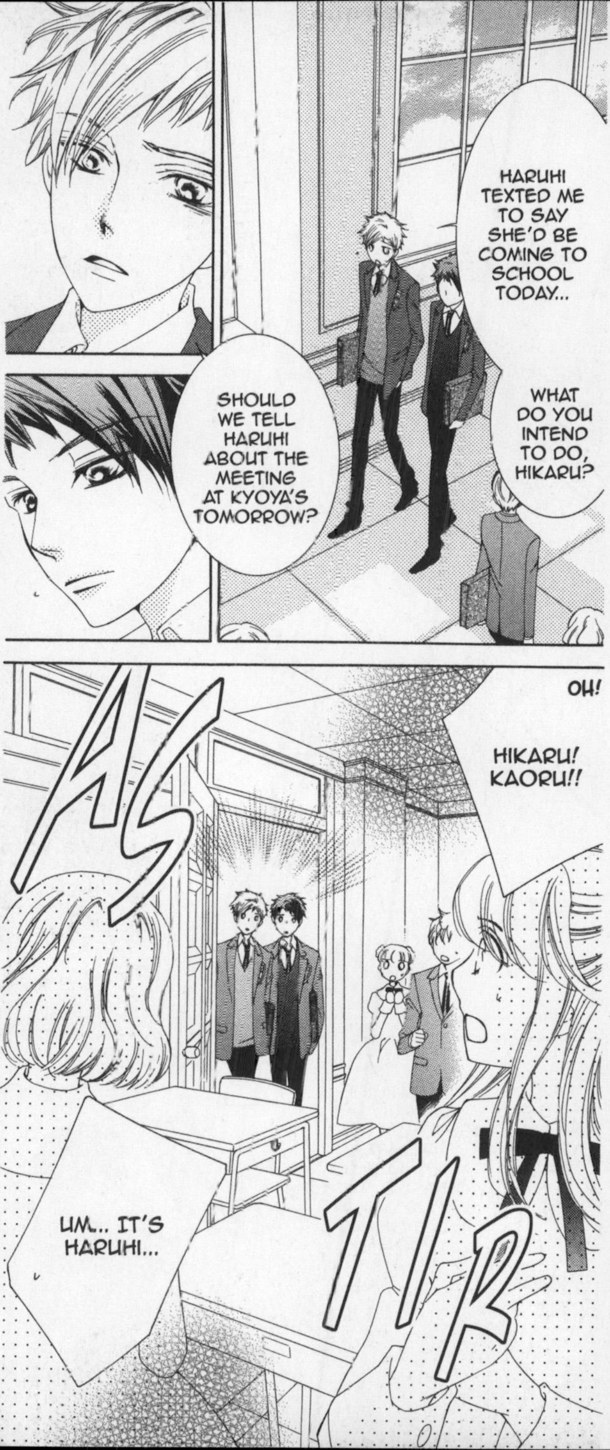
HARUHI TEXTED ME TO SAY SHE'D BE COMING TO SCHOOL TODAY...
SHOULD WE TELL HARUHI ABOUT THE MEETING AT KYOYA'S TOMORROW?
WHAT DO YOU INTEND TO DO, HIKARU?
OH!
HIKARU! KAORU!!
HAS
UM... IT'S HARUHI...
TIR

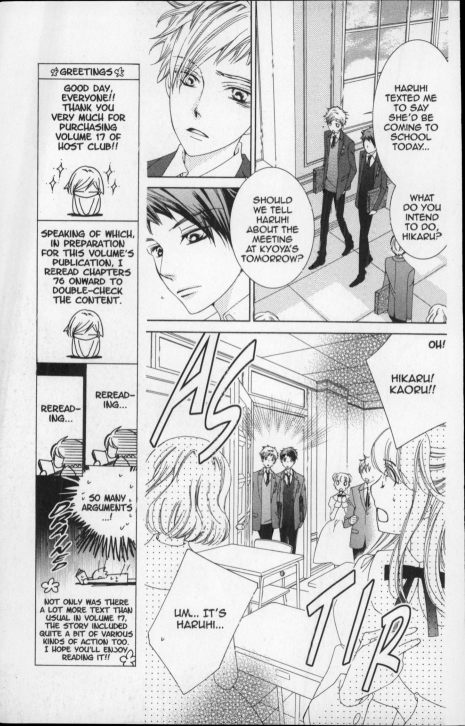

GREETINGS

GOOD DAY, EVERYONE!! THANK YOU VERY MUCH FOR PURCHASING VOLUME 17 OF HOST CLUB!!

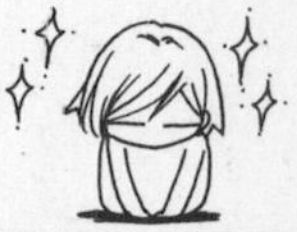

SPEAKING OF WHICH, IN PREPARATION FOR THIS VOLUME'S PUBLICATION, I REREAD CHAPTERS 76 ONWARD TO DOUBLE-CHECK THE CONTENT.

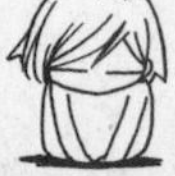

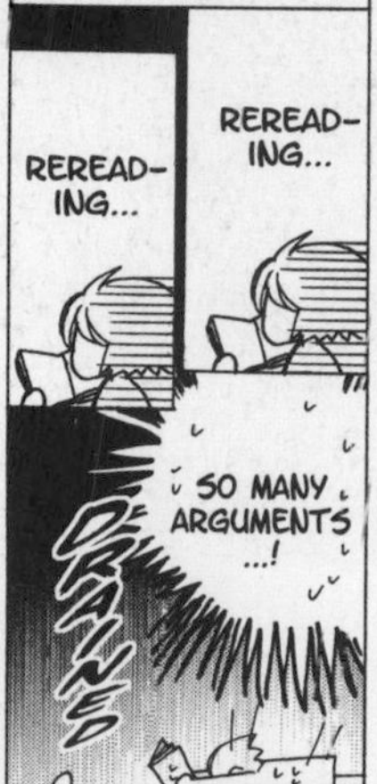
REREADING...
REREADING...
SO MANY ARGUMENTS ...!
DRAINED

NOT ONLY WAS THERE A LOT MORE TEXT THAN USUAL IN VOLUME 17, THE STORY INCLUDED QUITE A BIT OF VARIOUS KINDS OF ACTION TOO. I HOPE YOU'LL ENJOY READING IT!!

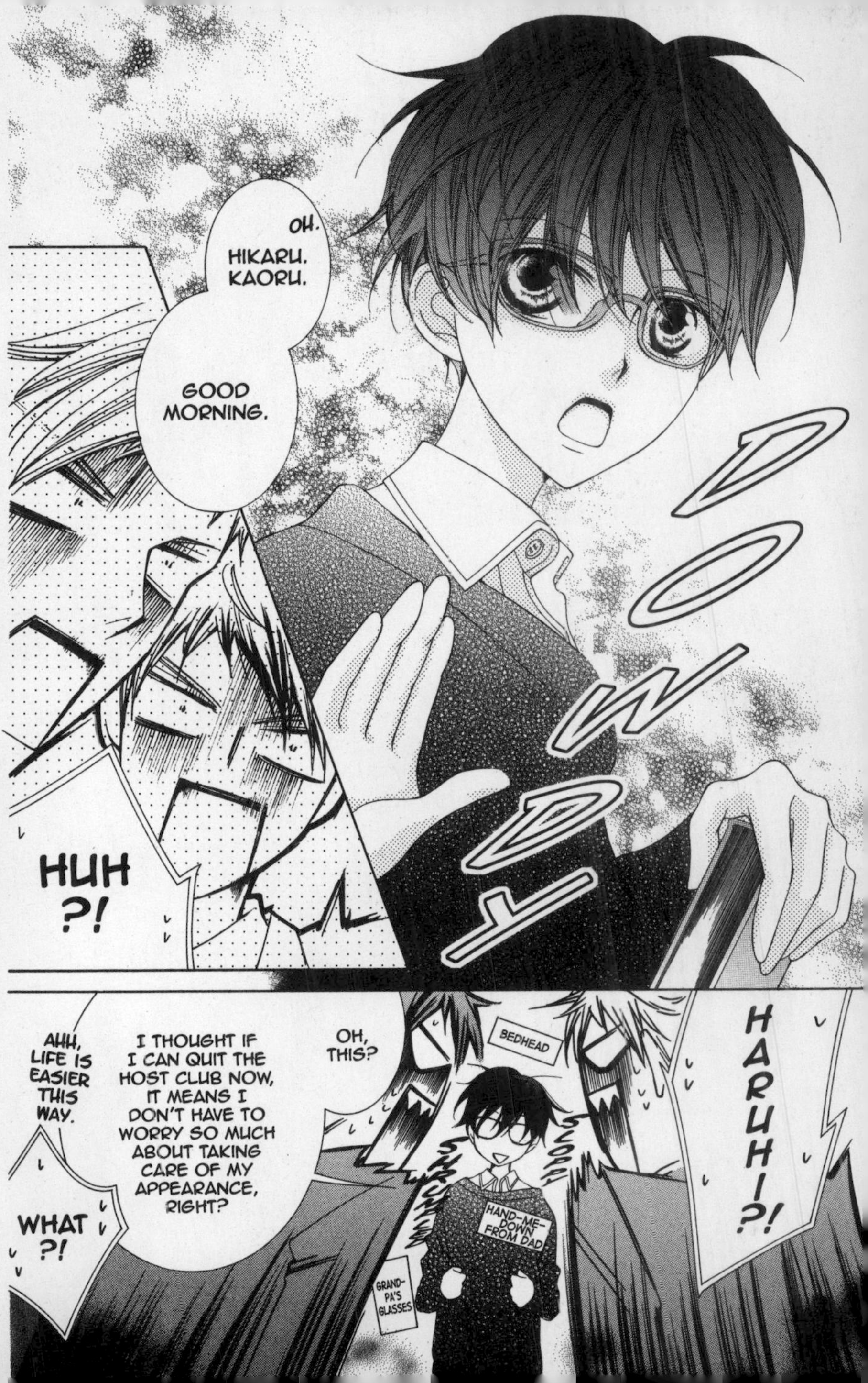
OH. HIKARU. KAORU.
GOOD MORNING.
DOWDY
HUH?!
HARUHI?!
BEDHEAD
HAND-ME-DOWN FROM DAD
GRAND-PA'S GLASSES
OH, THIS?
I THOUGHT IF I CAN QUIT THE HOST CLUB NOW, IT MEANS I DON'T HAVE TO WORRY SO MUCH ABOUT TAKING CARE OF MY APPEARANCE, RIGHT?
AHH, LIFE IS EASIER THIS WAY.
WHAT?!

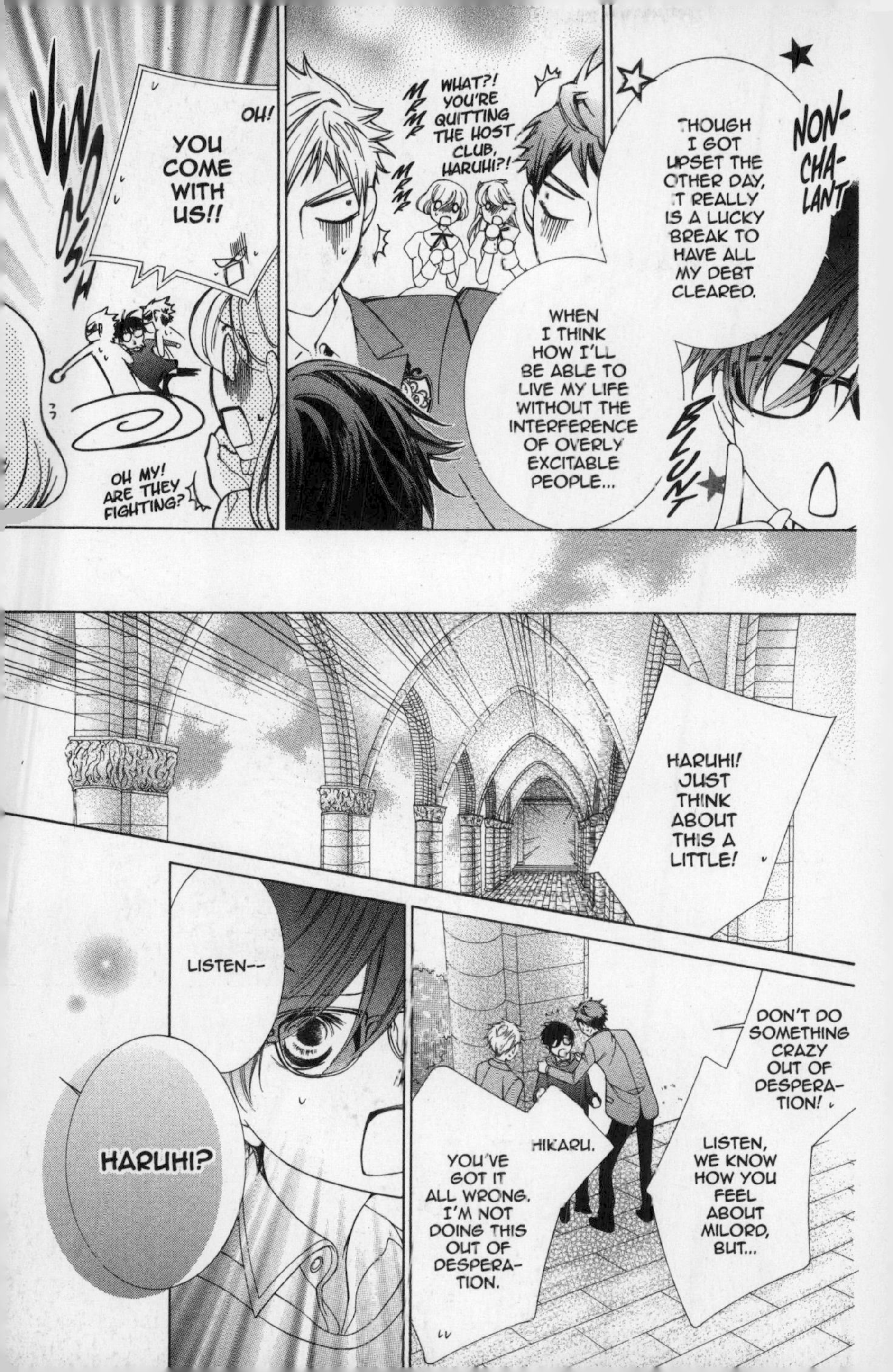
NON-CHALANT
THOUGH I GOT UPSET THE OTHER DAY, IT REALLY IS A LUCKY BREAK TO HAVE ALL MY DEBT CLEARED.
BLUNT
WHEN I THINK HOW I'LL BE ABLE TO LIVE MY LIFE WITHOUT THE INTERFERENCE OF OVERLY EXCITABLE PEOPLE...
WHAT?! YOU'RE QUITTING THE HOST CLUB, HARUHI?!
MRMR
MRMR
OH!
YOU COME WITH US!!
VWOOSH
OH MY! ARE THEY FIGHTING?
HARUHI! JUST THINK ABOUT THIS A LITTLE!
DON'T DO SOMETHING CRAZY OUT OF DESPERATION!
LISTEN, WE KNOW HOW YOU FEEL ABOUT MILORD, BUT...
HIKARU.
YOU'VE GOT IT ALL WRONG. I'M NOT DOING THIS OUT OF DESPERATION.
LISTEN--
HARUHI?

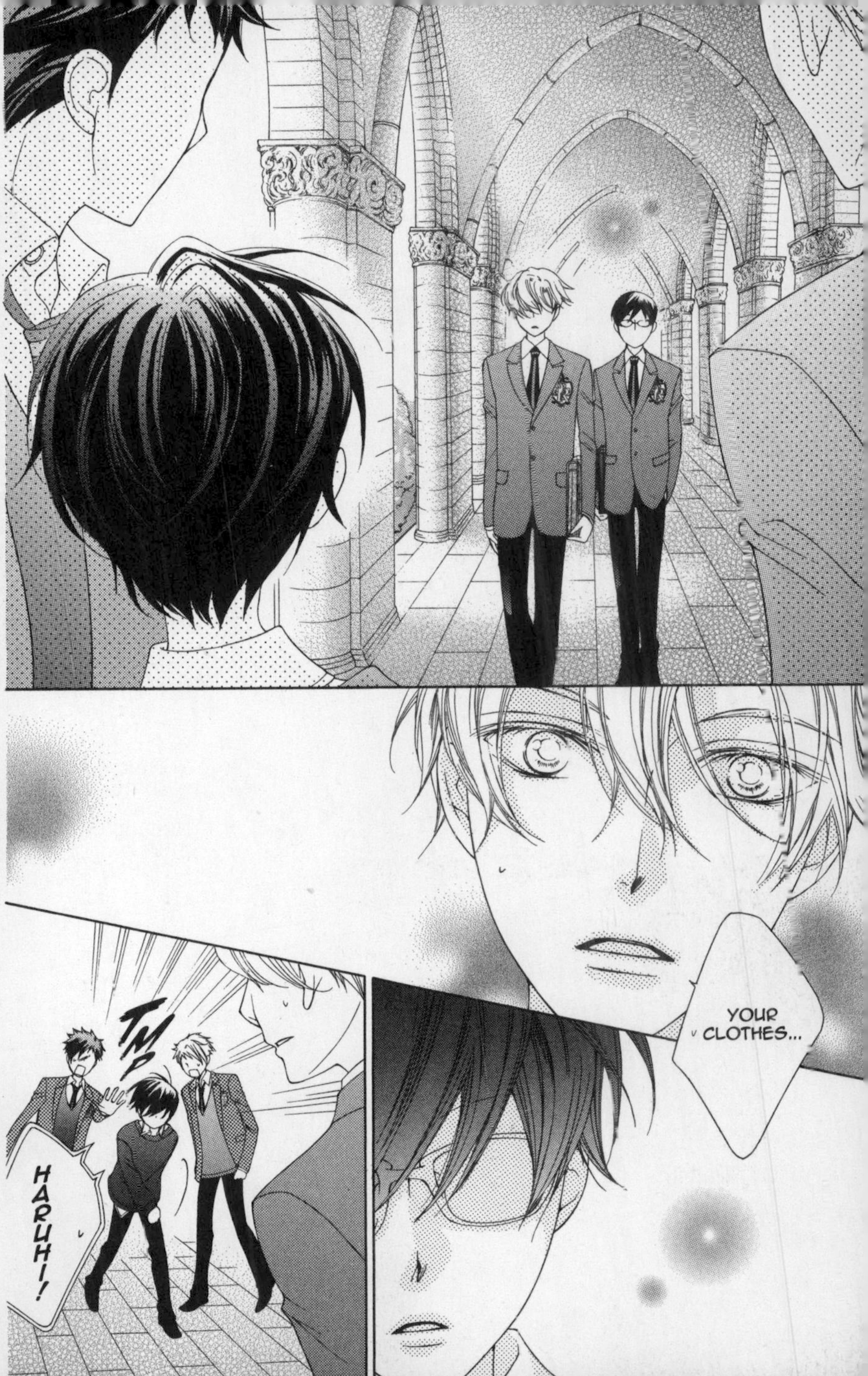
YOUR CLOTHES...
TMP
HARUHI!

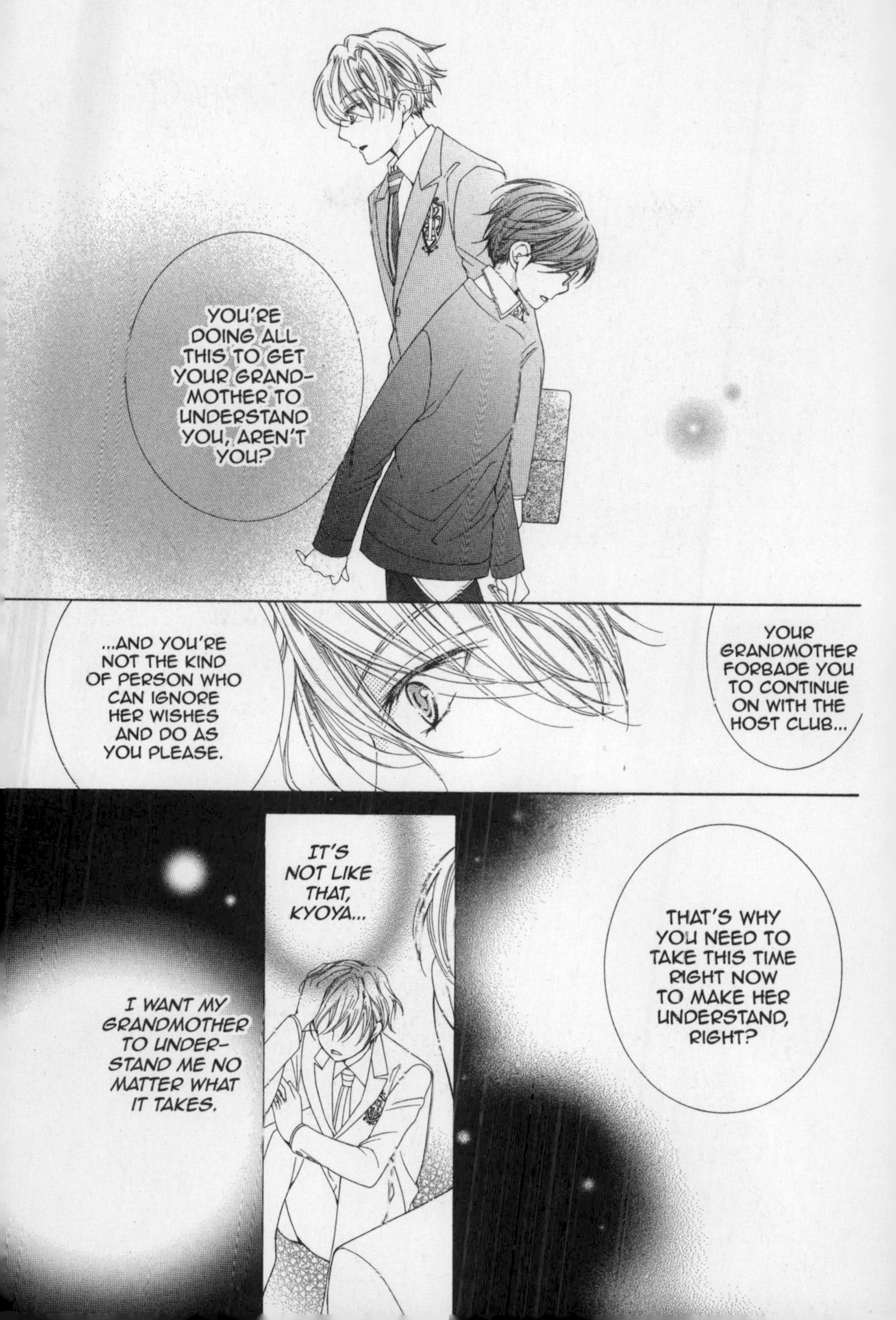
YOU'RE DOING ALL THIS TO GET YOUR GRAND-MOTHER TO UNDERSTAND YOU, AREN'T YOU?
YOUR GRANDMOTHER FORBADE YOU TO CONTINUE ON WITH THE HOST CLUB...
...AND YOU'RE NOT THE KIND OF PERSON WHO CAN IGNORE HER WISHES AND DO AS YOU PLEASE.
THAT'S WHY YOU NEED TO TAKE THIS TIME RIGHT NOW TO MAKE HER UNDERSTAND, RIGHT?
IT'S NOT LIKE THAT, KYOYA...
I WANT MY GRANDMOTHER TO UNDER-STAND ME NO MATTER WHAT IT TAKES.

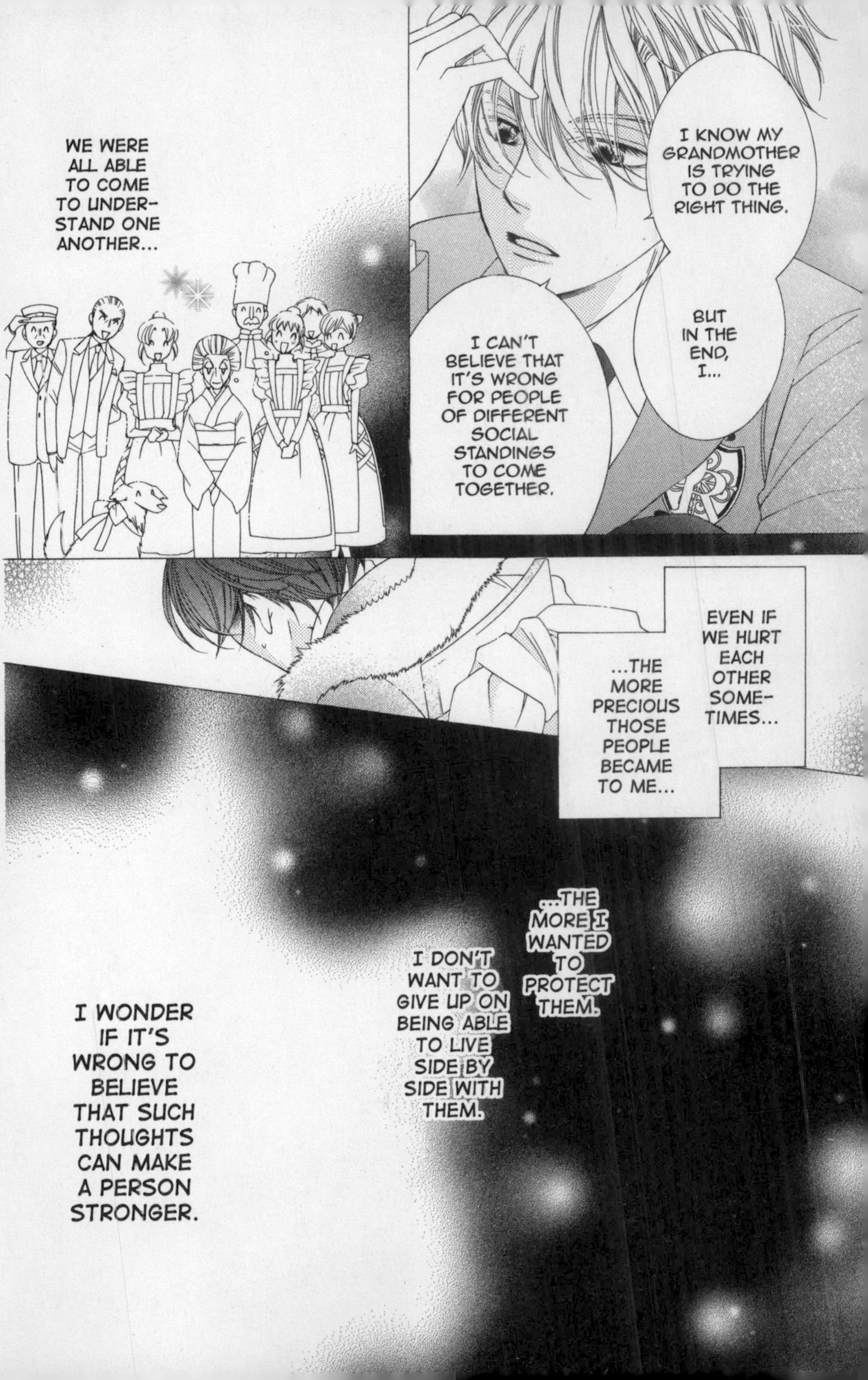
I KNOW MY GRANDMOTHER IS TRYING TO DO THE RIGHT THING.
BUT IN THE END, I...
I CAN'T BELIEVE THAT IT'S WRONG FOR PEOPLE OF DIFFERENT SOCIAL STANDINGS TO COME TOGETHER.
WE WERE ALL ABLE TO COME TO UNDER-STAND ONE ANOTHER...
EVEN IF WE HURT EACH OTHER SOME-TIMES...
...THE MORE PRECIOUS THOSE PEOPLE BECAME TO ME...
...THE MORE I WANTED TO PROTECT THEM.
I DON'T WANT TO GIVE UP ON BEING ABLE TO LIVE SIDE BY SIDE WITH THEM.
I WONDER IF IT'S WRONG TO BELIEVE THAT SUCH THOUGHTS CAN MAKE A PERSON STRONGER.

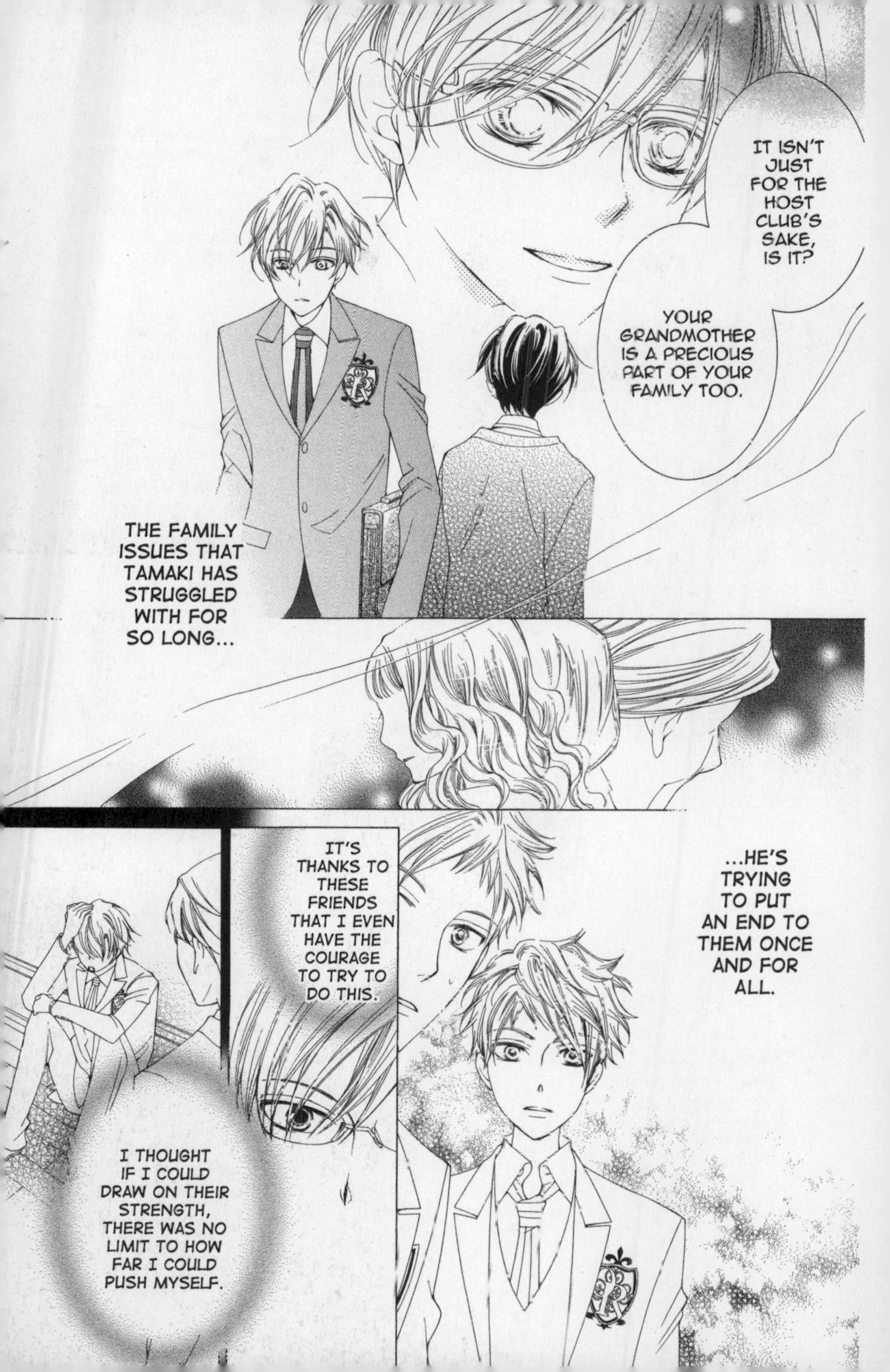
IT ISN'T JUST FOR THE HOST CLUB'S SAKE, IS IT?
YOUR GRANDMOTHER IS A PRECIOUS PART OF YOUR FAMILY TOO.
THE FAMILY ISSUES THAT TAMAKI HAS STRUGGLED WITH FOR SO LONG...
...HE'S TRYING TO PUT AN END TO THEM ONCE AND FOR ALL.
IT'S THANKS TO THESE FRIENDS THAT I EVEN HAVE THE COURAGE TO TRY TO DO THIS.
I THOUGHT IF I COULD DRAW ON THEIR STRENGTH, THERE WAS NO LIMIT TO HOW FAR I COULD PUSH MYSELF.

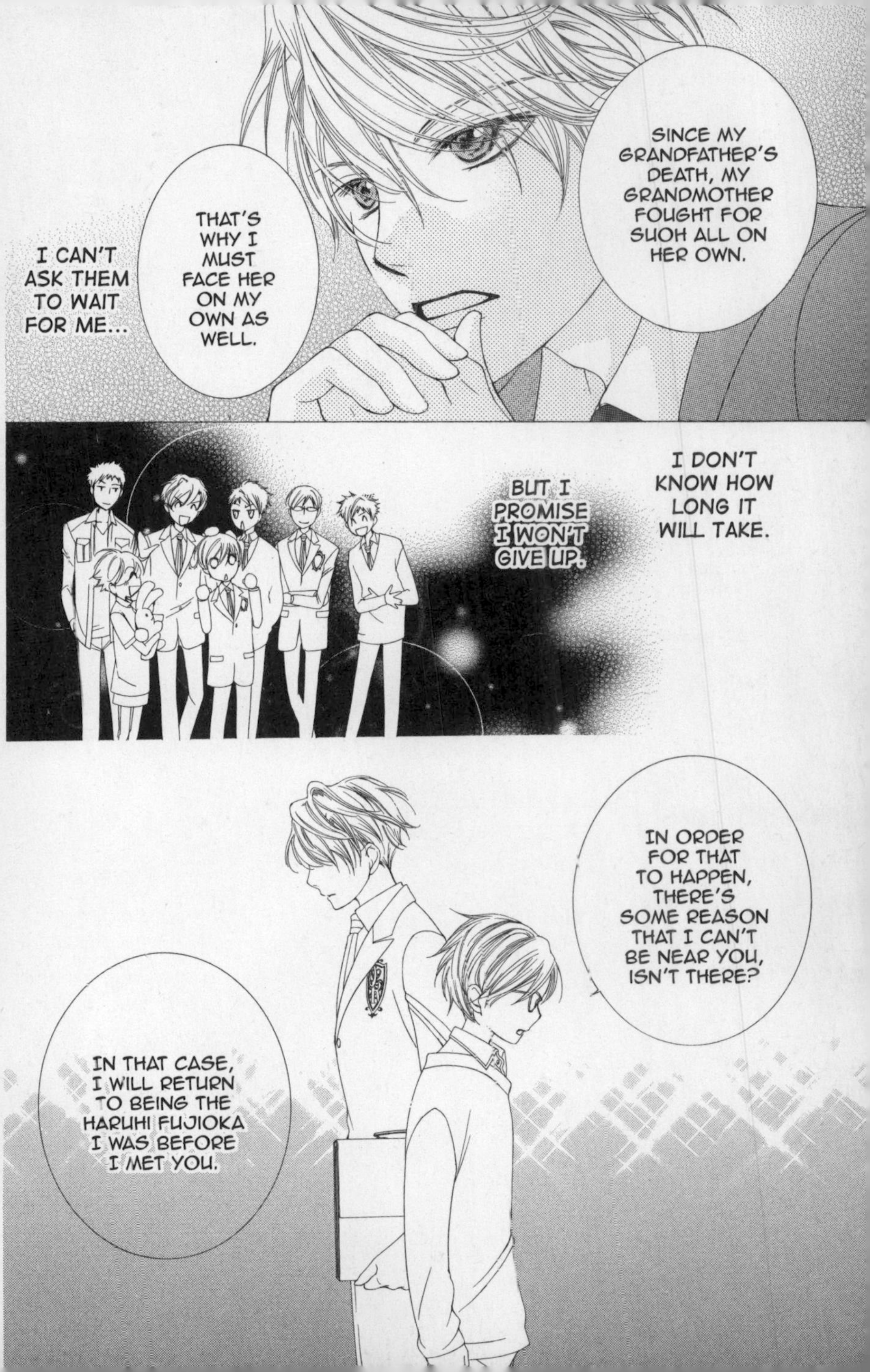
SINCE MY GRANDFATHER'S DEATH, MY GRANDMOTHER FOUGHT FOR SUOH ALL ON HER OWN.
THAT'S WHY I MUST FACE HER ON MY OWN AS WELL.
I CAN'T ASK THEM TO WAIT FOR ME...
I DON'T KNOW HOW LONG IT WILL TAKE.
BUT I PROMISE I WON'T GIVE UP.
IN ORDER FOR THAT TO HAPPEN, THERE'S SOME REASON THAT I CAN'T BE NEAR YOU, ISN'T THERE?
IN THAT CASE, I WILL RETURN TO BEING THE HARUHI FUJIOKA I WAS BEFORE I MET YOU.

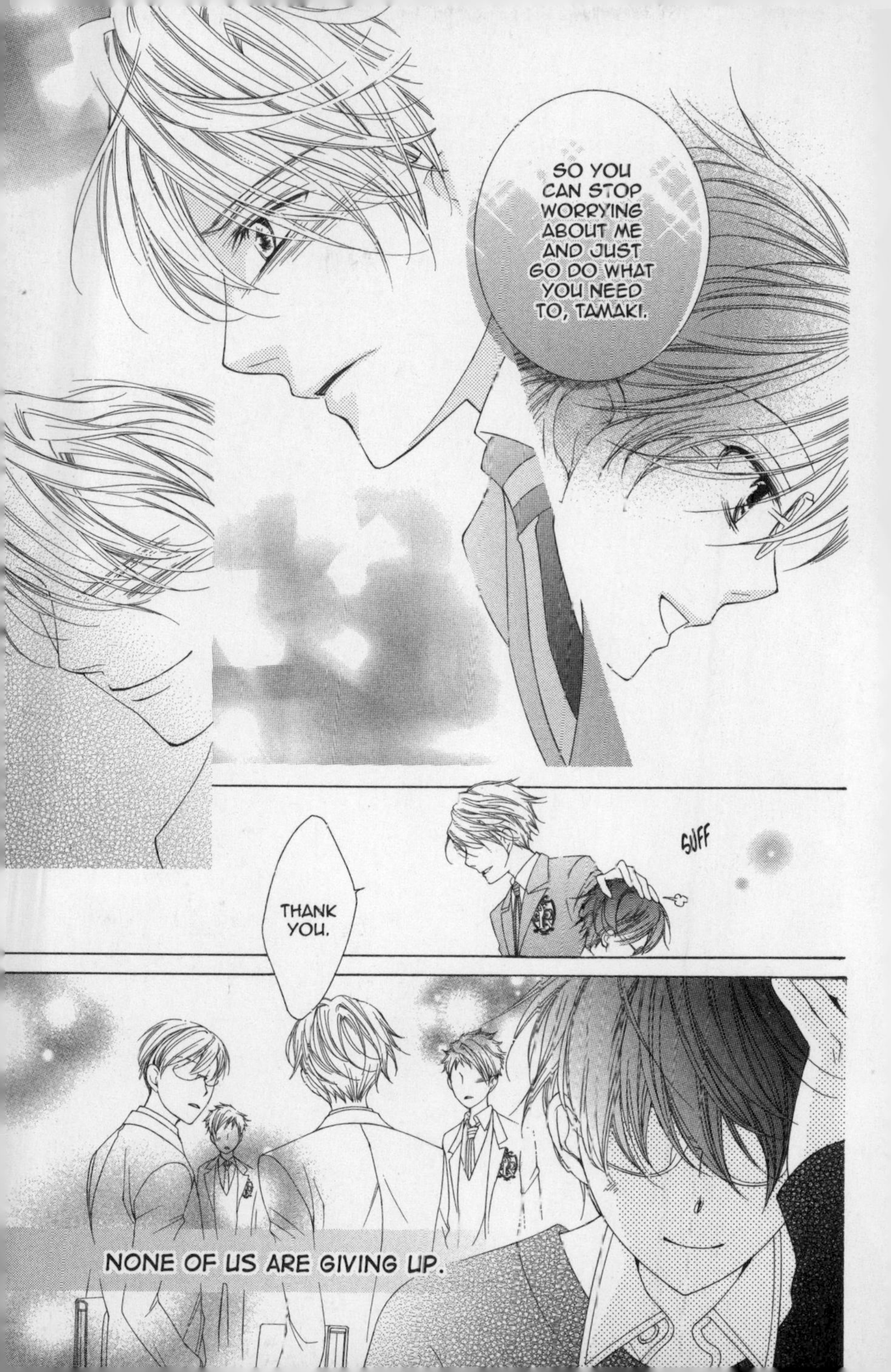
SO YOU CAN STOP WORRYING ABOUT ME AND JUST GO DO WHAT YOU NEED TO, TAMAKI.
SUFF
THANK YOU.
NONE OF US ARE GIVING UP.

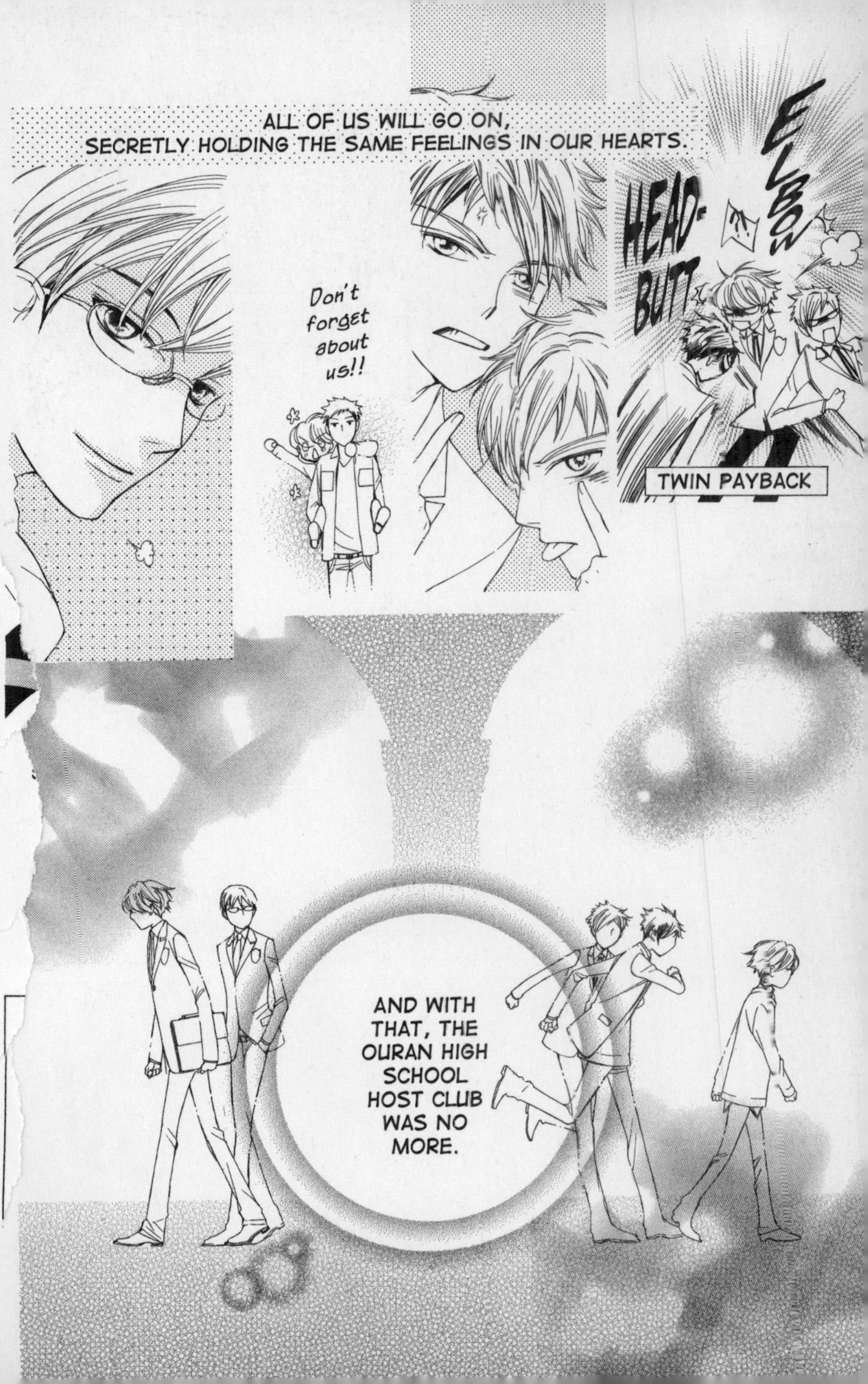
ALL OF US WILL GO ON, SECRETLY HOLDING THE SAME FEELINGS IN OUR HEARTS.
ELBOW
?!
HEAD-BUTT
TWIN PAYBACK
Don't forget about us!!
AND WITH THAT, THE OURAN HIGH SCHOOL HOST CLUB WAS NO MORE.

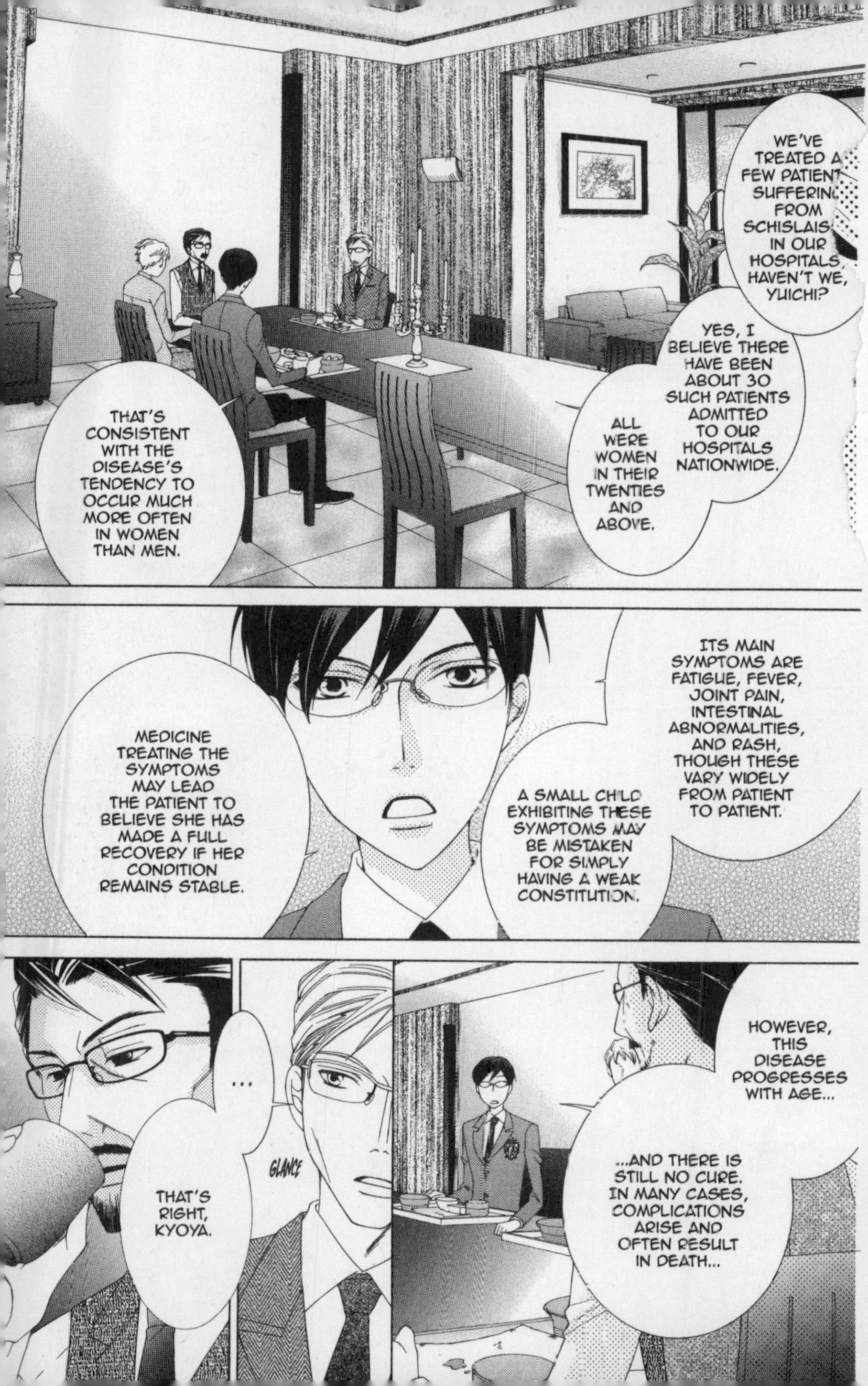
WE'VE TREATED A FEW PATIENT SUFFERIN FROM SCHISLAIS IN OUR HOSPITALS, HAVEN'T WE, YUICHI?
YES, I BELIEVE THERE HAVE BEEN ABOUT 30 SUCH PATIENTS ADMITTED TO OUR HOSPITALS NATIONWIDE.
ALL WERE WOMEN IN THEIR TWENTIES AND ABOVE.
THAT'S CONSISTENT WITH THE DISEASE'S TENDENCY TO OCCUR MUCH MORE OFTEN IN WOMEN THAN MEN.
ITS MAIN SYMPTOMS ARE FATIGUE, FEVER, JOINT PAIN, INTESTINAL ABNORMALITIES, AND RASH, THOUGH THESE VARY WIDELY FROM PATIENT TO PATIENT.
A SMALL CHILD EXHIBITING THESE SYMPTOMS MAY BE MISTAKEN FOR SIMPLY HAVING A WEAK CONSTITUTION.
MEDICINE TREATING THE SYMPTOMS MAY LEAD THE PATIENT TO BELIEVE SHE HAS MADE A FULL RECOVERY IF HER CONDITION REMAINS STABLE.
HOWEVER, THIS DISEASE PROGRESSES WITH AGE...
...AND THERE IS STILL NO CURE. IN MANY CASES, COMPLICATIONS ARISE AND OFTEN RESULT IN DEATH...
...
GLANCE
THAT'S RIGHT, KYOYA.

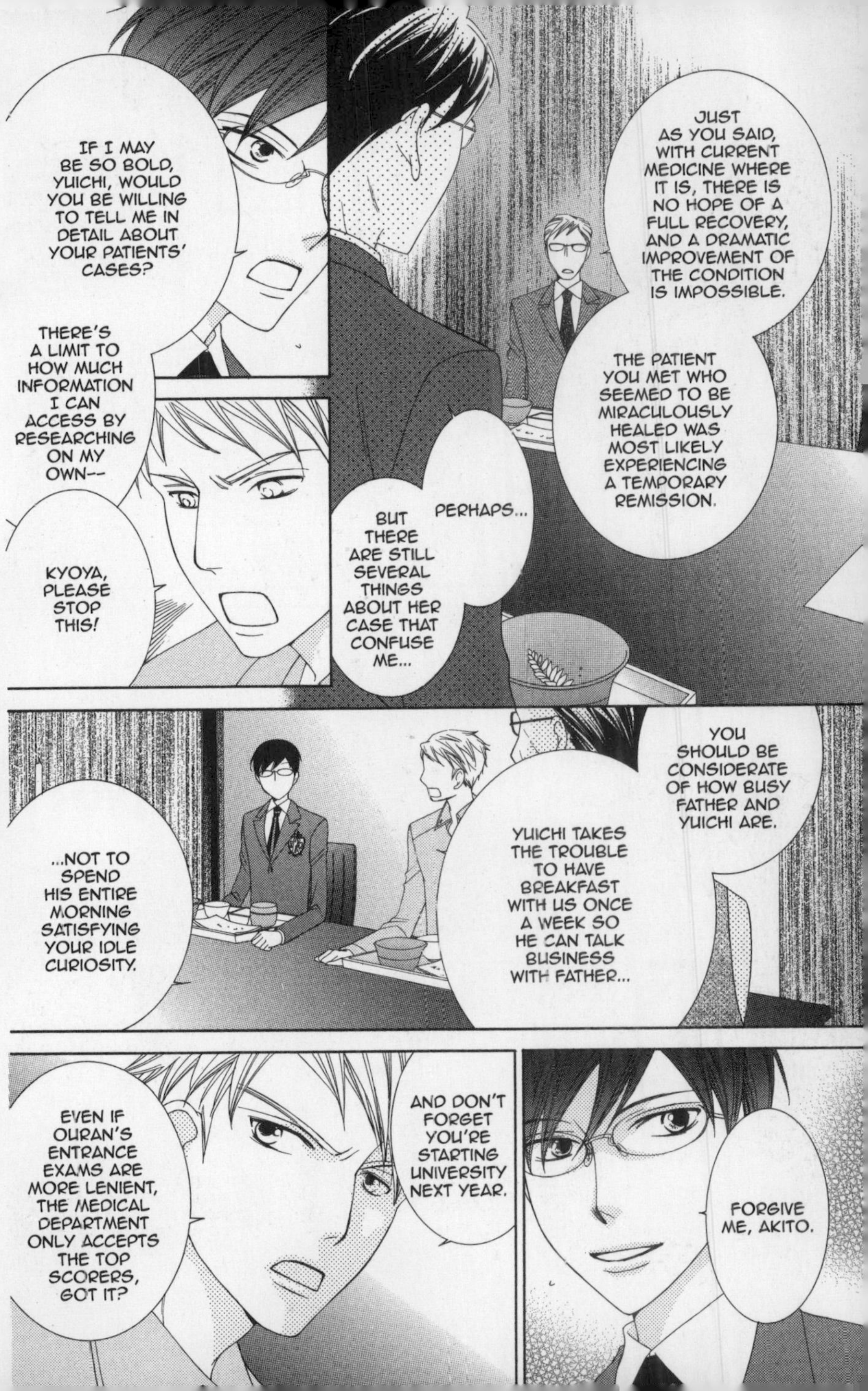
JUST AS YOU SAID, WITH CURRENT MEDICINE WHERE IT IS, THERE IS NO HOPE OF A FULL RECOVERY, AND A DRAMATIC IMPROVEMENT OF THE CONDITION IS IMPOSSIBLE.
THE PATIENT YOU MET WHO SEEMED TO BE MIRACULOUSLY HEALED WAS MOST LIKELY EXPERIENCING A TEMPORARY REMISSION.
PERHAPS...
BUT THERE ARE STILL SEVERAL THINGS ABOUT HER CASE THAT CONFUSE ME...
IF I MAY BE SO BOLD, YUICHI, WOULD YOU BE WILLING TO TELL ME IN DETAIL ABOUT YOUR PATIENTS' CASES?
THERE'S A LIMIT TO HOW MUCH INFORMATION I CAN ACCESS BY RESEARCHING ON MY OWN--
KYOYA, PLEASE STOP THIS!
YOU SHOULD BE CONSIDERATE OF HOW BUSY FATHER AND YUICHI ARE.
YUICHI TAKES THE TROUBLE TO HAVE BREAKFAST WITH US ONCE A WEEK SO HE CAN TALK BUSINESS WITH FATHER...
...NOT TO SPEND HIS ENTIRE MORNING SATISFYING YOUR IDLE CURIOSITY.
FORGIVE ME, AKITO.
AND DON'T FORGET YOU'RE STARTING UNIVERSITY NEXT YEAR.
EVEN IF OURAN'S ENTRANCE EXAMS ARE MORE LENIENT, THE MEDICAL DEPARTMENT ONLY ACCEPTS THE TOP SCORERS, GOT IT?

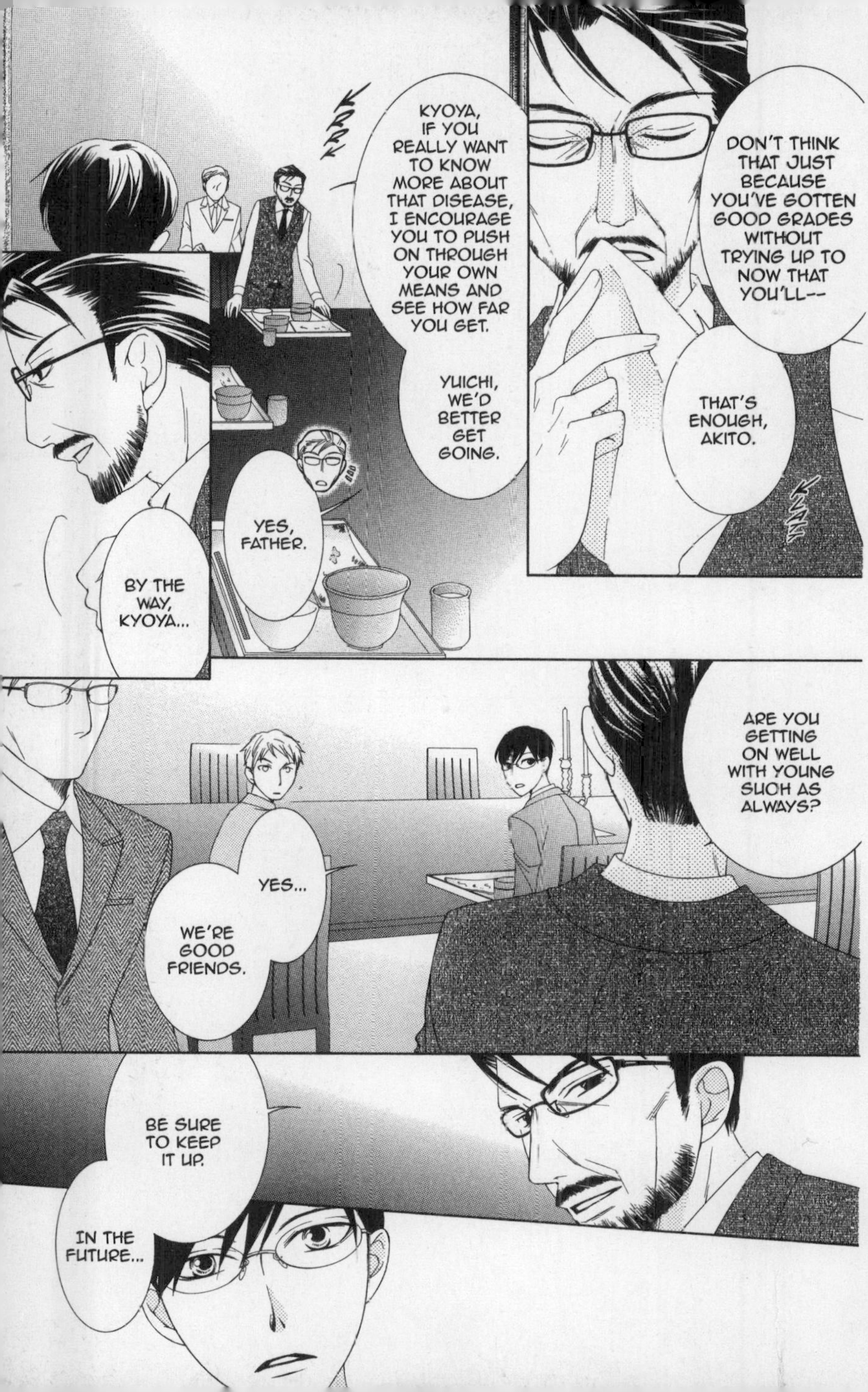
DON'T THINK THAT JUST BECAUSE YOU'VE GOTTEN GOOD GRADES WITHOUT TRYING UP TO NOW THAT YOU'LL--
THAT'S ENOUGH, AKITO.
KRRK
KRRK
KYOYA, IF YOU REALLY WANT TO KNOW MORE ABOUT THAT DISEASE, I ENCOURAGE YOU TO PUSH ON THROUGH YOUR OWN MEANS AND SEE HOW FAR YOU GET.
YUICHI, WE'D BETTER GET GOING.
YES, FATHER.
BY THE WAY, KYOYA...
ARE YOU GETTING ON WELL WITH YOUNG SUOH AS ALWAYS?
YES...
WE'RE GOOD FRIENDS.
BE SURE TO KEEP IT UP.
IN THE FUTURE...

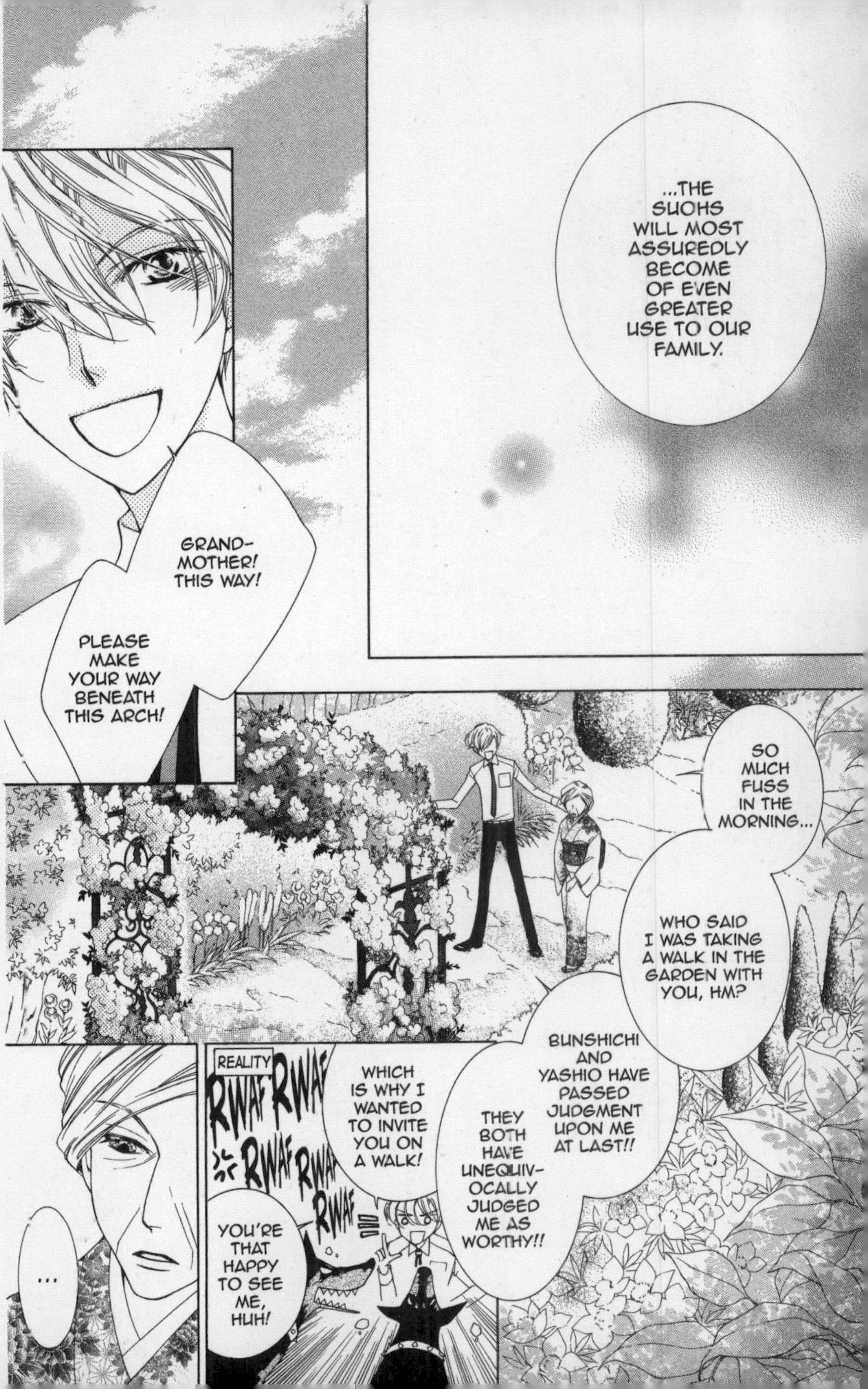
...THE SUOHS WILL MOST ASSUREDLY BECOME OF EVEN GREATER USE TO OUR FAMILY.
GRAND-MOTHER! THIS WAY!
PLEASE MAKE YOUR WAY BENEATH THIS ARCH!
SO MUCH FUSS IN THE MORNING...
WHO SAID I WAS TAKING A WALK IN THE GARDEN WITH YOU, HM?
BUNSHICHI AND YASHIO HAVE PASSED JUDGMENT UPON ME AT LAST!!
THEY BOTH HAVE UNEQUIV-OCALLY JUDGED ME AS WORTHY!!
WHICH IS WHY I WANTED TO INVITE YOU ON A WALK!
REALITY
RWAF RWAF
RWAF RWAF
RWAF
YOU'RE THAT HAPPY TO SEE ME, HUH!
...

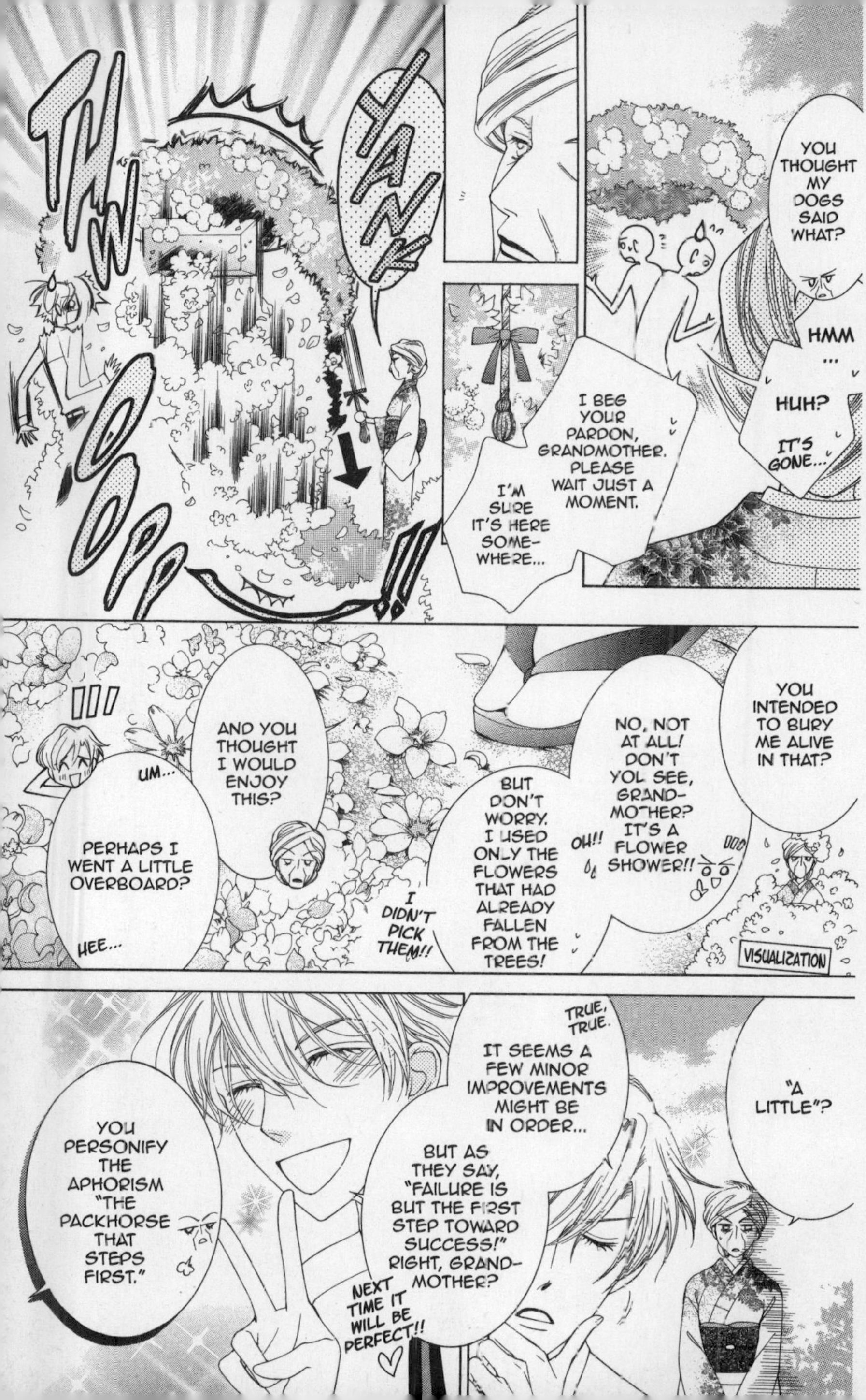
YOU THOUGHT MY DOGS SAID WHAT?
HMM...
HUH?
IT'S GONE...
I BEG YOUR PARDON, GRANDMOTHER. PLEASE WAIT JUST A MOMENT.
I'M SURE IT'S HERE SOMEWHERE...
YANK
THWOOP!!
YOU INTENDED TO BURY ME ALIVE IN THAT?
VISUALIZATION
NO, NOT AT ALL! DON'T YOU SEE, GRANDMOTHER? IT'S A FLOWER SHOWER!!
OH!!
BUT DON'T WORRY. I USED ONLY THE FLOWERS THAT HAD ALREADY FALLEN FROM THE TREES!
I DIDN'T PICK THEM!!
AND YOU THOUGHT I WOULD ENJOY THIS?
UM...
PERHAPS I WENT A LITTLE OVERBOARD?
HEE...
"A LITTLE"?
TRUE, TRUE.
IT SEEMS A FEW MINOR IMPROVEMENTS MIGHT BE IN ORDER...
BUT AS THEY SAY, "FAILURE IS BUT THE FIRST STEP TOWARD SUCCESS!" RIGHT, GRANDMOTHER?
NEXT TIME IT WILL BE PERFECT!!
YOU PERSONIFY THE APHORISM "THE PACKHORSE THAT STEPS FIRST."

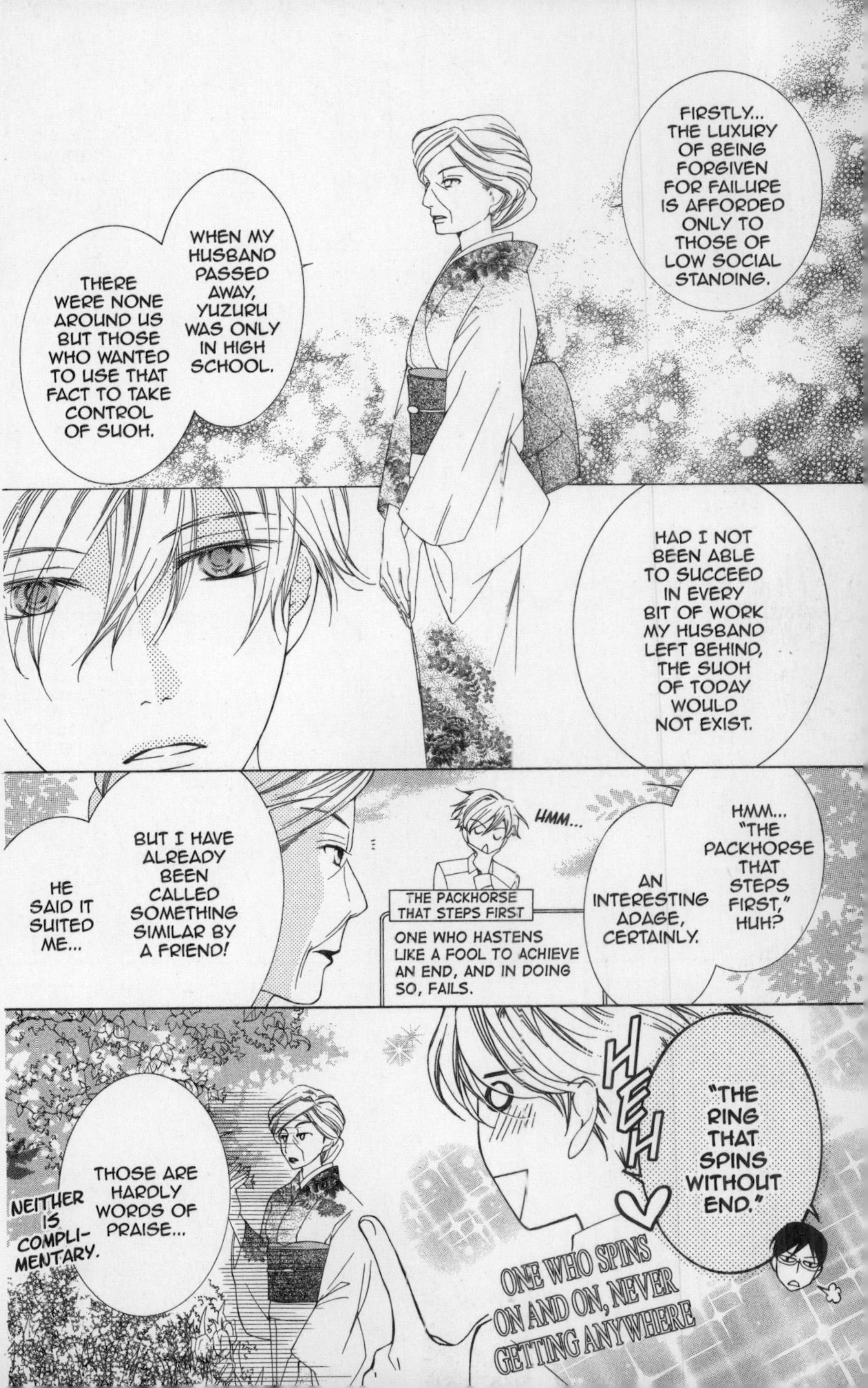
FIRSTLY... THE LUXURY OF BEING FORGIVEN FOR FAILURE IS AFFORDED ONLY TO THOSE OF LOW SOCIAL STANDING.
WHEN MY HUSBAND PASSED AWAY, YUZURU WAS ONLY IN HIGH SCHOOL.
THERE WERE NONE AROUND US BUT THOSE WHO WANTED TO USE THAT FACT TO TAKE CONTROL OF SUOH.
HAD I NOT BEEN ABLE TO SUCCEED IN EVERY BIT OF WORK MY HUSBAND LEFT BEHIND, THE SUOH OF TODAY WOULD NOT EXIST.
HMM... "THE PACKHORSE THAT STEPS FIRST," HUH?
AN INTERESTING ADAGE, CERTAINLY.
HMM...
THE PACKHORSE THAT STEPS FIRST
ONE WHO HASTENS LIKE A FOOL TO ACHIEVE AN END, AND IN DOING SO, FAILS.
BUT I HAVE ALREADY BEEN CALLED SOMETHING SIMILAR BY A FRIEND!
HE SAID IT SUITED ME...
"THE RING THAT SPINS WITHOUT END."
HEH
ONE WHO SPINS ON AND ON, NEVER GETTING ANYWHERE
THOSE ARE HARDLY WORDS OF PRAISE...
NEITHER IS COMPLI-MENTARY.

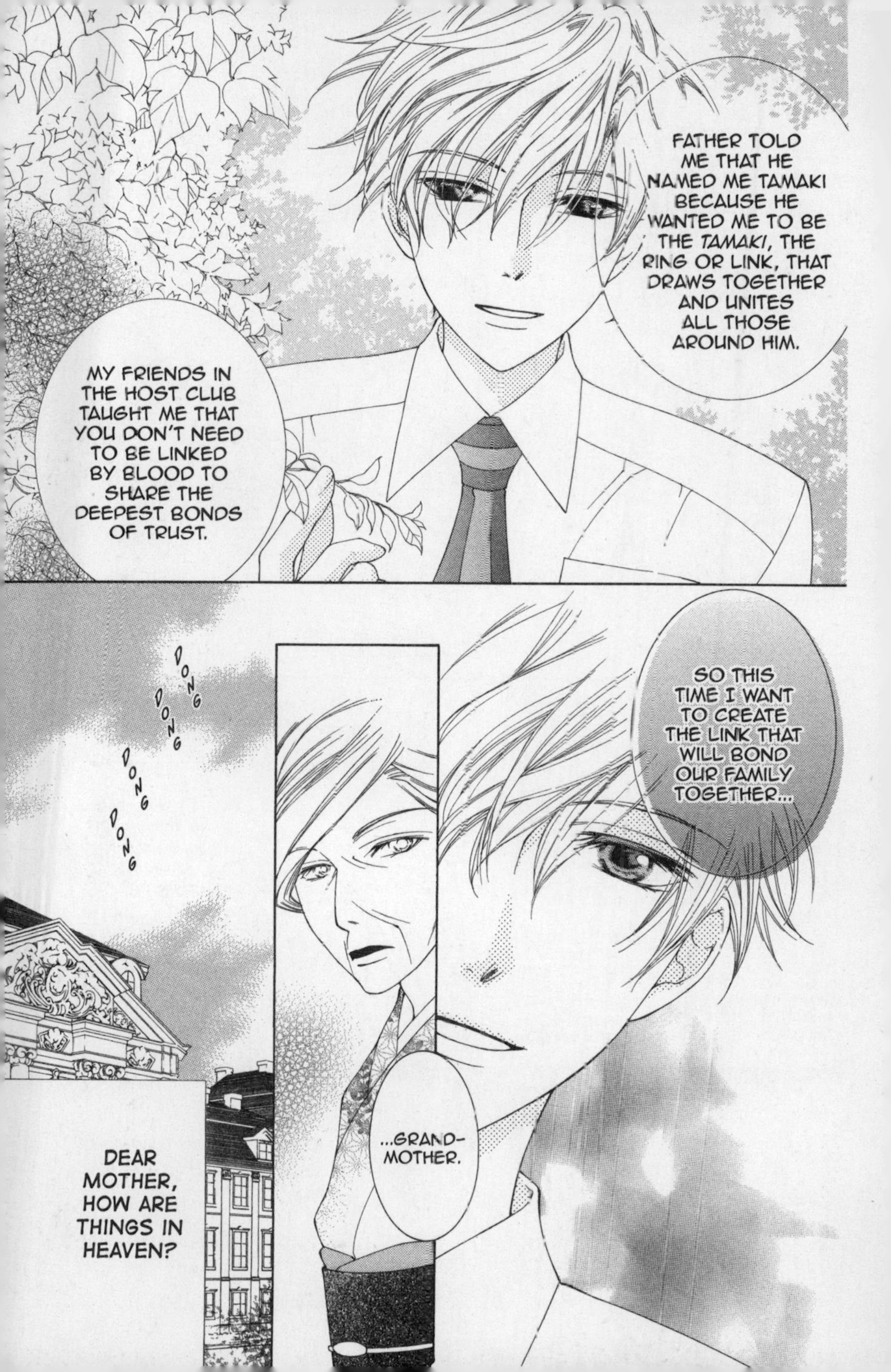
FATHER TOLD ME THAT HE NAMED ME TAMAKI BECAUSE HE WANTED ME TO BE THE *TAMAKI*, THE RING OR LINK, THAT DRAWS TOGETHER AND UNITES ALL THOSE AROUND HIM.
MY FRIENDS IN THE HOST CLUB TAUGHT ME THAT YOU DON'T NEED TO BE LINKED BY BLOOD TO SHARE THE DEEPEST BONDS OF TRUST.
SO THIS TIME I WANT TO CREATE THE LINK THAT WILL BOND OUR FAMILY TOGETHER...
...GRAND-MOTHER.
DONG
DONG
DONG
DONG
DEAR MOTHER, HOW ARE THINGS IN HEAVEN?

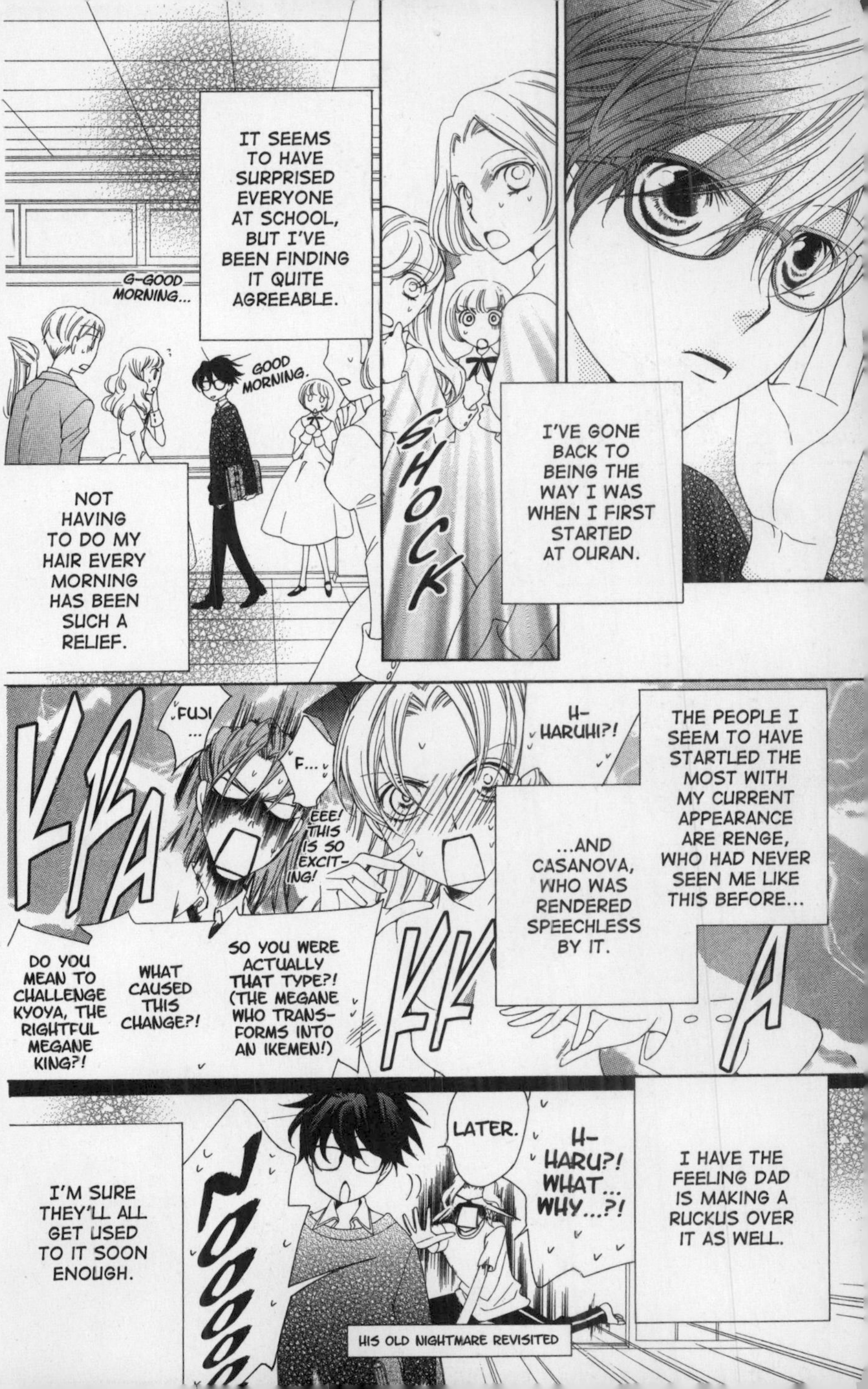
I'VE GONE BACK TO BEING THE WAY I WAS WHEN I FIRST STARTED AT OURAN.
SHOCK
IT SEEMS TO HAVE SURPRISED EVERYONE AT SCHOOL, BUT I'VE BEEN FINDING IT QUITE AGREEABLE.
GOOD MORNING.
G-GOOD MORNING...
NOT HAVING TO DO MY HAIR EVERY MORNING HAS BEEN SUCH A RELIEF.
THE PEOPLE I SEEM TO HAVE STARTLED THE MOST WITH MY CURRENT APPEARANCE ARE RENGE, WHO HAD NEVER SEEN ME LIKE THIS BEFORE...
...AND CASANOVA, WHO WAS RENDERED SPEECHLESS BY IT.
H-HARUHI?!
A
KY
F...
FUJI...
KYA
EEE! THIS IS SO EXCITING!
SO YOU WERE ACTUALLY THAT TYPE?! (THE MEGANE WHO TRANSFORMS INTO AN IKEMEN!)
WHAT CAUSED THIS CHANGE?!
DO YOU MEAN TO CHALLENGE KYOYA, THE RIGHTFUL MEGANE KING?!
I HAVE THE FEELING DAD IS MAKING A RUCKUS OVER IT AS WELL.
H-HARU?! WHAT... WHY...?!
LATER.
NOOOOO
I'M SURE THEY'LL ALL GET USED TO IT SOON ENOUGH.
HIS OLD NIGHTMARE REVISITED

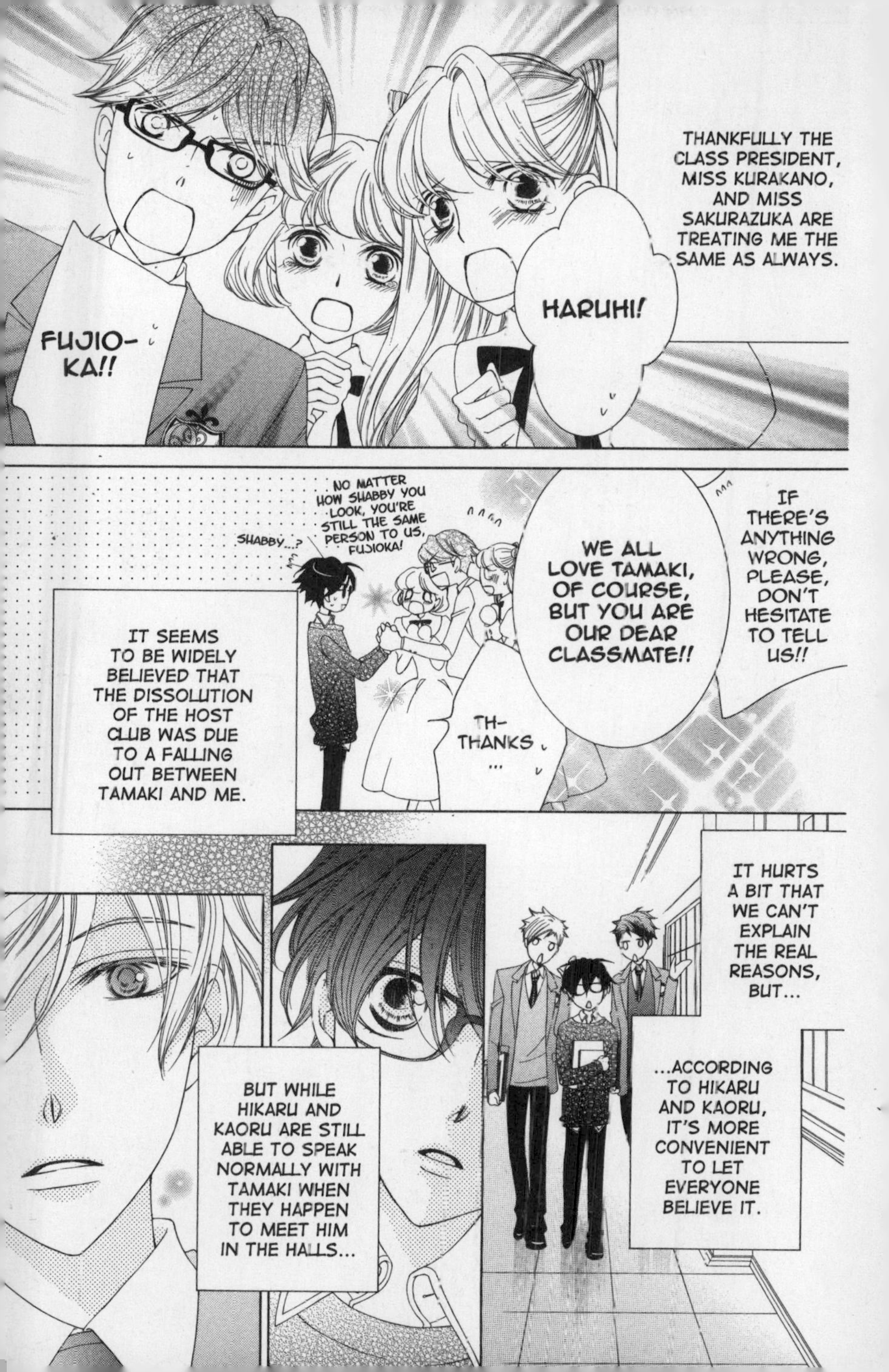
THANKFULLY THE CLASS PRESIDENT, MISS KURAKANO, AND MISS SAKURAZUKA ARE TREATING ME THE SAME AS ALWAYS.
HARUHI!
FUJIO-KA!!
IF THERE'S ANYTHING WRONG, PLEASE, DON'T HESITATE TO TELL US!!
WE ALL LOVE TAMAKI, OF COURSE, BUT YOU ARE OUR DEAR CLASSMATE!!
TH-THANKS...
NO MATTER HOW SHABBY YOU LOOK, YOU'RE STILL THE SAME PERSON TO US, FUJIOKA!
SHABBY...?
IT SEEMS TO BE WIDELY BELIEVED THAT THE DISSOLUTION OF THE HOST CLUB WAS DUE TO A FALLING OUT BETWEEN TAMAKI AND ME.
IT HURTS A BIT THAT WE CAN'T EXPLAIN THE REAL REASONS, BUT...
...ACCORDING TO HIKARU AND KAORU, IT'S MORE CONVENIENT TO LET EVERYONE BELIEVE IT.
BUT WHILE HIKARU AND KAORU ARE STILL ABLE TO SPEAK NORMALLY WITH TAMAKI WHEN THEY HAPPEN TO MEET HIM IN THE HALLS...

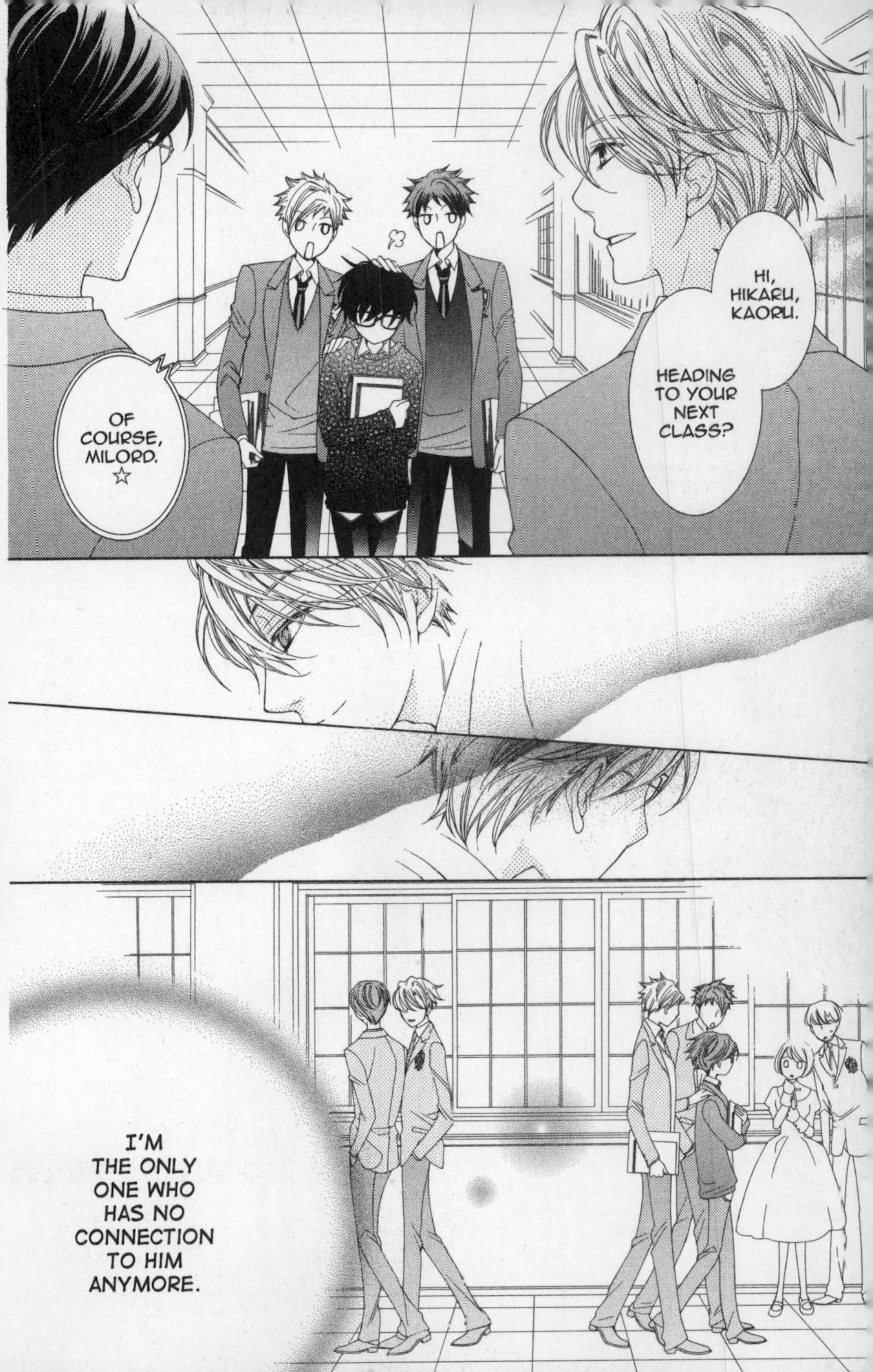
HI, HIKARU, KAORU.
HEADING TO YOUR NEXT CLASS?
OF COURSE, MILORD. ☆
I'M THE ONLY ONE WHO HAS NO CONNECTION TO HIM ANYMORE.

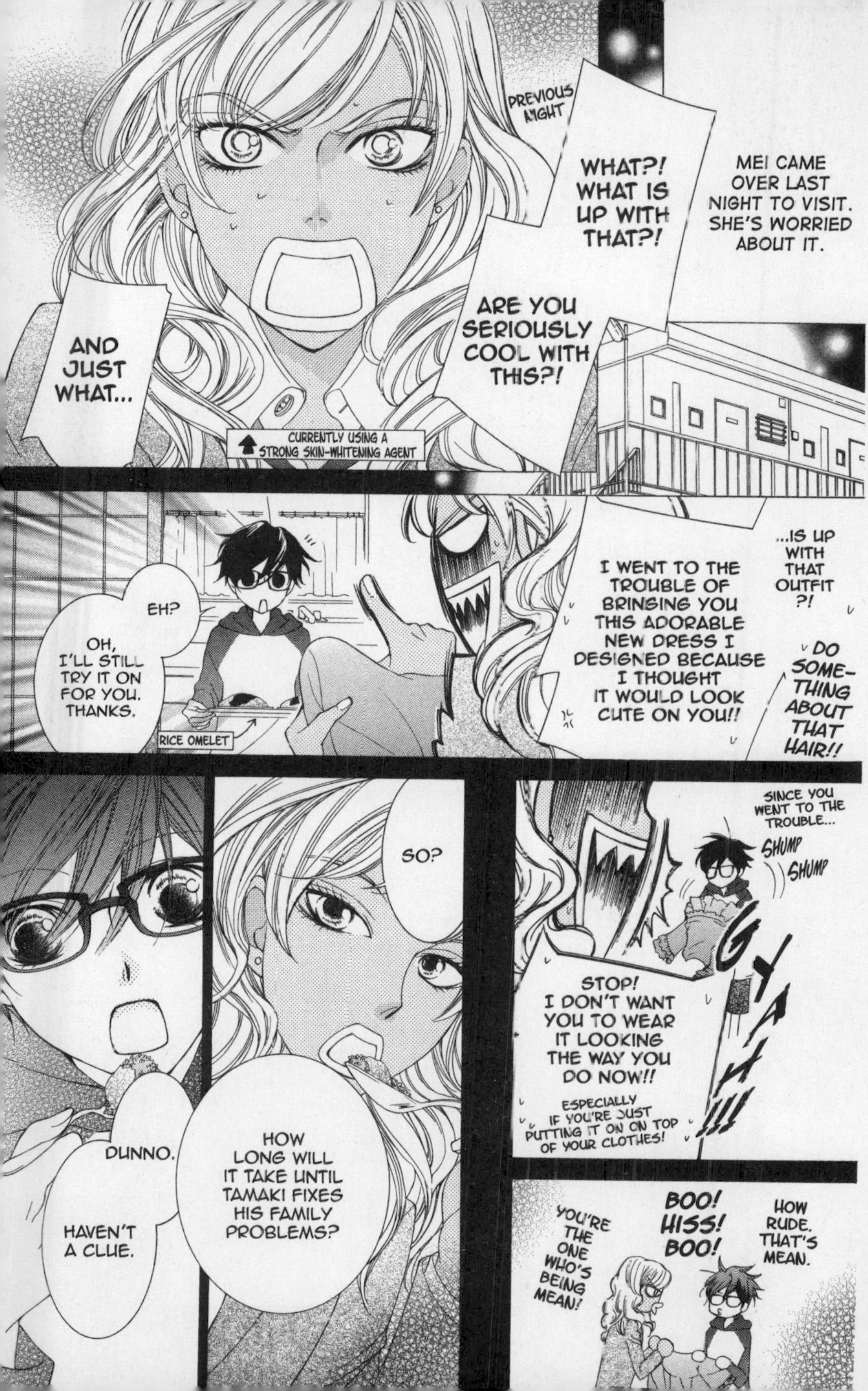
MEI CAME OVER LAST NIGHT TO VISIT. SHE'S WORRIED ABOUT IT.
PREVIOUS NIGHT
WHAT?! WHAT IS UP WITH THAT?!
ARE YOU SERIOUSLY COOL WITH THIS?!
AND JUST WHAT...
CURRENTLY USING A STRONG SKIN-WHITENING AGENT
...IS UP WITH THAT OUTFIT?!
DO SOME-THING ABOUT THAT HAIR!!
I WENT TO THE TROUBLE OF BRINGING YOU THIS ADORABLE NEW DRESS I DESIGNED BECAUSE I THOUGHT IT WOULD LOOK CUTE ON YOU!!
EH?
OH, I'LL STILL TRY IT ON FOR YOU. THANKS.
RICE OMELET
SINCE YOU WENT TO THE TROUBLE...
SHUMP
SHUMP
STOP! I DON'T WANT YOU TO WEAR IT LOOKING THE WAY YOU DO NOW!!
ESPECIALLY IF YOU'RE JUST PUTTING IT ON ON TOP OF YOUR CLOTHES!
HOW RUDE. THAT'S MEAN.
BOO! HISS! BOO!
YOU'RE THE ONE WHO'S BEING MEAN!
SO?
HOW LONG WILL IT TAKE UNTIL TAMAKI FIXES HIS FAMILY PROBLEMS?
DUNNO.
HAVEN'T A CLUE.

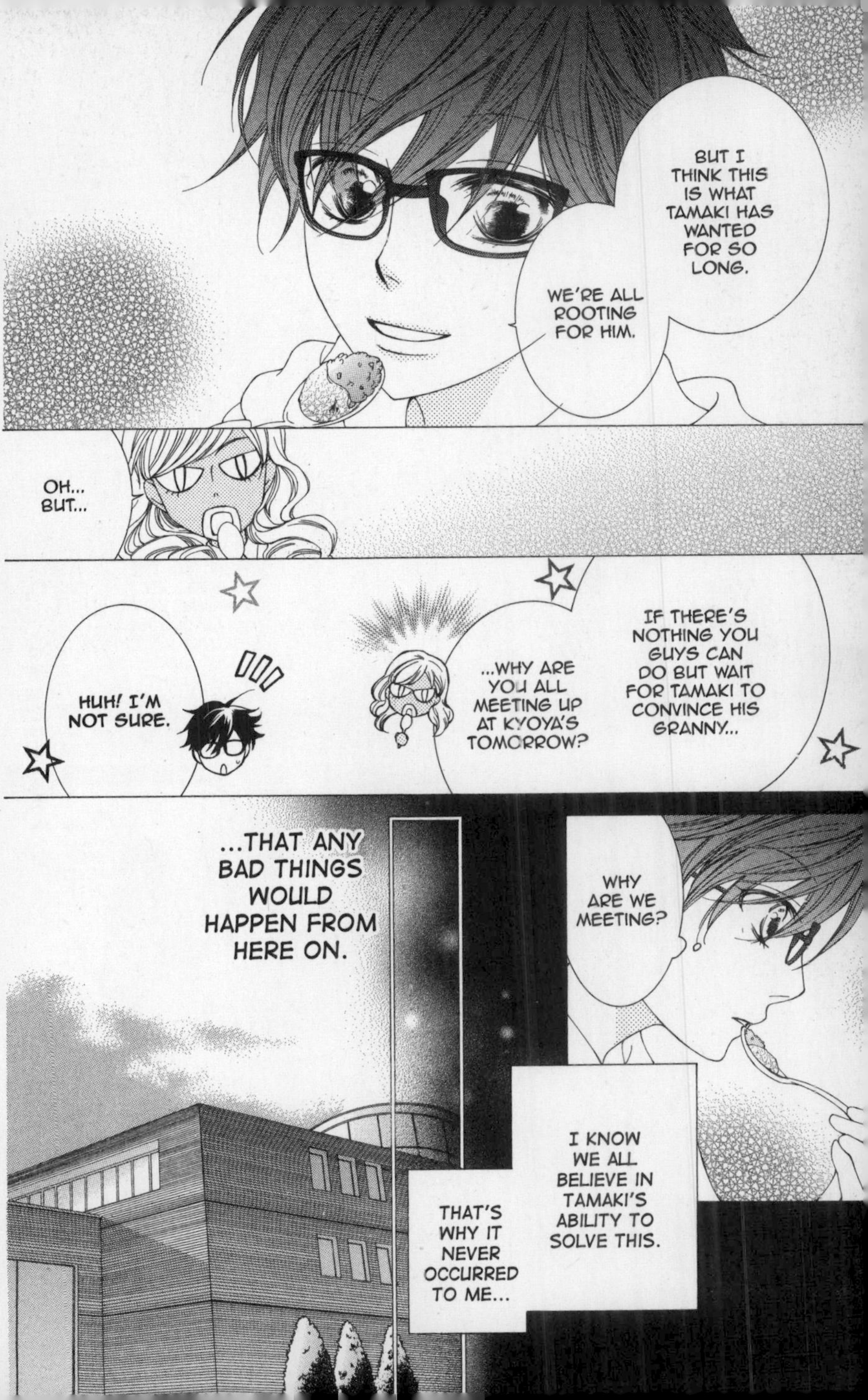
BUT I THINK THIS IS WHAT TAMAKI HAS WANTED FOR SO LONG.
WE'RE ALL ROOTING FOR HIM.
OH... BUT...
IF THERE'S NOTHING YOU GUYS CAN DO BUT WAIT FOR TAMAKI TO CONVINCE HIS GRANNY...
...WHY ARE YOU ALL MEETING UP AT KYOYA'S TOMORROW?
HUH! I'M NOT SURE.
WHY ARE WE MEETING?
I KNOW WE ALL BELIEVE IN TAMAKI'S ABILITY TO SOLVE THIS.
THAT'S WHY IT NEVER OCCURRED TO ME...
...THAT ANY BAD THINGS WOULD HAPPEN FROM HERE ON.

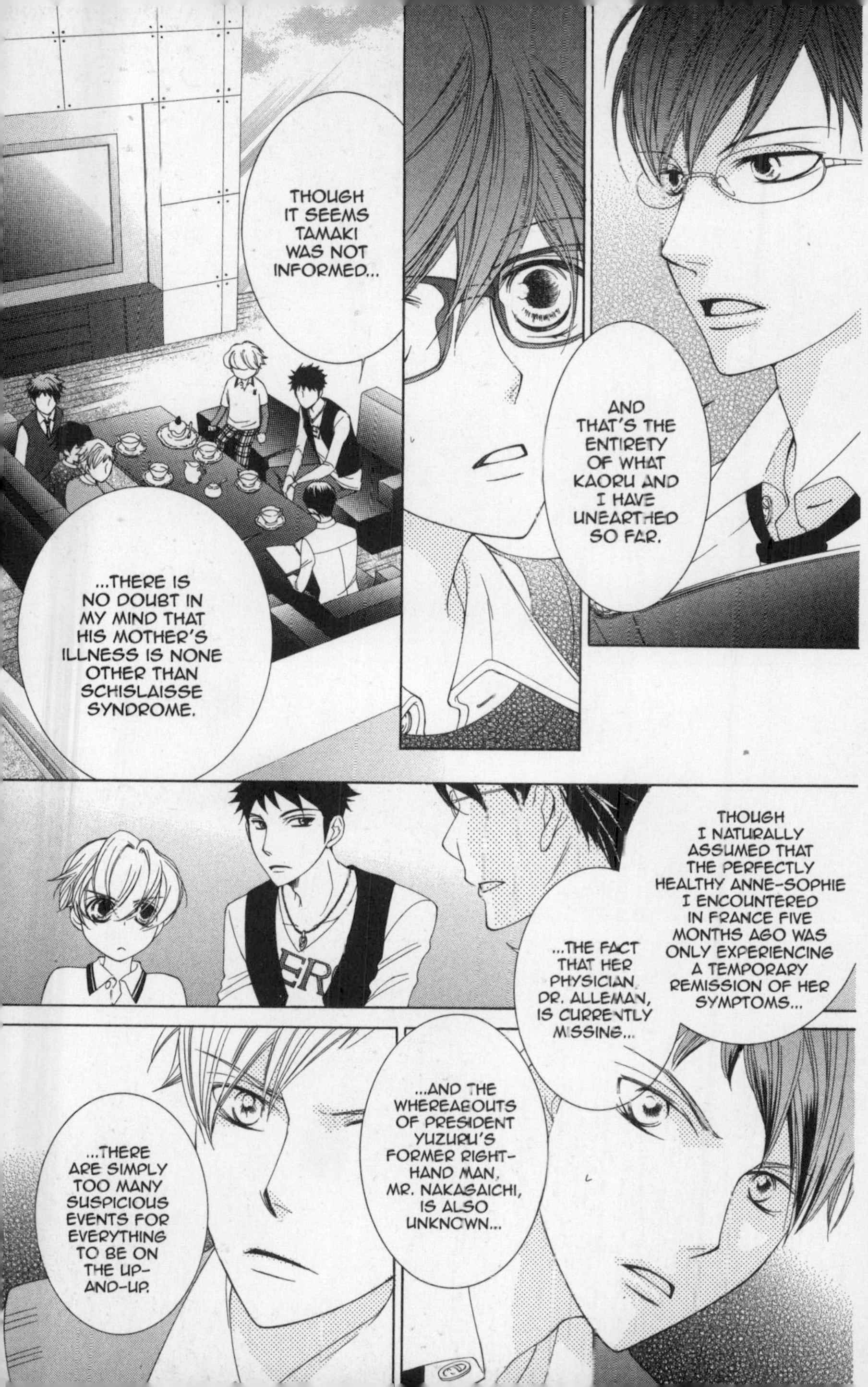
AND THAT'S THE ENTIRETY OF WHAT KAORU AND I HAVE UNEARTHED SO FAR.
THOUGH IT SEEMS TAMAKI WAS NOT INFORMED...
...THERE IS NO DOUBT IN MY MIND THAT HIS MOTHER'S ILLNESS IS NONE OTHER THAN SCHISLAISSE SYNDROME.
THOUGH I NATURALLY ASSUMED THAT THE PERFECTLY HEALTHY ANNE-SOPHIE I ENCOUNTERED IN FRANCE FIVE MONTHS AGO WAS ONLY EXPERIENCING A TEMPORARY REMISSION OF HER SYMPTOMS...
...THE FACT THAT HER PHYSICIAN, DR. ALLEMAN, IS CURRENTLY MISSING...
...AND THE WHEREABOUTS OF PRESIDENT YUZURU'S FORMER RIGHT-HAND MAN, MR. NAKASAICHI, IS ALSO UNKNOWN...
...THERE ARE SIMPLY TOO MANY SUSPICIOUS EVENTS FOR EVERYTHING TO BE ON THE UP-AND-UP.

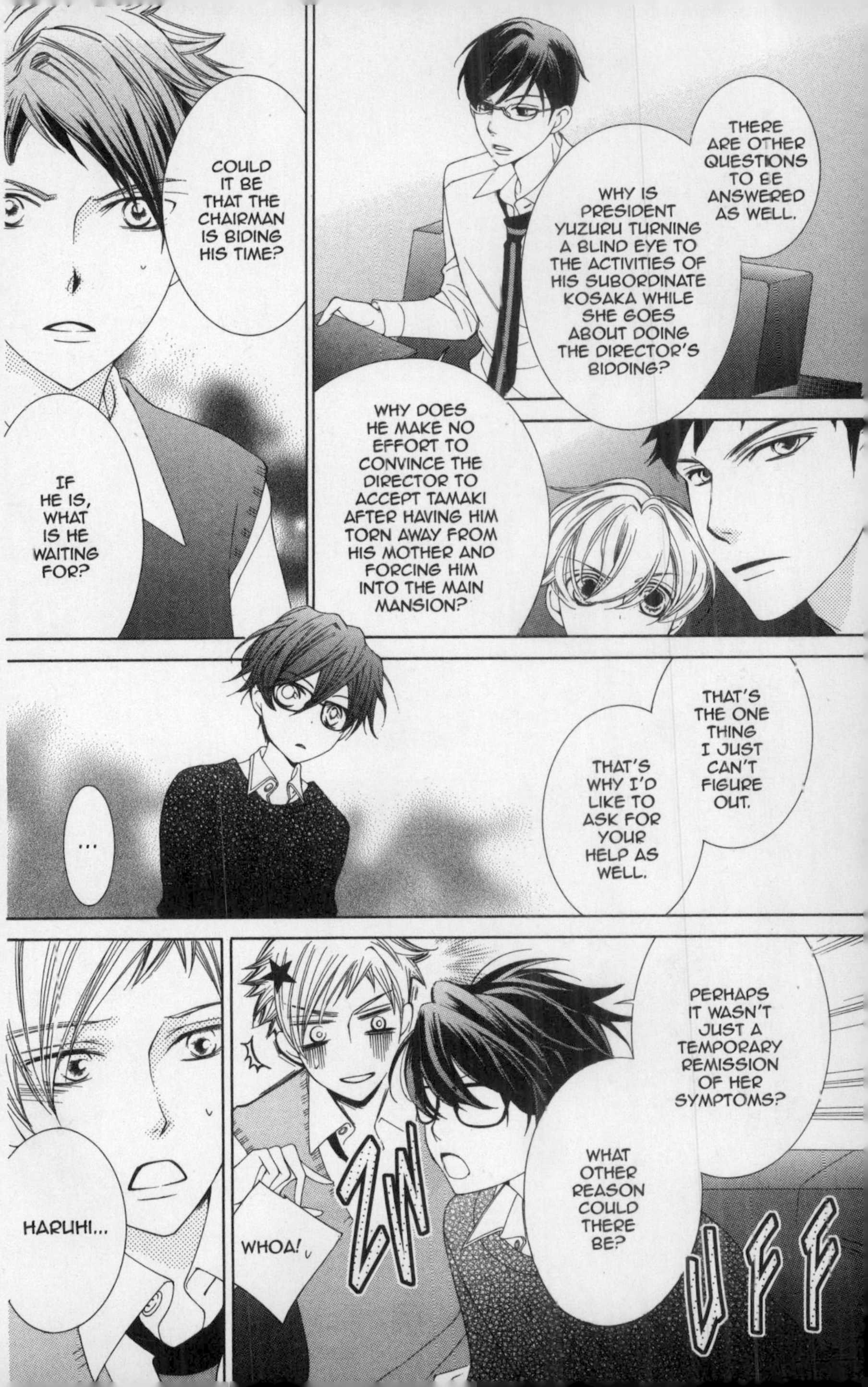
THERE ARE OTHER QUESTIONS TO BE ANSWERED AS WELL.
WHY IS PRESIDENT YUZURU TURNING A BLIND EYE TO THE ACTIVITIES OF HIS SUBORDINATE KOSAKA WHILE SHE GOES ABOUT DOING THE DIRECTOR'S BIDDING?
WHY DOES HE MAKE NO EFFORT TO CONVINCE THE DIRECTOR TO ACCEPT TAMAKI AFTER HAVING HIM TORN AWAY FROM HIS MOTHER AND FORCING HIM INTO THE MAIN MANSION?
COULD IT BE THAT THE CHAIRMAN IS BIDING HIS TIME?
IF HE IS, WHAT IS HE WAITING FOR?
THAT'S THE ONE THING I JUST CAN'T FIGURE OUT.
THAT'S WHY I'D LIKE TO ASK FOR YOUR HELP AS WELL.
...
PERHAPS IT WASN'T JUST A TEMPORARY REMISSION OF HER SYMPTOMS?
WHAT OTHER REASON COULD THERE BE?
WHOA!
HARUHI...

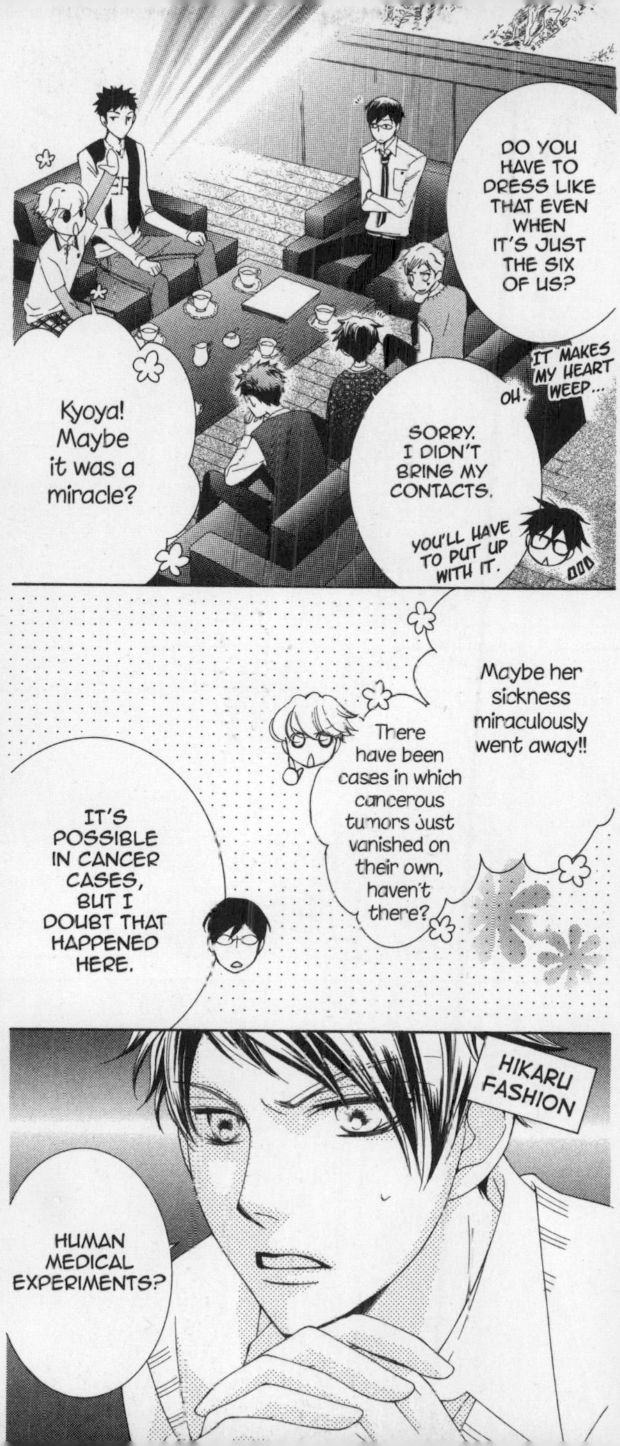

DO YOU HAVE TO DRESS LIKE THAT EVEN WHEN IT'S JUST THE SIX OF US?
OH.
IT MAKES MY HEART WEEP...
SORRY. I DIDN'T BRING MY CONTACTS.
YOU'LL HAVE TO PUT UP WITH IT.
Kyoya! Maybe it was a miracle?
Maybe her sickness miraculously went away!!
There have been cases in which cancerous tumors just vanished on their own, haven't there?
IT'S POSSIBLE IN CANCER CASES, BUT I DOUBT THAT HAPPENED HERE.
HIKARU FASHION
HUMAN MEDICAL EXPERIMENTS?

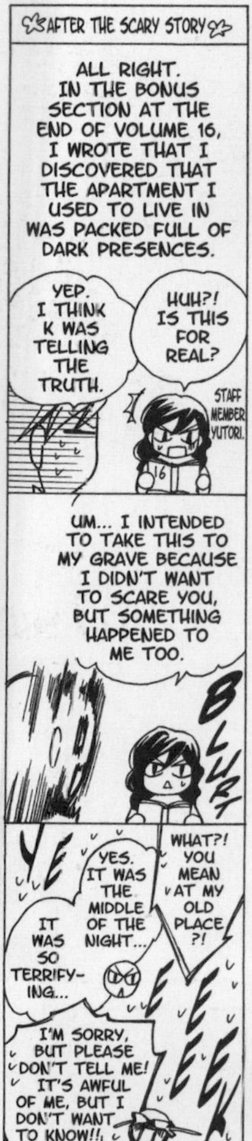

AFTER THE SCARY STORY
ALL RIGHT. IN THE BONUS SECTION AT THE END OF VOLUME 16, I WROTE THAT I DISCOVERED THAT THE APARTMENT I USED TO LIVE IN WAS PACKED FULL OF DARK PRESENCES.
HUH?! IS THIS FOR REAL?
YEP. I THINK K WAS TELLING THE TRUTH.
STAFF MEMBER YUTORI
16
UM... I INTENDED TO TAKE THIS TO MY GRAVE BECAUSE I DIDN'T WANT TO SCARE YOU, BUT SOMETHING HAPPENED TO ME TOO.
BLURT
WHAT?! YOU MEAN AT MY OLD PLACE?!
YES. IT WAS THE MIDDLE OF THE NIGHT...
IT WAS SO TERRIFYING...
YEEEEEK
I'M SORRY, BUT PLEASE DON'T TELL ME! IT'S AWFUL OF ME, BUT I DON'T WANT TO KNOW!!
LATER
YUI
OH MY GOD! YUTORI JUST TOLD ME!
SO, SO SCARY!!
EEK! EEK! EEK! EEK!
I STILL DON'T KNOW WHAT HAPPENED.

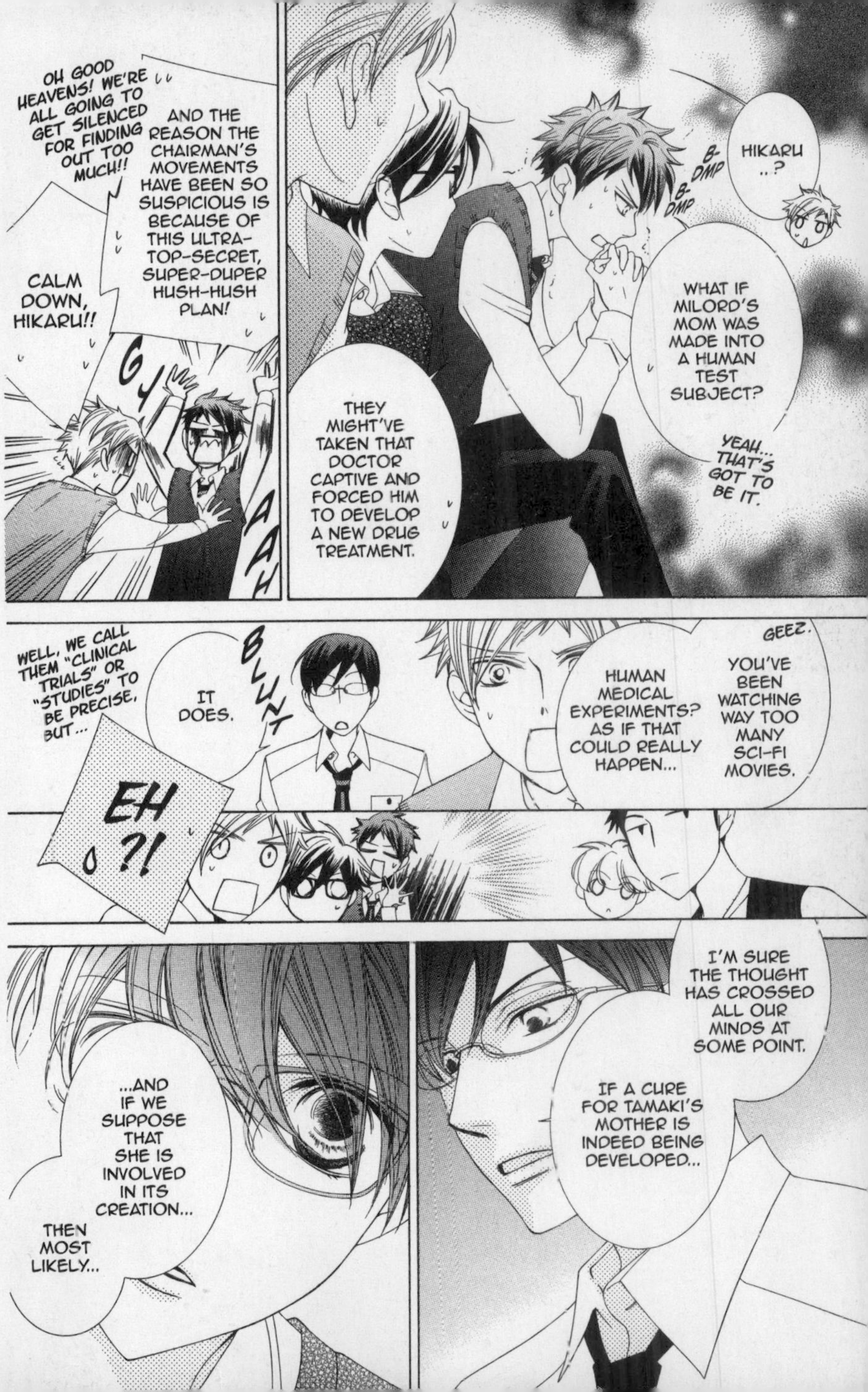
HIKARU ..?
B-DMP
B-DMP
WHAT IF MILORD'S MOM WAS MADE INTO A HUMAN TEST SUBJECT?
YEAH... THAT'S GOT TO BE IT.
THEY MIGHT'VE TAKEN THAT DOCTOR CAPTIVE AND FORCED HIM TO DEVELOP A NEW DRUG TREATMENT.
AND THE REASON THE CHAIRMAN'S MOVEMENTS HAVE BEEN SO SUSPICIOUS IS BECAUSE OF THIS ULTRA-TOP-SECRET, SUPER-DUPER HUSH-HUSH PLAN!
OH GOOD HEAVENS! WE'RE ALL GOING TO GET SILENCED FOR FINDING OUT TOO MUCH!!
GYAAH
CALM DOWN, HIKARU!!
GEEZ.
YOU'VE BEEN WATCHING WAY TOO MANY SCI-FI MOVIES.
HUMAN MEDICAL EXPERIMENTS? AS IF THAT COULD REALLY HAPPEN...
BLUNT
IT DOES.
WELL, WE CALL THEM "CLINICAL TRIALS" OR "STUDIES" TO BE PRECISE, BUT...
EH ?!
I'M SURE THE THOUGHT HAS CROSSED ALL OUR MINDS AT SOME POINT.
IF A CURE FOR TAMAKI'S MOTHER IS INDEED BEING DEVELOPED...
...AND IF WE SUPPOSE THAT SHE IS INVOLVED IN ITS CREATION...
THEN MOST LIKELY...

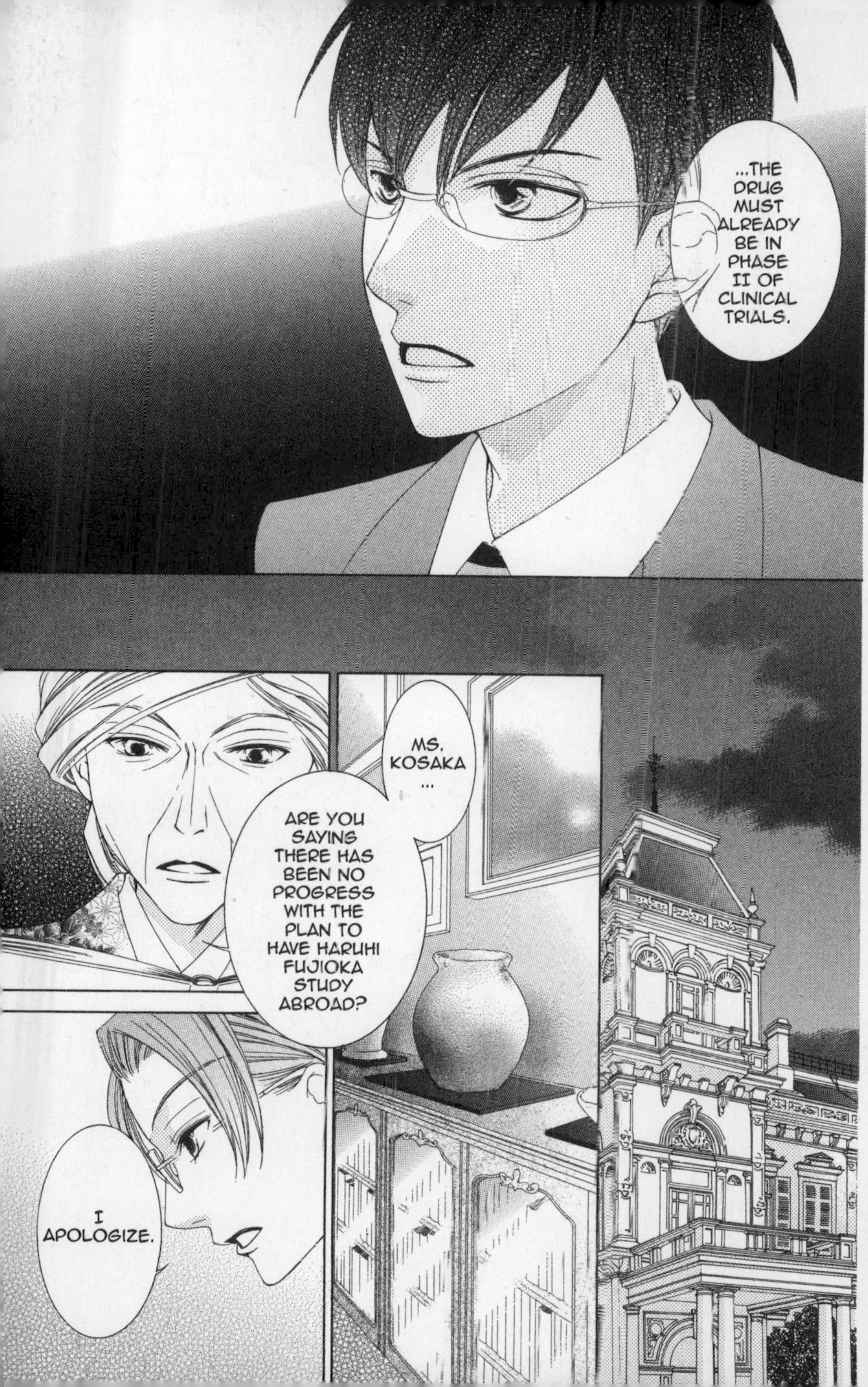
...THE DRUG MUST ALREADY BE IN PHASE II OF CLINICAL TRIALS.
MS. KOSAKA ...
ARE YOU SAYING THERE HAS BEEN NO PROGRESS WITH THE PLAN TO HAVE HARUHI FUJIOKA STUDY ABROAD?
I APOLOGIZE.

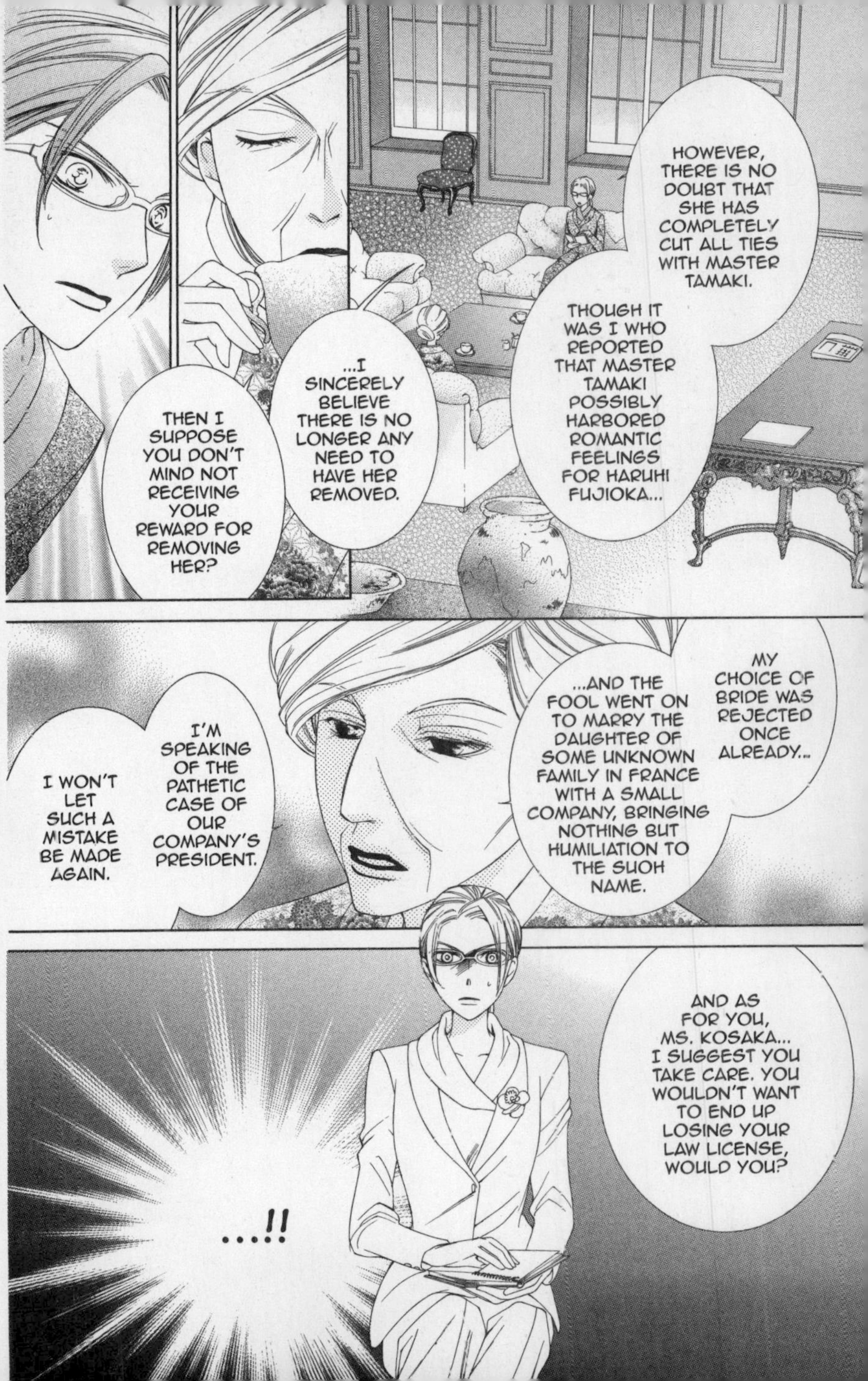
HOWEVER, THERE IS NO DOUBT THAT SHE HAS COMPLETELY CUT ALL TIES WITH MASTER TAMAKI.
THOUGH IT WAS I WHO REPORTED THAT MASTER TAMAKI POSSIBLY HARBORED ROMANTIC FEELINGS FOR HARUHI FUJIOKA...
...I SINCERELY BELIEVE THERE IS NO LONGER ANY NEED TO HAVE HER REMOVED.
THEN I SUPPOSE YOU DON'T MIND NOT RECEIVING YOUR REWARD FOR REMOVING HER?
MY CHOICE OF BRIDE WAS REJECTED ONCE ALREADY...
...AND THE FOOL WENT ON TO MARRY THE DAUGHTER OF SOME UNKNOWN FAMILY IN FRANCE WITH A SMALL COMPANY, BRINGING NOTHING BUT HUMILIATION TO THE SUOH NAME.
I'M SPEAKING OF THE PATHETIC CASE OF OUR COMPANY'S PRESIDENT.
I WON'T LET SUCH A MISTAKE BE MADE AGAIN.
AND AS FOR YOU, MS. KOSAKA... I SUGGEST YOU TAKE CARE. YOU WOULDN'T WANT TO END UP LOSING YOUR LAW LICENSE, WOULD YOU?
...!!

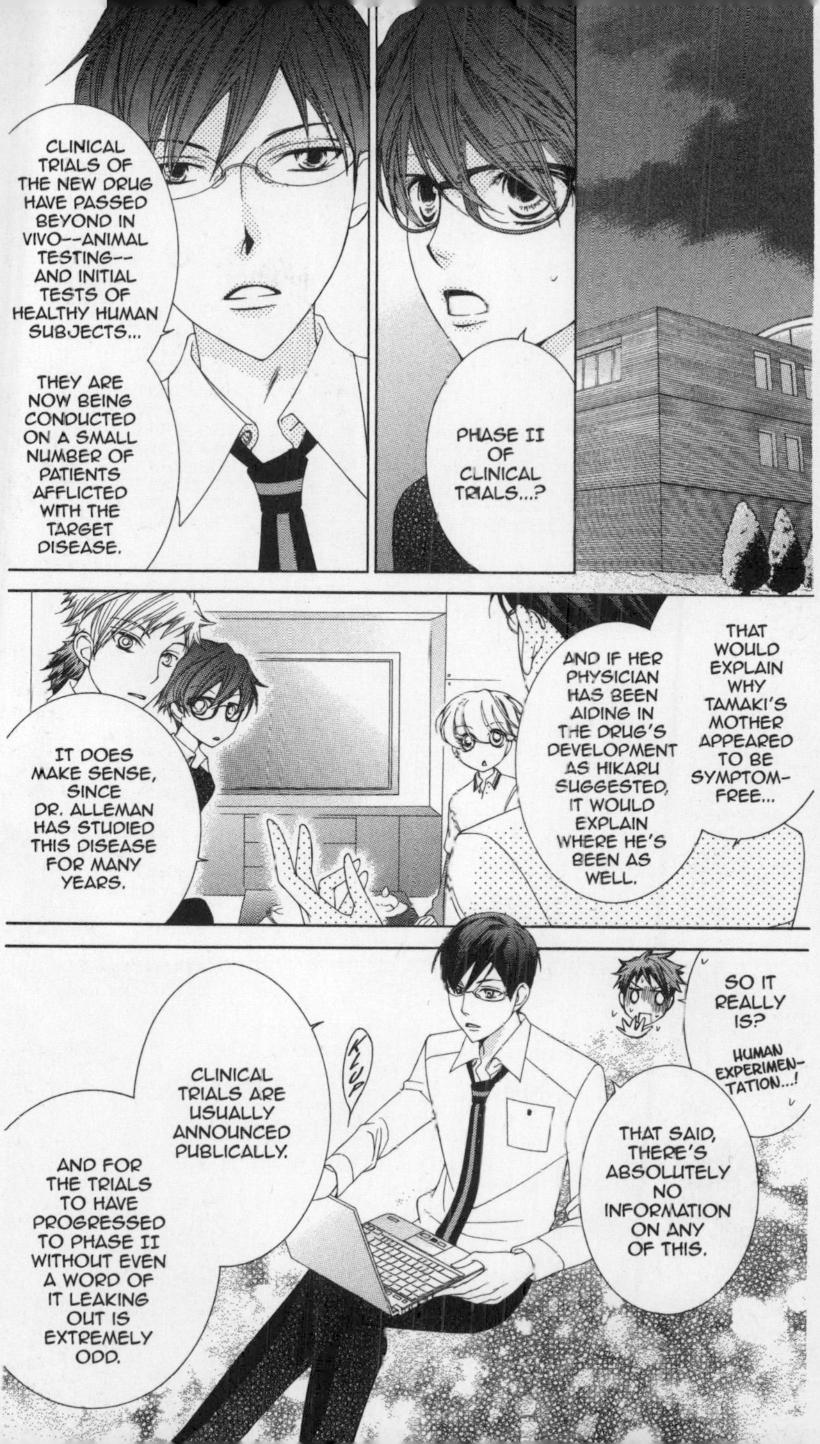
PHASE II OF CLINICAL TRIALS...?
CLINICAL TRIALS OF THE NEW DRUG HAVE PASSED BEYOND IN VIVO--ANIMAL TESTING--AND INITIAL TESTS OF HEALTHY HUMAN SUBJECTS...
THEY ARE NOW BEING CONDUCTED ON A SMALL NUMBER OF PATIENTS AFFLICTED WITH THE TARGET DISEASE.
THAT WOULD EXPLAIN WHY TAMAKI'S MOTHER APPEARED TO BE SYMPTOM-FREE...
AND IF HER PHYSICIAN HAS BEEN AIDING IN THE DRUG'S DEVELOPMENT AS HIKARU SUGGESTED, IT WOULD EXPLAIN WHERE HE'S BEEN AS WELL.
IT DOES MAKE SENSE, SINCE DR. ALLEMAN HAS STUDIED THIS DISEASE FOR MANY YEARS.
SO IT REALLY IS?
HUMAN EXPERIMENTATION...!
THAT SAID, THERE'S ABSOLUTELY NO INFORMATION ON ANY OF THIS.
CLINICAL TRIALS ARE USUALLY ANNOUNCED PUBLICALLY.
AND FOR THE TRIALS TO HAVE PROGRESSED TO PHASE II WITHOUT EVEN A WORD OF IT LEAKING OUT IS EXTREMELY ODD.

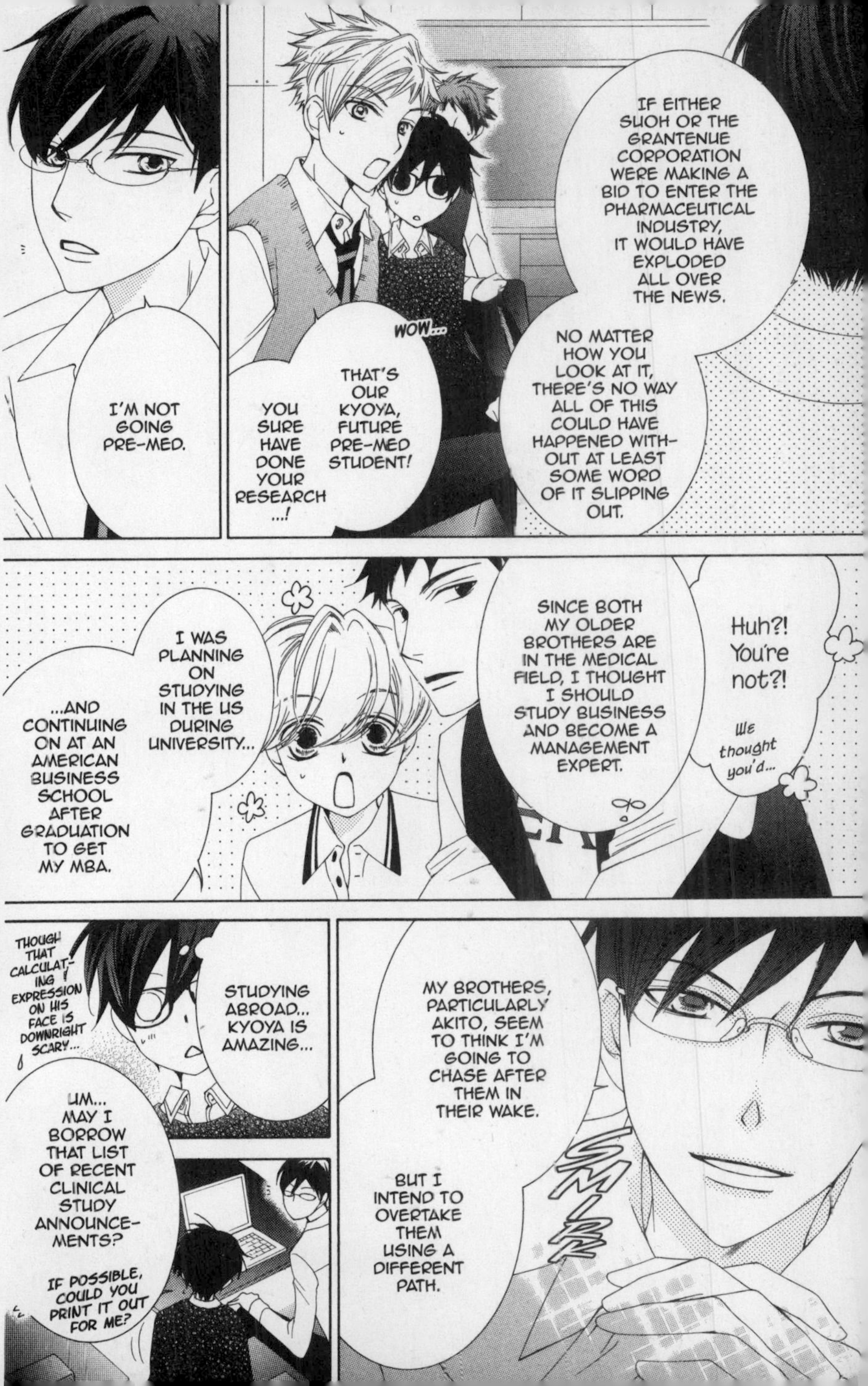
IF EITHER SUOH OR THE GRANTENUE CORPORATION WERE MAKING A BID TO ENTER THE PHARMACEUTICAL INDUSTRY, IT WOULD HAVE EXPLODED ALL OVER THE NEWS.
NO MATTER HOW YOU LOOK AT IT, THERE'S NO WAY ALL OF THIS COULD HAVE HAPPENED WITH-OUT AT LEAST SOME WORD OF IT SLIPPING OUT.
WOW...
THAT'S OUR KYOYA, FUTURE PRE-MED STUDENT!
YOU SURE HAVE DONE YOUR RESEARCH ...!
I'M NOT GOING PRE-MED.
Huh?! You're not?!
We thought you'd...
SINCE BOTH MY OLDER BROTHERS ARE IN THE MEDICAL FIELD, I THOUGHT I SHOULD STUDY BUSINESS AND BECOME A MANAGEMENT EXPERT.
I WAS PLANNING ON STUDYING IN THE US DURING UNIVERSITY...
...AND CONTINUING ON AT AN AMERICAN BUSINESS SCHOOL AFTER GRADUATION TO GET MY MBA.
MY BROTHERS, PARTICULARLY AKITO, SEEM TO THINK I'M GOING TO CHASE AFTER THEM IN THEIR WAKE.
BUT I INTEND TO OVERTAKE THEM USING A DIFFERENT PATH.
SMIRK
STUDYING ABROAD... KYOYA IS AMAZING...
THOUGH THAT CALCULAT-ING EXPRESSION ON HIS FACE IS DOWNRIGHT SCARY...
UM... MAY I BORROW THAT LIST OF RECENT CLINICAL STUDY ANNOUNCE-MENTS?
IF POSSIBLE, COULD YOU PRINT IT OUT FOR ME?

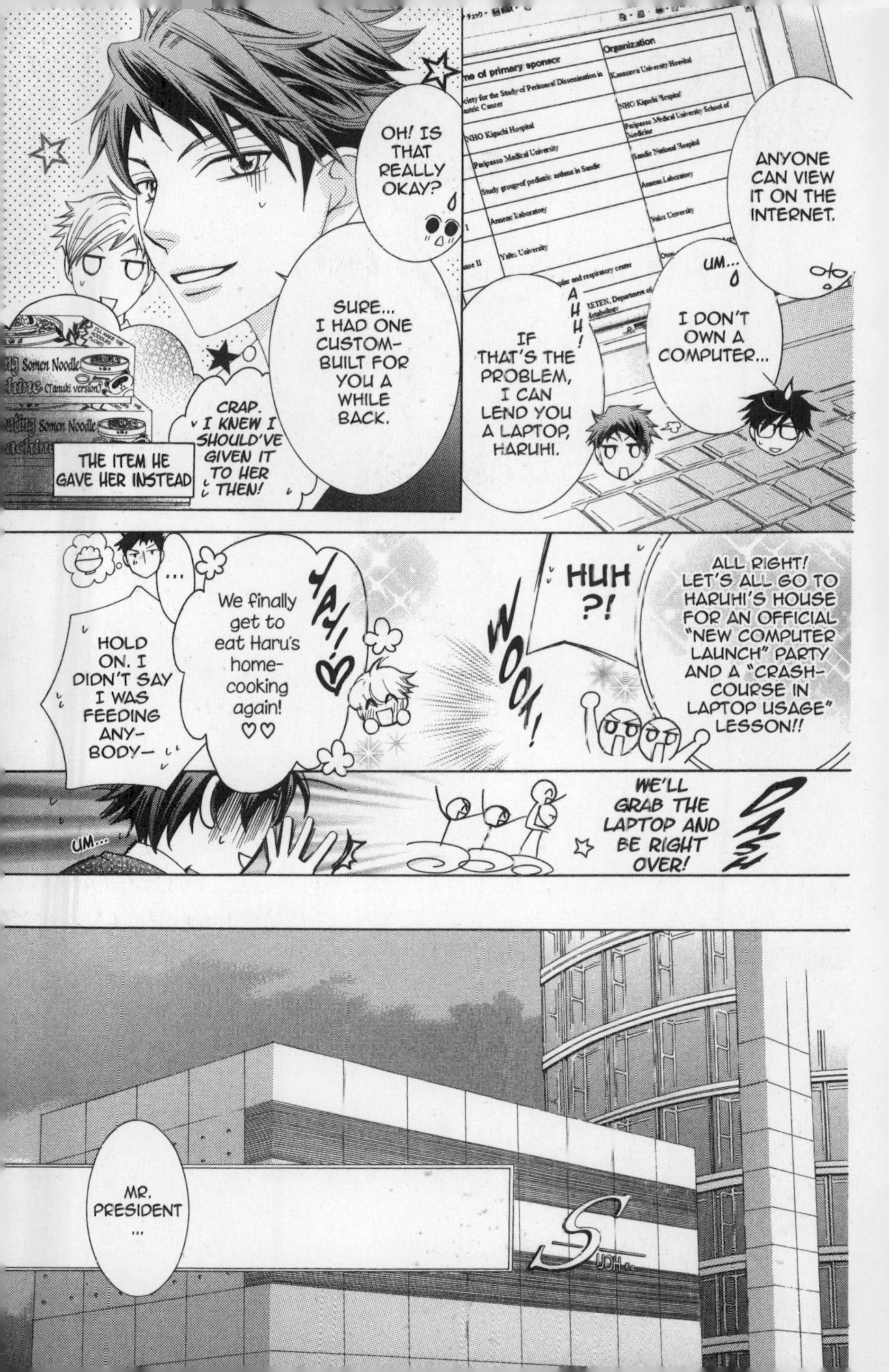
ANYONE CAN VIEW IT ON THE INTERNET.
UM...
I DON'T OWN A COMPUTER...
AHH!
IF THAT'S THE PROBLEM, I CAN LEND YOU A LAPTOP, HARUHI.
OH! IS THAT REALLY OKAY?
SURE... I HAD ONE CUSTOM-BUILT FOR YOU A WHILE BACK.
CRAP. I KNEW I SHOULD'VE GIVEN IT TO HER THEN!
THE ITEM HE GAVE HER INSTEAD
ALL RIGHT! LET'S ALL GO TO HARUHI'S HOUSE FOR AN OFFICIAL "NEW COMPUTER LAUNCH" PARTY AND A "CRASH-COURSE IN LAPTOP USAGE" LESSON!!
HUH ?!
WOOH!
YAY!♡
We finally get to eat Haru's home-cooking again! ♡♡
...
HOLD ON. I DIDN'T SAY I WAS FEEDING ANYBODY—
DASH
WE'LL GRAB THE LAPTOP AND BE RIGHT OVER!
UM...
MR. PRESIDENT ...

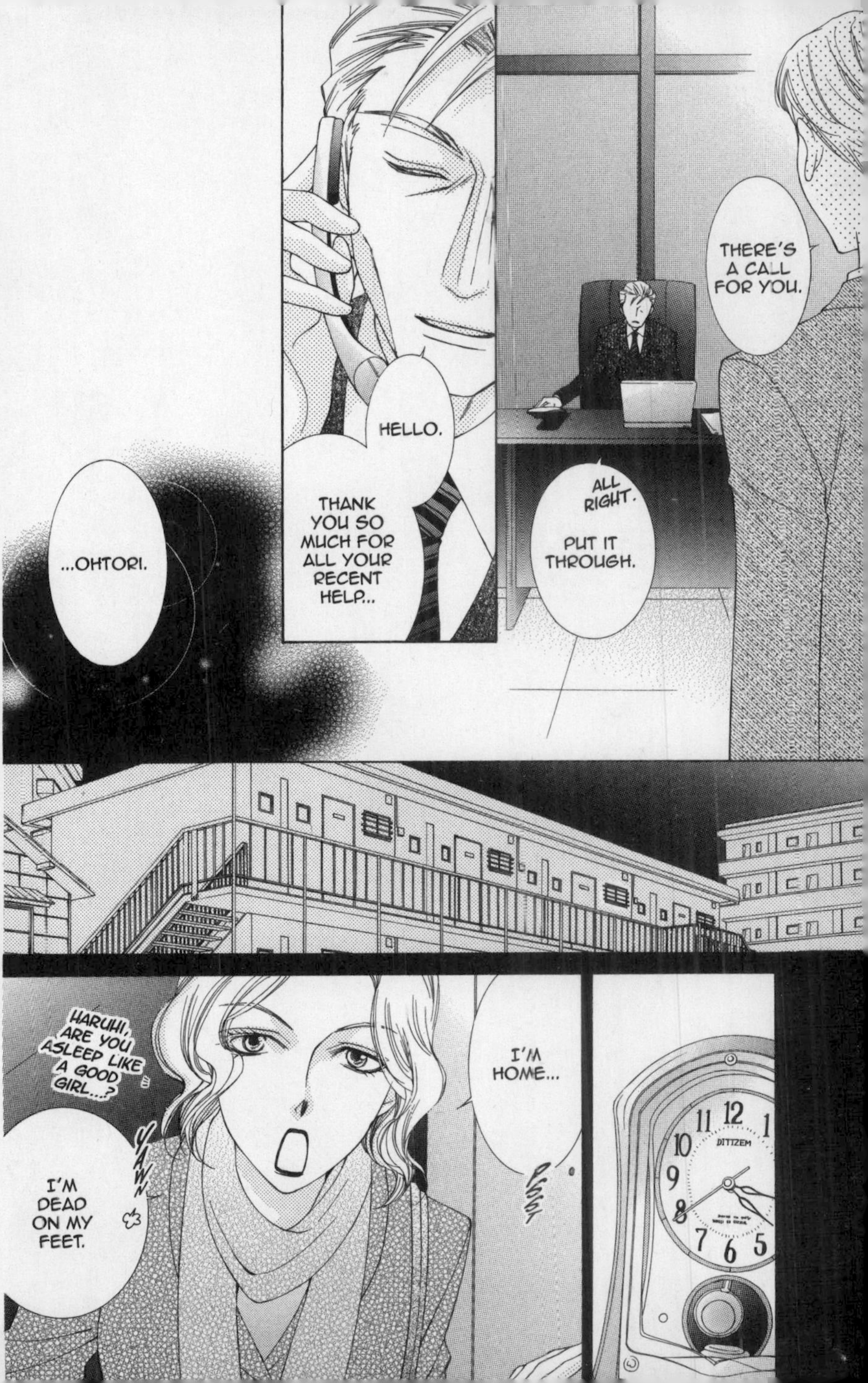
THERE'S A CALL FOR YOU.
ALL RIGHT.
PUT IT THROUGH.
HELLO.
THANK YOU SO MUCH FOR ALL YOUR RECENT HELP...
...OHTORI.
DITTZEM
I'M HOME...
HARUHI, ARE YOU ASLEEP LIKE A GOOD GIRL...?
YAWN
I'M DEAD ON MY FEET.

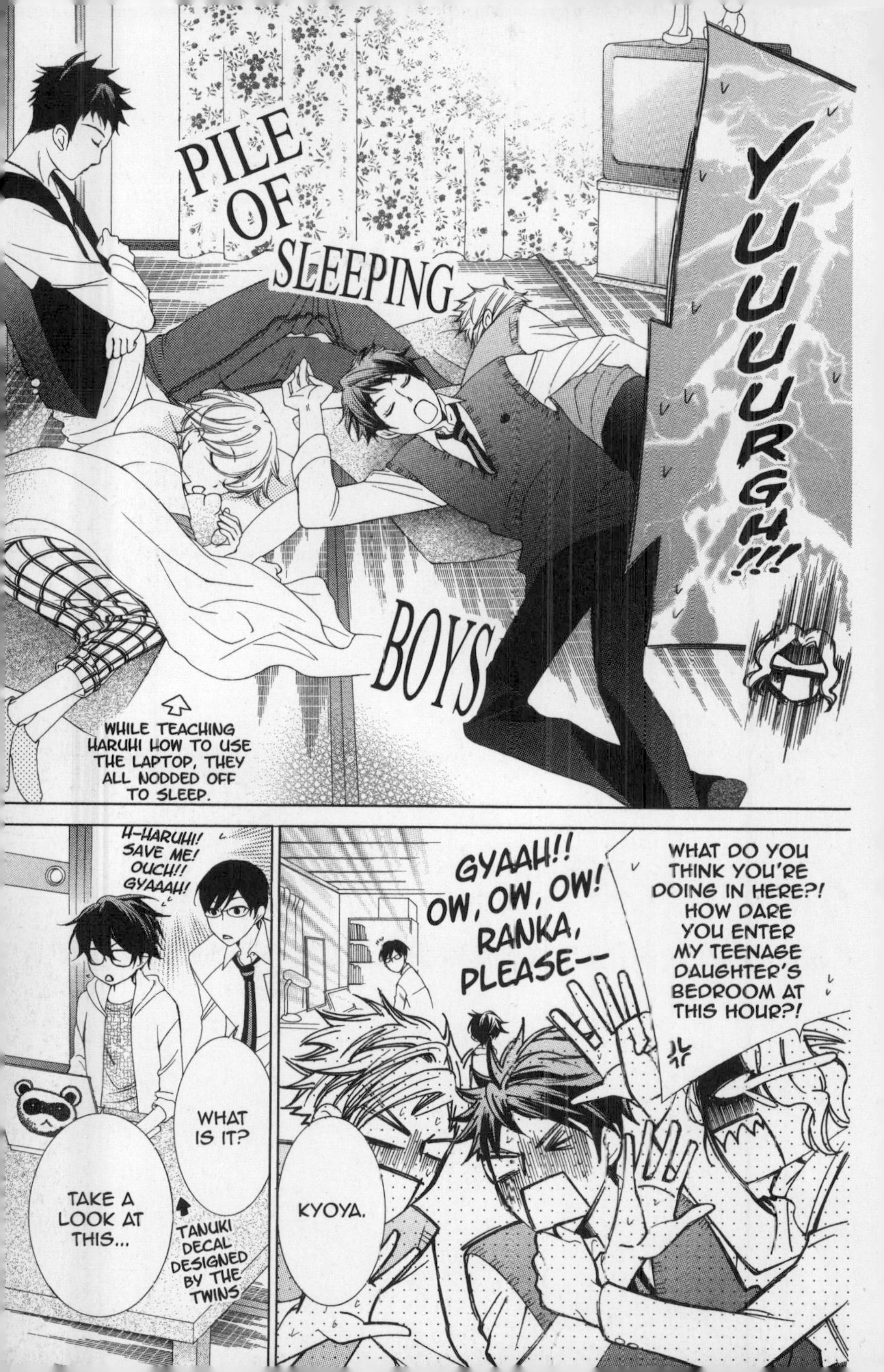
YUUURGH!!!
PILE OF SLEEPING BOYS
WHILE TEACHING HARUHI HOW TO USE THE LAPTOP, THEY ALL NODDED OFF TO SLEEP.
WHAT DO YOU THINK YOU'RE DOING IN HERE?! HOW DARE YOU ENTER MY TEENAGE DAUGHTER'S BEDROOM AT THIS HOUR?!
GYAAH!! OW, OW, OW! RANKA, PLEASE--
KYOYA.
H-HARUHI! SAVE ME! OUCH!! GYAAAH!
WHAT IS IT?
TAKE A LOOK AT THIS...
TANUKI DECAL DESIGNED BY THE TWINS

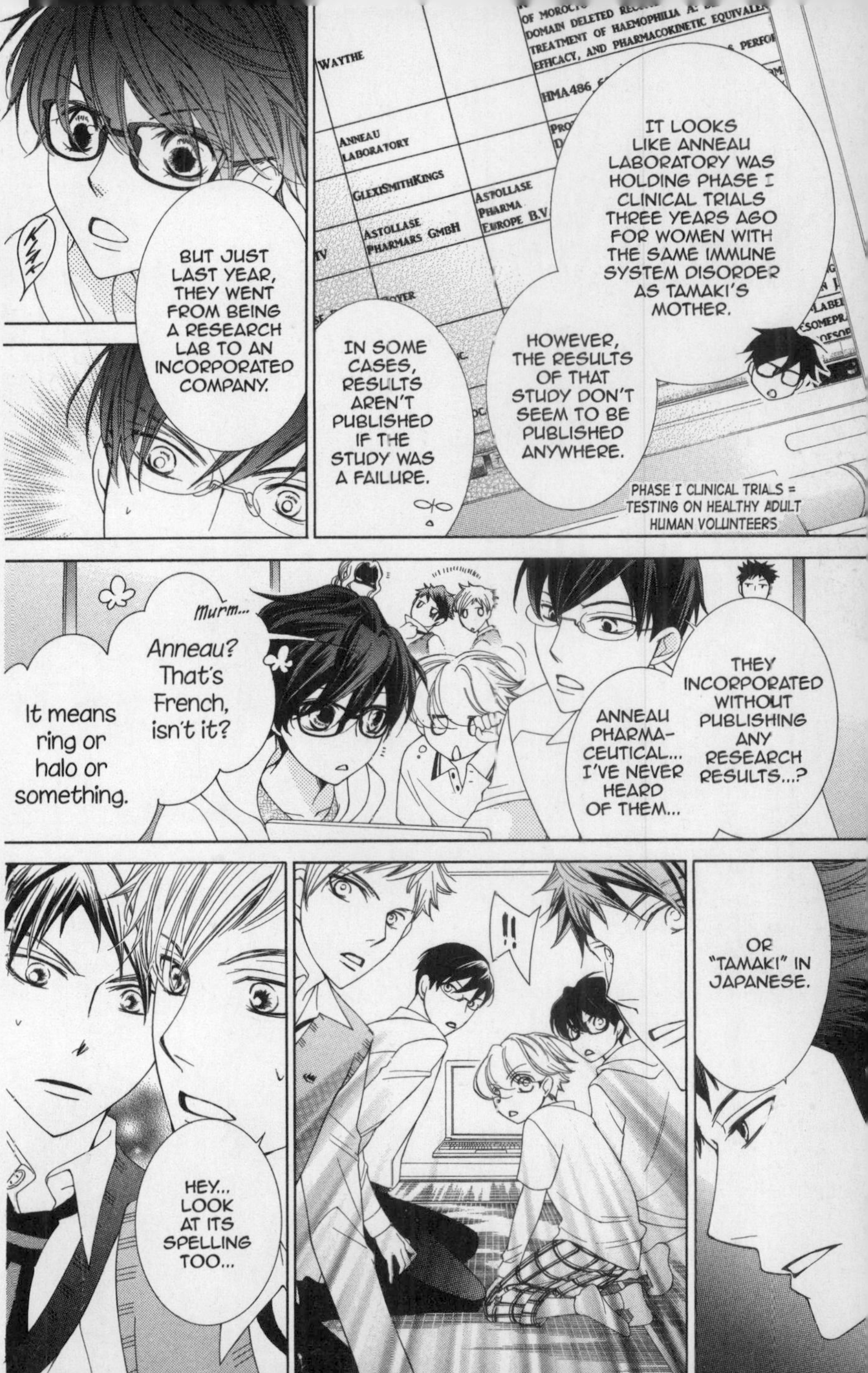

WAYTHE
HMA486
ANNEAU LABORATORY
GLEXISMITHKINGS
ASTOLLASE PHARMA EUROPE B.V
ASTOLLASE PHARMARS GMBH
IT LOOKS LIKE ANNEAU LABORATORY WAS HOLDING PHASE I CLINICAL TRIALS THREE YEARS AGO FOR WOMEN WITH THE SAME IMMUNE SYSTEM DISORDER AS TAMAKI'S MOTHER.
HOWEVER, THE RESULTS OF THAT STUDY DON'T SEEM TO BE PUBLISHED ANYWHERE.
IN SOME CASES, RESULTS AREN'T PUBLISHED IF THE STUDY WAS A FAILURE.
PHASE I CLINICAL TRIALS = TESTING ON HEALTHY ADULT HUMAN VOLUNTEERS
BUT JUST LAST YEAR, THEY WENT FROM BEING A RESEARCH LAB TO AN INCORPORATED COMPANY.
THEY INCORPORATED WITHOUT PUBLISHING ANY RESEARCH RESULTS...?
ANNEAU PHARMACEUTICAL... I'VE NEVER HEARD OF THEM...
Murm...
Anneau? That's French, isn't it?
It means ring or halo or something.
OR "TAMAKI" IN JAPANESE.
!!
HEY... LOOK AT ITS SPELLING TOO...

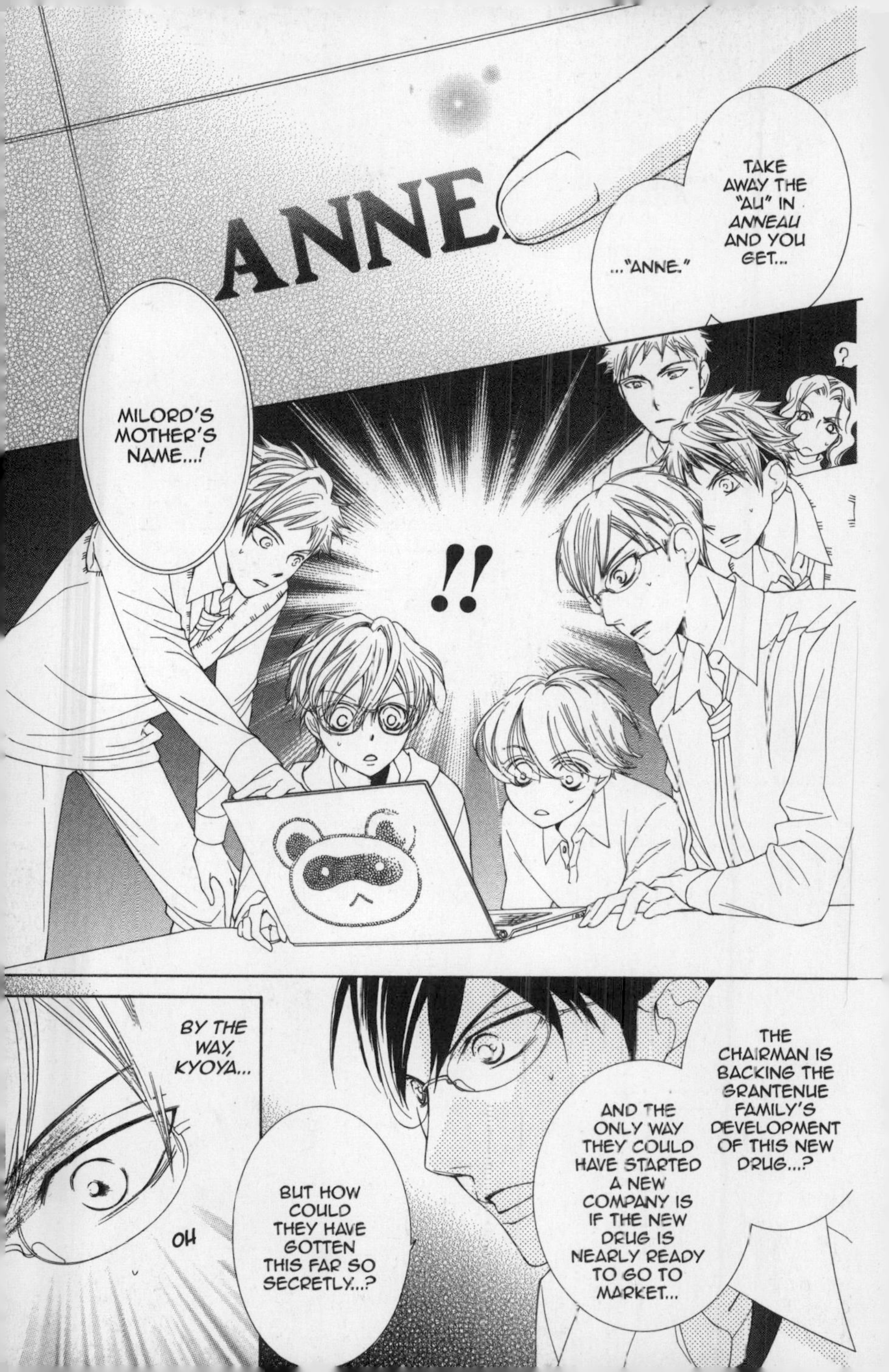
ANNE
TAKE AWAY THE "AU" IN ANNEAU AND YOU GET...
..."ANNE."
?
MILORD'S MOTHER'S NAME...!
!!
THE CHAIRMAN IS BACKING THE GRANTENUE FAMILY'S DEVELOPMENT OF THIS NEW DRUG...?
AND THE ONLY WAY THEY COULD HAVE STARTED A NEW COMPANY IS IF THE NEW DRUG IS NEARLY READY TO GO TO MARKET...
BUT HOW COULD THEY HAVE GOTTEN THIS FAR SO SECRETLY...?
BY THE WAY, KYOYA...
OH

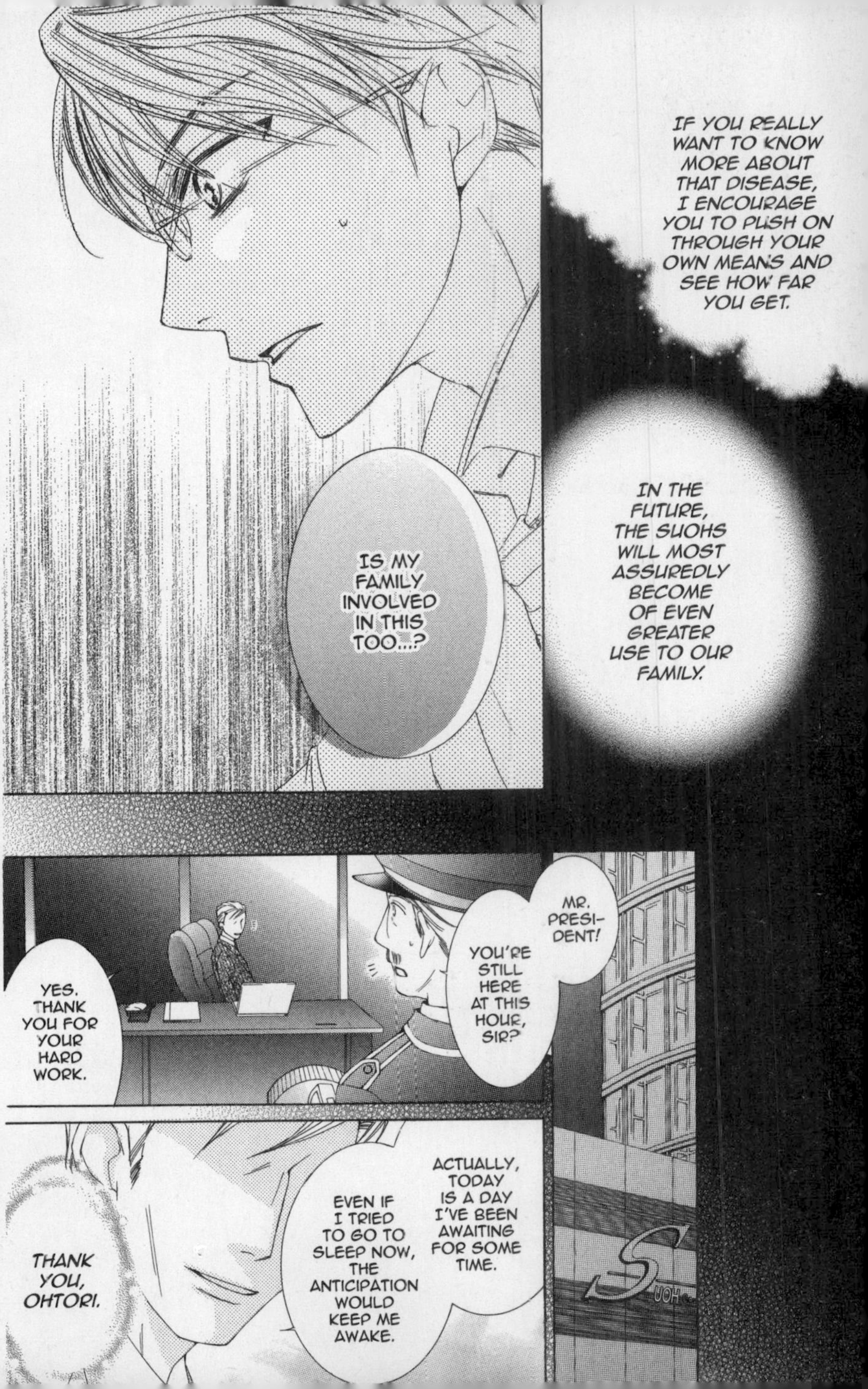
IF YOU REALLY WANT TO KNOW MORE ABOUT THAT DISEASE, I ENCOURAGE YOU TO PUSH ON THROUGH YOUR OWN MEANS AND SEE HOW FAR YOU GET.
IN THE FUTURE, THE SUOHS WILL MOST ASSUREDLY BECOME OF EVEN GREATER USE TO OUR FAMILY.
IS MY FAMILY INVOLVED IN THIS TOO...?
SUOH
MR. PRESIDENT!
YOU'RE STILL HERE AT THIS HOUR, SIR?
YES. THANK YOU FOR YOUR HARD WORK.
ACTUALLY, TODAY IS A DAY I'VE BEEN AWAITING FOR SOME TIME.
EVEN IF I TRIED TO GO TO SLEEP NOW, THE ANTICIPATION WOULD KEEP ME AWAKE.
THANK YOU, OHTORI.

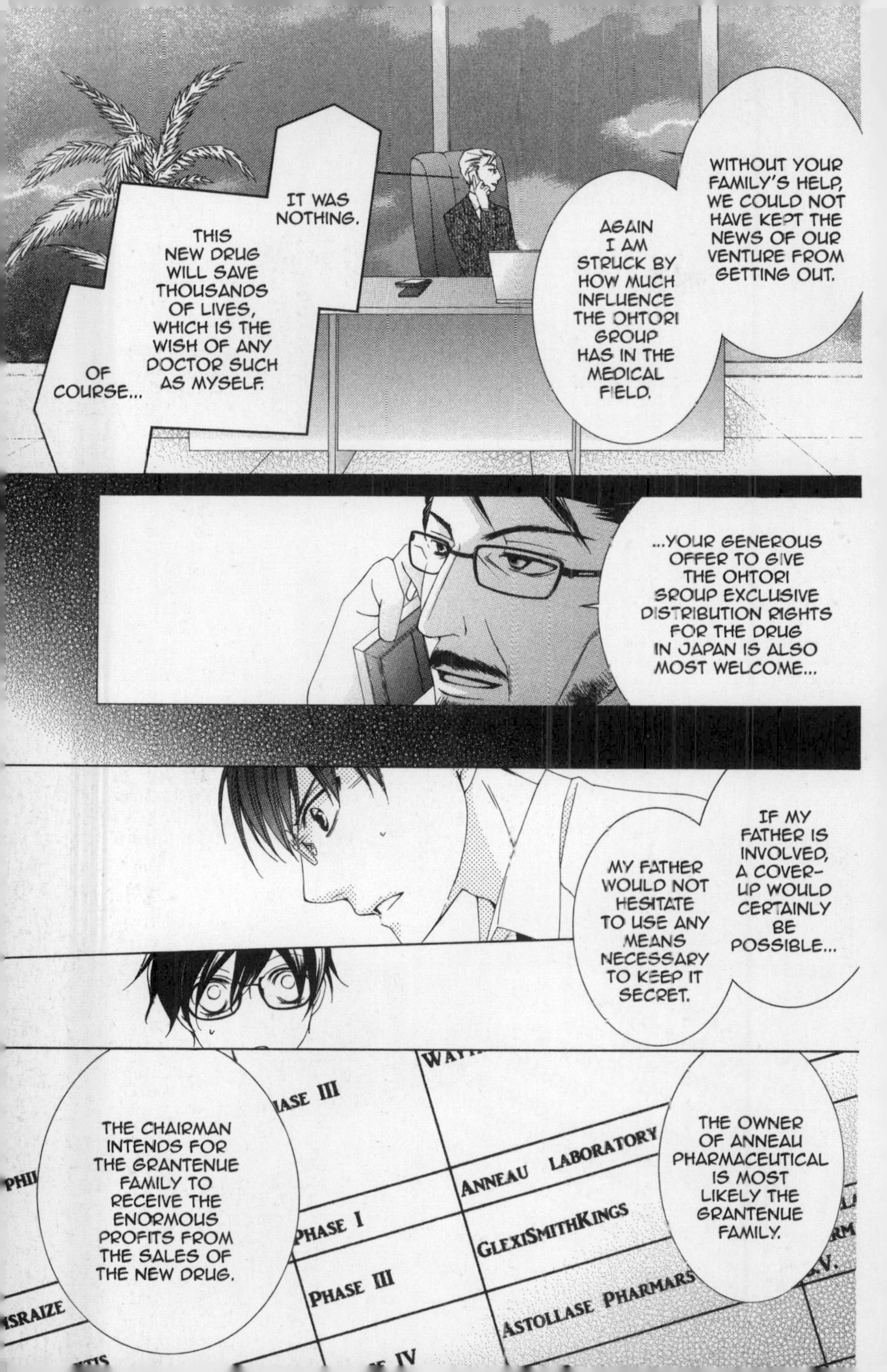
WITHOUT YOUR FAMILY'S HELP, WE COULD NOT HAVE KEPT THE NEWS OF OUR VENTURE FROM GETTING OUT.
AGAIN I AM STRUCK BY HOW MUCH INFLUENCE THE OHTORI GROUP HAS IN THE MEDICAL FIELD.
IT WAS NOTHING.
THIS NEW DRUG WILL SAVE THOUSANDS OF LIVES, WHICH IS THE WISH OF ANY DOCTOR SUCH AS MYSELF.
OF COURSE...
...YOUR GENEROUS OFFER TO GIVE THE OHTORI GROUP EXCLUSIVE DISTRIBUTION RIGHTS FOR THE DRUG IN JAPAN IS ALSO MOST WELCOME...
IF MY FATHER IS INVOLVED, A COVER-UP WOULD CERTAINLY BE POSSIBLE...
MY FATHER WOULD NOT HESITATE TO USE ANY MEANS NECESSARY TO KEEP IT SECRET.
THE OWNER OF ANNEAU PHARMACEUTICAL IS MOST LIKELY THE GRANTENUE FAMILY.
ANNEAU LABORATORY
GLEXISMITHKINGS
ASTOLLASE PHARMARS
PHASE I
PHASE III
THE CHAIRMAN INTENDS FOR THE GRANTENUE FAMILY TO RECEIVE THE ENORMOUS PROFITS FROM THE SALES OF THE NEW DRUG.

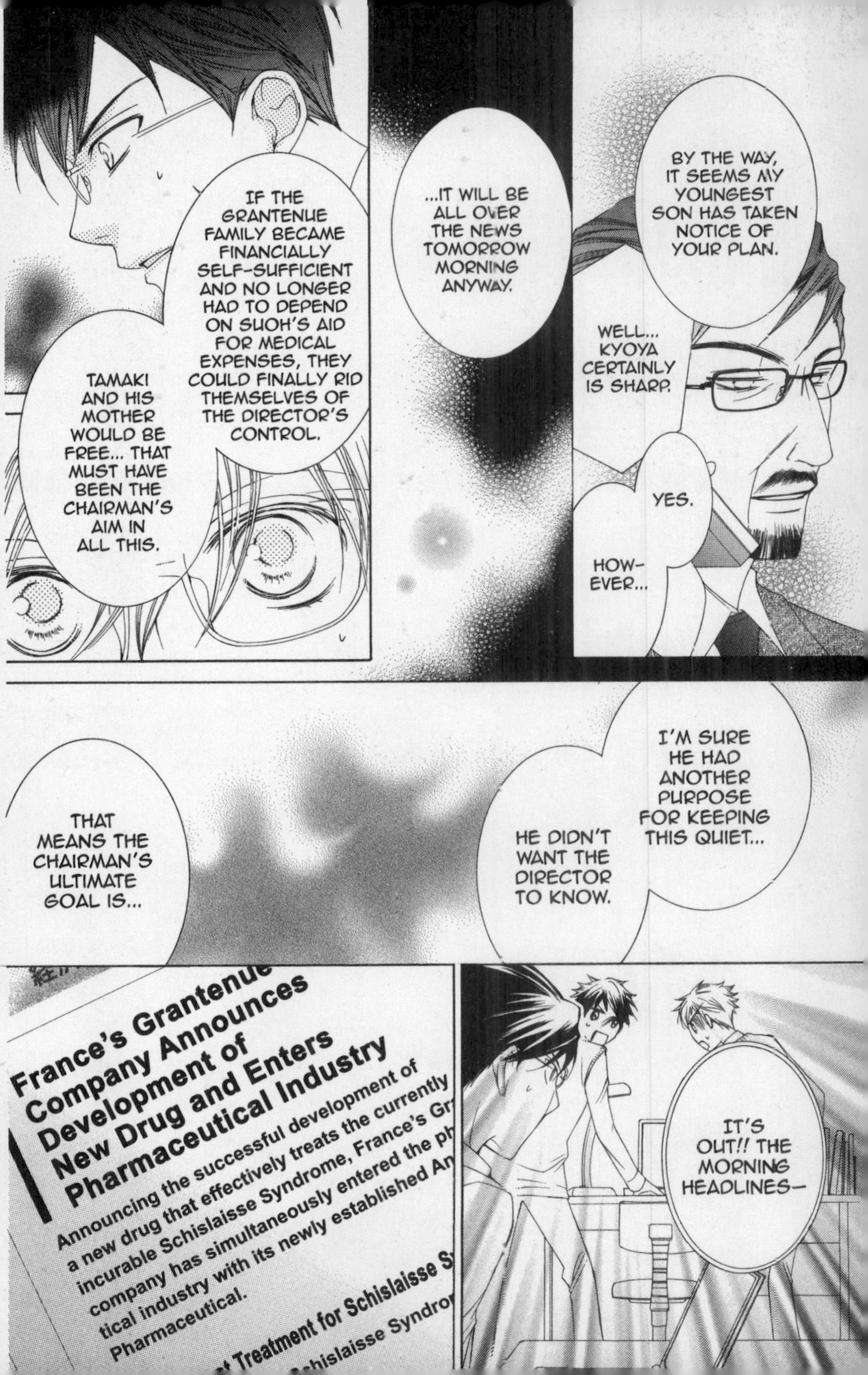
BY THE WAY, IT SEEMS MY YOUNGEST SON HAS TAKEN NOTICE OF YOUR PLAN.
WELL... KYOYA CERTAINLY IS SHARP.
YES.
HOW-EVER...
...IT WILL BE ALL OVER THE NEWS TOMORROW MORNING ANYWAY.
IF THE GRANTENUE FAMILY BECAME FINANCIALLY SELF-SUFFICIENT AND NO LONGER HAD TO DEPEND ON SUOH'S AID FOR MEDICAL EXPENSES, THEY COULD FINALLY RID THEMSELVES OF THE DIRECTOR'S CONTROL.
TAMAKI AND HIS MOTHER WOULD BE FREE... THAT MUST HAVE BEEN THE CHAIRMAN'S AIM IN ALL THIS.
I'M SURE HE HAD ANOTHER PURPOSE FOR KEEPING THIS QUIET...
HE DIDN'T WANT THE DIRECTOR TO KNOW.
THAT MEANS THE CHAIRMAN'S ULTIMATE GOAL IS...
IT'S OUT!! THE MORNING HEADLINES—
France's Grantenue Company Announces Development of New Drug and Enters Pharmaceutical Industry
Announcing the successful development of a new drug that effectively treats the currently incurable Schislaisse Syndrome, France's Gr company has simultaneously entered the ph tical industry with its newly established An Pharmaceutical.
Treatment for Schislaisse Sy
Schislaisse Syndro

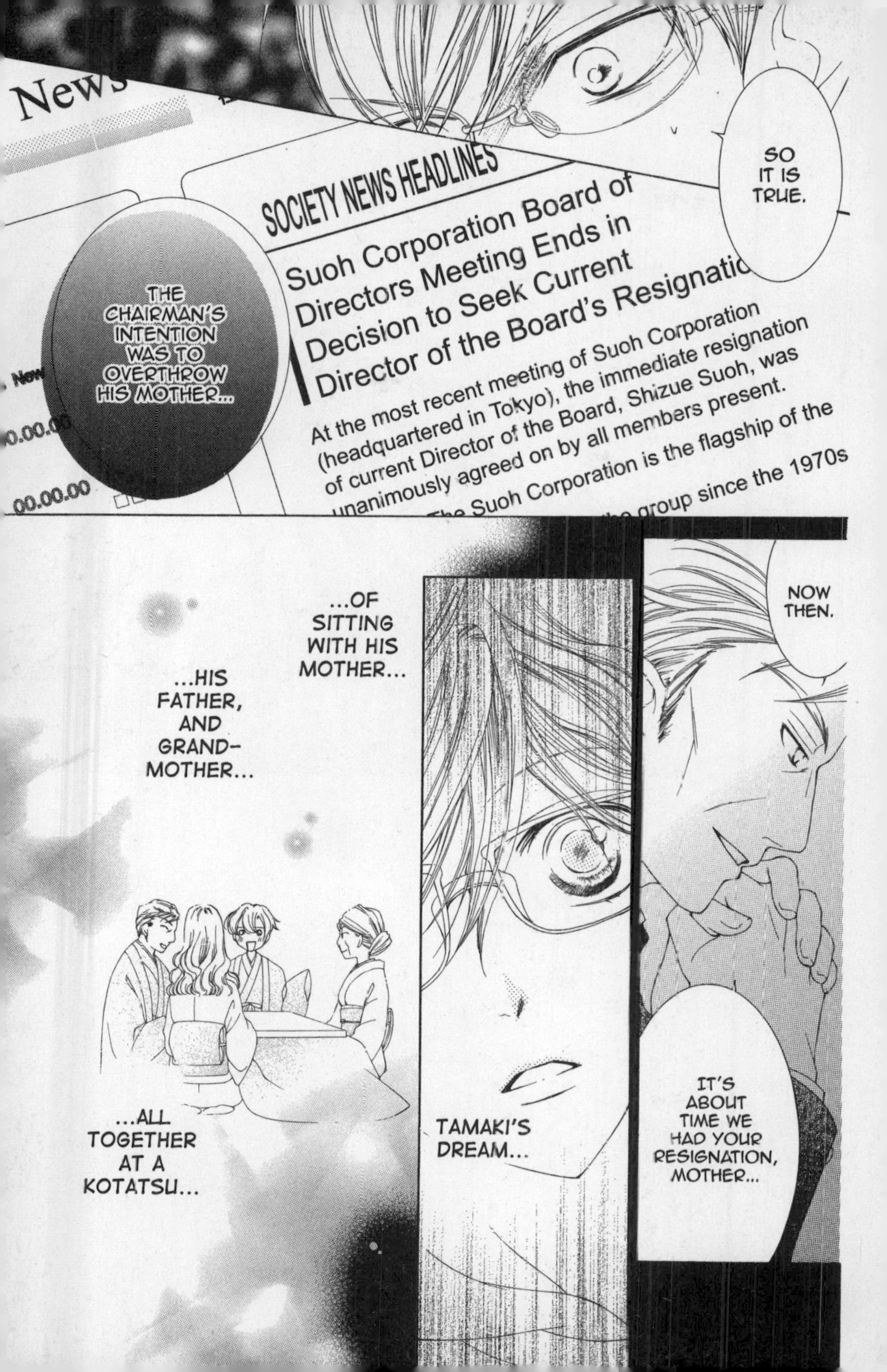
SO IT IS TRUE.
News
SOCIETY NEWS HEADLINES
Suoh Corporation Board of Directors Meeting Ends in Decision to Seek Current Director of the Board's Resignatio
At the most recent meeting of Suoh Corporation (headquartered in Tokyo), the immediate resignation of current Director of the Board, Shizue Suoh, was unanimously agreed on by all members present.
The Suoh Corporation is the flagship of the group since the 1970s
THE CHAIRMAN'S INTENTION WAS TO OVERTHROW HIS MOTHER...
NOW THEN.
IT'S ABOUT TIME WE HAD YOUR RESIGNATION, MOTHER...
TAMAKI'S DREAM...
...OF SITTING WITH HIS MOTHER...
...HIS FATHER, AND GRAND-MOTHER...
...ALL TOGETHER AT A KOTATSU...

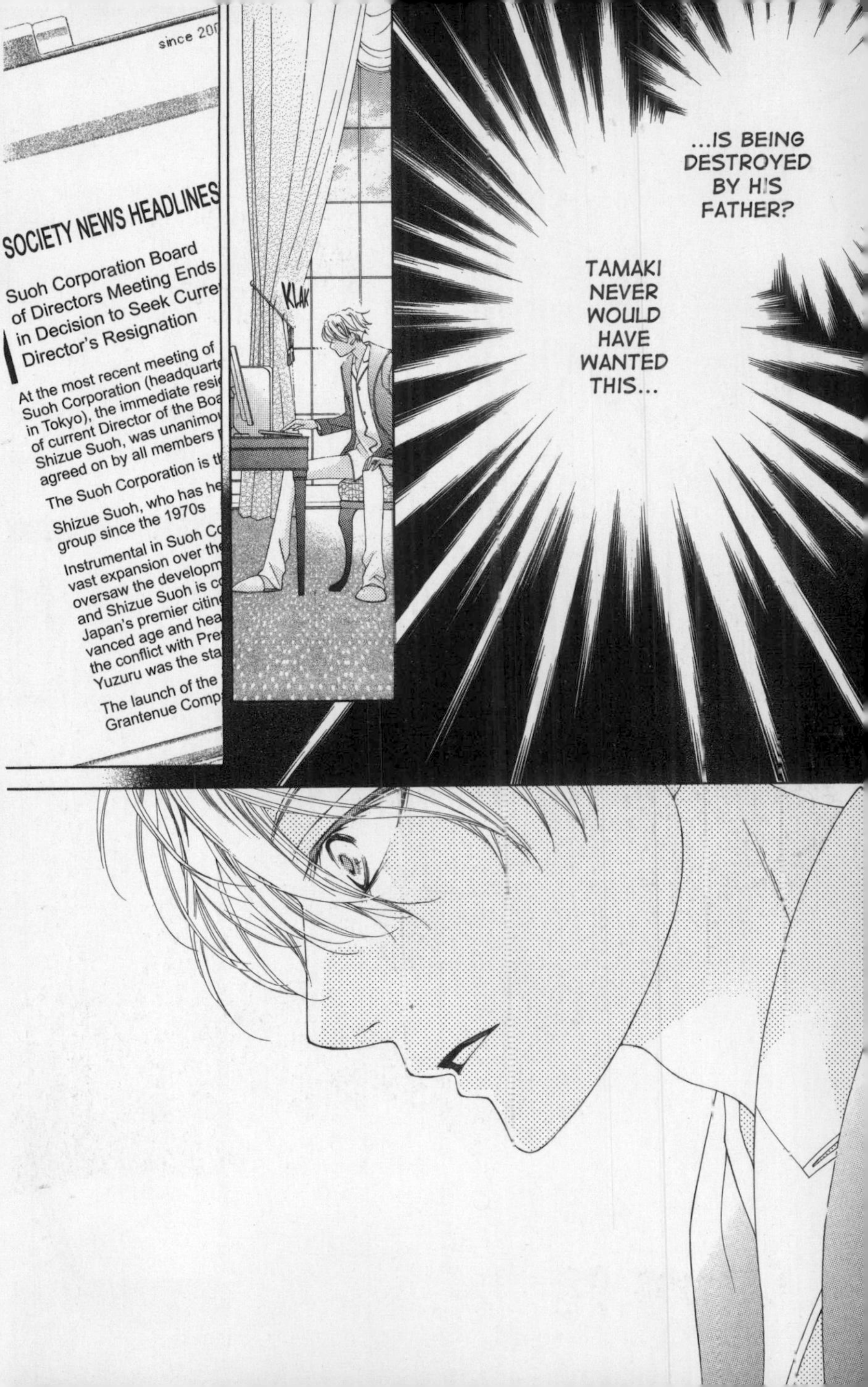
...IS BEING DESTROYED BY HIS FATHER?
TAMAKI NEVER WOULD HAVE WANTED THIS...
KLAK
since 20
SOCIETY NEWS HEADLINES
Suoh Corporation Board of Directors Meeting Ends in Decision to Seek Curre Director's Resignation
At the most recent meeting of Suoh Corporation (headquarte in Tokyo), the immediate resi of current Director of the Boa Shizue Suoh, was unanimo agreed on by all members
The Suoh Corporation is t
Shizue Suoh, who has he group since the 1970s
Instrumental in Suoh Co vast expansion over the oversaw the developm and Shizue Suoh is co Japan's premier citin vanced age and hea the conflict with Pre Yuzuru was the sta
The launch of the Grantenue Comp

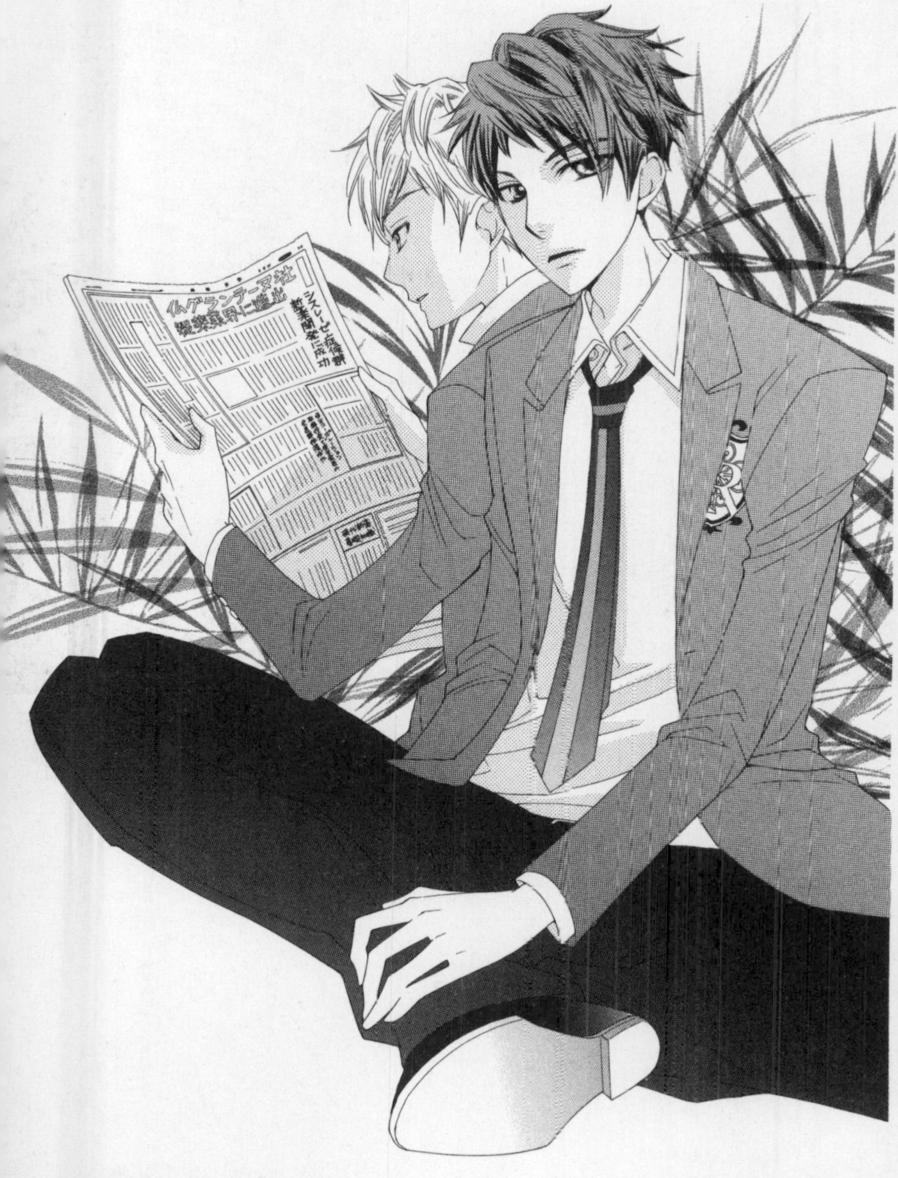
仏グランテーヌ社
製薬業界に進出
シスレーゼ症候群
新薬開発に成功

EPISODE 78

France's Grantenue Company Announces Development of New Drug and Enters Pharmaceutical Industry

Announcing the successful development of a new drug that effectively treats the currently incurable Schislaisse Syndrome, France's Grantenue Company has simultaneously entered the pharmaceutical industry with its newly established Annue Pharmaceutical.

...Schislaisse Sy

SOCIETY NEWS HEADLINES

Suoh Corporation Board of Directors Meeting Ends in Decision to Seek Current Director of the Board's Resignation

At the most recent meeting of Suoh Corporation (headquartered in Tokyo), the immediate resignation of current Director of the Board, Shizue Suoh, was unanimously agreed on by all members pr...

The Suoh Corporation is the...

...ho has be...

WHAT IS THIS...?

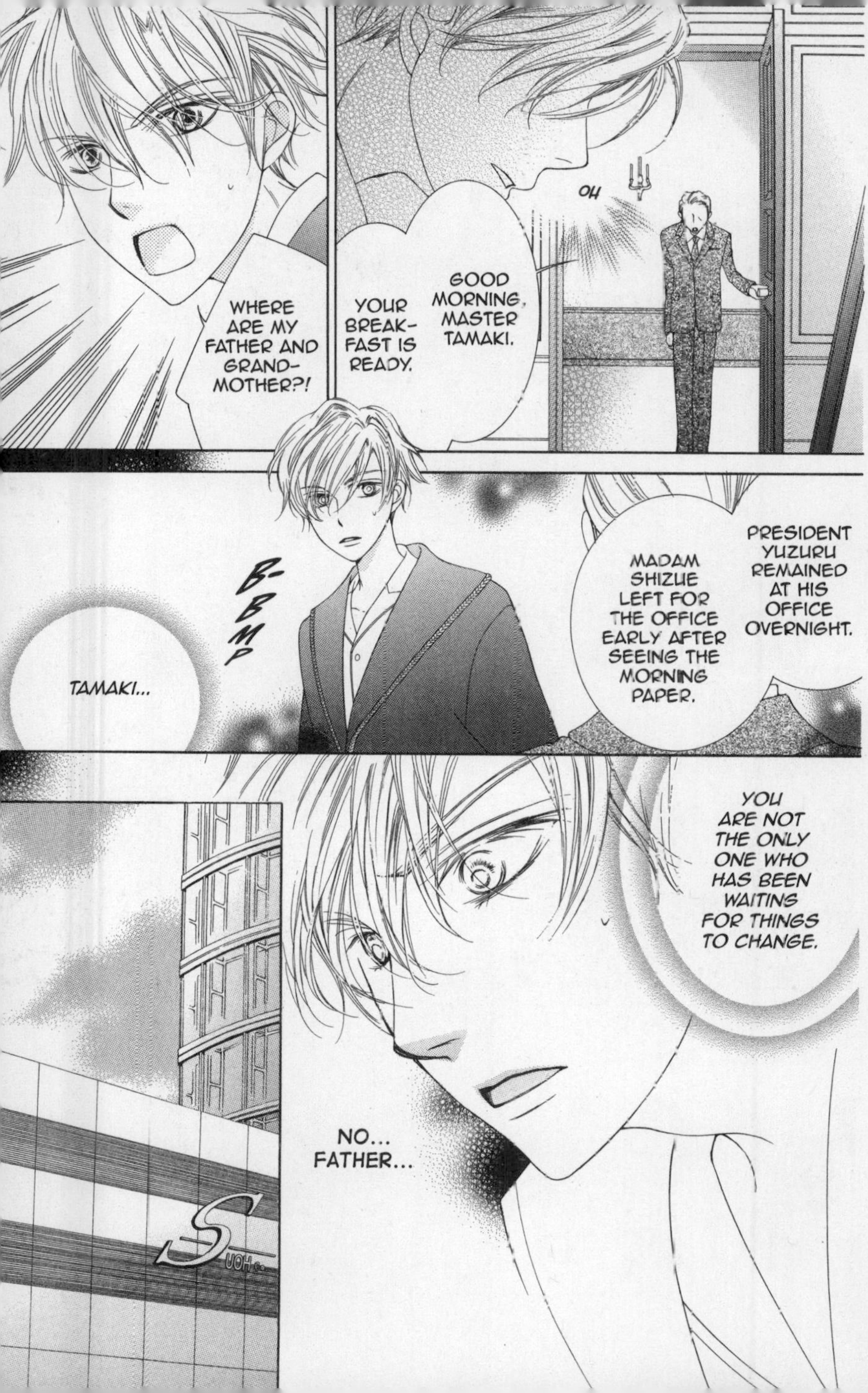
OH
GOOD MORNING, MASTER TAMAKI.
YOUR BREAK-FAST IS READY.
WHERE ARE MY FATHER AND GRAND-MOTHER?!
PRESIDENT YUZURU REMAINED AT HIS OFFICE OVERNIGHT.
MADAM SHIZUE LEFT FOR THE OFFICE EARLY AFTER SEEING THE MORNING PAPER.
B-BMP
TAMAKI...
YOU ARE NOT THE ONLY ONE WHO HAS BEEN WAITING FOR THINGS TO CHANGE.
NO... FATHER...
SUOH

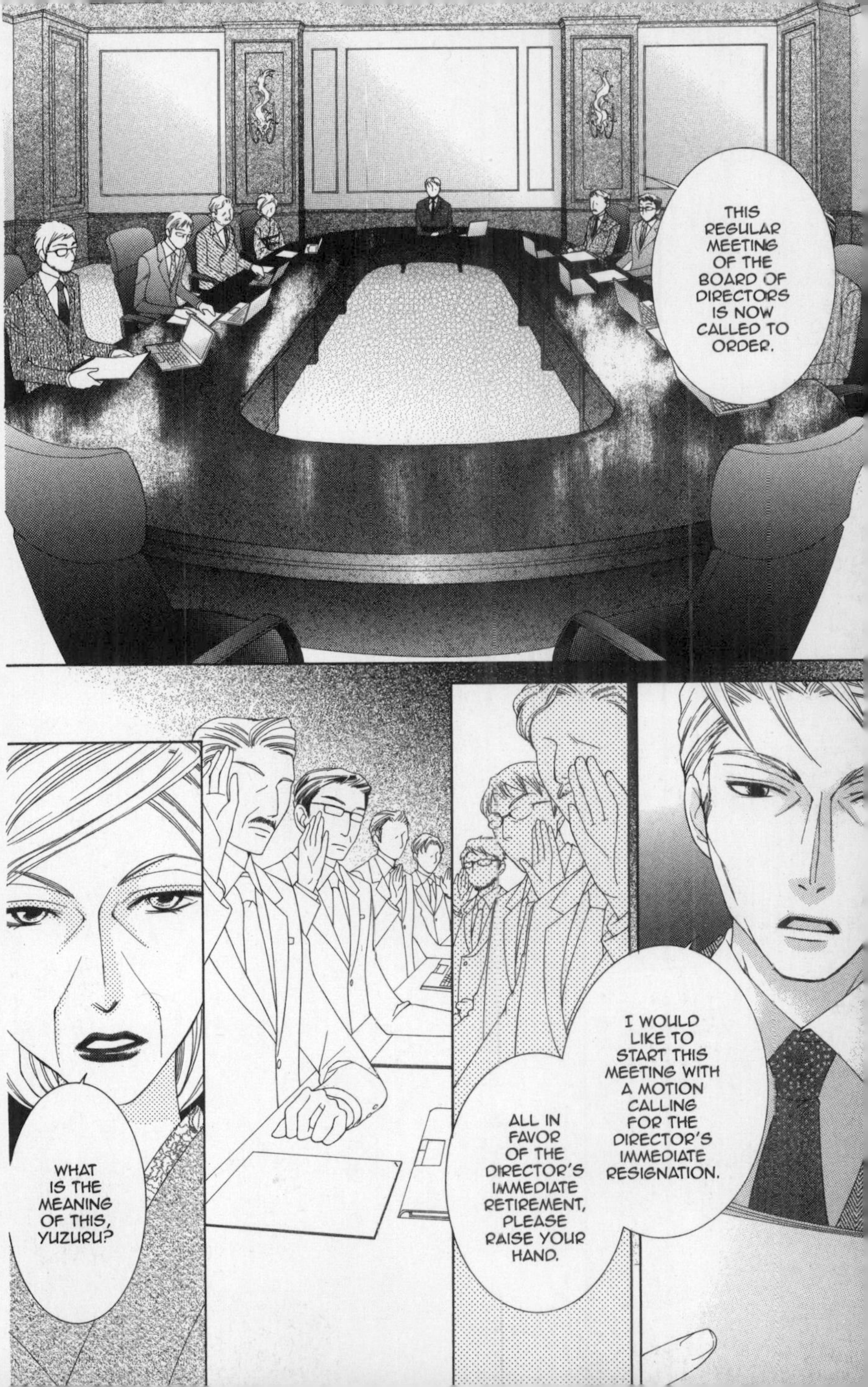
THIS REGULAR MEETING OF THE BOARD OF DIRECTORS IS NOW CALLED TO ORDER.
I WOULD LIKE TO START THIS MEETING WITH A MOTION CALLING FOR THE DIRECTOR'S IMMEDIATE RESIGNATION.
ALL IN FAVOR OF THE DIRECTOR'S IMMEDIATE RETIREMENT, PLEASE RAISE YOUR HAND.
WHAT IS THE MEANING OF THIS, YUZURU?

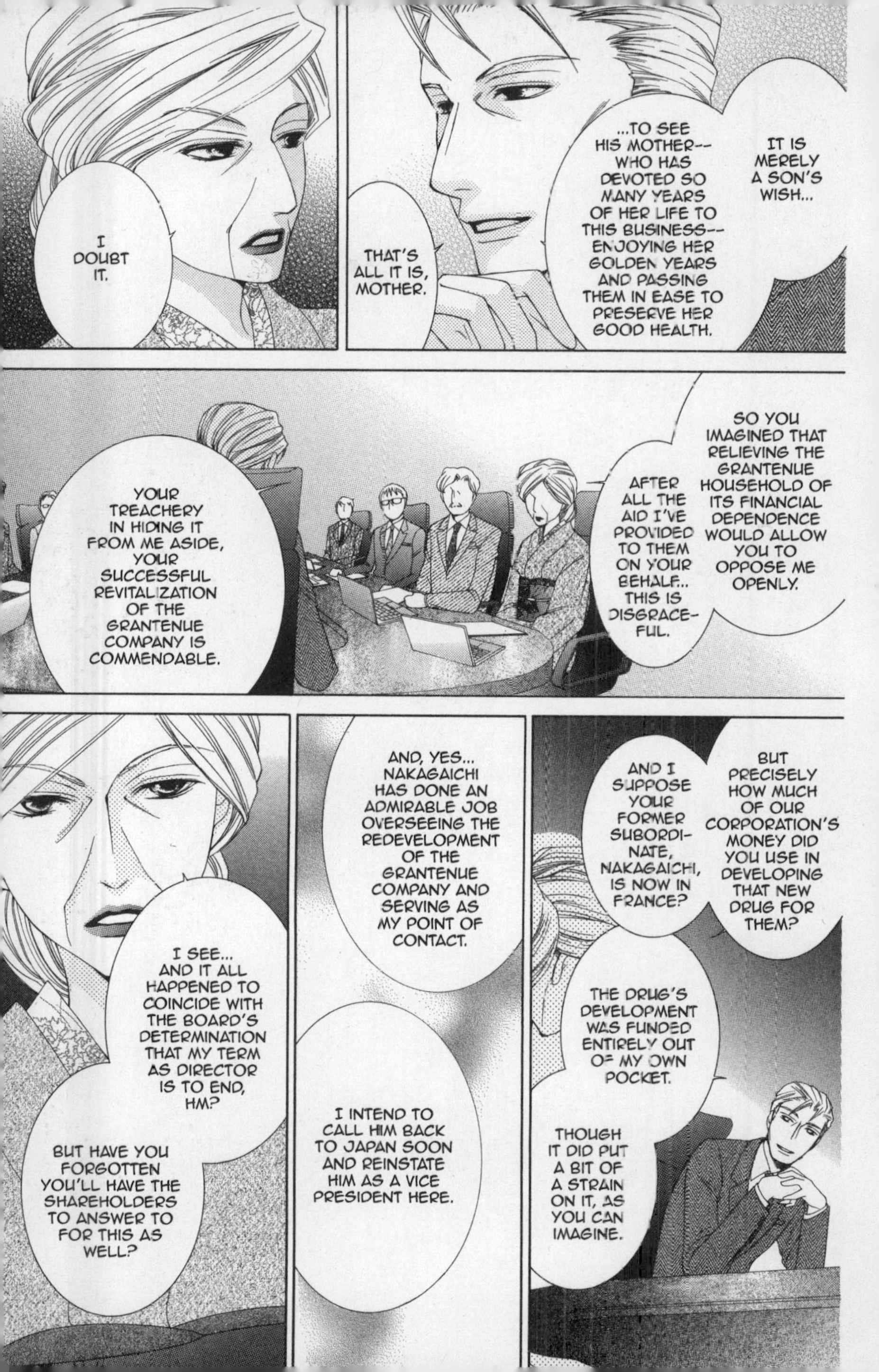
IT IS MERELY A SON'S WISH...
...TO SEE HIS MOTHER-- WHO HAS DEVOTED SO MANY YEARS OF HER LIFE TO THIS BUSINESS-- ENJOYING HER GOLDEN YEARS AND PASSING THEM IN EASE TO PRESERVE HER GOOD HEALTH.
THAT'S ALL IT IS, MOTHER.
I DOUBT IT.
SO YOU IMAGINED THAT RELIEVING THE GRANTENUE HOUSEHOLD OF ITS FINANCIAL DEPENDENCE WOULD ALLOW YOU TO OPPOSE ME OPENLY.
AFTER ALL THE AID I'VE PROVIDED TO THEM ON YOUR BEHALF... THIS IS DISGRACE-FUL.
YOUR TREACHERY IN HIDING IT FROM ME ASIDE, YOUR SUCCESSFUL REVITALIZATION OF THE GRANTENUE COMPANY IS COMMENDABLE.
BUT PRECISELY HOW MUCH OF OUR CORPORATION'S MONEY DID YOU USE IN DEVELOPING THAT NEW DRUG FOR THEM?
AND I SUPPOSE YOUR FORMER SUBORDI-NATE, NAKAGAICHI, IS NOW IN FRANCE?
THE DRUG'S DEVELOPMENT WAS FUNDED ENTIRELY OUT OF MY OWN POCKET.
THOUGH IT DID PUT A BIT OF A STRAIN ON IT, AS YOU CAN IMAGINE.
AND, YES... NAKAGAICHI HAS DONE AN ADMIRABLE JOB OVERSEEING THE REDEVELOPMENT OF THE GRANTENUE COMPANY AND SERVING AS MY POINT OF CONTACT.
I INTEND TO CALL HIM BACK TO JAPAN SOON AND REINSTATE HIM AS A VICE PRESIDENT HERE.
I SEE... AND IT ALL HAPPENED TO COINCIDE WITH THE BOARD'S DETERMINATION THAT MY TERM AS DIRECTOR IS TO END, HM?
BUT HAVE YOU FORGOTTEN YOU'LL HAVE THE SHAREHOLDERS TO ANSWER TO FOR THIS AS WELL?

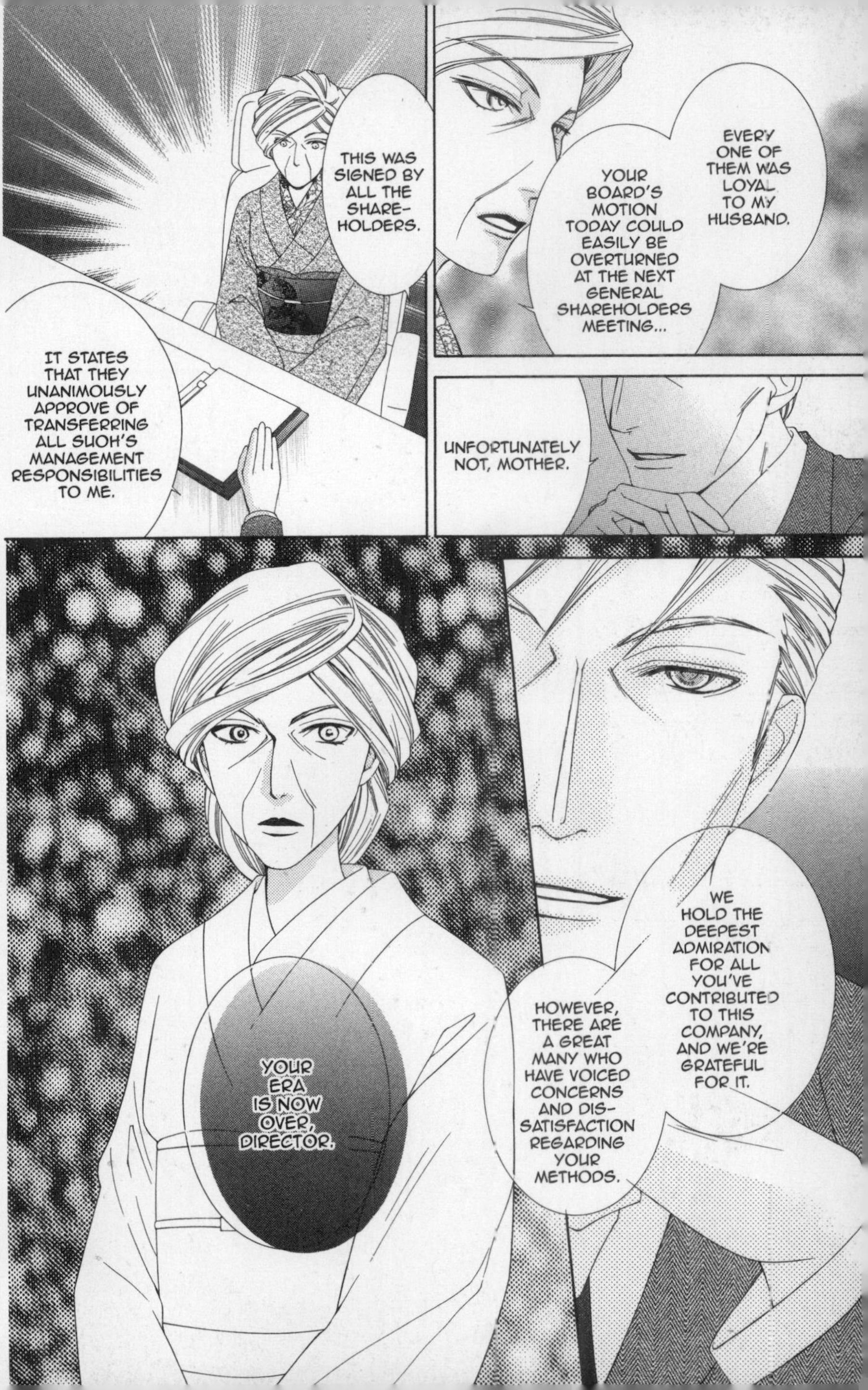
EVERY ONE OF THEM WAS LOYAL TO MY HUSBAND.
YOUR BOARD'S MOTION TODAY COULD EASILY BE OVERTURNED AT THE NEXT GENERAL SHAREHOLDERS MEETING...
UNFORTUNATELY NOT, MOTHER.
THIS WAS SIGNED BY ALL THE SHARE-HOLDERS.
IT STATES THAT THEY UNANIMOUSLY APPROVE OF TRANSFERRING ALL SUOH'S MANAGEMENT RESPONSIBILITIES TO ME.
WE HOLD THE DEEPEST ADMIRATION FOR ALL YOU'VE CONTRIBUTED TO THIS COMPANY, AND WE'RE GRATEFUL FOR IT.
HOWEVER, THERE ARE A GREAT MANY WHO HAVE VOICED CONCERNS AND DIS-SATISFACTION REGARDING YOUR METHODS.
YOUR ERA IS NOW OVER, DIRECTOR.

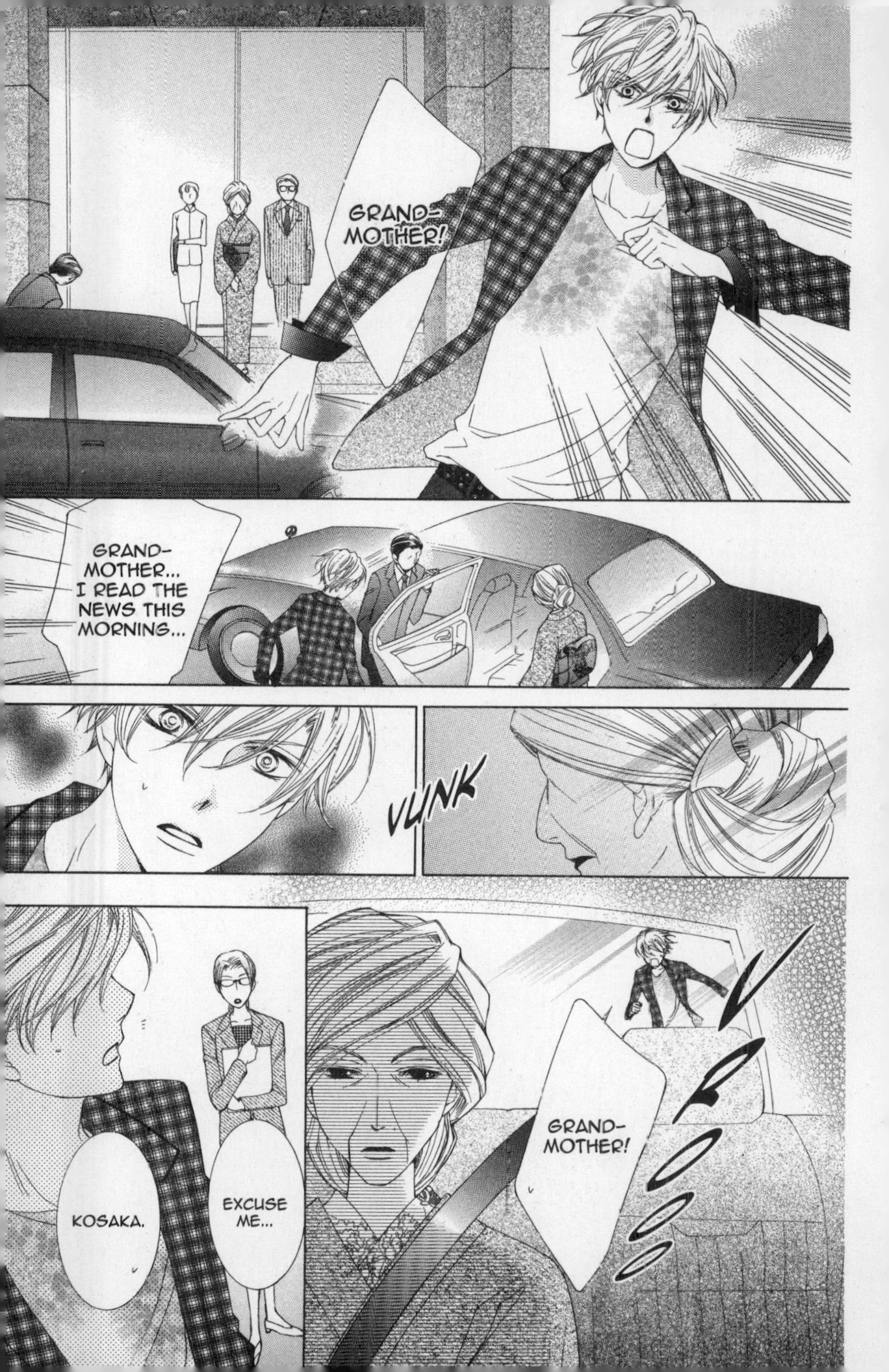
GRAND-MOTHER!
GRAND-MOTHER... I READ THE NEWS THIS MORNING...
VUNK
VROOOO
GRAND-MOTHER!
EXCUSE ME...
KOSAKA.

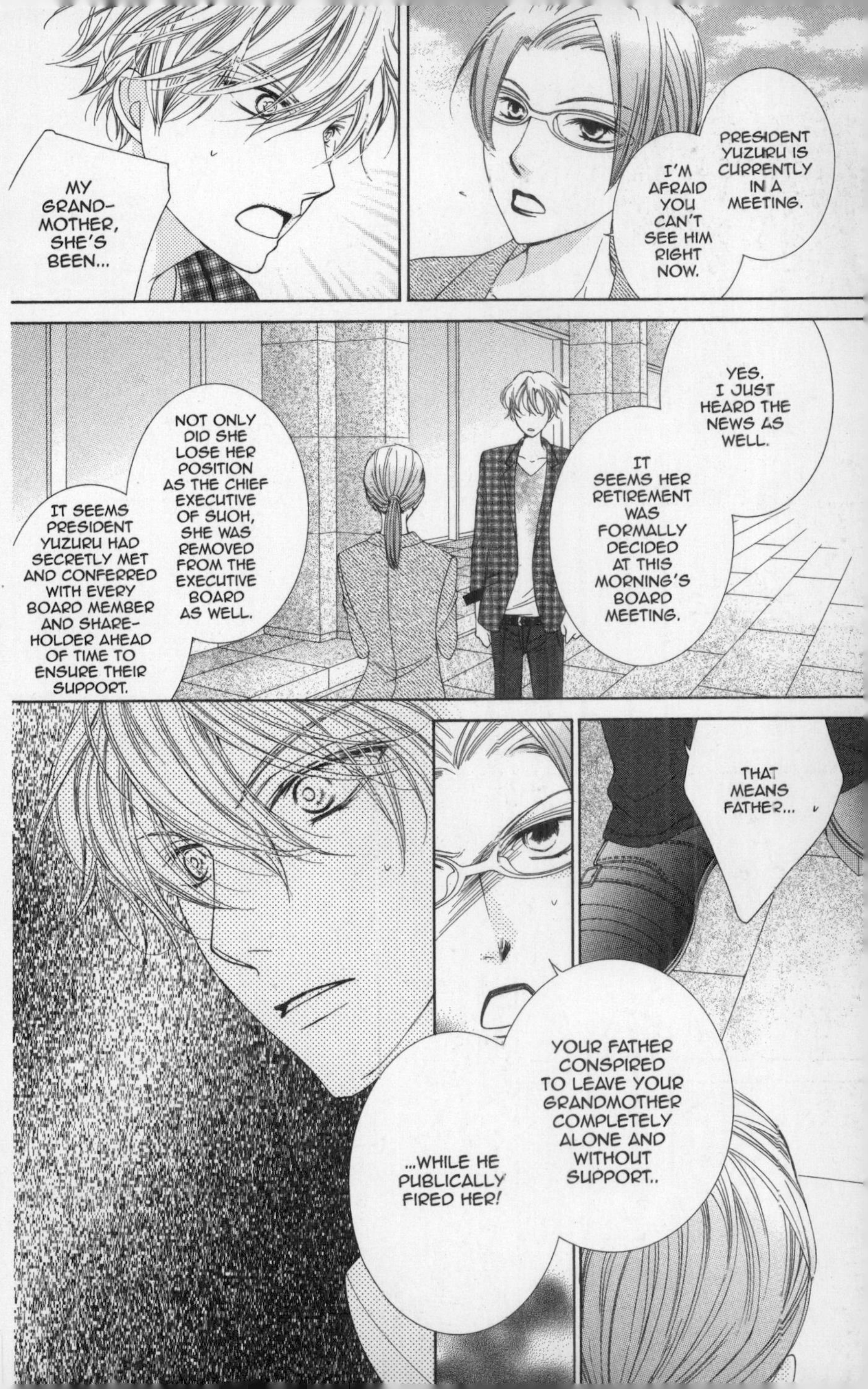
PRESIDENT YUZURU IS CURRENTLY IN A MEETING.
I'M AFRAID YOU CAN'T SEE HIM RIGHT NOW.
MY GRAND-MOTHER, SHE'S BEEN...
YES. I JUST HEARD THE NEWS AS WELL.
IT SEEMS HER RETIREMENT WAS FORMALLY DECIDED AT THIS MORNING'S BOARD MEETING.
NOT ONLY DID SHE LOSE HER POSITION AS THE CHIEF EXECUTIVE OF SUOH, SHE WAS REMOVED FROM THE EXECUTIVE BOARD AS WELL.
IT SEEMS PRESIDENT YUZURU HAD SECRETLY MET AND CONFERRED WITH EVERY BOARD MEMBER AND SHARE-HOLDER AHEAD OF TIME TO ENSURE THEIR SUPPORT.
THAT MEANS FATHER?...
YOUR FATHER CONSPIRED TO LEAVE YOUR GRANDMOTHER COMPLETELY ALONE AND WITHOUT SUPPORT..
...WHILE HE PUBLICALLY FIRED HER!

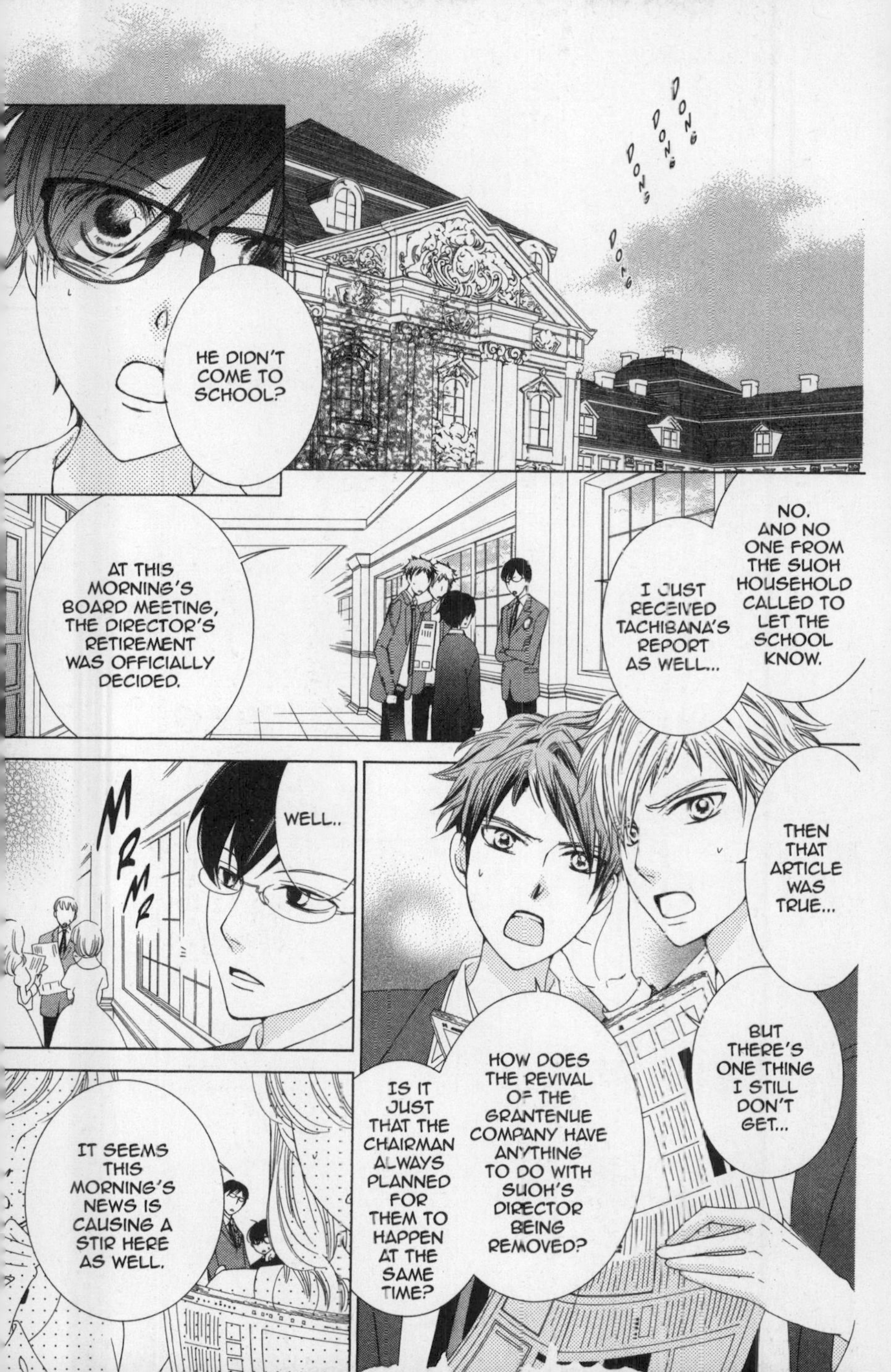
DONG DONG DONG DONG
HE DIDN'T COME TO SCHOOL?
NO. AND NO ONE FROM THE SUOH HOUSEHOLD CALLED TO LET THE SCHOOL KNOW.
I JUST RECEIVED TACHIBANA'S REPORT AS WELL...
AT THIS MORNING'S BOARD MEETING, THE DIRECTOR'S RETIREMENT WAS OFFICIALLY DECIDED.
THEN THAT ARTICLE WAS TRUE...
BUT THERE'S ONE THING I STILL DON'T GET...
HOW DOES THE REVIVAL OF THE GRANTENUE COMPANY HAVE ANYTHING TO DO WITH SUOH'S DIRECTOR BEING REMOVED?
IS IT JUST THAT THE CHAIRMAN ALWAYS PLANNED FOR THEM TO HAPPEN AT THE SAME TIME?
MRMR
WELL..
IT SEEMS THIS MORNING'S NEWS IS CAUSING A STIR HERE AS WELL.

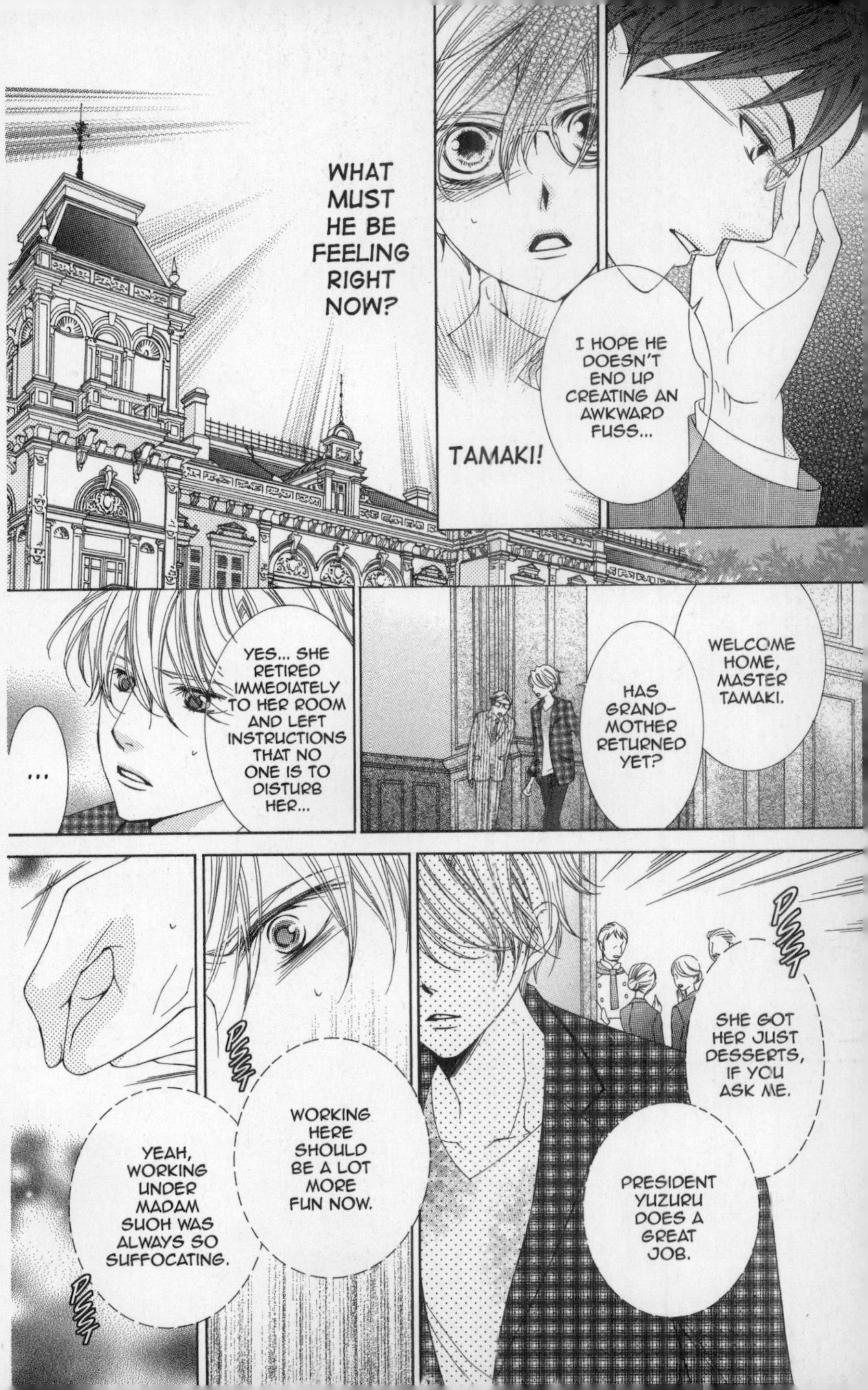
I HOPE HE DOESN'T END UP CREATING AN AWKWARD FUSS...
TAMAKI!
WHAT MUST HE BE FEELING RIGHT NOW?
WELCOME HOME, MASTER TAMAKI.
HAS GRAND-MOTHER RETURNED YET?
YES... SHE RETIRED IMMEDIATELY TO HER ROOM AND LEFT INSTRUCTIONS THAT NO ONE IS TO DISTURB HER...
...
SHE GOT HER JUST DESSERTS, IF YOU ASK ME.
PRESIDENT YUZURU DOES A GREAT JOB.
WORKING HERE SHOULD BE A LOT MORE FUN NOW.
YEAH, WORKING UNDER MADAM SUOH WAS ALWAYS SO SUFFOCATING.

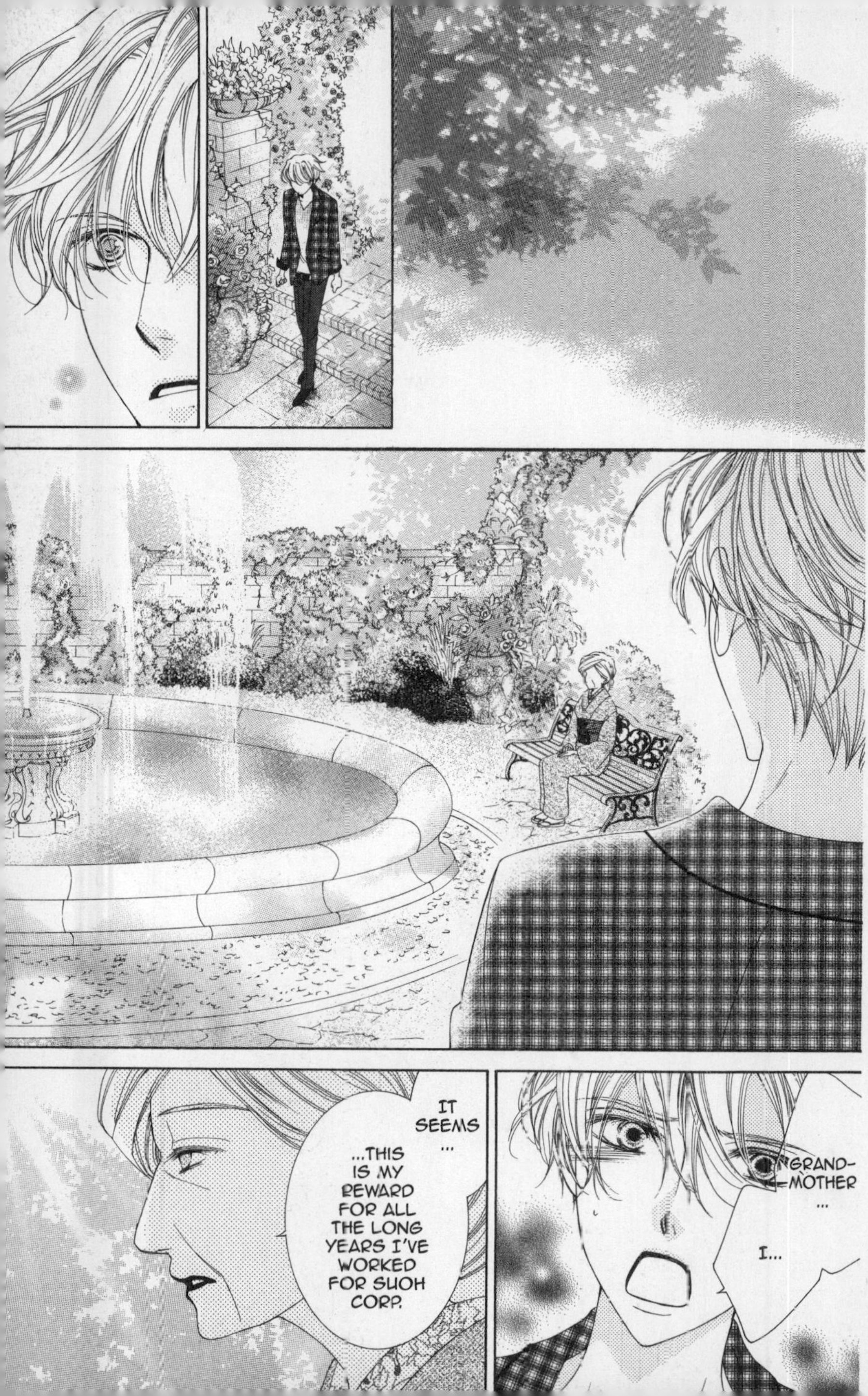
GRAND-MOTHER ...
I...
IT SEEMS ...
...THIS IS MY REWARD FOR ALL THE LONG YEARS I'VE WORKED FOR SUOH CORP.

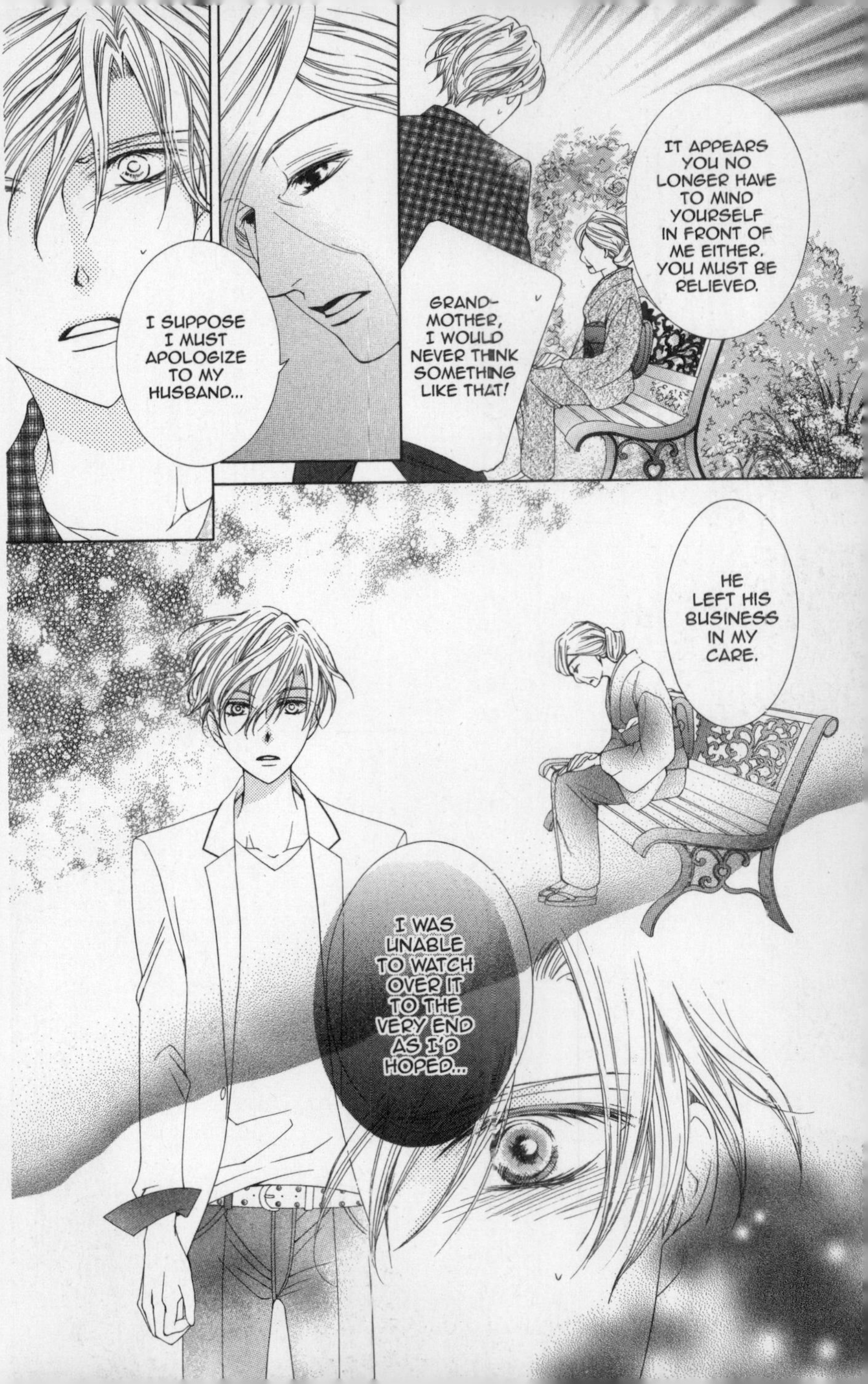

IT APPEARS YOU NO LONGER HAVE TO MIND YOURSELF IN FRONT OF ME EITHER. YOU MUST BE RELIEVED.
GRAND-MOTHER, I WOULD NEVER THINK SOMETHING LIKE THAT!
I SUPPOSE I MUST APOLOGIZE TO MY HUSBAND...
HE LEFT HIS BUSINESS IN MY CARE.
I WAS UNABLE TO WATCH OVER IT TO THE VERY END AS I'D HOPED...

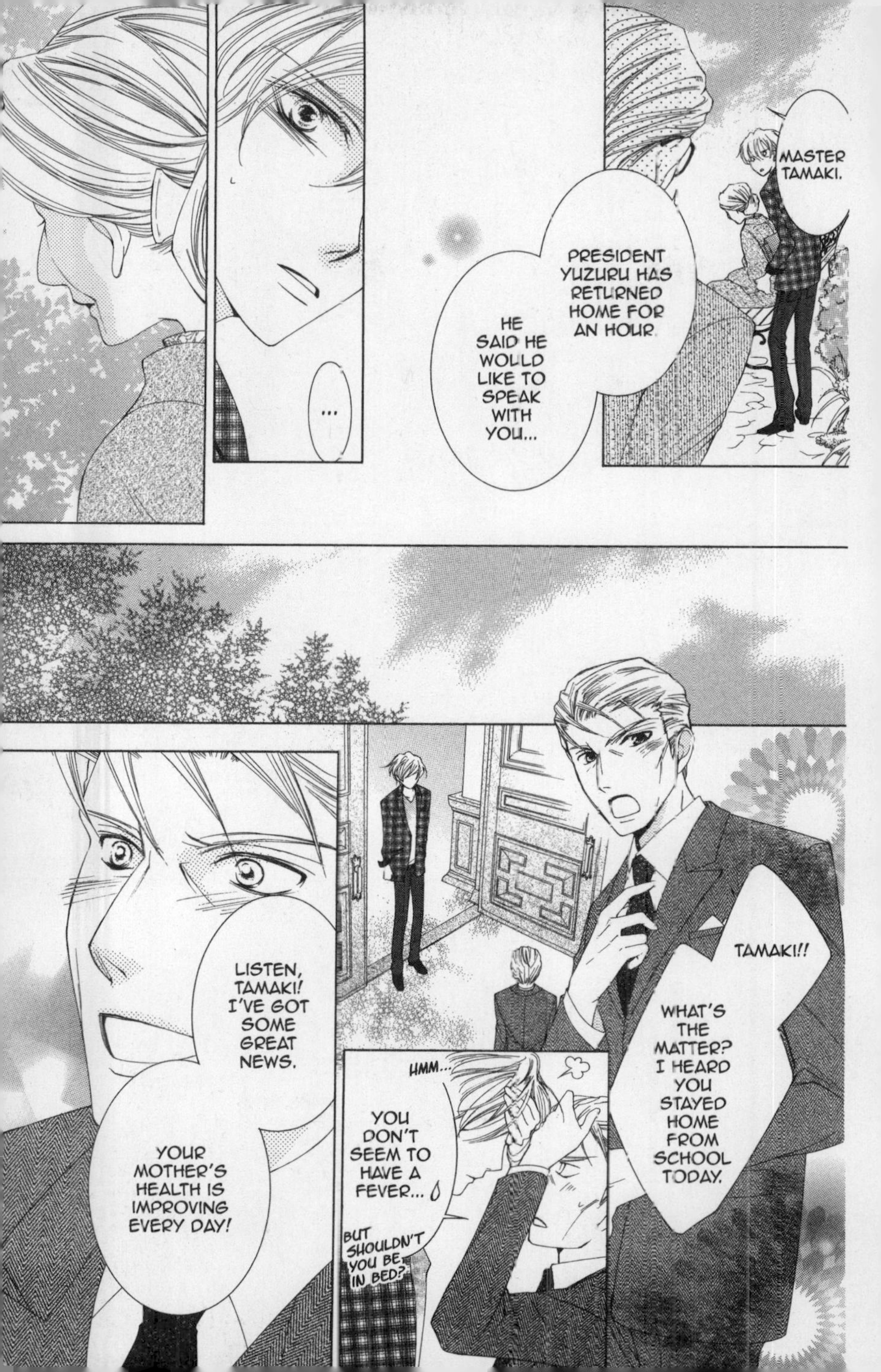
MASTER TAMAKI.
PRESIDENT YUZURU HAS RETURNED HOME FOR AN HOUR.
HE SAID HE WOULD LIKE TO SPEAK WITH YOU...
...
TAMAKI!!
WHAT'S THE MATTER? I HEARD YOU STAYED HOME FROM SCHOOL TODAY.
HMM...
YOU DON'T SEEM TO HAVE A FEVER...
BUT SHOULDN'T YOU BE IN BED?
LISTEN, TAMAKI! I'VE GOT SOME GREAT NEWS.
YOUR MOTHER'S HEALTH IS IMPROVING EVERY DAY!

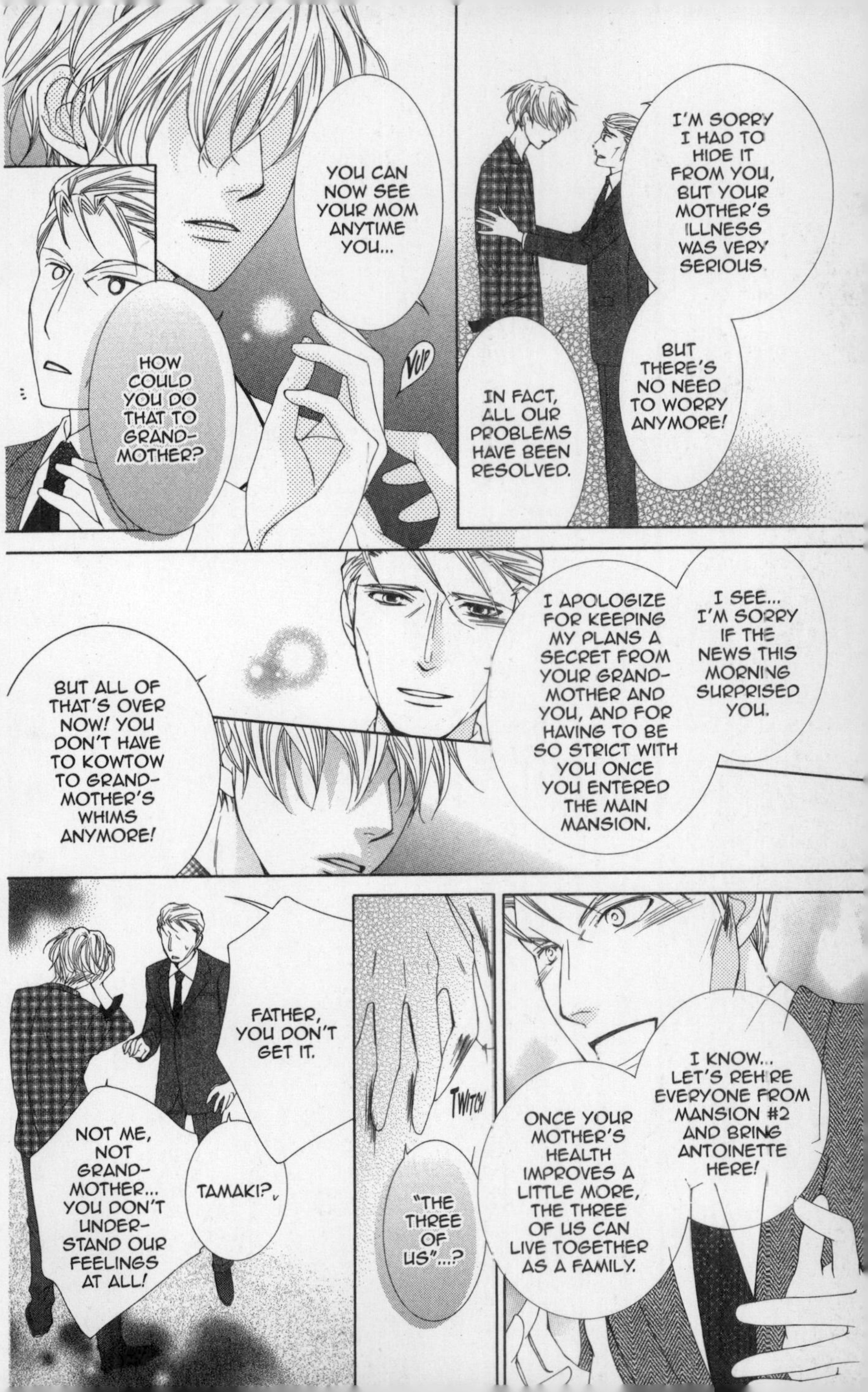
I'M SORRY I HAD TO HIDE IT FROM YOU, BUT YOUR MOTHER'S ILLNESS WAS VERY SERIOUS.
BUT THERE'S NO NEED TO WORRY ANYMORE!
IN FACT, ALL OUR PROBLEMS HAVE BEEN RESOLVED.
YOU CAN NOW SEE YOUR MOM ANYTIME YOU...
VUP
HOW COULD YOU DO THAT TO GRAND-MOTHER?
I SEE... I'M SORRY IF THE NEWS THIS MORNING SURPRISED YOU.
I APOLOGIZE FOR KEEPING MY PLANS A SECRET FROM YOUR GRAND-MOTHER AND YOU, AND FOR HAVING TO BE SO STRICT WITH YOU ONCE YOU ENTERED THE MAIN MANSION.
BUT ALL OF THAT'S OVER NOW! YOU DON'T HAVE TO KOWTOW TO GRAND-MOTHER'S WHIMS ANYMORE!
I KNOW... LET'S REHIRE EVERYONE FROM MANSION #2 AND BRING ANTOINETTE HERE!
ONCE YOUR MOTHER'S HEALTH IMPROVES A LITTLE MORE, THE THREE OF US CAN LIVE TOGETHER AS A FAMILY.
TWITCH
"THE THREE OF US"...?
FATHER, YOU DON'T GET IT.
TAMAKI?
NOT ME, NOT GRAND-MOTHER... YOU DON'T UNDER-STAND OUR FEELINGS AT ALL!

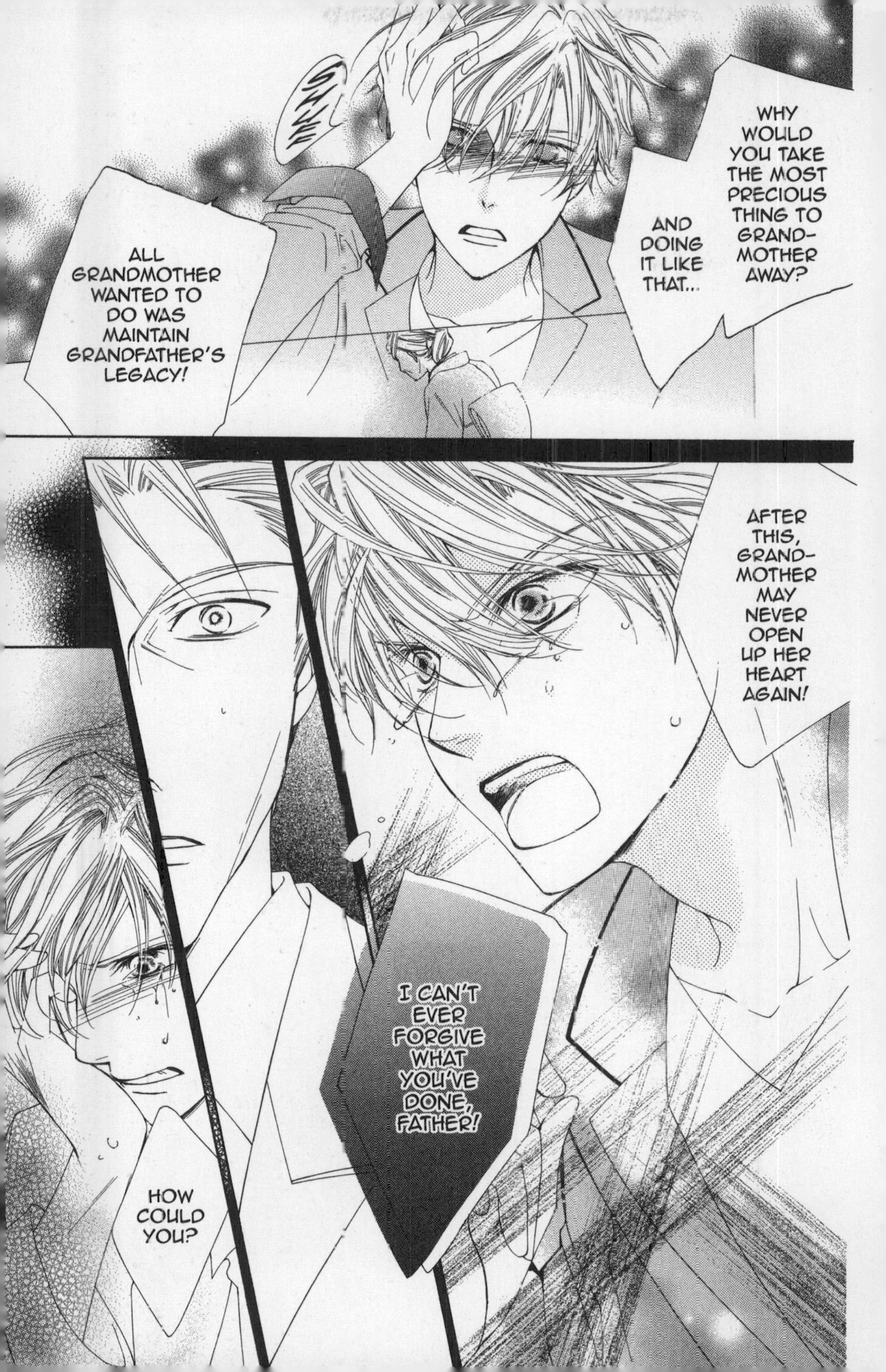
WHY WOULD YOU TAKE THE MOST PRECIOUS THING TO GRAND-MOTHER AWAY?
AND DOING IT LIKE THAT...
SHAKE
ALL GRANDMOTHER WANTED TO DO WAS MAINTAIN GRANDFATHER'S LEGACY!
AFTER THIS, GRAND-MOTHER MAY NEVER OPEN UP HER HEART AGAIN!
I CAN'T EVER FORGIVE WHAT YOU'VE DONE, FATHER!
HOW COULD YOU?

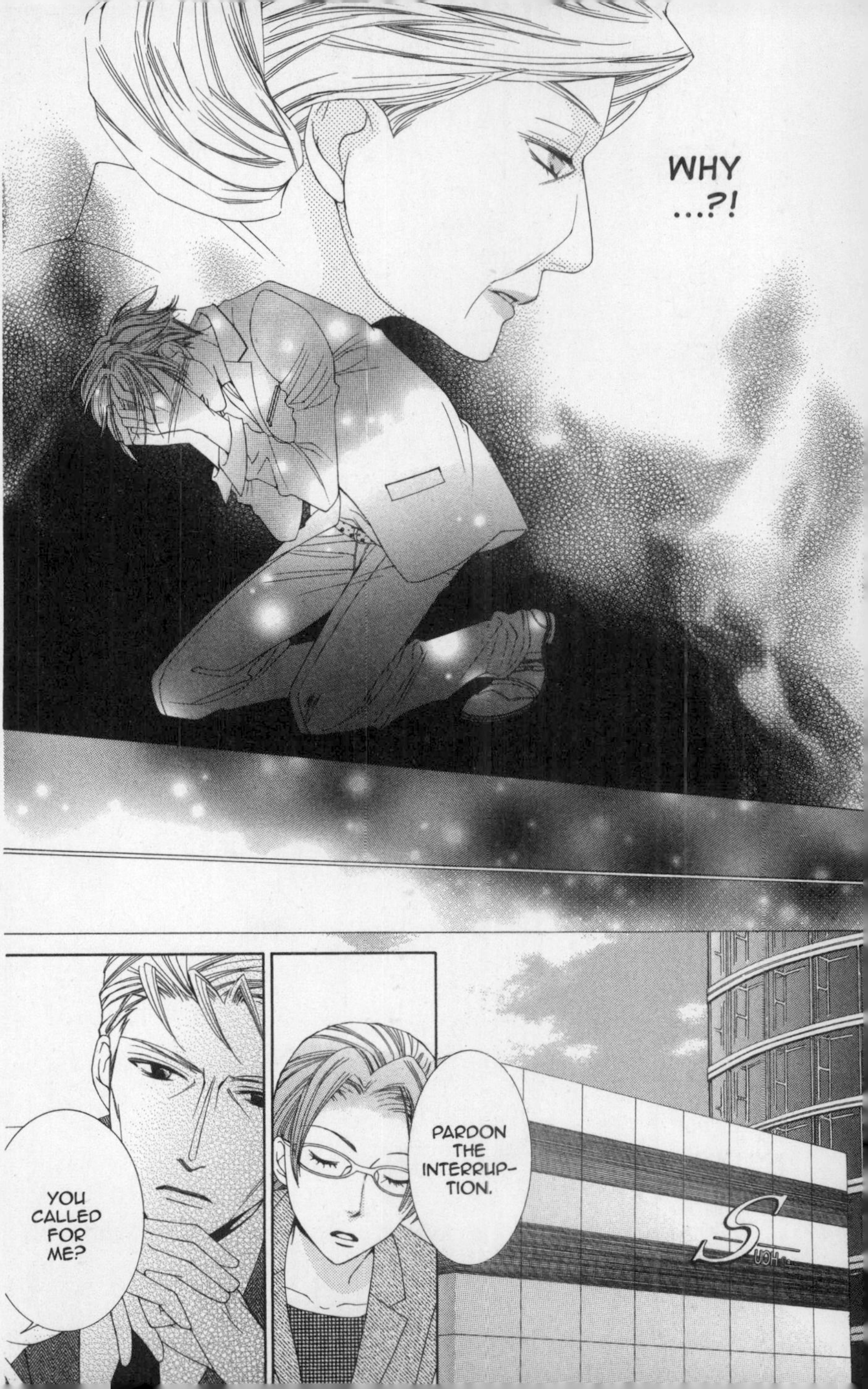
WHY ...?!
PARDON THE INTERRUPTION.
YOU CALLED FOR ME?

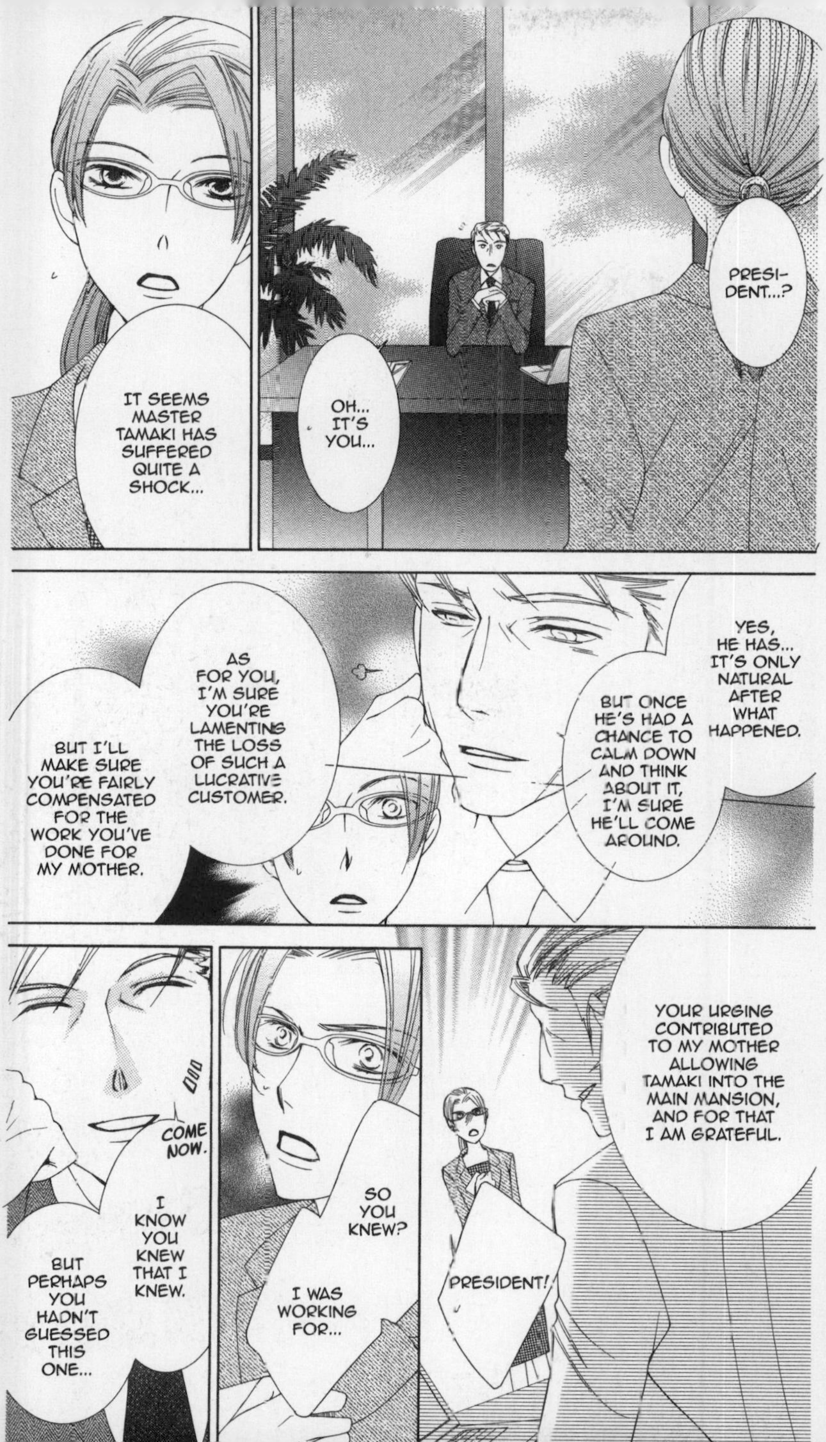
PRESIDENT...?
OH... IT'S YOU...
IT SEEMS MASTER TAMAKI HAS SUFFERED QUITE A SHOCK...
YES, HE HAS... IT'S ONLY NATURAL AFTER WHAT HAPPENED.
BUT ONCE HE'S HAD A CHANCE TO CALM DOWN AND THINK ABOUT IT, I'M SURE HE'LL COME AROUND.
AS FOR YOU, I'M SURE YOU'RE LAMENTING THE LOSS OF SUCH A LUCRATIVE CUSTOMER.
BUT I'LL MAKE SURE YOU'RE FAIRLY COMPENSATED FOR THE WORK YOU'VE DONE FOR MY MOTHER.
YOUR URGING CONTRIBUTED TO MY MOTHER ALLOWING TAMAKI INTO THE MAIN MANSION, AND FOR THAT I AM GRATEFUL.
PRESIDENT!
SO YOU KNEW?
I WAS WORKING FOR...
COME NOW.
I KNOW YOU KNEW THAT I KNEW.
BUT PERHAPS YOU HADN'T GUESSED THIS ONE...

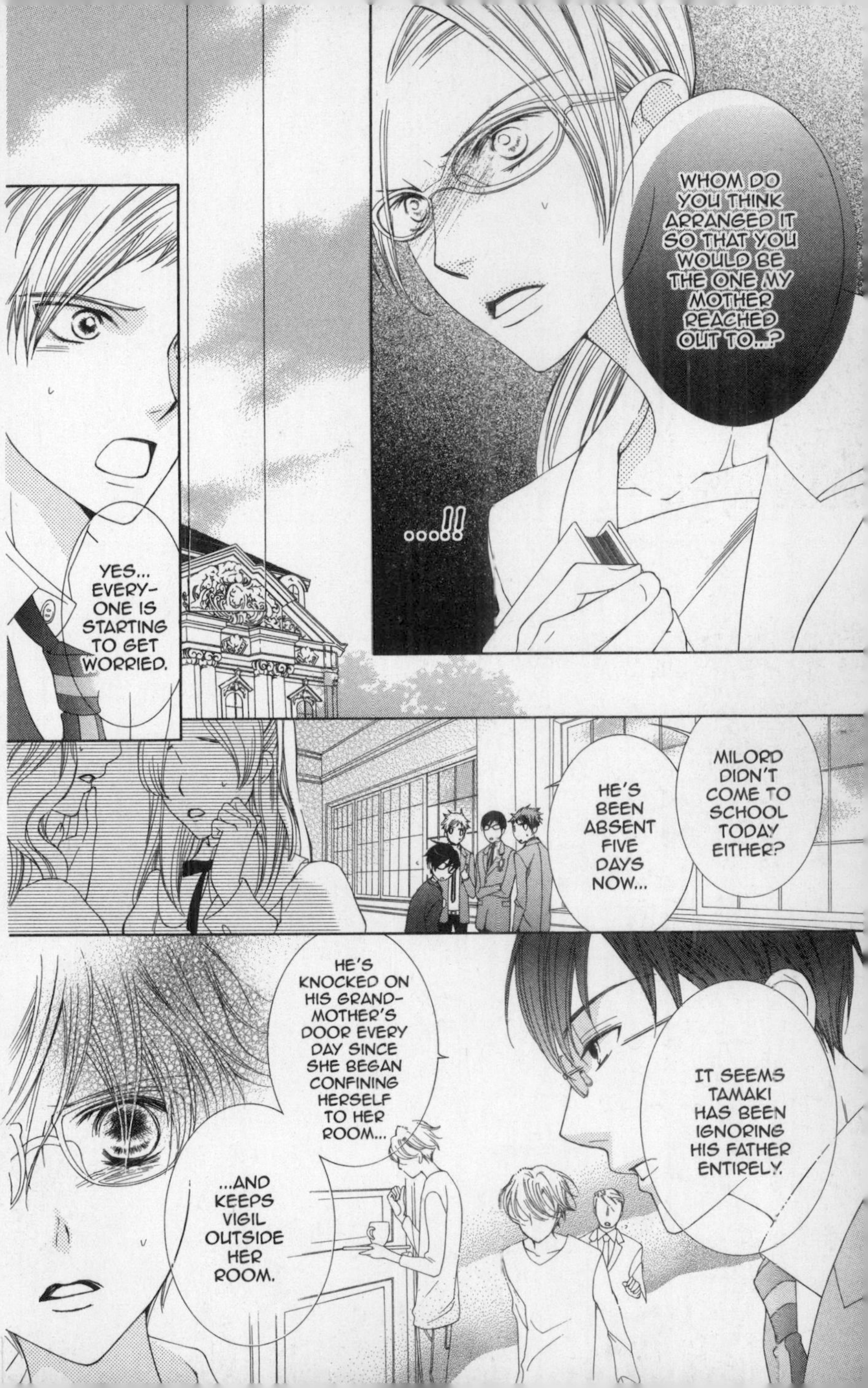
WHOM DO YOU THINK ARRANGED IT SO THAT YOU WOULD BE THE ONE MY MOTHER REACHED OUT TO...?
.....!!
YES... EVERYONE IS STARTING TO GET WORRIED.
MILORD DIDN'T COME TO SCHOOL TODAY EITHER?
HE'S BEEN ABSENT FIVE DAYS NOW...
IT SEEMS TAMAKI HAS BEEN IGNORING HIS FATHER ENTIRELY.
HE'S KNOCKED ON HIS GRANDMOTHER'S DOOR EVERY DAY SINCE SHE BEGAN CONFINING HERSELF TO HER ROOM...
...AND KEEPS VIGIL OUTSIDE HER ROOM.

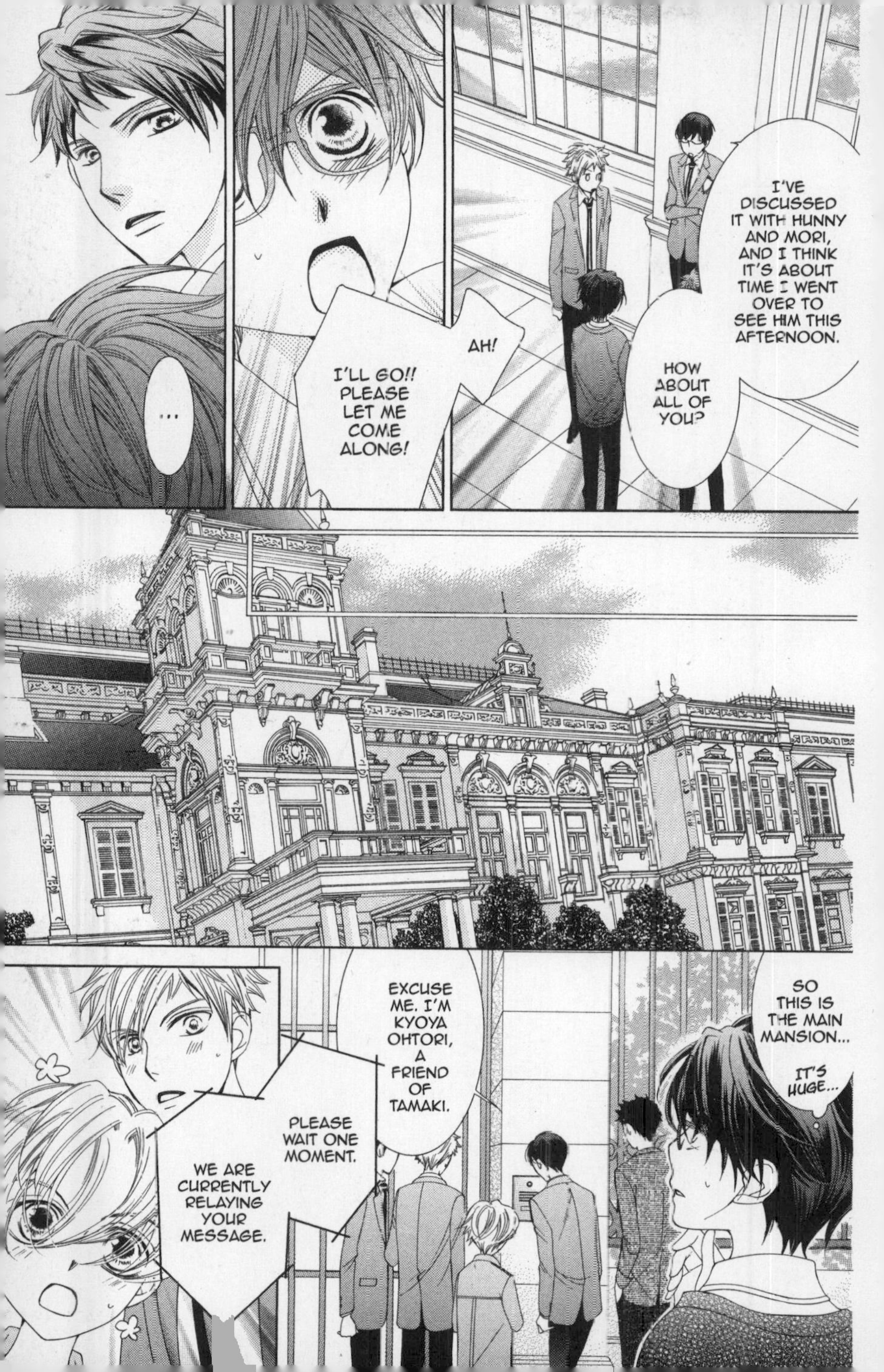
I'VE DISCUSSED IT WITH HUNNY AND MORI, AND I THINK IT'S ABOUT TIME I WENT OVER TO SEE HIM THIS AFTERNOON.
HOW ABOUT ALL OF YOU?
AH!
I'LL GO!! PLEASE LET ME COME ALONG!
...
SO THIS IS THE MAIN MANSION...
IT'S HUGE...
EXCUSE ME. I'M KYOYA OHTORI, A FRIEND OF TAMAKI.
PLEASE WAIT ONE MOMENT.
WE ARE CURRENTLY RELAYING YOUR MESSAGE.

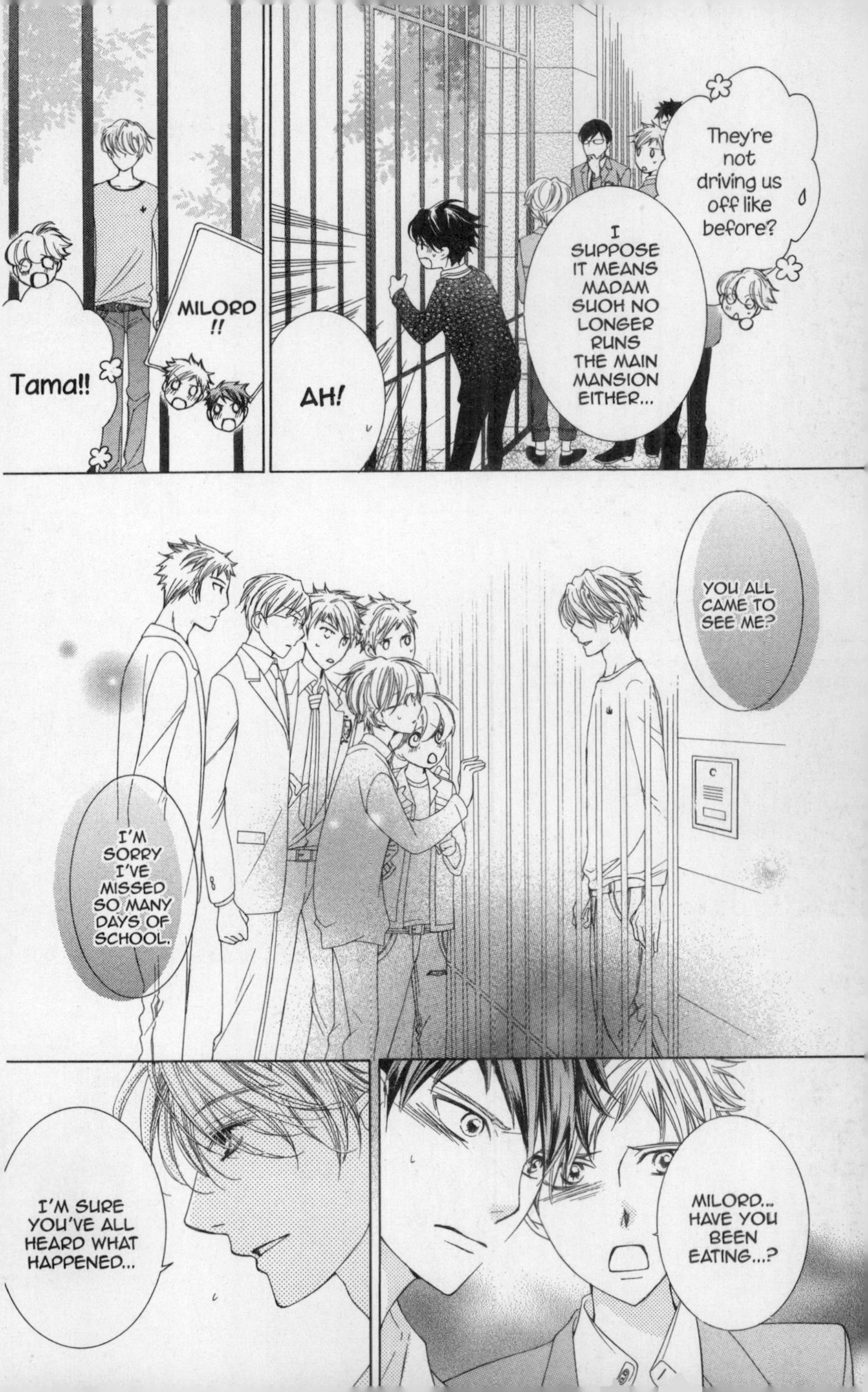
They're not driving us off like before?
I SUPPOSE IT MEANS MADAM SUOH NO LONGER RUNS THE MAIN MANSION EITHER...
AH!
MILORD !!
Tama!!
YOU ALL CAME TO SEE ME?
I'M SORRY I'VE MISSED SO MANY DAYS OF SCHOOL.
MILORD... HAVE YOU BEEN EATING...?
I'M SURE YOU'VE ALL HEARD WHAT HAPPENED...

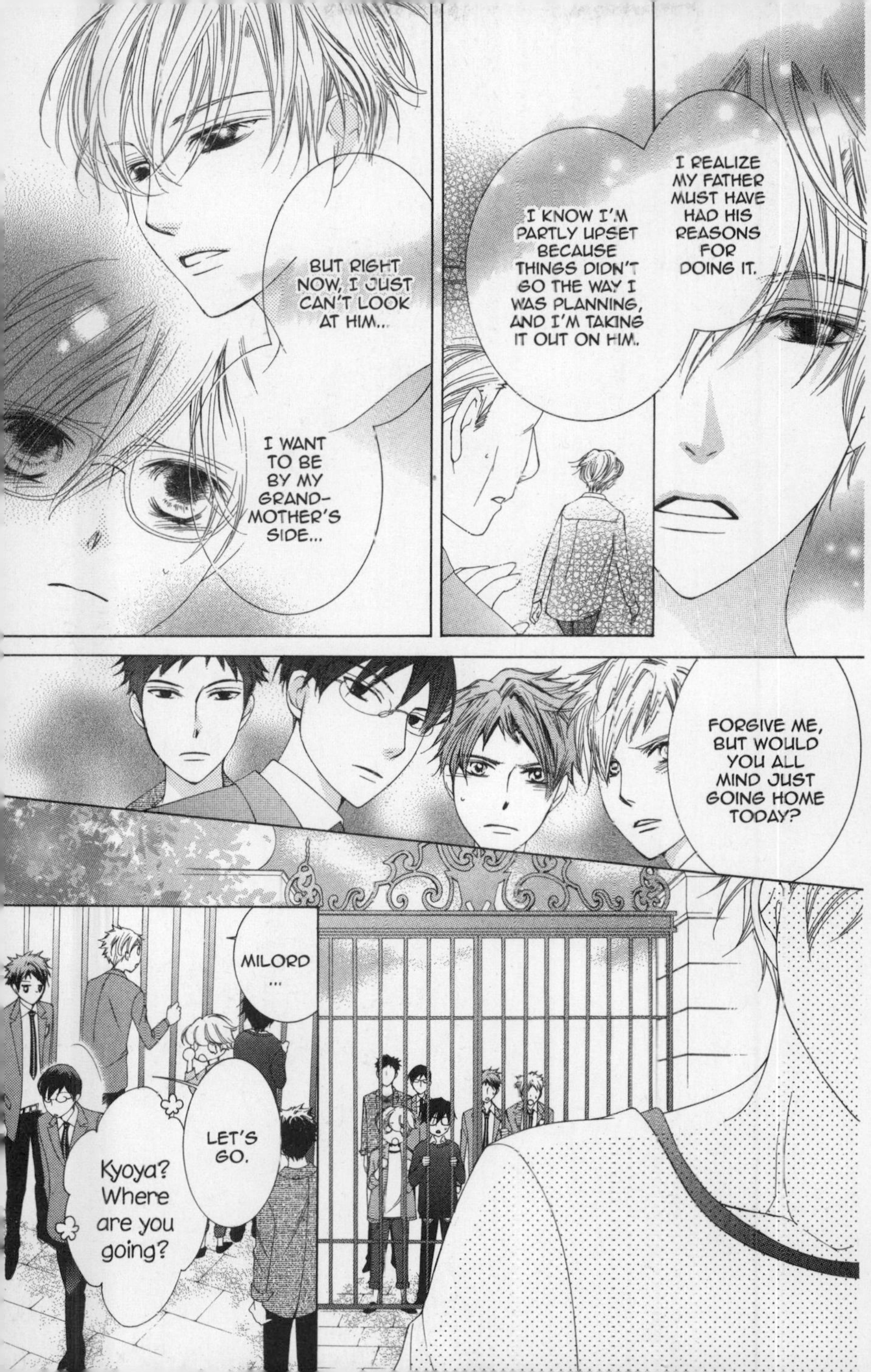
I REALIZE MY FATHER MUST HAVE HAD HIS REASONS FOR DOING IT.
I KNOW I'M PARTLY UPSET BECAUSE THINGS DIDN'T GO THE WAY I WAS PLANNING, AND I'M TAKING IT OUT ON HIM.
BUT RIGHT NOW, I JUST CAN'T LOOK AT HIM...
I WANT TO BE BY MY GRAND-MOTHER'S SIDE...
FORGIVE ME, BUT WOULD YOU ALL MIND JUST GOING HOME TODAY?
MILORD ...
LET'S GO.
Kyoya? Where are you going?

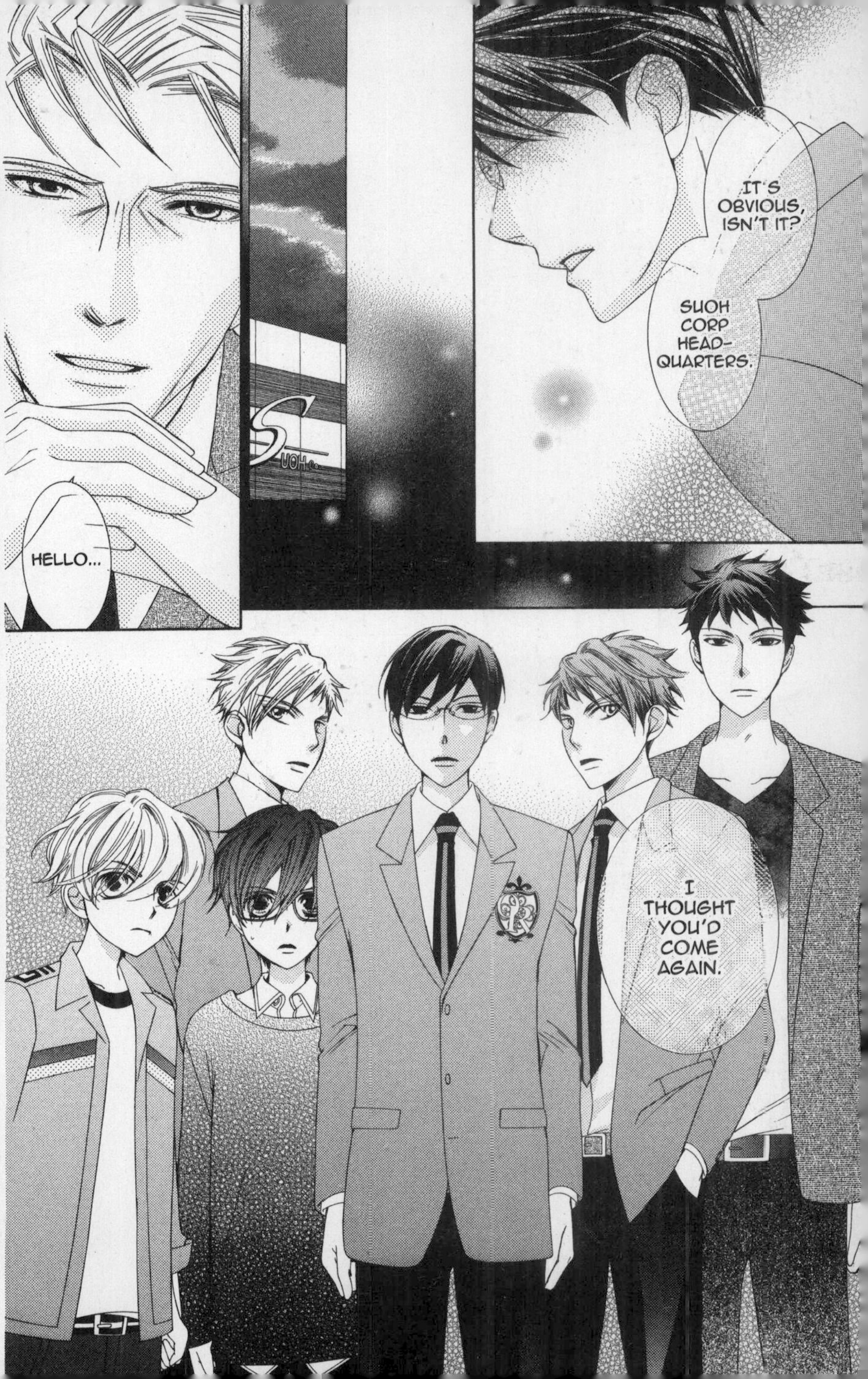
IT'S OBVIOUS, ISN'T IT?
SUOH CORP HEAD-QUARTERS.
HELLO...
I THOUGHT YOU'D COME AGAIN.

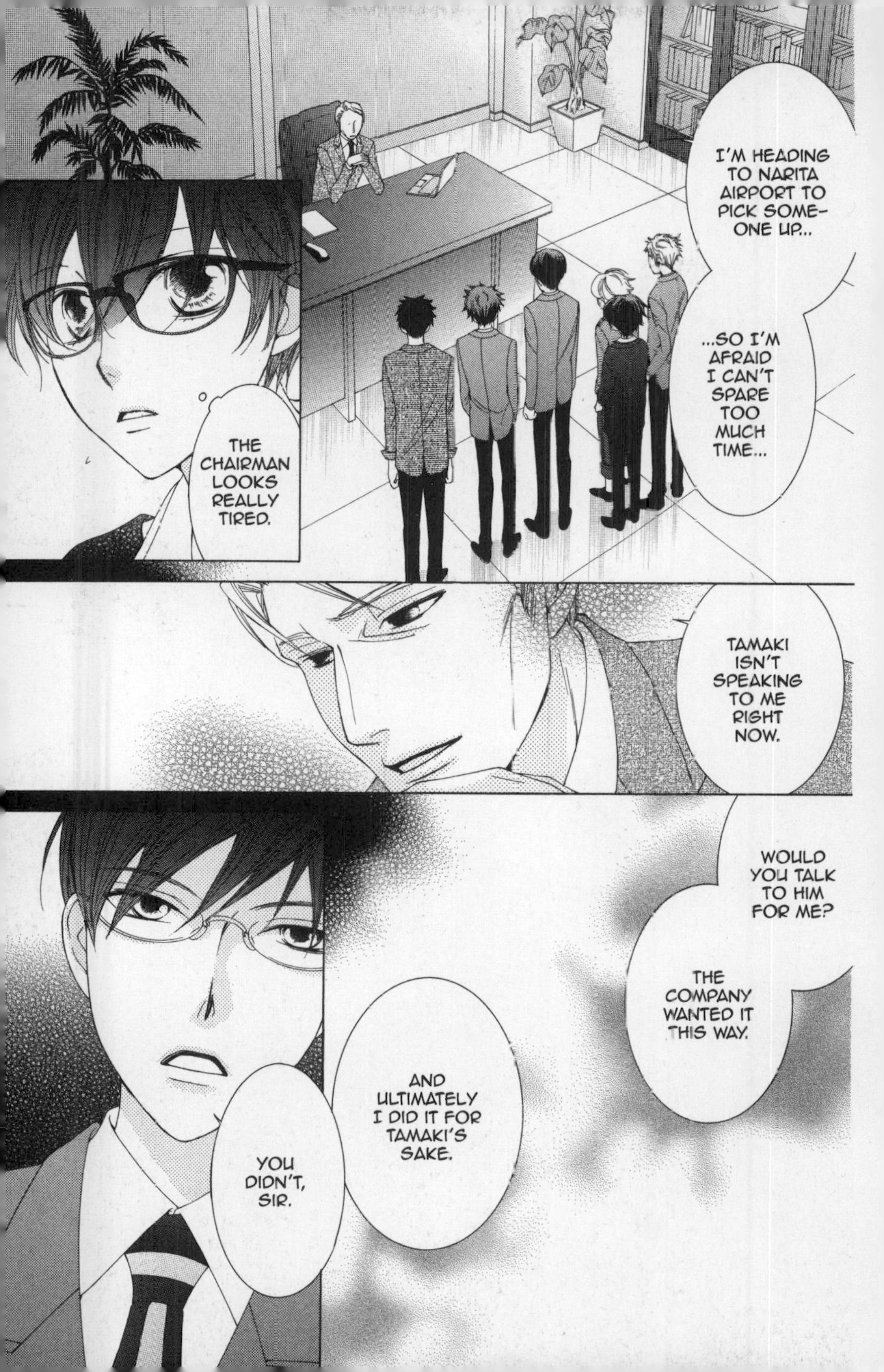
I'M HEADING TO NARITA AIRPORT TO PICK SOME-ONE UP...
...SO I'M AFRAID I CAN'T SPARE TOO MUCH TIME...
THE CHAIRMAN LOOKS REALLY TIRED.
TAMAKI ISN'T SPEAKING TO ME RIGHT NOW.
WOULD YOU TALK TO HIM FOR ME?
THE COMPANY WANTED IT THIS WAY.
AND ULTIMATELY I DID IT FOR TAMAKI'S SAKE.
YOU DIDN'T, SIR.

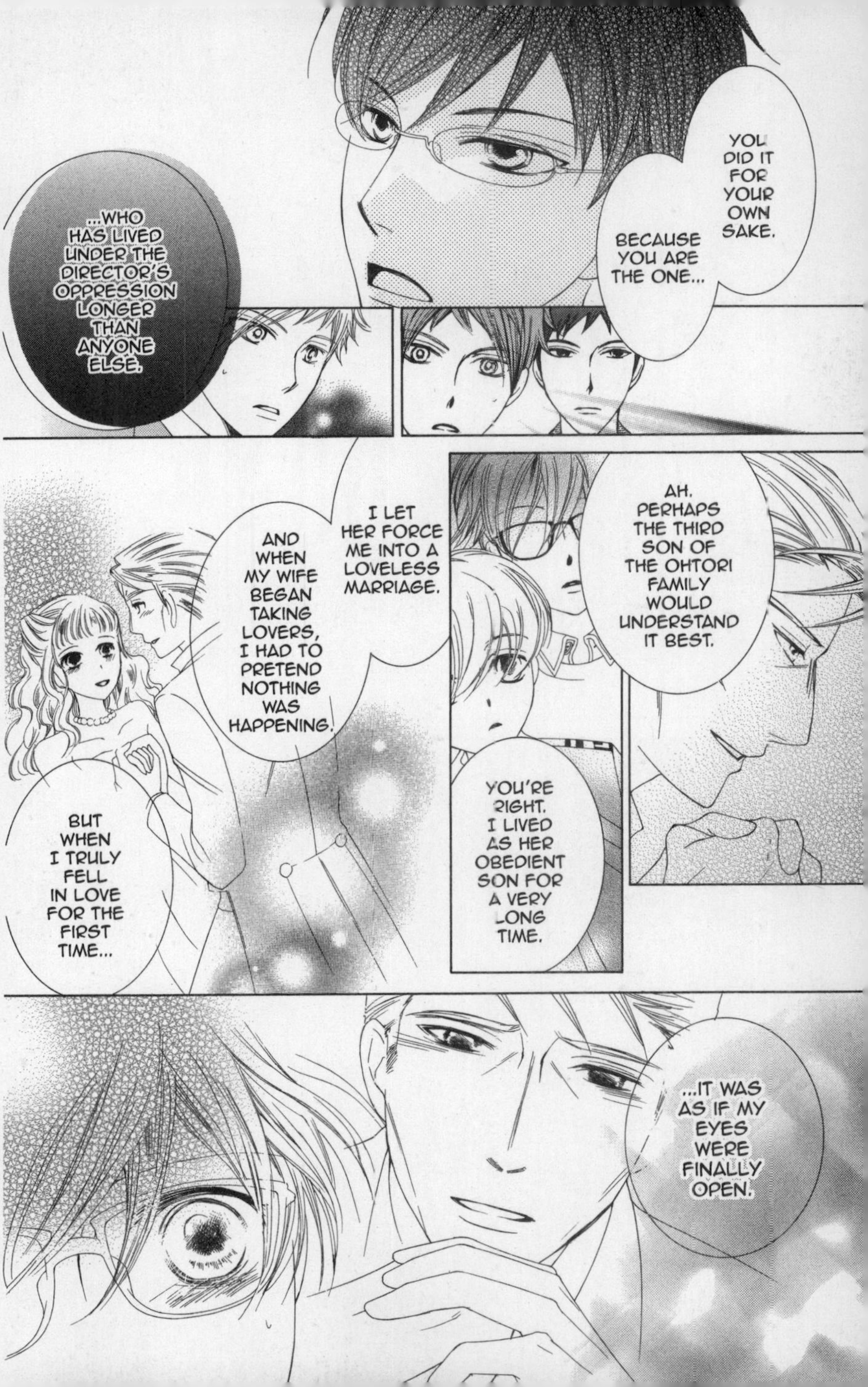
YOU DID IT FOR YOUR OWN SAKE.
BECAUSE YOU ARE THE ONE...
...WHO HAS LIVED UNDER THE DIRECTOR'S OPPRESSION LONGER THAN ANYONE ELSE.
AH. PERHAPS THE THIRD SON OF THE OHTORI FAMILY WOULD UNDERSTAND IT BEST.
YOU'RE RIGHT. I LIVED AS HER OBEDIENT SON FOR A VERY LONG TIME.
I LET HER FORCE ME INTO A LOVELESS MARRIAGE.
AND WHEN MY WIFE BEGAN TAKING LOVERS, I HAD TO PRETEND NOTHING WAS HAPPENING.
BUT WHEN I TRULY FELL IN LOVE FOR THE FIRST TIME...
...IT WAS AS IF MY EYES WERE FINALLY OPEN.

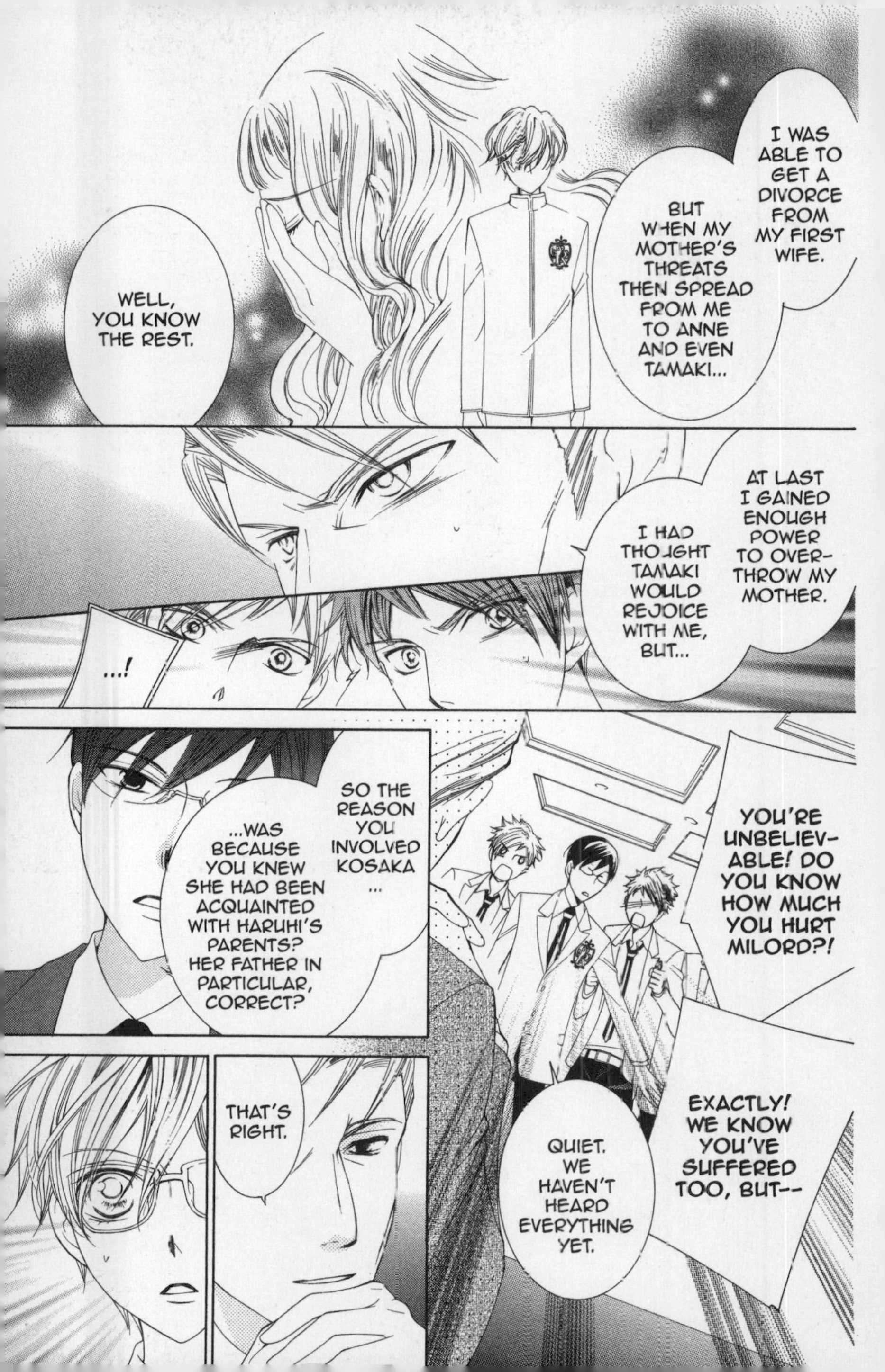
I WAS ABLE TO GET A DIVORCE FROM MY FIRST WIFE.
BUT WHEN MY MOTHER'S THREATS THEN SPREAD FROM ME TO ANNE AND EVEN TAMAKI...
WELL, YOU KNOW THE REST.
AT LAST I GAINED ENOUGH POWER TO OVER-THROW MY MOTHER.
I HAD THOUGHT TAMAKI WOULD REJOICE WITH ME, BUT...
...!
YOU'RE UNBELIEV-ABLE! DO YOU KNOW HOW MUCH YOU HURT MILORD?!
EXACTLY! WE KNOW YOU'VE SUFFERED TOO, BUT--
QUIET. WE HAVEN'T HEARD EVERYTHING YET.
SO THE REASON YOU INVOLVED KOSAKA ...
...WAS BECAUSE YOU KNEW SHE HAD BEEN ACQUAINTED WITH HARUHI'S PARENTS? HER FATHER IN PARTICULAR, CORRECT?
THAT'S RIGHT.

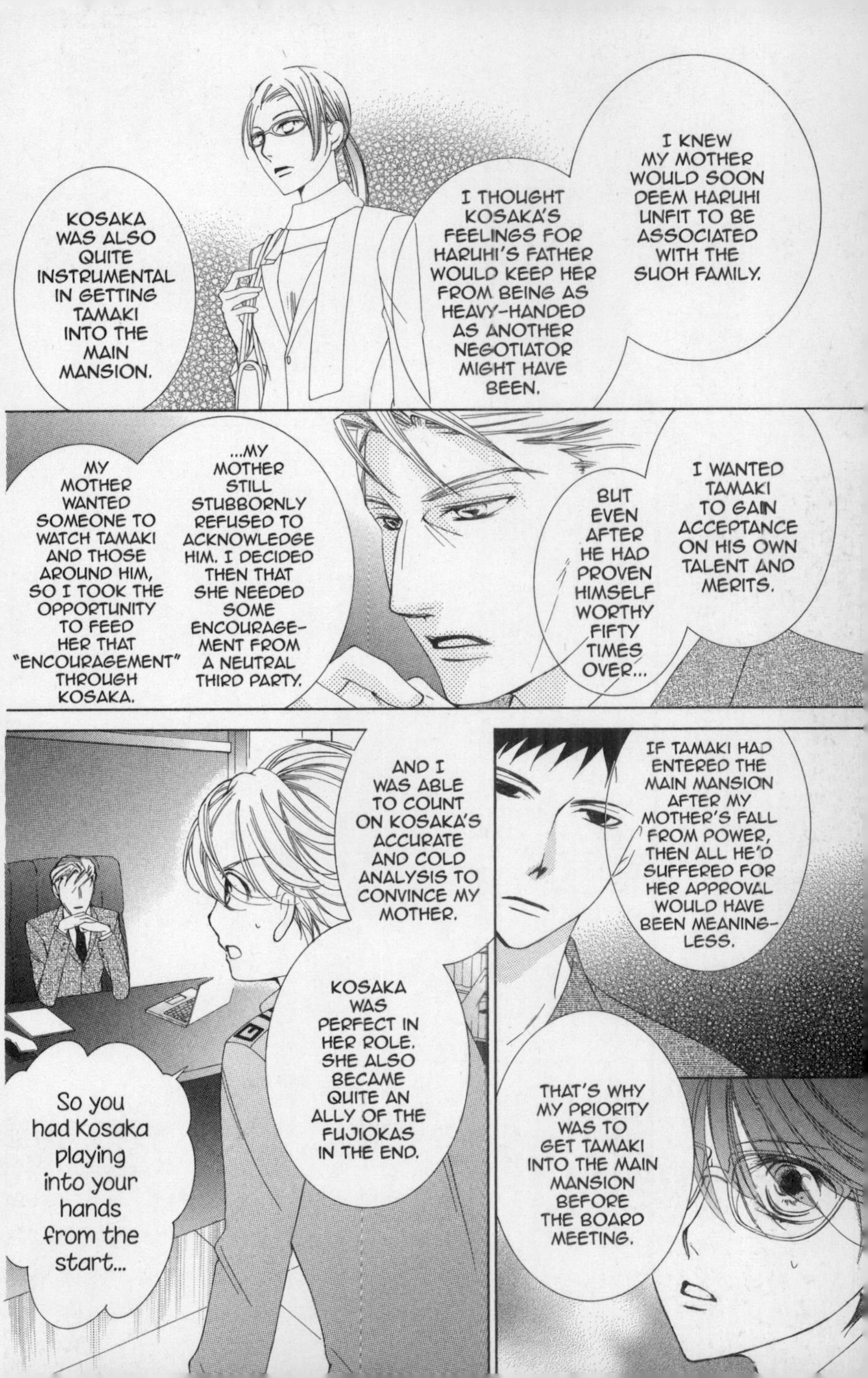
I KNEW MY MOTHER WOULD SOON DEEM HARUHI UNFIT TO BE ASSOCIATED WITH THE SUOH FAMILY.
I THOUGHT KOSAKA'S FEELINGS FOR HARUHI'S FATHER WOULD KEEP HER FROM BEING AS HEAVY-HANDED AS ANOTHER NEGOTIATOR MIGHT HAVE BEEN.
KOSAKA WAS ALSO QUITE INSTRUMENTAL IN GETTING TAMAKI INTO THE MAIN MANSION.
I WANTED TAMAKI TO GAIN ACCEPTANCE ON HIS OWN TALENT AND MERITS.
BUT EVEN AFTER HE HAD PROVEN HIMSELF WORTHY FIFTY TIMES OVER...
...MY MOTHER STILL STUBBORNLY REFUSED TO ACKNOWLEDGE HIM. I DECIDED THEN THAT SHE NEEDED SOME ENCOURAGE-MENT FROM A NEUTRAL THIRD PARTY.
MY MOTHER WANTED SOMEONE TO WATCH TAMAKI AND THOSE AROUND HIM, SO I TOOK THE OPPORTUNITY TO FEED HER THAT "ENCOURAGEMENT" THROUGH KOSAKA.
IF TAMAKI HAD ENTERED THE MAIN MANSION AFTER MY MOTHER'S FALL FROM POWER, THEN ALL HE'D SUFFERED FOR HER APPROVAL WOULD HAVE BEEN MEANING-LESS.
THAT'S WHY MY PRIORITY WAS TO GET TAMAKI INTO THE MAIN MANSION BEFORE THE BOARD MEETING.
AND I WAS ABLE TO COUNT ON KOSAKA'S ACCURATE AND COLD ANALYSIS TO CONVINCE MY MOTHER.
KOSAKA WAS PERFECT IN HER ROLE. SHE ALSO BECAME QUITE AN ALLY OF THE FUJIOKAS IN THE END.
So you had Kosaka playing into your hands from the start...

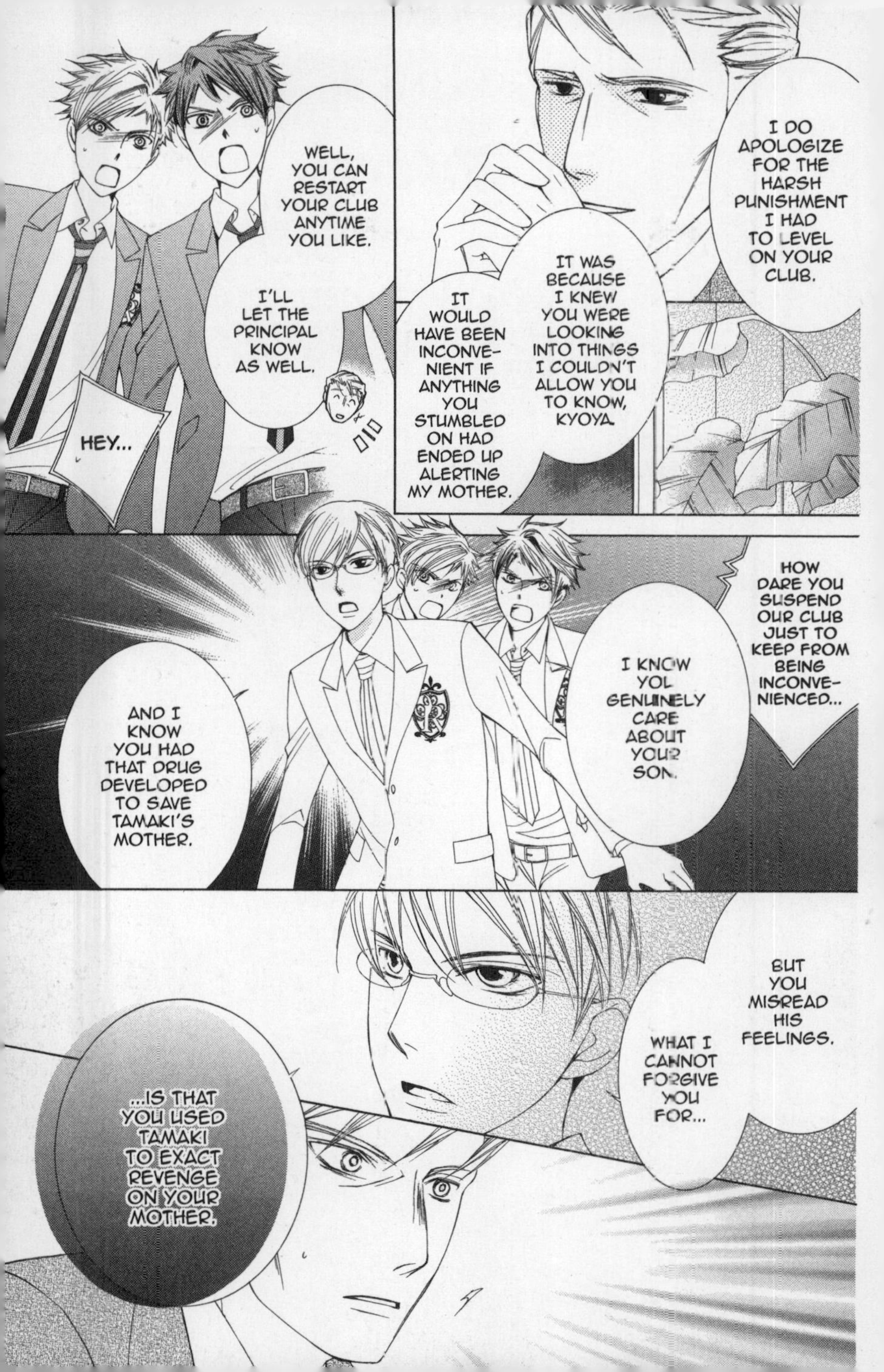
I DO APOLOGIZE FOR THE HARSH PUNISHMENT I HAD TO LEVEL ON YOUR CLUB.
IT WAS BECAUSE I KNEW YOU WERE LOOKING INTO THINGS I COULDN'T ALLOW YOU TO KNOW, KYOYA.
IT WOULD HAVE BEEN INCONVE-NIENT IF ANYTHING YOU STUMBLED ON HAD ENDED UP ALERTING MY MOTHER.
WELL, YOU CAN RESTART YOUR CLUB ANYTIME YOU LIKE.
I'LL LET THE PRINCIPAL KNOW AS WELL.
HEY...
HOW DARE YOU SUSPEND OUR CLUB JUST TO KEEP FROM BEING INCONVE-NIENCED...
I KNOW YOU GENUINELY CARE ABOUT YOUR SON.
AND I KNOW YOU HAD THAT DRUG DEVELOPED TO SAVE TAMAKI'S MOTHER.
BUT YOU MISREAD HIS FEELINGS.
WHAT I CANNOT FORGIVE YOU FOR...
...IS THAT YOU USED TAMAKI TO EXACT REVENGE ON YOUR MOTHER.

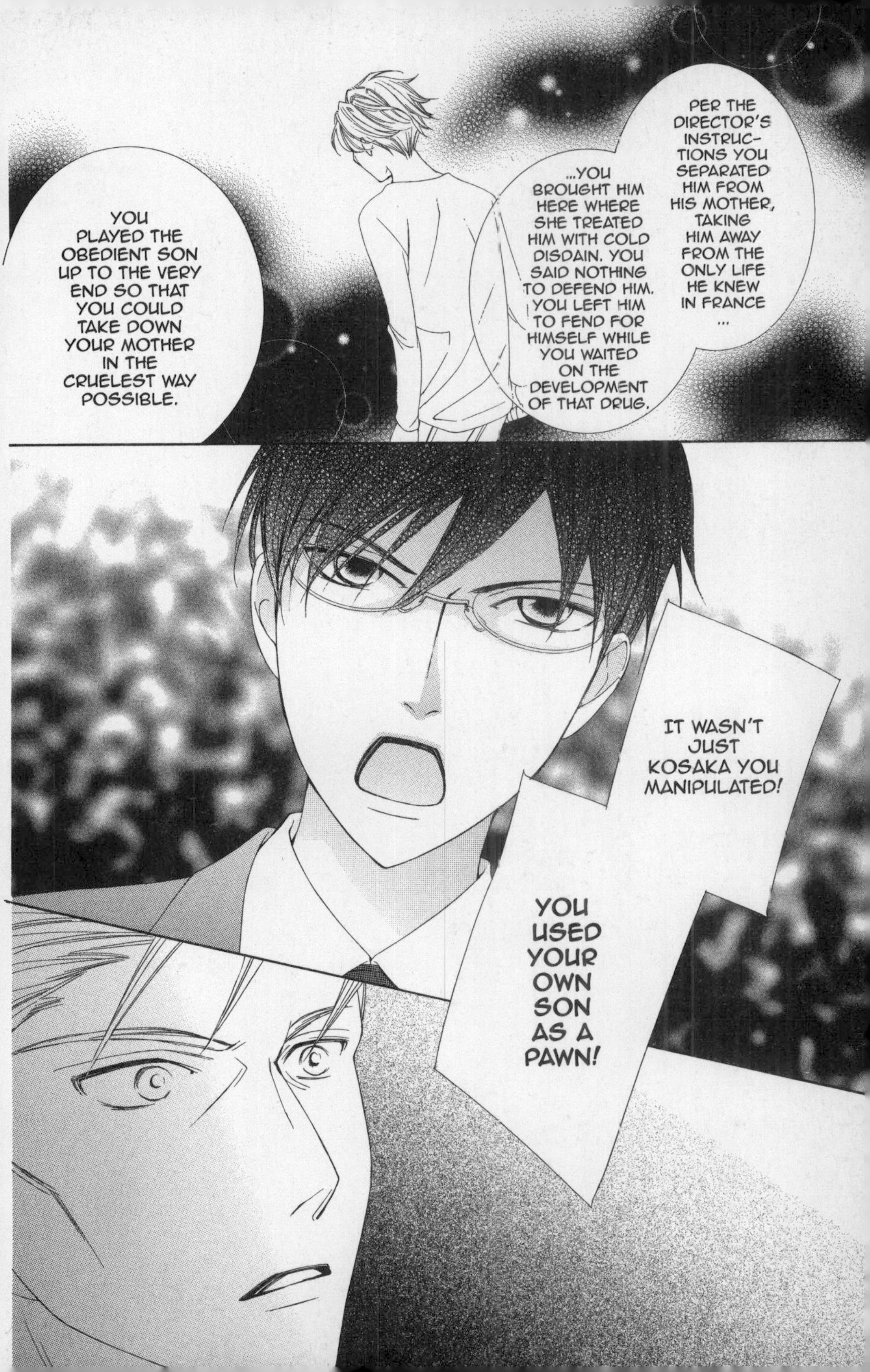
PER THE DIRECTOR'S INSTRUCTIONS YOU SEPARATED HIM FROM HIS MOTHER, TAKING HIM AWAY FROM THE ONLY LIFE HE KNEW IN FRANCE ...
...YOU BROUGHT HIM HERE WHERE SHE TREATED HIM WITH COLD DISDAIN. YOU SAID NOTHING TO DEFEND HIM. YOU LEFT HIM TO FEND FOR HIMSELF WHILE YOU WAITED ON THE DEVELOPMENT OF THAT DRUG.
YOU PLAYED THE OBEDIENT SON UP TO THE VERY END SO THAT YOU COULD TAKE DOWN YOUR MOTHER IN THE CRUELEST WAY POSSIBLE.
IT WASN'T JUST KOSAKA YOU MANIPULATED!
YOU USED YOUR OWN SON AS A PAWN!

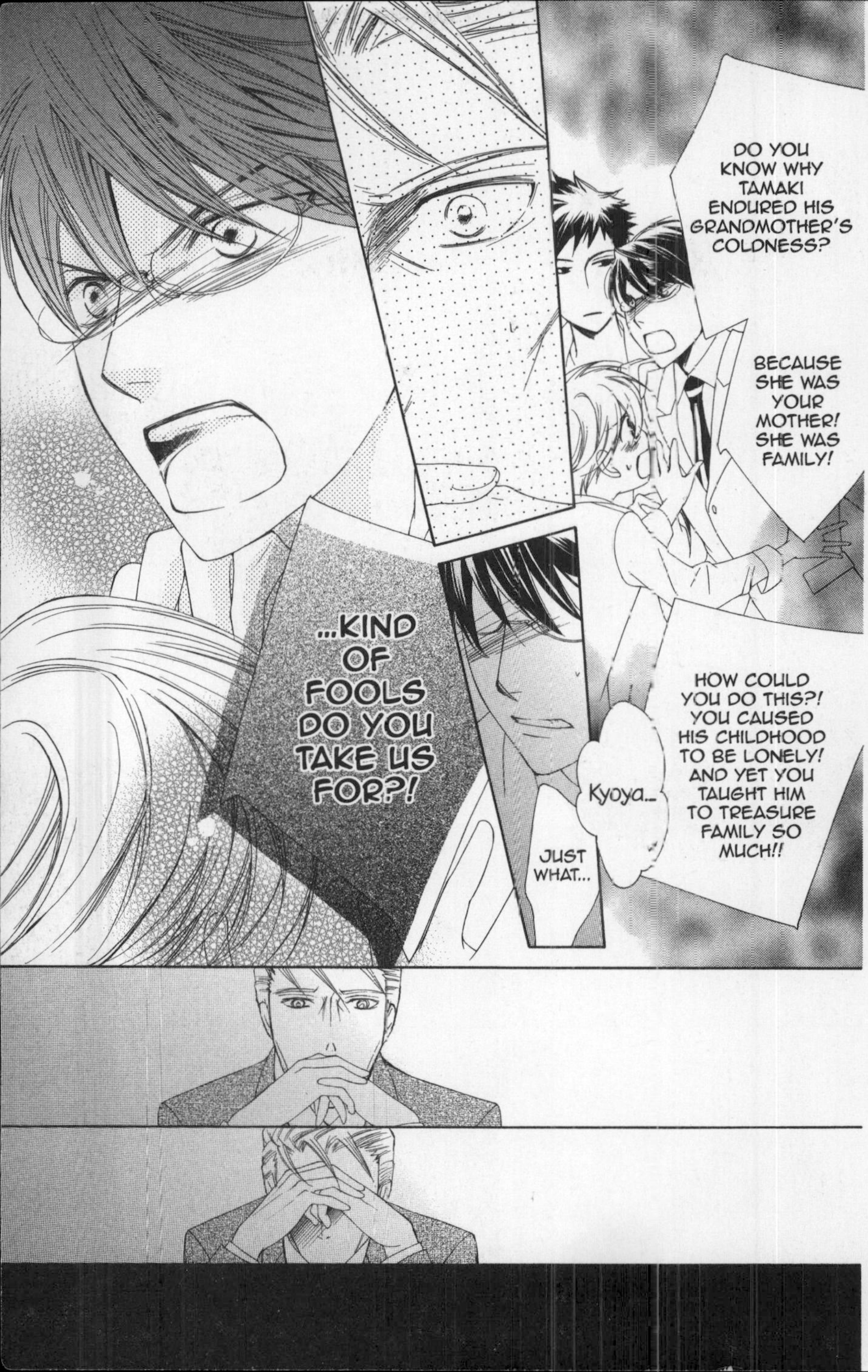
DO YOU KNOW WHY TAMAKI ENDURED HIS GRANDMOTHER'S COLDNESS?
BECAUSE SHE WAS YOUR MOTHER! SHE WAS FAMILY!
HOW COULD YOU DO THIS?! YOU CAUSED HIS CHILDHOOD TO BE LONELY! AND YET YOU TAUGHT HIM TO TREASURE FAMILY SO MUCH!!
Kyoya...
JUST WHAT...
...KIND OF FOOLS DO YOU TAKE US FOR?!

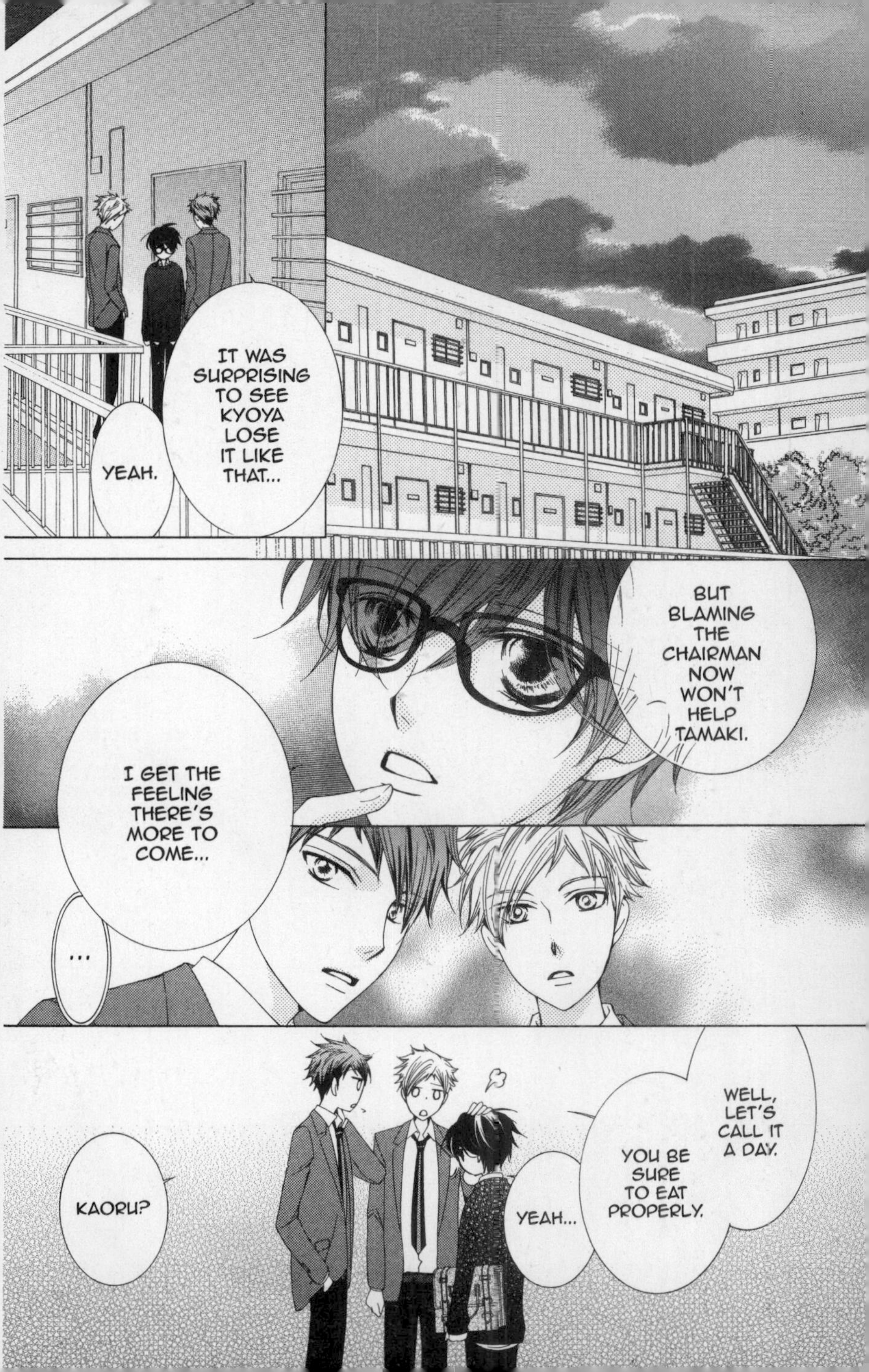
IT WAS SURPRISING TO SEE KYOYA LOSE IT LIKE THAT...
YEAH.
BUT BLAMING THE CHAIRMAN NOW WON'T HELP TAMAKI.
I GET THE FEELING THERE'S MORE TO COME...
...
WELL, LET'S CALL IT A DAY.
YOU BE SURE TO EAT PROPERLY.
YEAH...
KAORU?

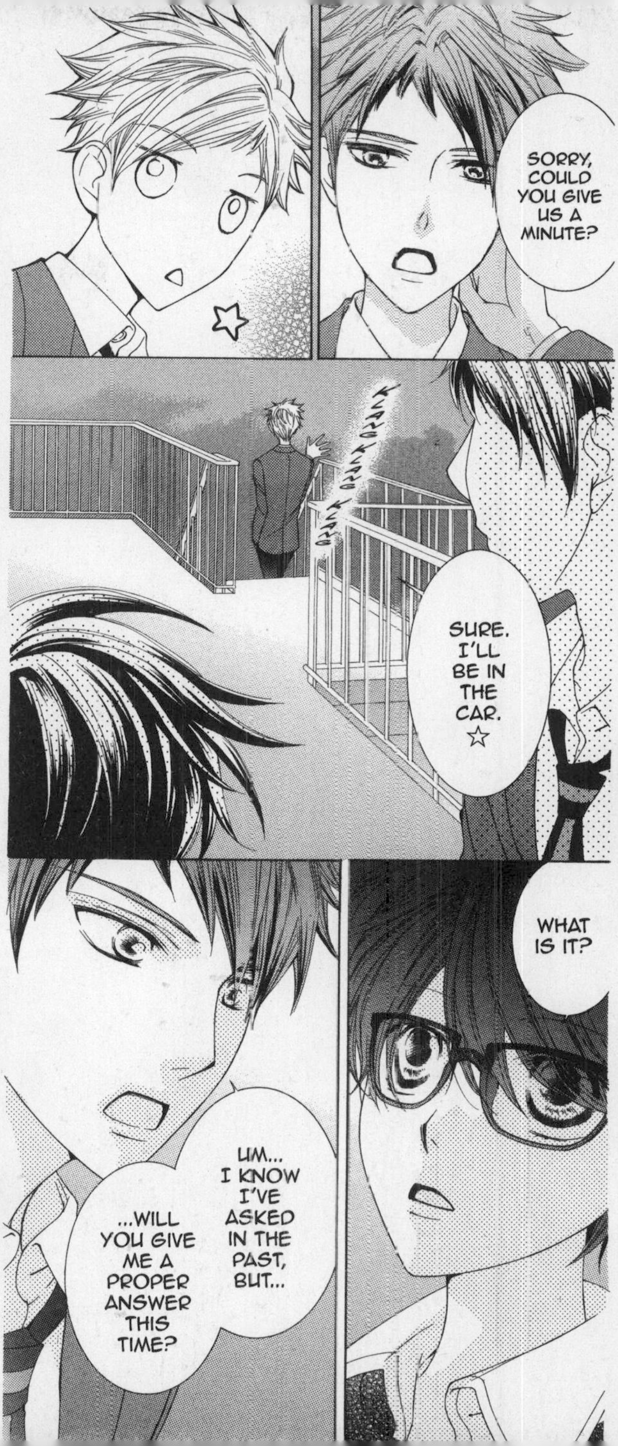
SORRY, COULD YOU GIVE US A MINUTE?
SURE. I'LL BE IN THE CAR. ☆
WHAT IS IT?
UM... I KNOW I'VE ASKED IN THE PAST, BUT...
...WILL YOU GIVE ME A PROPER ANSWER THIS TIME?

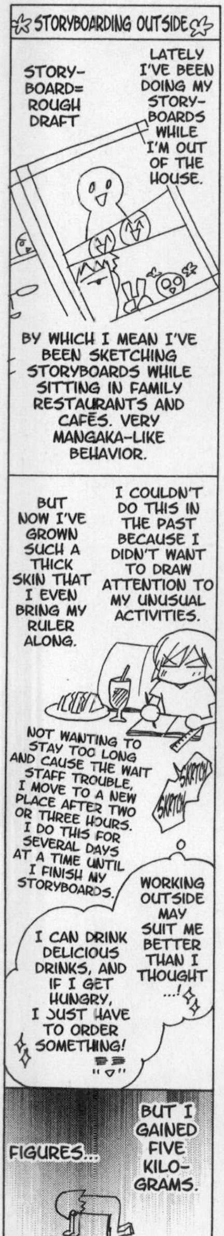
STORYBOARDING OUTSIDE
LATELY I'VE BEEN DOING MY STORY-BOARDS WHILE I'M OUT OF THE HOUSE.
STORY-BOARD= ROUGH DRAFT
BY WHICH I MEAN I'VE BEEN SKETCHING STORYBOARDS WHILE SITTING IN FAMILY RESTAURANTS AND CAFÉS. VERY MANGAKA-LIKE BEHAVIOR.
I COULDN'T DO THIS IN THE PAST BECAUSE I DIDN'T WANT TO DRAW ATTENTION TO MY UNUSUAL ACTIVITIES.
BUT NOW I'VE GROWN SUCH A THICK SKIN THAT I EVEN BRING MY RULER ALONG.
NOT WANTING TO STAY TOO LONG AND CAUSE THE WAIT STAFF TROUBLE, I MOVE TO A NEW PLACE AFTER TWO OR THREE HOURS. I DO THIS FOR SEVERAL DAYS AT A TIME UNTIL I FINISH MY STORYBOARDS.
SKRTCH SKRTCH
WORKING OUTSIDE MAY SUIT ME BETTER THAN I THOUGHT...!
I CAN DRINK DELICIOUS DRINKS, AND IF I GET HUNGRY, I JUST HAVE TO ORDER SOMETHING!
BUT I GAINED FIVE KILO-GRAMS.
FIGURES...

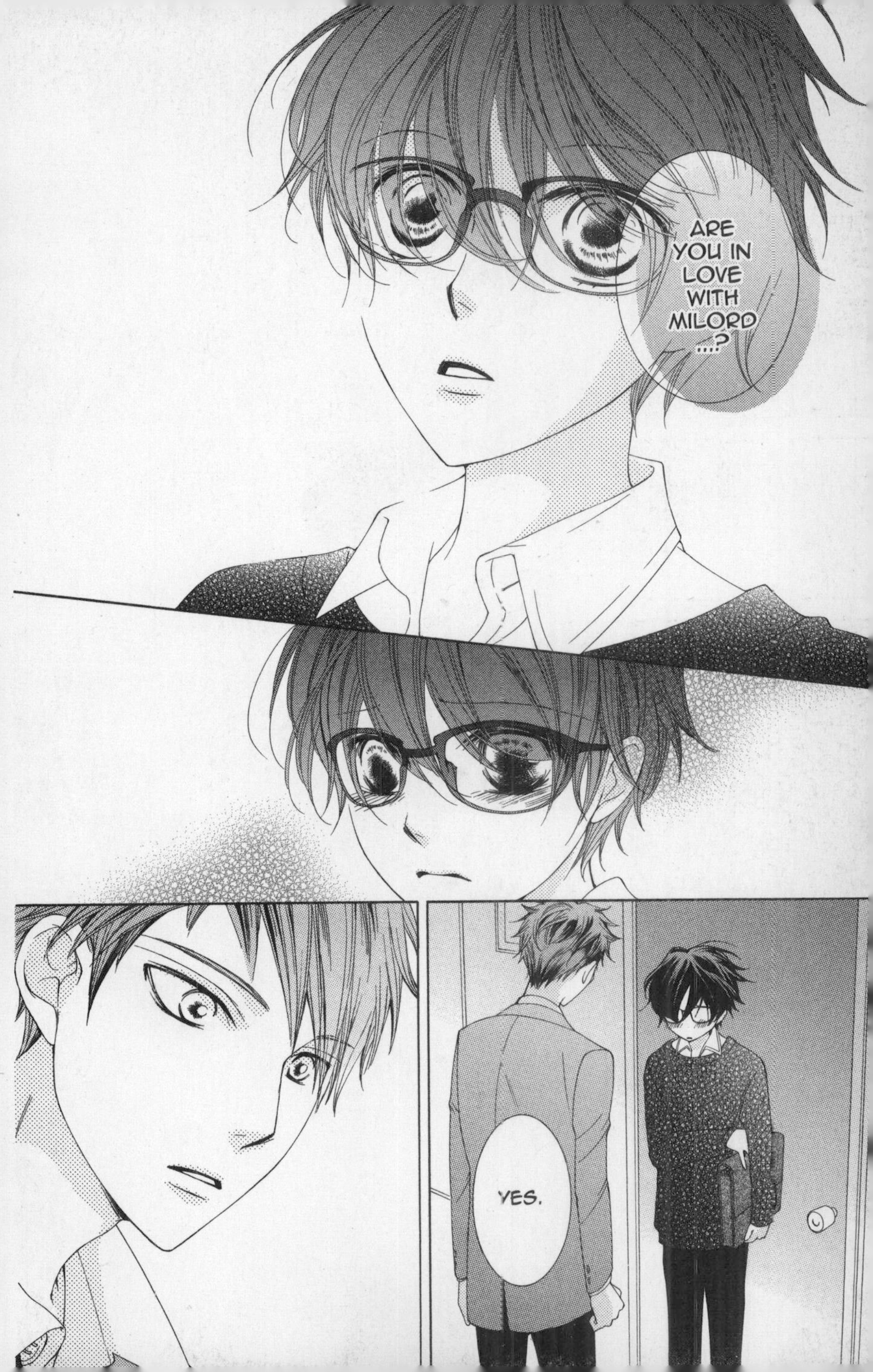
ARE YOU IN LOVE WITH MILORD ...?
YES.

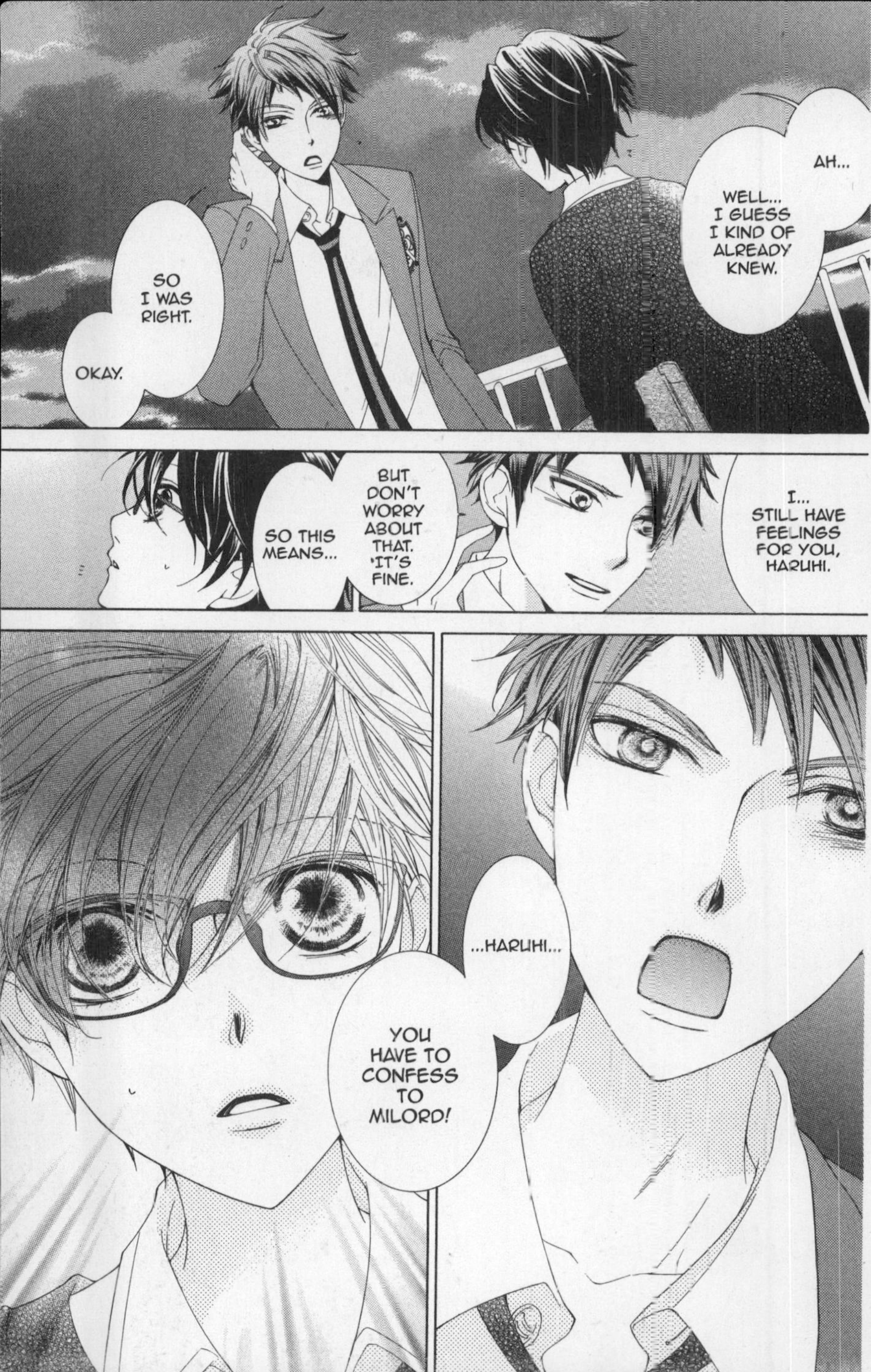
AH...
WELL... I GUESS I KIND OF ALREADY KNEW.
SO I WAS RIGHT.
OKAY.
I... STILL HAVE FEELINGS FOR YOU, HARUHI.
BUT DON'T WORRY ABOUT THAT. IT'S FINE.
SO THIS MEANS...
...HARUHI...
YOU HAVE TO CONFESS TO MILORD!

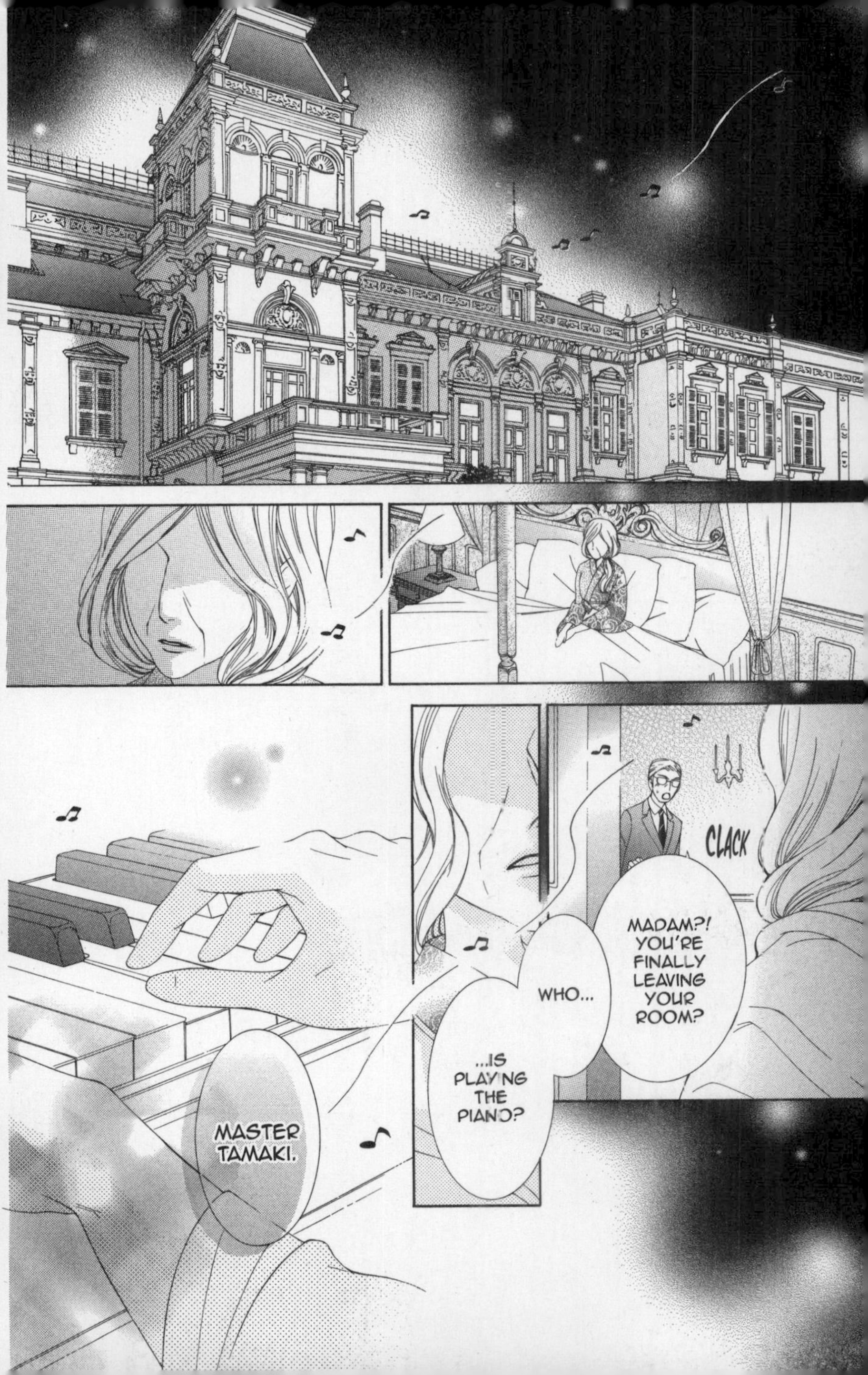
CLACK
MADAM?! YOU'RE FINALLY LEAVING YOUR ROOM?
WHO...
...IS PLAYING THE PIANO?
MASTER TAMAKI.

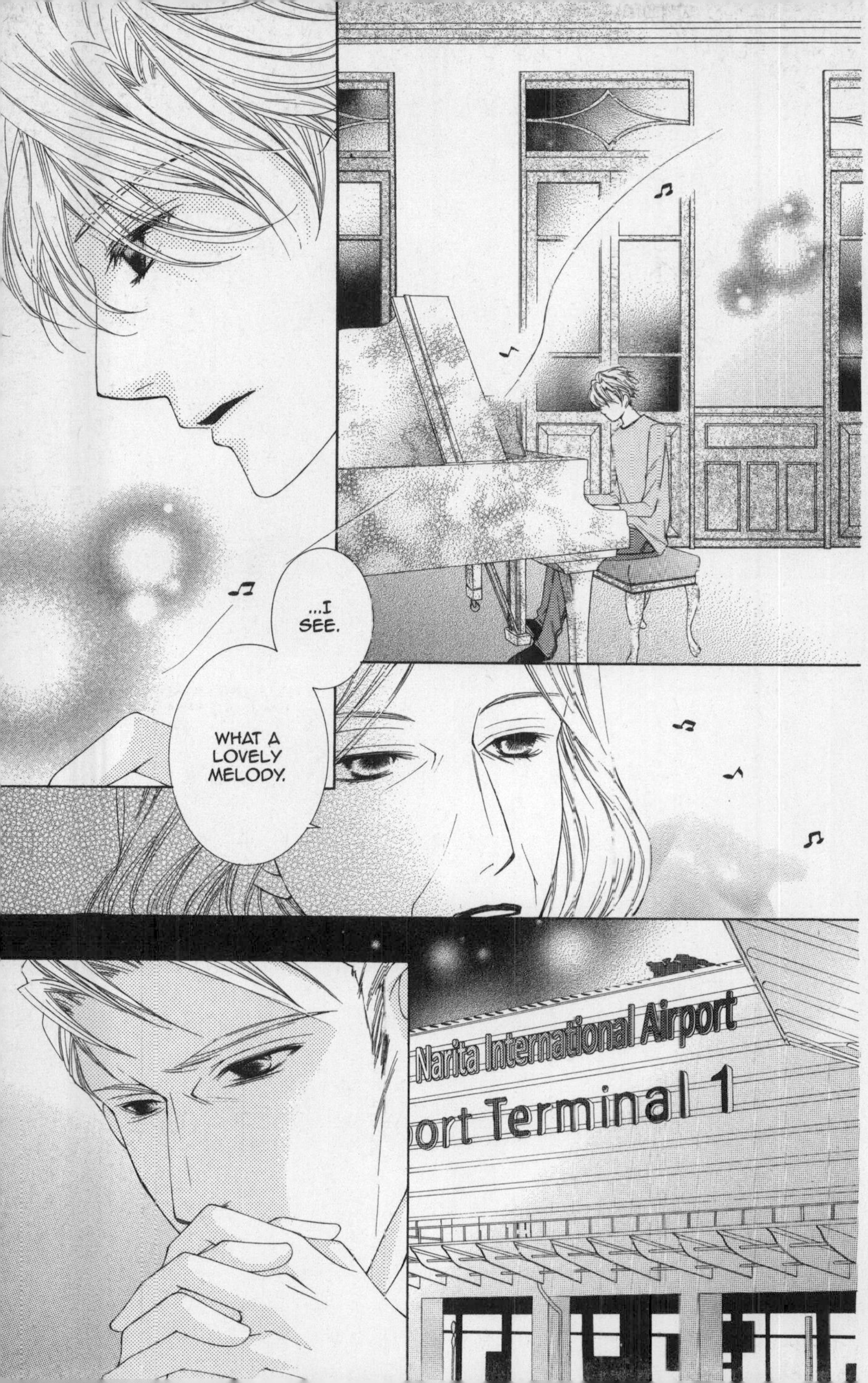
...I SEE.
WHAT A LOVELY MELODY.
Narita International Airport
ort Terminal 1

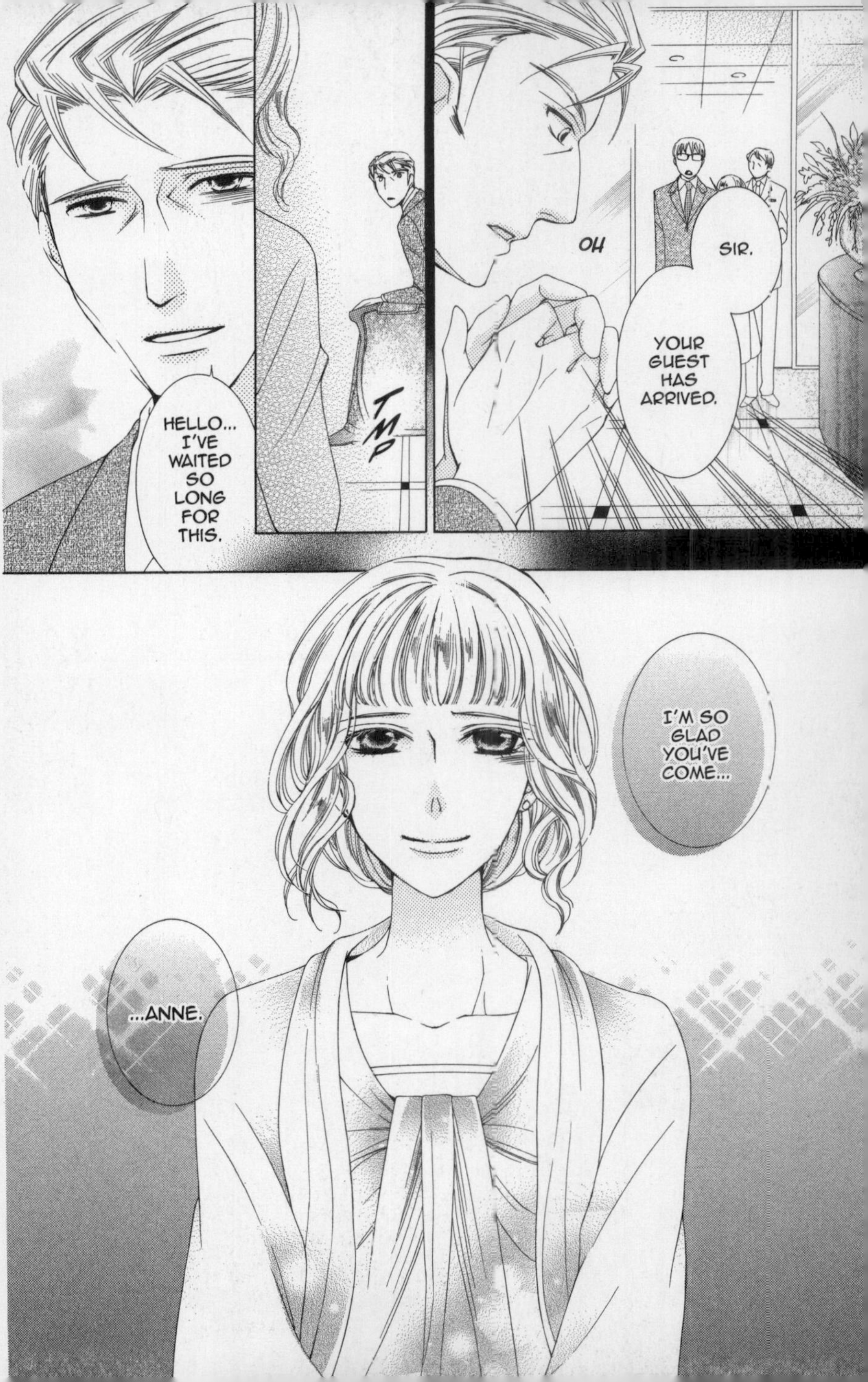
SIR.
YOUR GUEST HAS ARRIVED.
OH
TMP
HELLO... I'VE WAITED SO LONG FOR THIS.
I'M SO GLAD YOU'VE COME...
...ANNE.

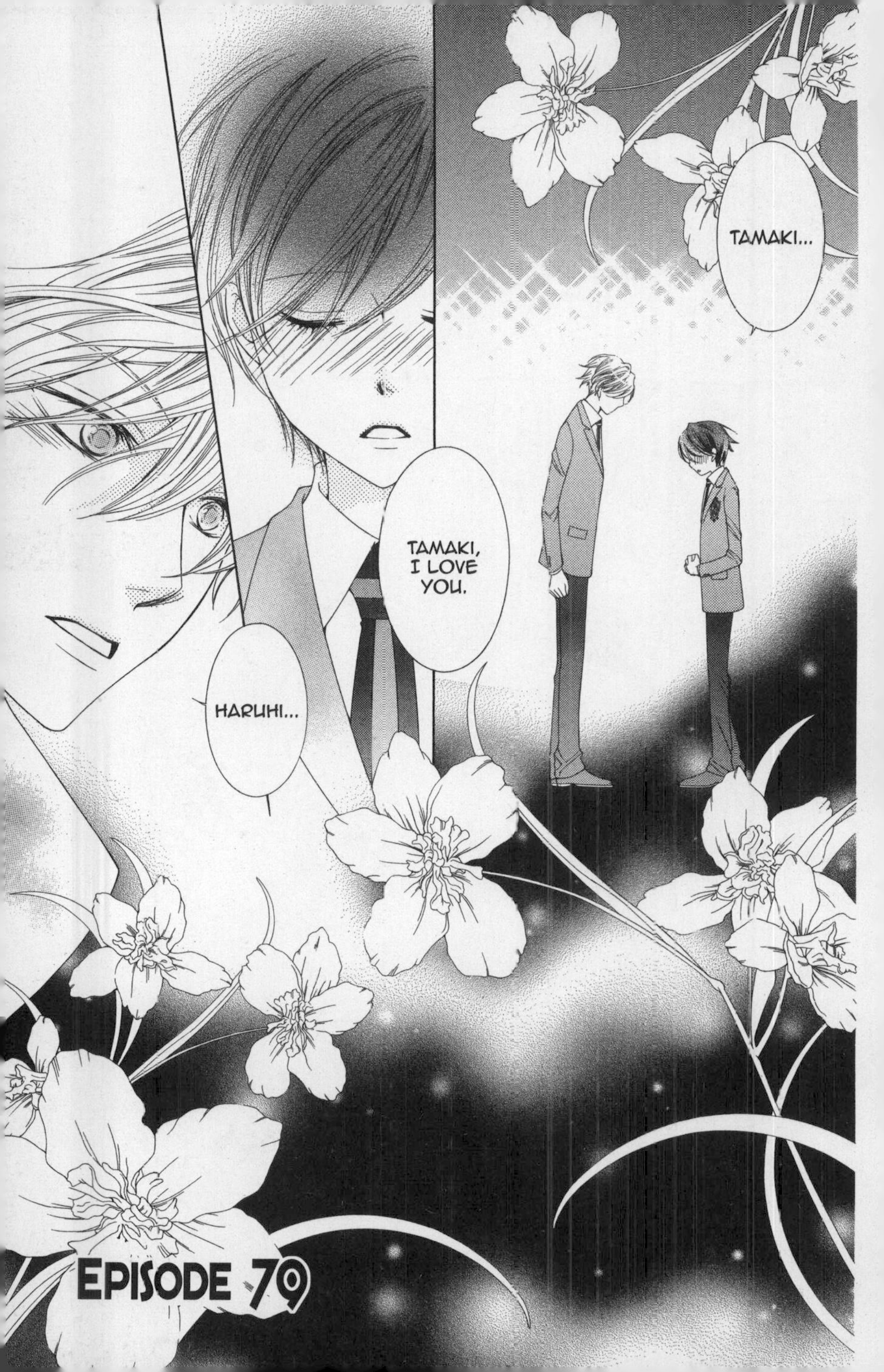
TAMAKI...
TAMAKI, I LOVE YOU.
HARUHI...
EPISODE 79

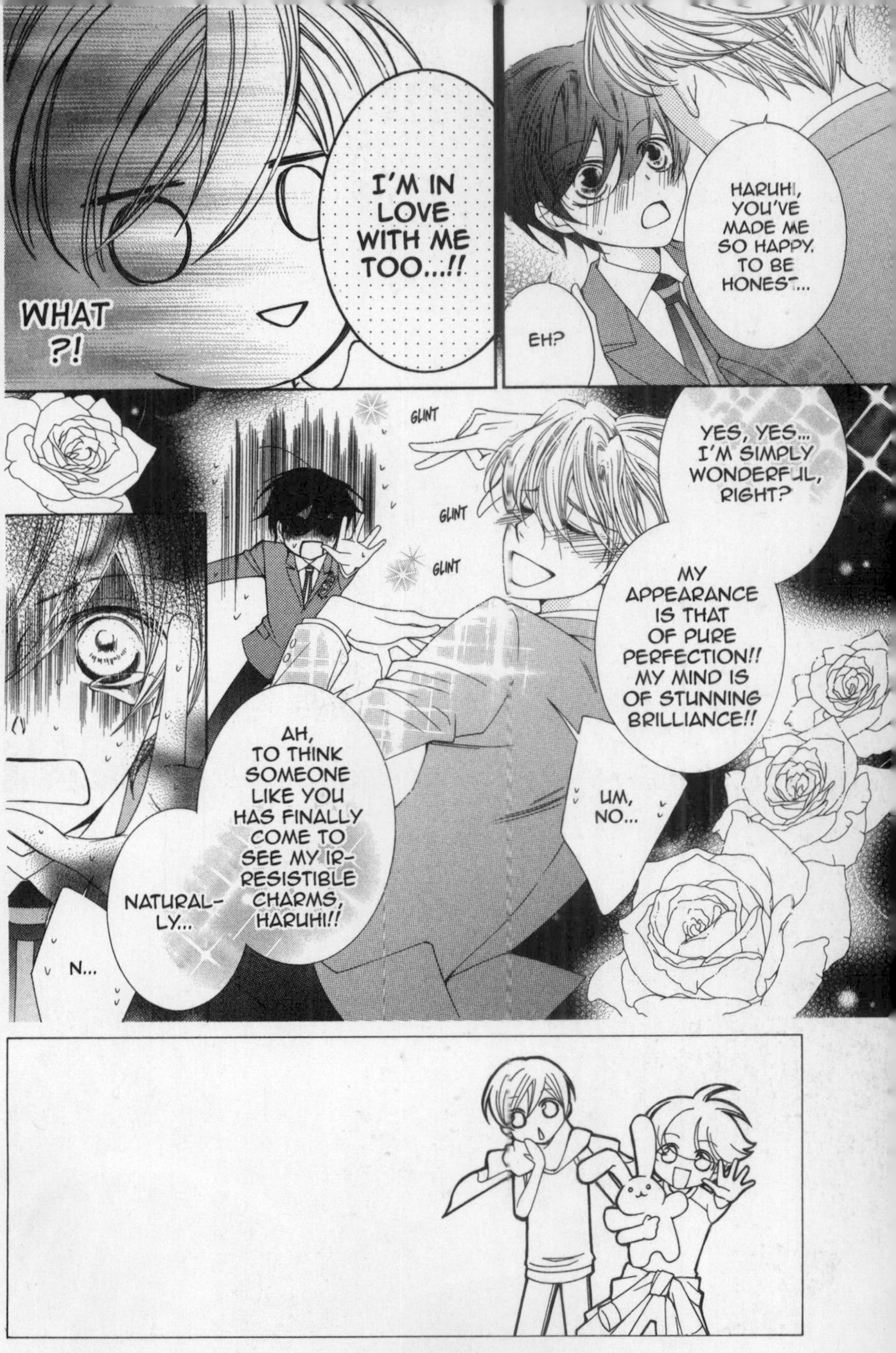
HARUHI, YOU'VE MADE ME SO HAPPY. TO BE HONEST...
EH?
I'M IN LOVE WITH ME TOO...!!
WHAT ?!
YES, YES... I'M SIMPLY WONDERFUL, RIGHT?
GLINT
GLINT
GLINT
MY APPEARANCE IS THAT OF PURE PERFECTION!! MY MIND IS OF STUNNING BRILLIANCE!!
UM, NO...
AH, TO THINK SOMEONE LIKE YOU HAS FINALLY COME TO SEE MY IR-RESISTIBLE CHARMS, HARUHI!!
NATURAL-LY...
N...

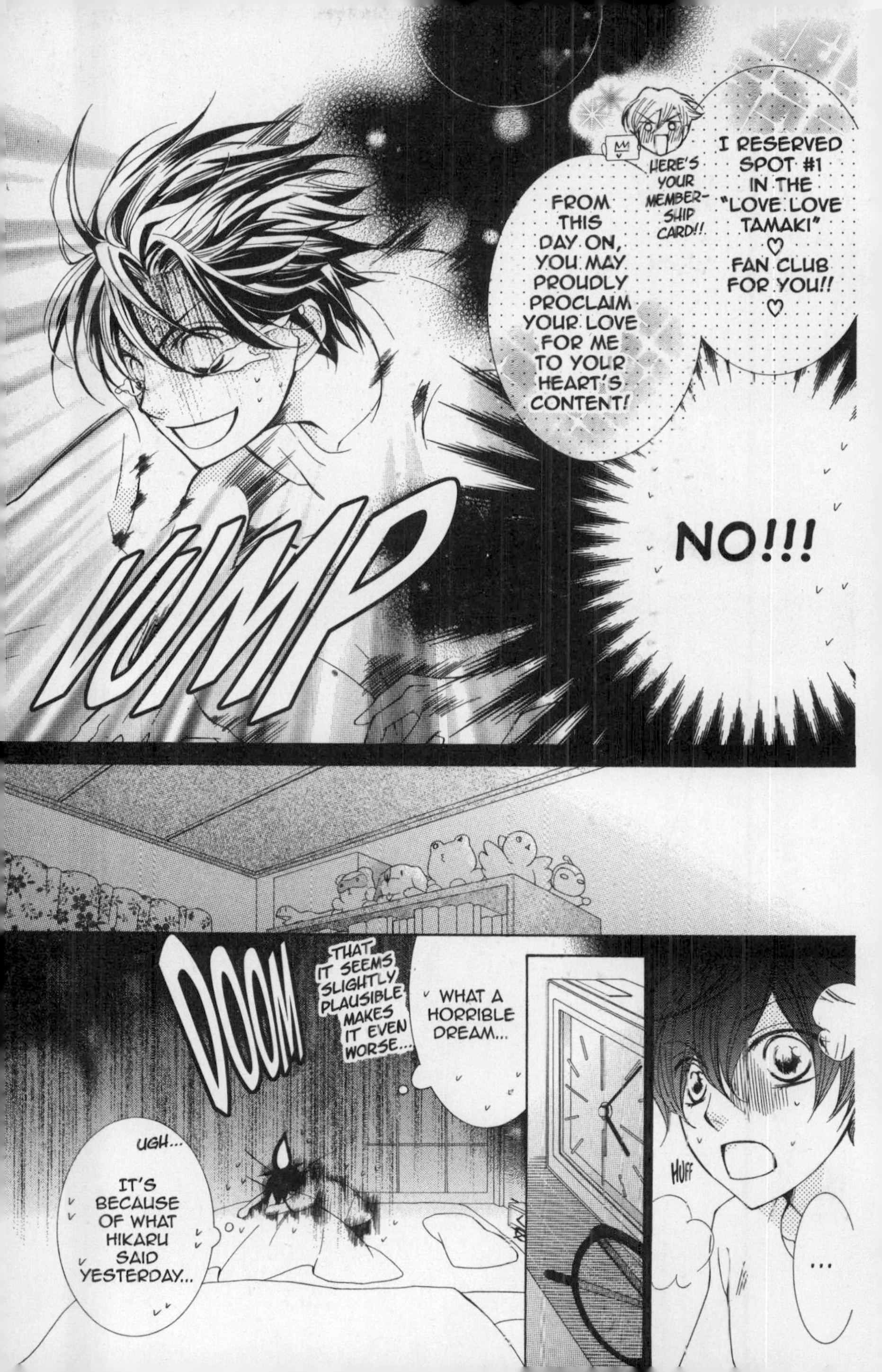
I RESERVED SPOT #1 IN THE "LOVE LOVE TAMAKI" ♡ FAN CLUB FOR YOU!! ♡
HERE'S YOUR MEMBERSHIP CARD!!
FROM THIS DAY ON, YOU MAY PROUDLY PROCLAIM YOUR LOVE FOR ME TO YOUR HEART'S CONTENT!
NO!!!
VOMP
...
HUFF
WHAT A HORRIBLE DREAM...
THAT IT SEEMS SLIGHTLY PLAUSIBLE MAKES IT EVEN WORSE...
DOOM
UGH...
IT'S BECAUSE OF WHAT HIKARU SAID YESTERDAY...

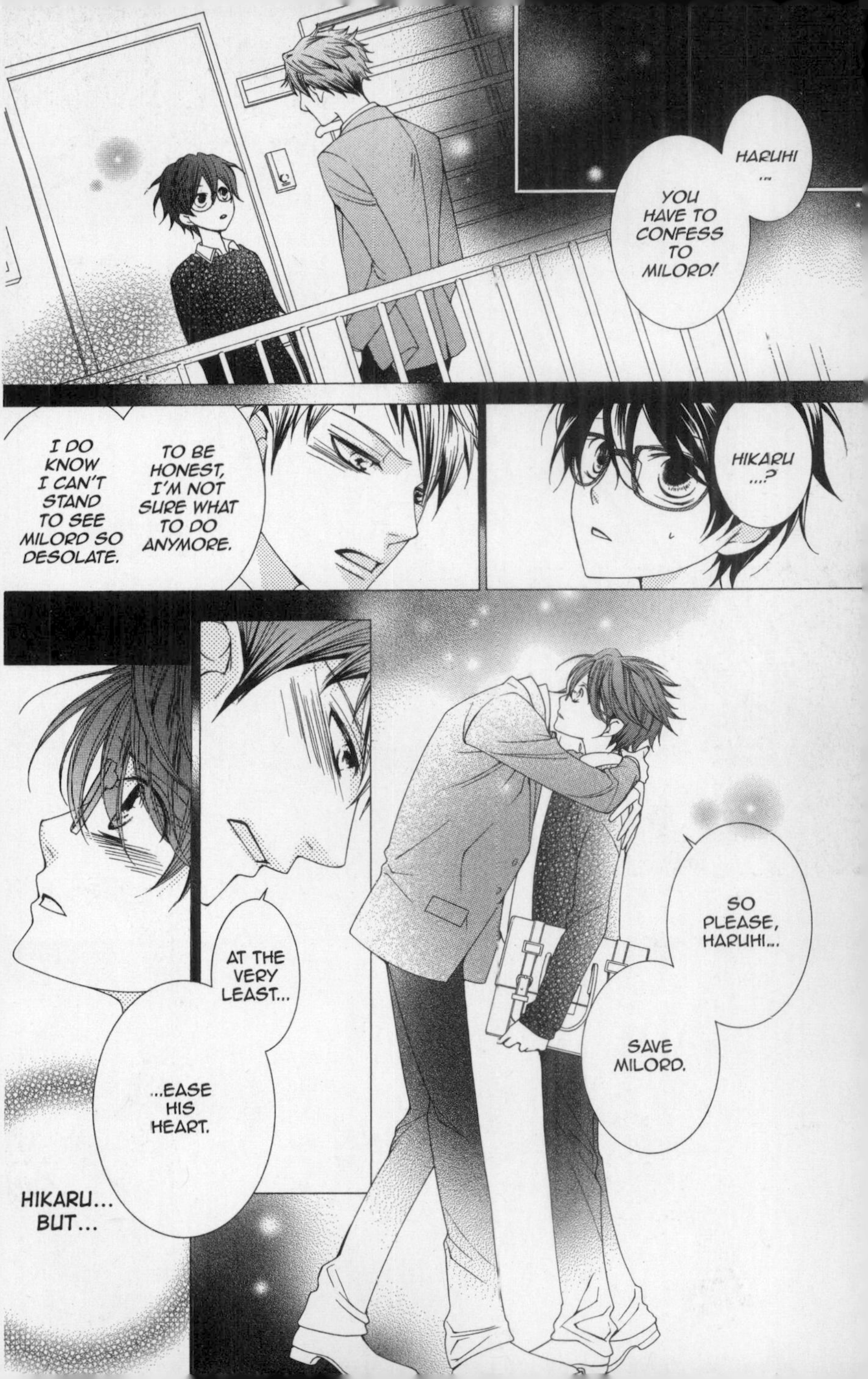
HARUHI...
YOU HAVE TO CONFESS TO MILORD!
HIKARU...?
TO BE HONEST, I'M NOT SURE WHAT TO DO ANYMORE.
I DO KNOW I CAN'T STAND TO SEE MILORD SO DESOLATE.
SO PLEASE, HARUHI...
SAVE MILORD.
AT THE VERY LEAST...
...EASE HIS HEART.
HIKARU... BUT...

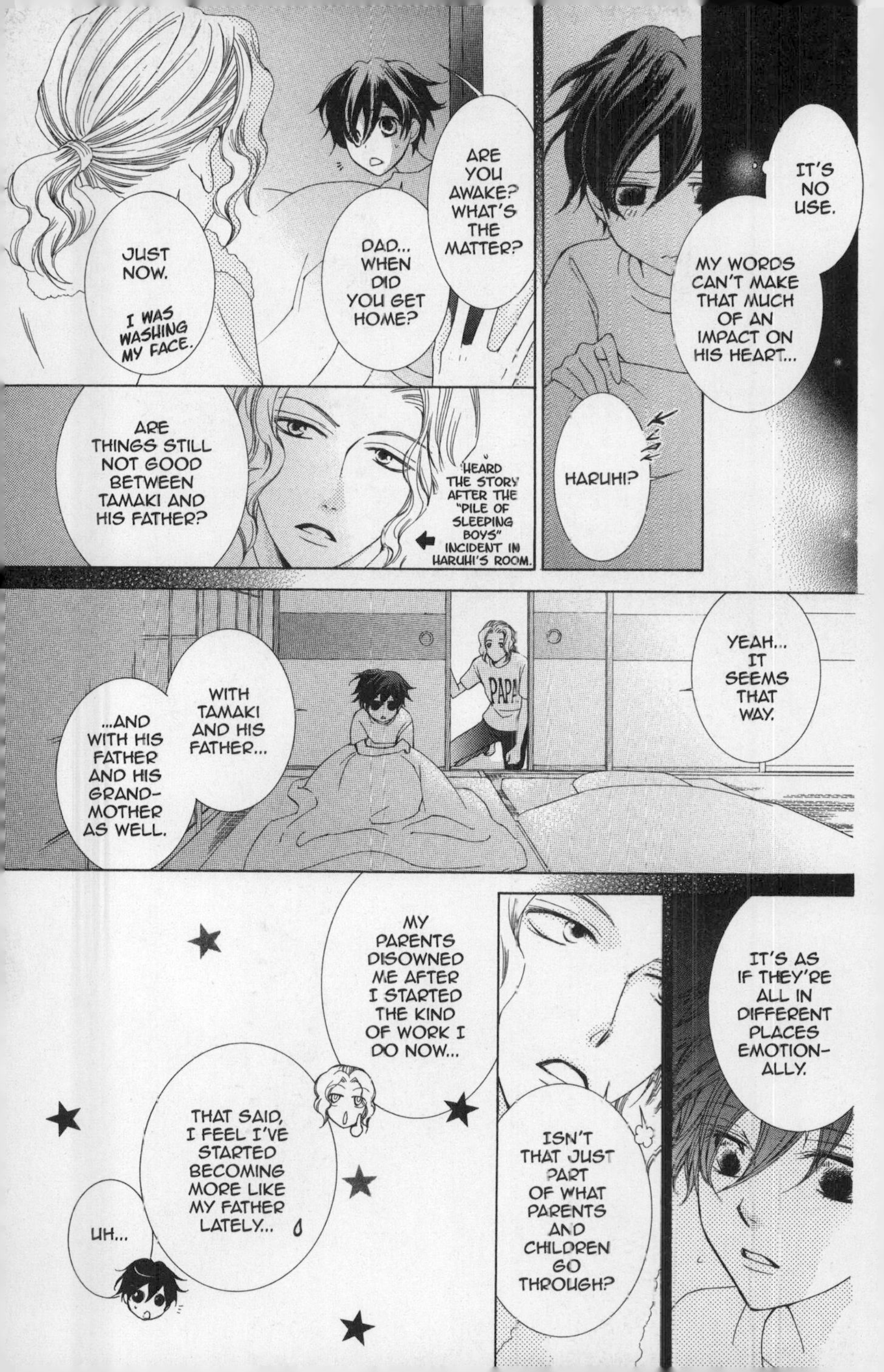
IT'S NO USE.
MY WORDS CAN'T MAKE THAT MUCH OF AN IMPACT ON HIS HEART...
HARUHI?
ARE YOU AWAKE? WHAT'S THE MATTER?
DAD... WHEN DID YOU GET HOME?
JUST NOW.
I WAS WASHING MY FACE.
HEARD THE STORY AFTER THE "PILE OF SLEEPING BOYS" INCIDENT IN HARUHI'S ROOM.
ARE THINGS STILL NOT GOOD BETWEEN TAMAKI AND HIS FATHER?
YEAH... IT SEEMS THAT WAY.
WITH TAMAKI AND HIS FATHER...
...AND WITH HIS FATHER AND HIS GRANDMOTHER AS WELL.
PAPA
IT'S AS IF THEY'RE ALL IN DIFFERENT PLACES EMOTIONALLY.
ISN'T THAT JUST PART OF WHAT PARENTS AND CHILDREN GO THROUGH?
MY PARENTS DISOWNED ME AFTER I STARTED THE KIND OF WORK I DO NOW...
THAT SAID, I FEEL I'VE STARTED BECOMING MORE LIKE MY FATHER LATELY...
UH...

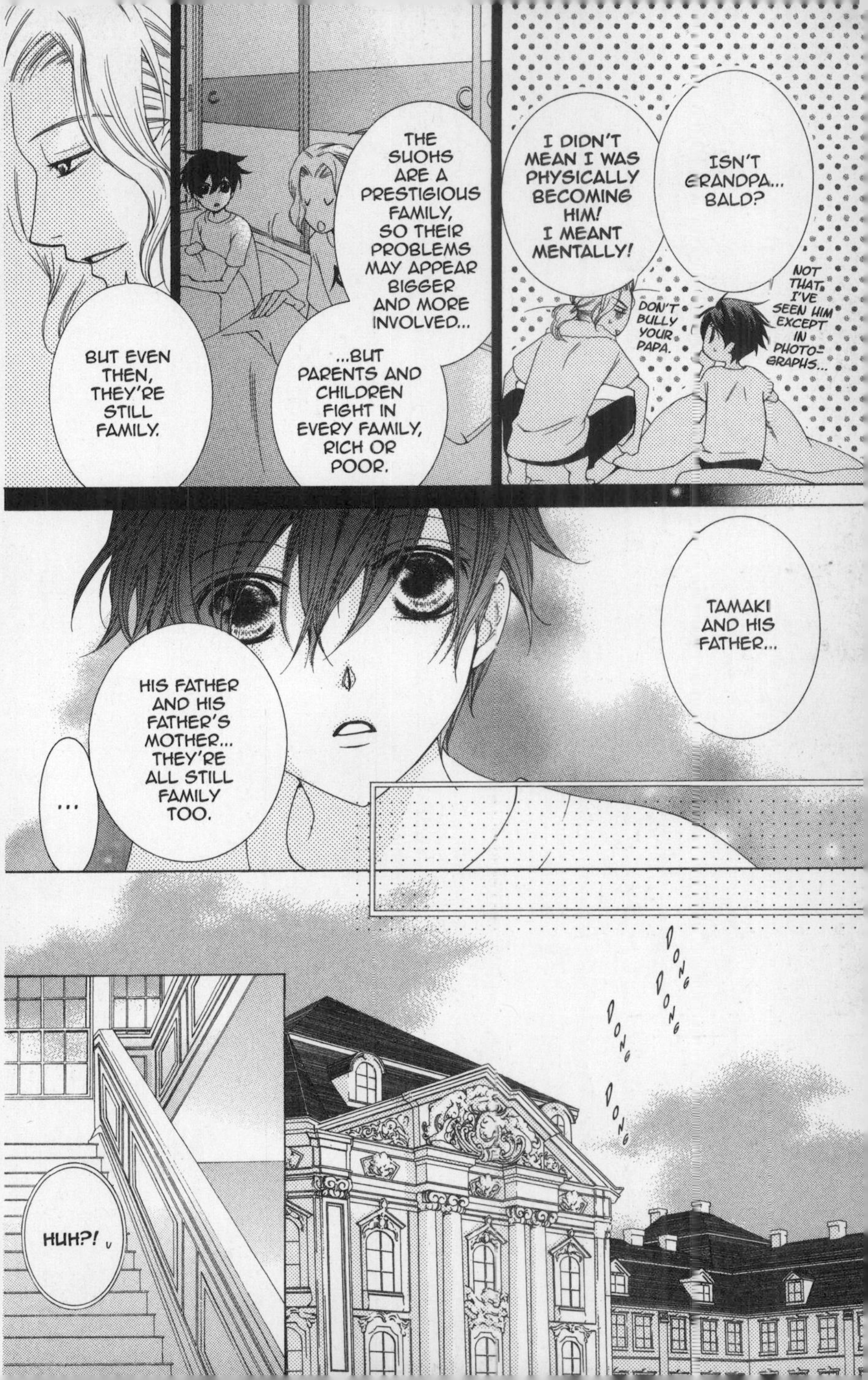
ISN'T GRANDPA... BALD?
I DIDN'T MEAN I WAS PHYSICALLY BECOMING HIM! I MEANT MENTALLY!
NOT THAT I'VE SEEN HIM EXCEPT IN PHOTO-GRAPHS...
DON'T BULLY YOUR PAPA.
THE SUOHS ARE A PRESTIGIOUS FAMILY, SO THEIR PROBLEMS MAY APPEAR BIGGER AND MORE INVOLVED...
...BUT PARENTS AND CHILDREN FIGHT IN EVERY FAMILY, RICH OR POOR.
BUT EVEN THEN, THEY'RE STILL FAMILY.
TAMAKI AND HIS FATHER...
HIS FATHER AND HIS FATHER'S MOTHER... THEY'RE ALL STILL FAMILY TOO.
...
DONG
DONG
DONG
DONG
HUH?!

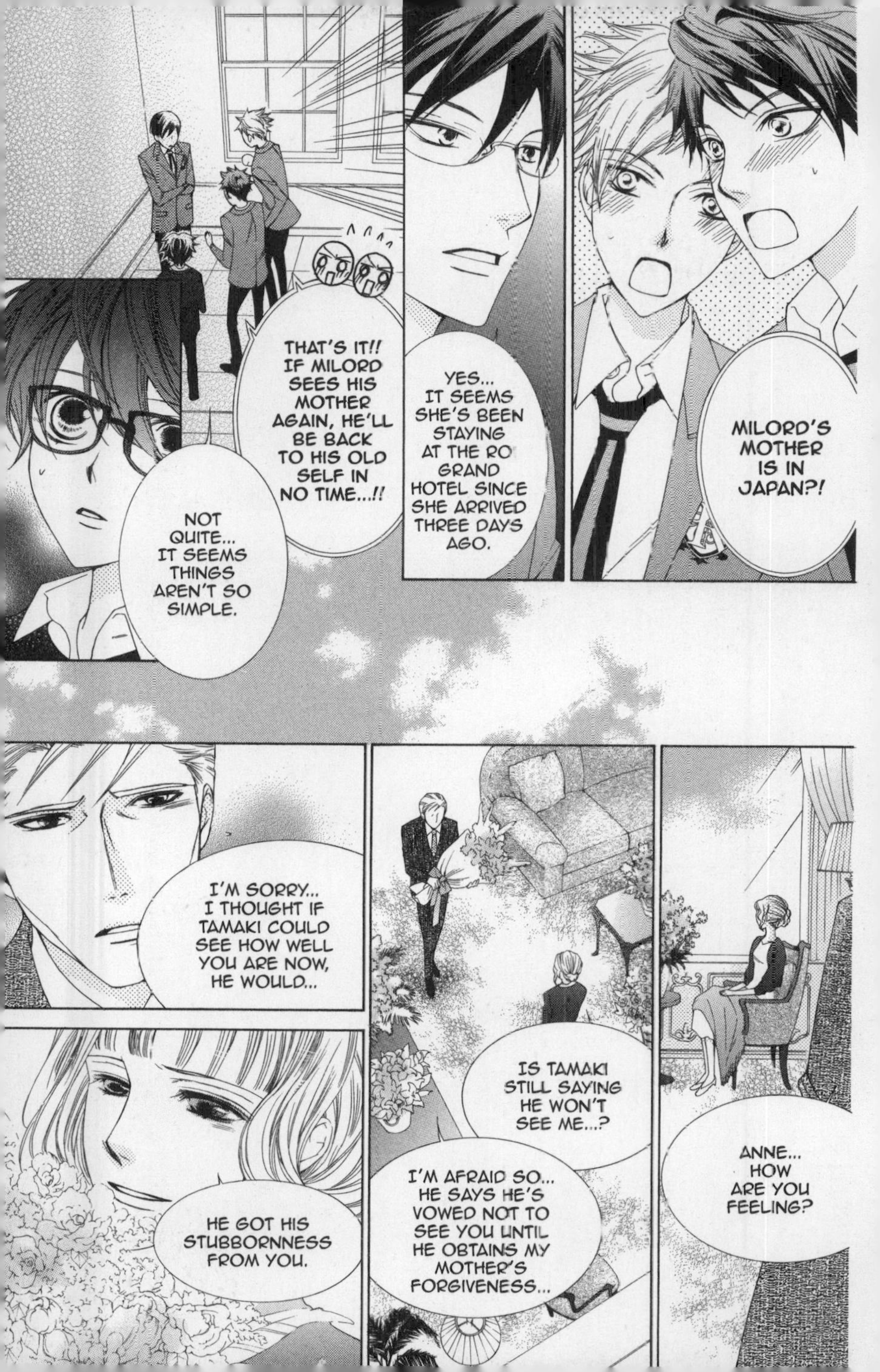
MILORD'S MOTHER IS IN JAPAN?!
YES... IT SEEMS SHE'S BEEN STAYING AT THE RO GRAND HOTEL SINCE SHE ARRIVED THREE DAYS AGO.
THAT'S IT!! IF MILORD SEES HIS MOTHER AGAIN, HE'LL BE BACK TO HIS OLD SELF IN NO TIME...!!
NOT QUITE... IT SEEMS THINGS AREN'T SO SIMPLE.
ANNE... HOW ARE YOU FEELING?
IS TAMAKI STILL SAYING HE WON'T SEE ME...?
I'M AFRAID SO... HE SAYS HE'S VOWED NOT TO SEE YOU UNTIL HE OBTAINS MY MOTHER'S FORGIVENESS...
I'M SORRY... I THOUGHT IF TAMAKI COULD SEE HOW WELL YOU ARE NOW, HE WOULD...
HE GOT HIS STUBBORNNESS FROM YOU.

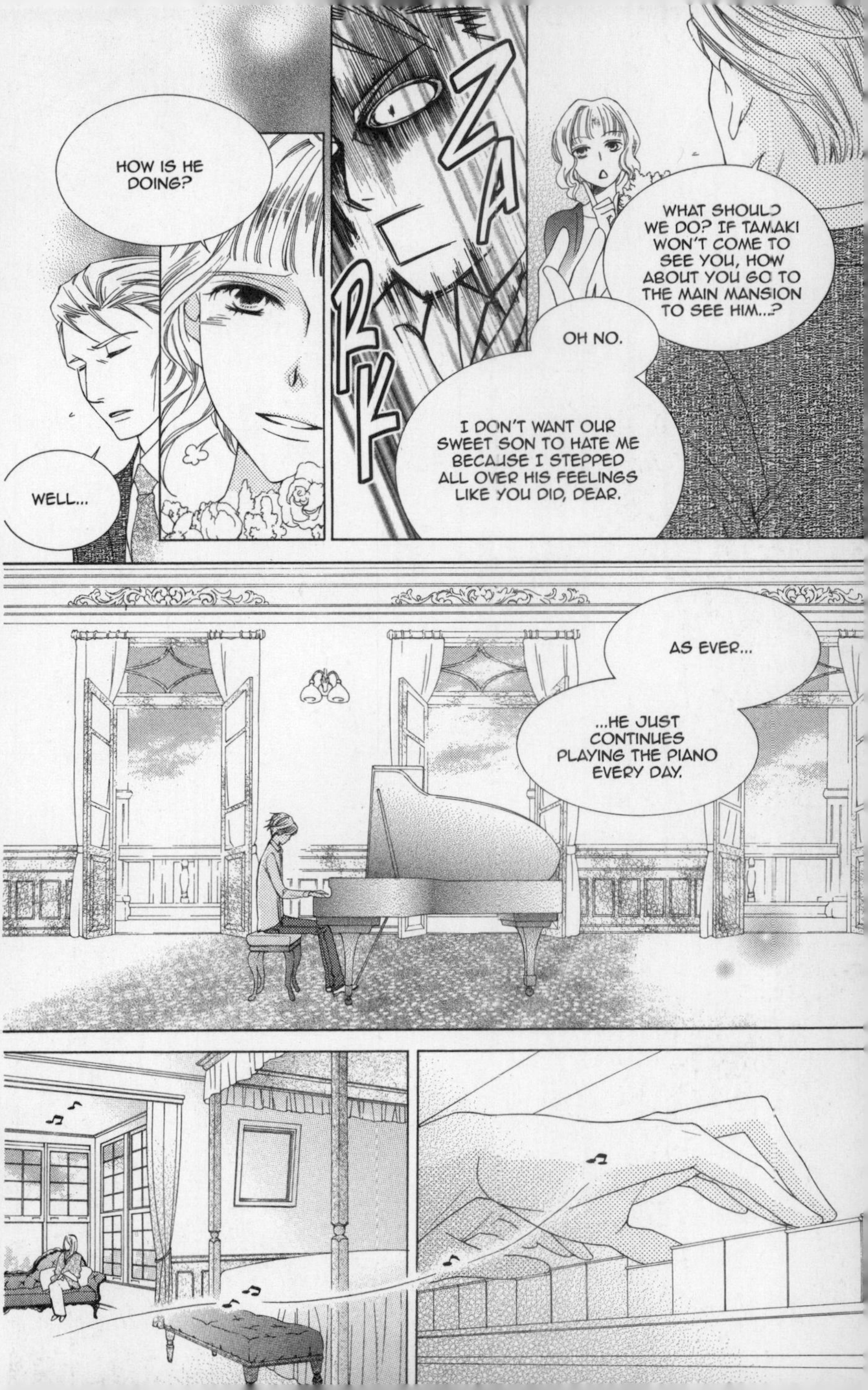
WHAT SHOULD WE DO? IF TAMAKI WON'T COME TO SEE YOU, HOW ABOUT YOU GO TO THE MAIN MANSION TO SEE HIM...?
OH NO.
I DON'T WANT OUR SWEET SON TO HATE ME BECAUSE I STEPPED ALL OVER HIS FEELINGS LIKE YOU DID, DEAR.
HOW IS HE DOING?
WELL...
AS EVER...
...HE JUST CONTINUES PLAYING THE PIANO EVERY DAY.

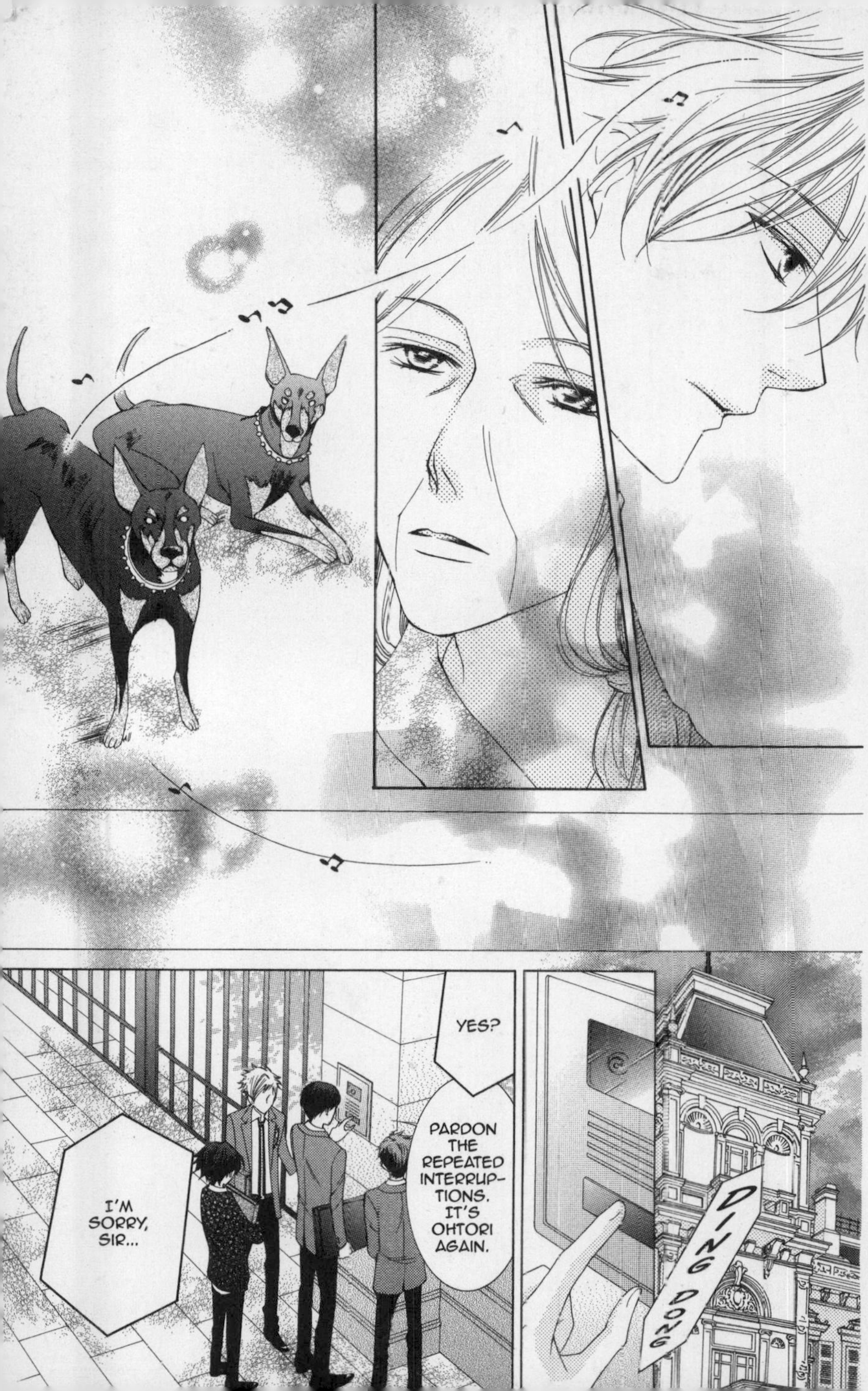
DING DONG
YES?
PARDON THE REPEATED INTERRUP-TIONS. IT'S OHTORI AGAIN.
I'M SORRY, SIR...

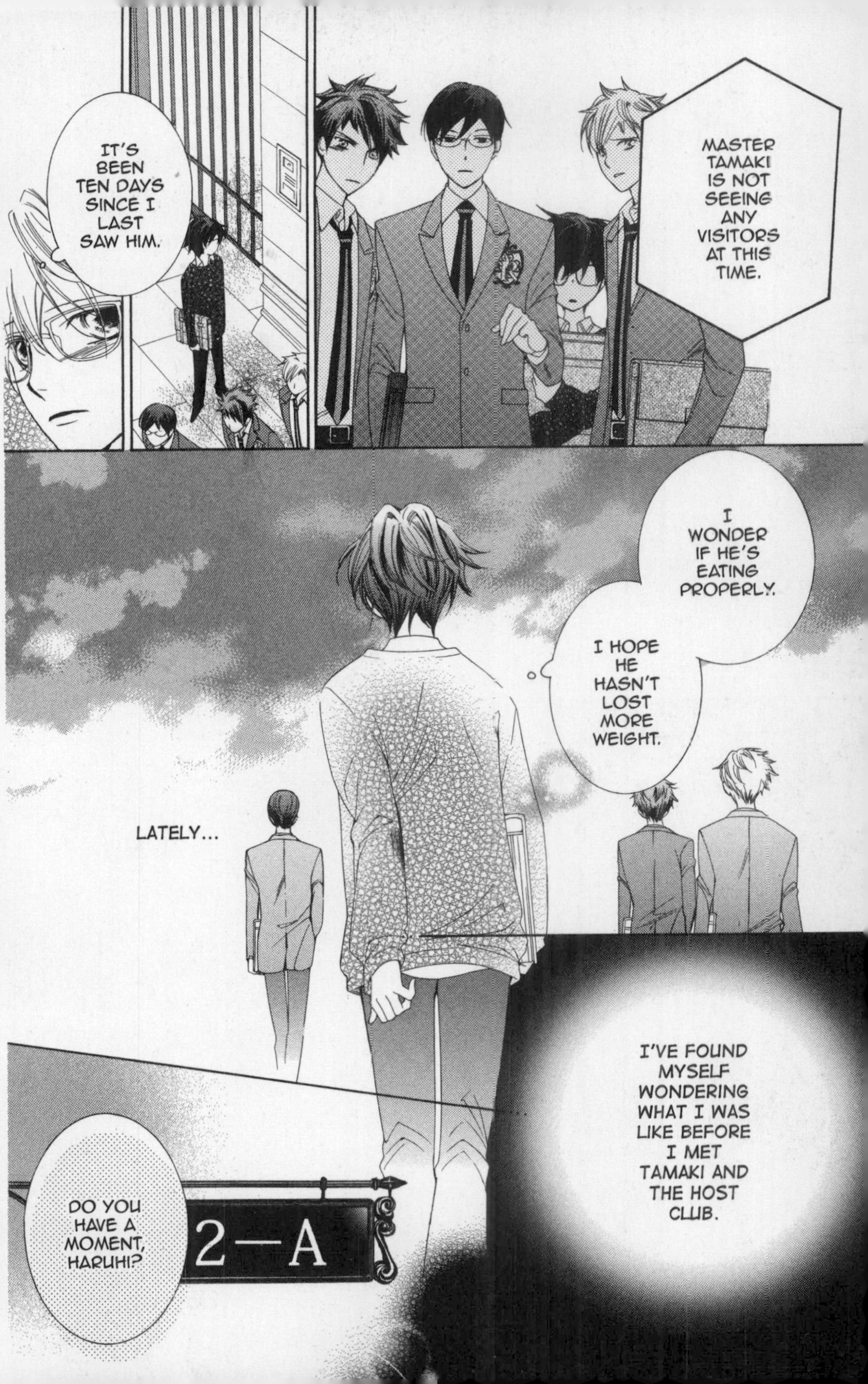
MASTER TAMAKI IS NOT SEEING ANY VISITORS AT THIS TIME.
IT'S BEEN TEN DAYS SINCE I LAST SAW HIM.
I WONDER IF HE'S EATING PROPERLY.
I HOPE HE HASN'T LOST MORE WEIGHT.
LATELY...
I'VE FOUND MYSELF WONDERING WHAT I WAS LIKE BEFORE I MET TAMAKI AND THE HOST CLUB.
2—A
DO YOU HAVE A MOMENT, HARUHI?

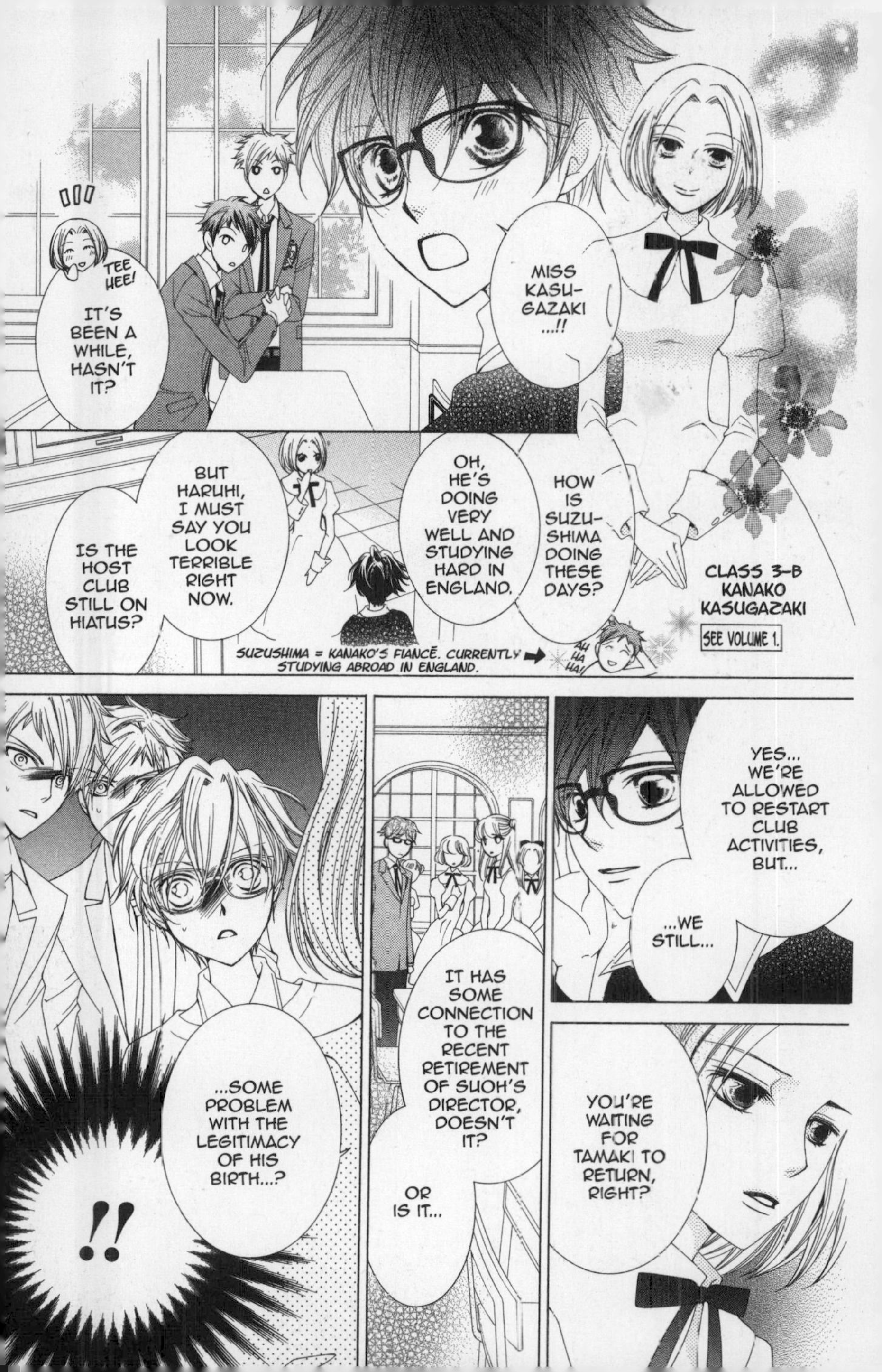
MISS KASUGAZAKI ...!!
TEE HEE!
IT'S BEEN A WHILE, HASN'T IT?
CLASS 3-B KANAKO KASUGAZAKI
SEE VOLUME 1.
HOW IS SUZUSHIMA DOING THESE DAYS?
AH HA HA!
OH, HE'S DOING VERY WELL AND STUDYING HARD IN ENGLAND.
SUZUSHIMA = KANAKO'S FIANCÉ. CURRENTLY STUDYING ABROAD IN ENGLAND.
BUT HARUHI, I MUST SAY YOU LOOK TERRIBLE RIGHT NOW.
IS THE HOST CLUB STILL ON HIATUS?
YES... WE'RE ALLOWED TO RESTART CLUB ACTIVITIES, BUT...
...WE STILL...
YOU'RE WAITING FOR TAMAKI TO RETURN, RIGHT?
IT HAS SOME CONNECTION TO THE RECENT RETIREMENT OF SUOH'S DIRECTOR, DOESN'T IT?
OR IS IT...
...SOME PROBLEM WITH THE LEGITIMACY OF HIS BIRTH...?
!!

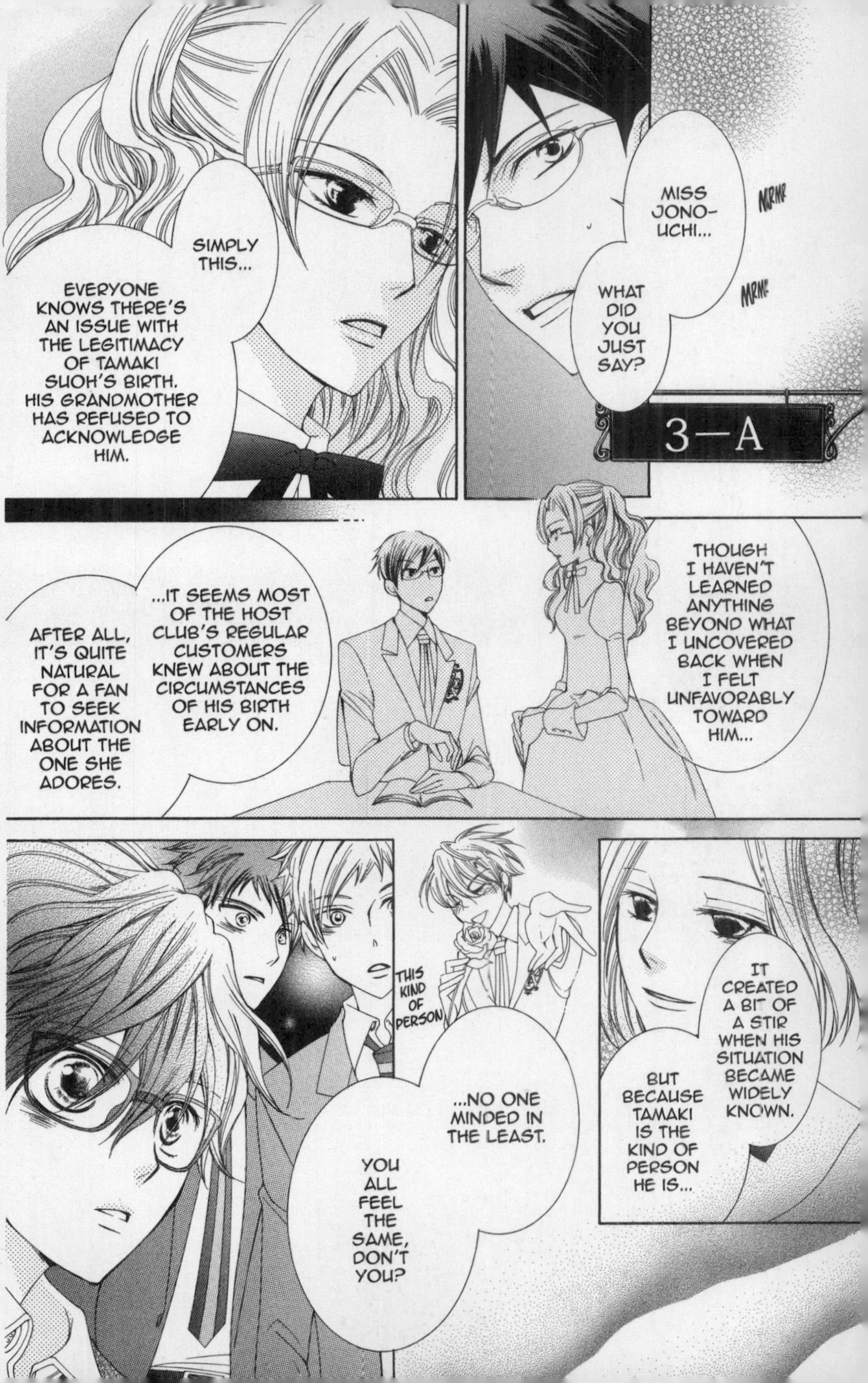
MISS JONO-UCHI...
WHAT DID YOU JUST SAY?
3—A
SIMPLY THIS...
EVERYONE KNOWS THERE'S AN ISSUE WITH THE LEGITIMACY OF TAMAKI SUOH'S BIRTH. HIS GRANDMOTHER HAS REFUSED TO ACKNOWLEDGE HIM.
THOUGH I HAVEN'T LEARNED ANYTHING BEYOND WHAT I UNCOVERED BACK WHEN I FELT UNFAVORABLY TOWARD HIM...
...IT SEEMS MOST OF THE HOST CLUB'S REGULAR CUSTOMERS KNEW ABOUT THE CIRCUMSTANCES OF HIS BIRTH EARLY ON.
AFTER ALL, IT'S QUITE NATURAL FOR A FAN TO SEEK INFORMATION ABOUT THE ONE SHE ADORES.
IT CREATED A BIT OF A STIR WHEN HIS SITUATION BECAME WIDELY KNOWN.
BUT BECAUSE TAMAKI IS THE KIND OF PERSON HE IS...
THIS KIND OF PERSON
...NO ONE MINDED IN THE LEAST.
YOU ALL FEEL THE SAME, DON'T YOU?

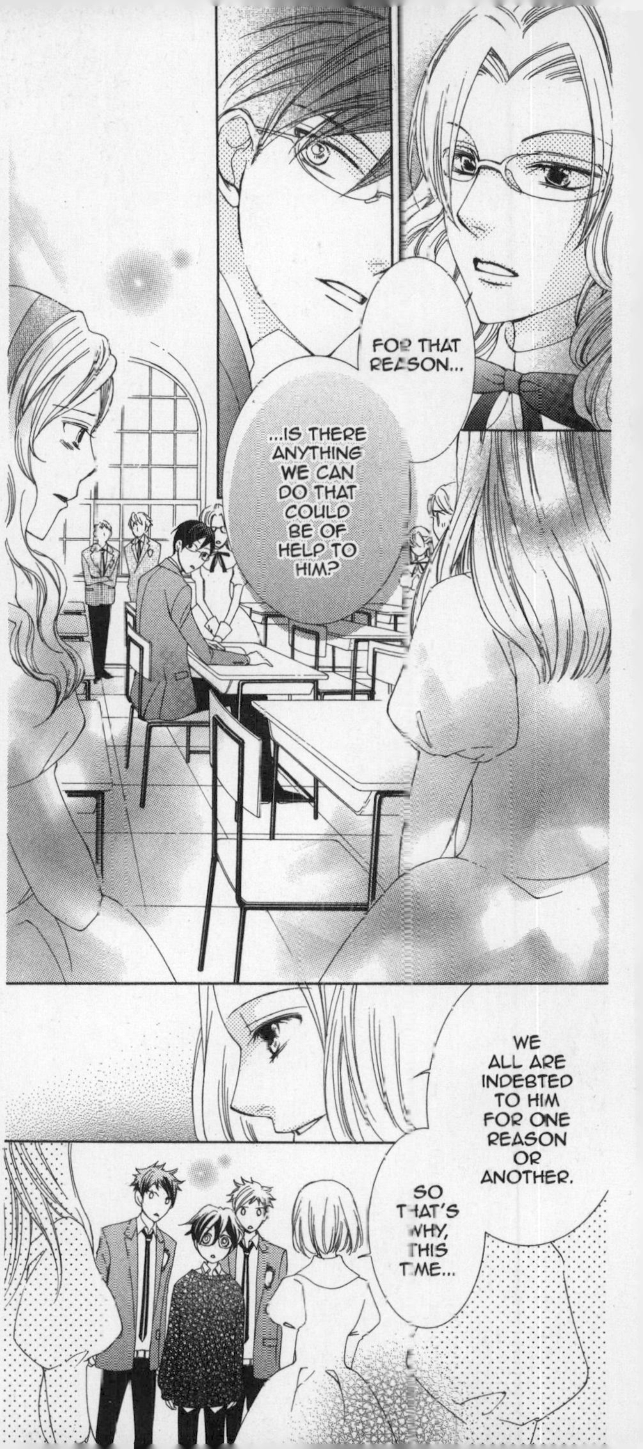
FOR THAT REASON...
...IS THERE ANYTHING WE CAN DO THAT COULD BE OF HELP TO HIM?
WE ALL ARE INDEBTED TO HIM FOR ONE REASON OR ANOTHER.
SO THAT'S WHY, THIS TIME...

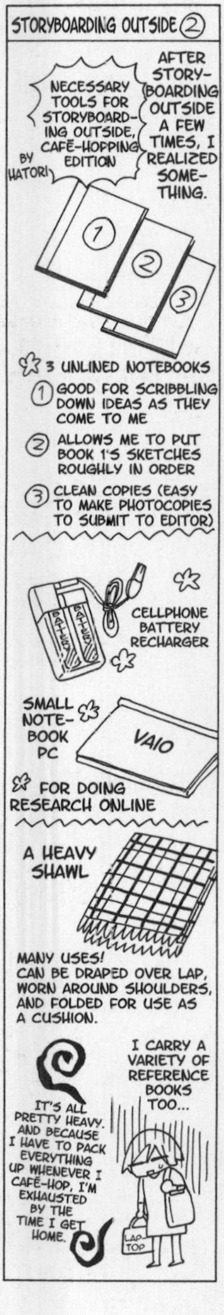
STORYBOARDING OUTSIDE ②
AFTER STORY-BOARDING OUTSIDE A FEW TIMES, I REALIZED SOME-THING.
NECESSARY TOOLS FOR STORYBOARD-ING OUTSIDE, CAFÉ-HOPPING EDITION
BY HATORI
3 UNLINED NOTEBOOKS
① GOOD FOR SCRIBBLING DOWN IDEAS AS THEY COME TO ME
② ALLOWS ME TO PUT BOOK 1'S SKETCHES ROUGHLY IN ORDER
③ CLEAN COPIES (EASY TO MAKE PHOTOCOPIES TO SUBMIT TO EDITOR)
CELLPHONE BATTERY RECHARGER
SMALL NOTE-BOOK PC
VAIO
FOR DOING RESEARCH ONLINE
A HEAVY SHAWL
MANY USES! CAN BE DRAPED OVER LAP, WORN AROUND SHOULDERS, AND FOLDED FOR USE AS A CUSHION.
I CARRY A VARIETY OF REFERENCE BOOKS TOO...
IT'S ALL PRETTY HEAVY. AND BECAUSE I HAVE TO PACK EVERYTHING UP WHENEVER I CAFÉ-HOP, I'M EXHAUSTED BY THE TIME I GET HOME.
LAP-TOP

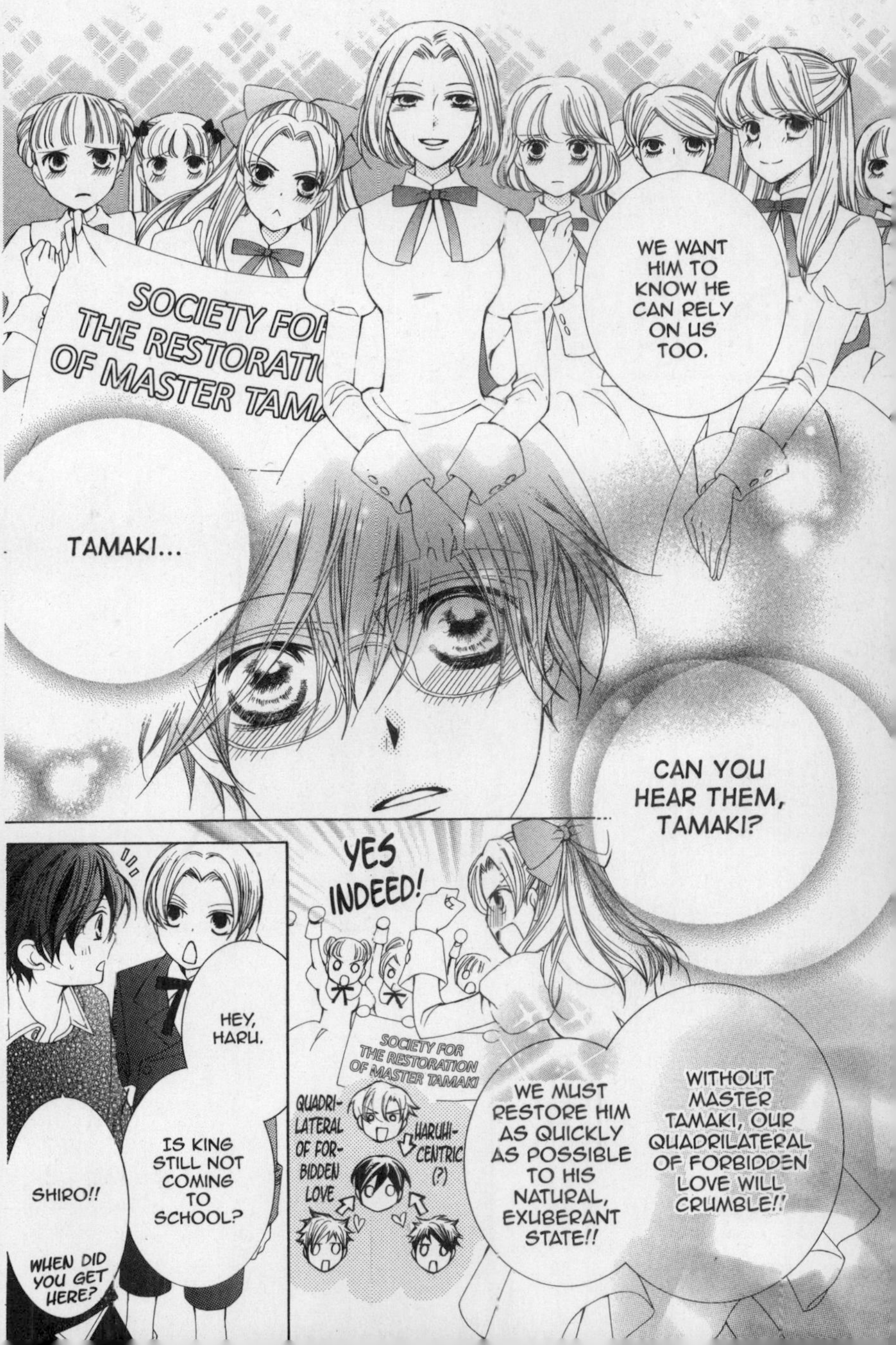
WE WANT HIM TO KNOW HE CAN RELY ON US TOO.
SOCIETY FO
THE RESTORATI
OF MASTER TAMA
TAMAKI...
CAN YOU HEAR THEM, TAMAKI?
YES INDEED!
WITHOUT MASTER TAMAKI, OUR QUADRILATERAL OF FORBIDDEN LOVE WILL CRUMBLE!!
WE MUST RESTORE HIM AS QUICKLY AS POSSIBLE TO HIS NATURAL, EXUBERANT STATE!!
SOCIETY FOR THE RESTORATION OF MASTER TAMAKI
QUADRILATERAL OF FORBIDDEN LOVE
HARUHI-CENTRIC (?)
HEY, HARU.
IS KING STILL NOT COMING TO SCHOOL?
SHIRO!!
WHEN DID YOU GET HERE?

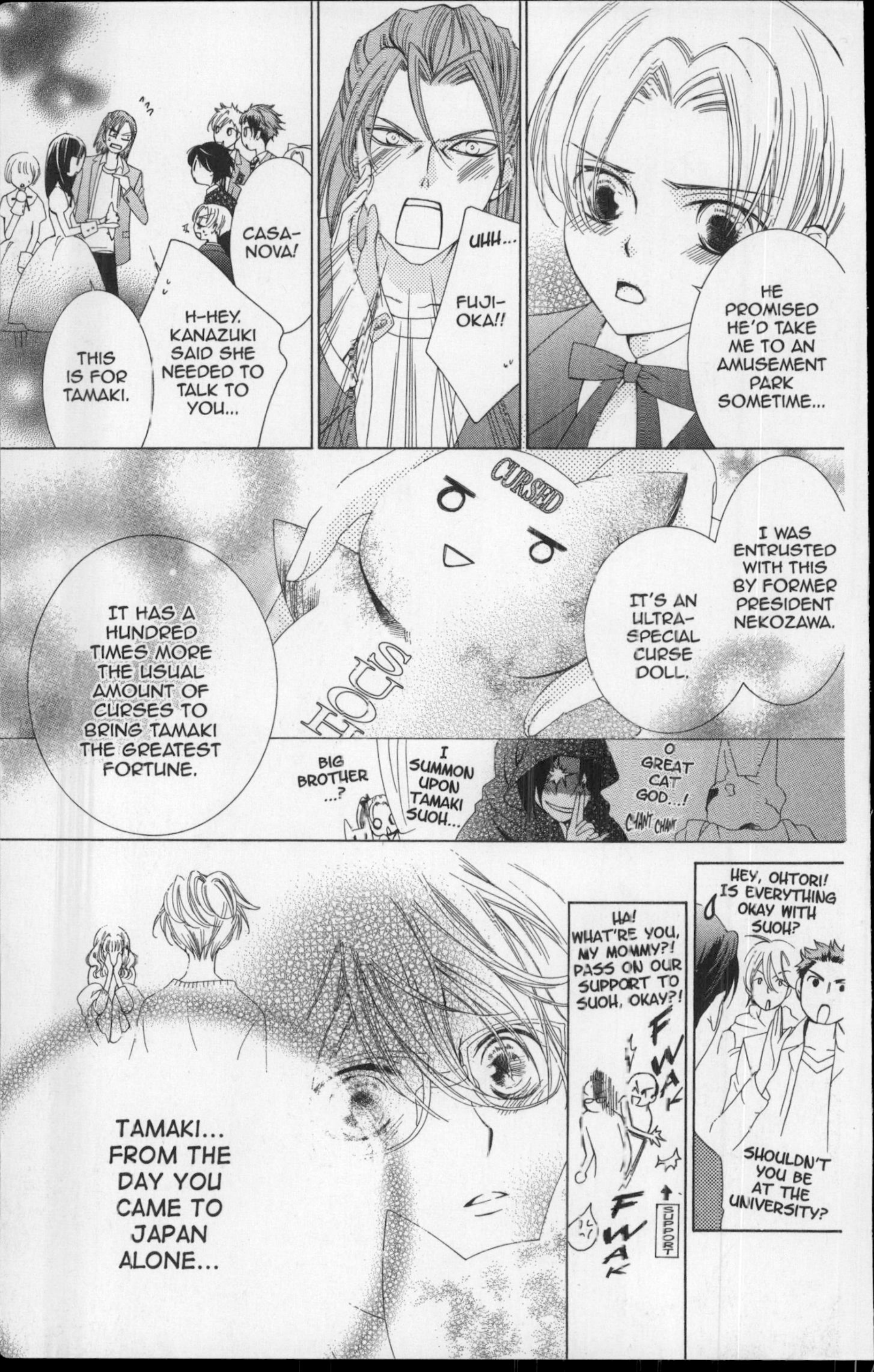
HE PROMISED HE'D TAKE ME TO AN AMUSEMENT PARK SOMETIME...
UHH...
FUJI-OKA!!
CASA-NOVA!
H-HEY. KANAZUKI SAID SHE NEEDED TO TALK TO YOU...
THIS IS FOR TAMAKI.
I WAS ENTRUSTED WITH THIS BY FORMER PRESIDENT NEKOZAWA.
IT'S AN ULTRA-SPECIAL CURSE DOLL.
CURSED
IT HAS A HUNDRED TIMES MORE THE USUAL AMOUNT OF CURSES TO BRING TAMAKI THE GREATEST FORTUNE.
O GREAT CAT GOD...!
CHANT CHANT
I SUMMON UPON TAMAKI SUOH...
BIG BROTHER ...?
HEY, OHTORI! IS EVERYTHING OKAY WITH SUOH?
SHOULDN'T YOU BE AT THE UNIVERSITY?
HA! WHAT'RE YOU, MY MOMMY?! PASS ON OUR SUPPORT TO SUOH, OKAY?!
FWAK
FWAK
SUPPORT
TAMAKI... FROM THE DAY YOU CAME TO JAPAN ALONE...

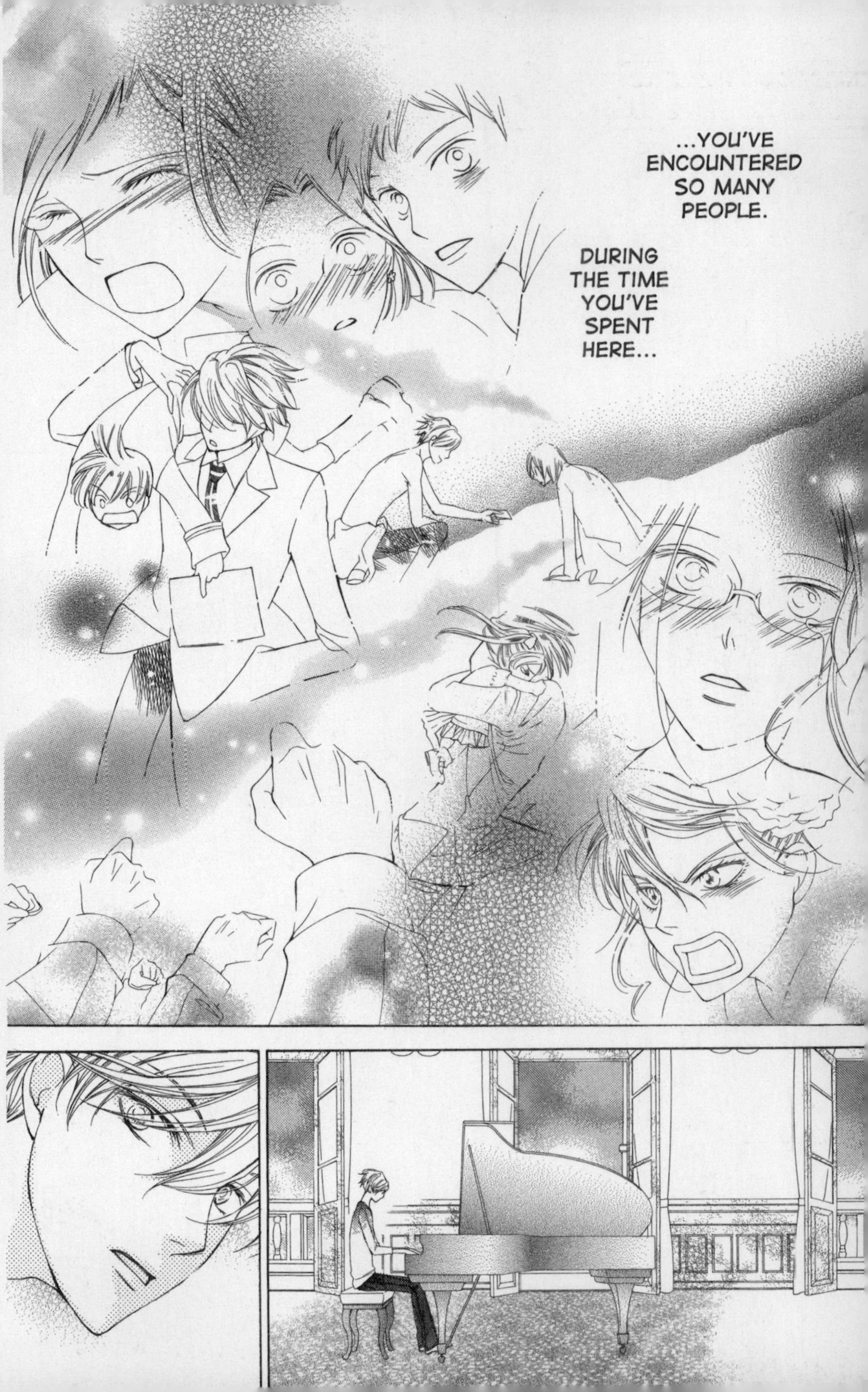
...YOU'VE ENCOUNTERED SO MANY PEOPLE.
DURING THE TIME YOU'VE SPENT HERE...

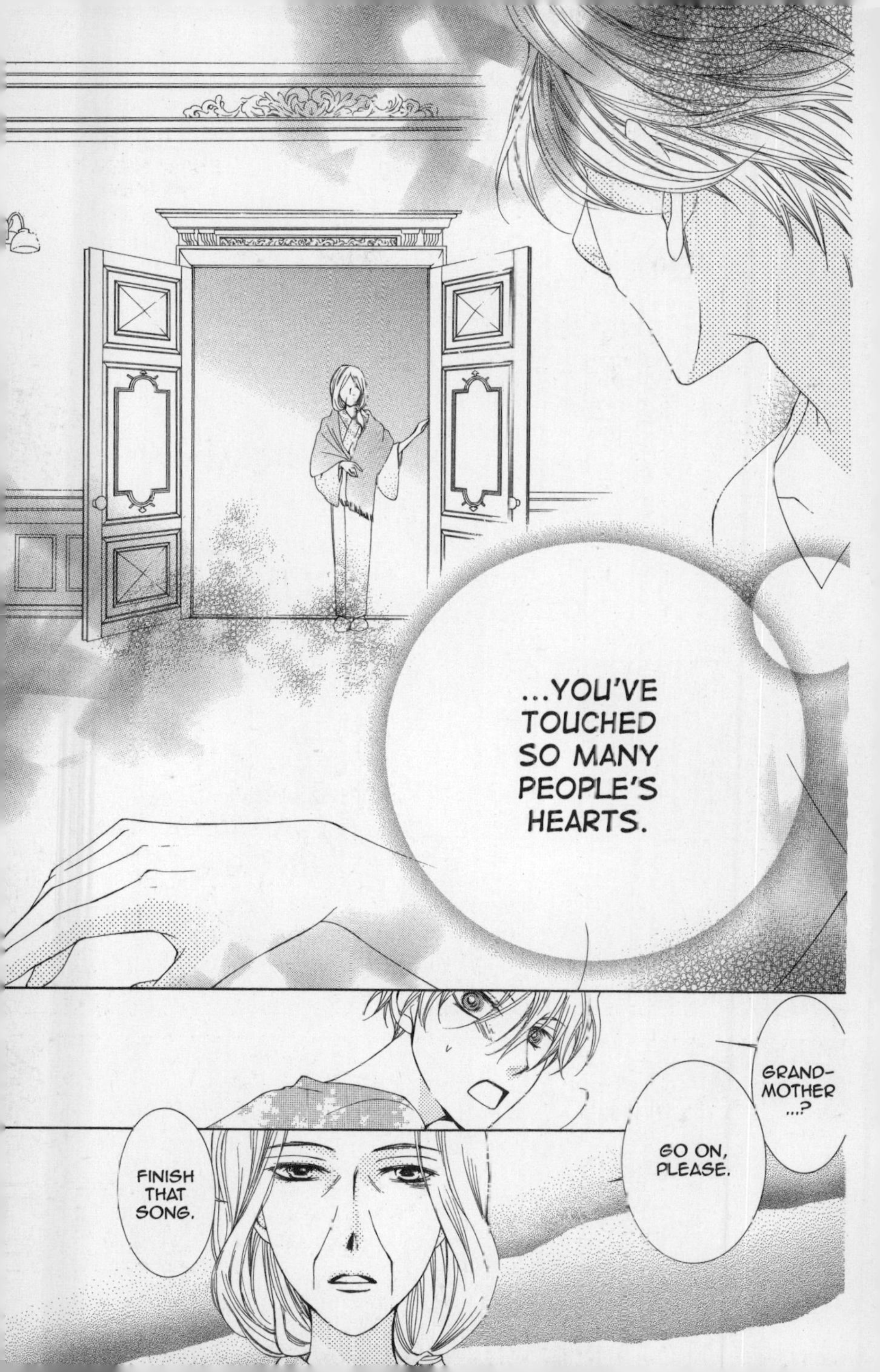
...YOU'VE TOUCHED SO MANY PEOPLE'S HEARTS.
GRAND-MOTHER ...?
GO ON, PLEASE.
FINISH THAT SONG.

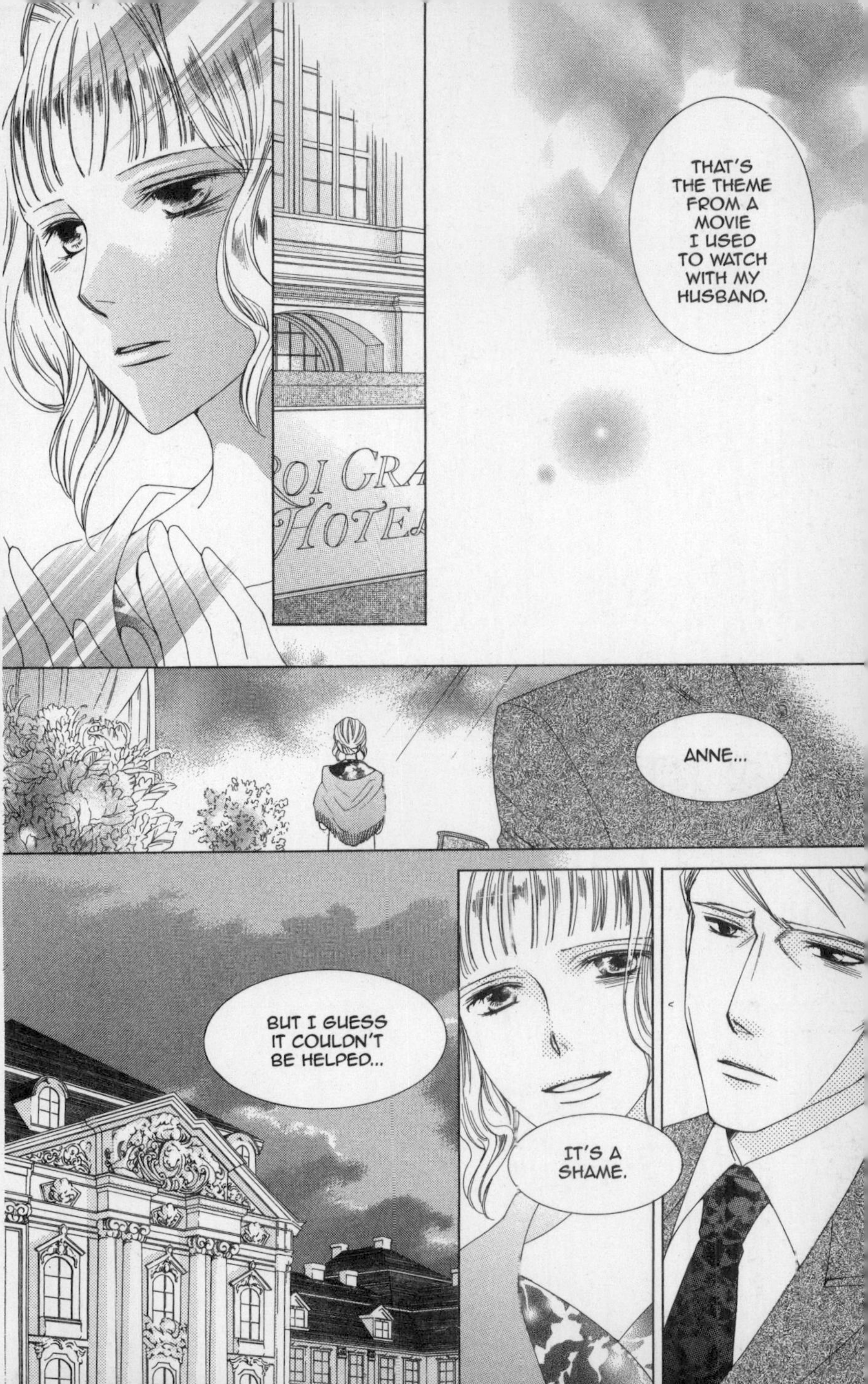
THAT'S THE THEME FROM A MOVIE I USED TO WATCH WITH MY HUSBAND.
ANNE...
IT'S A SHAME.
BUT I GUESS IT COULDN'T BE HELPED...

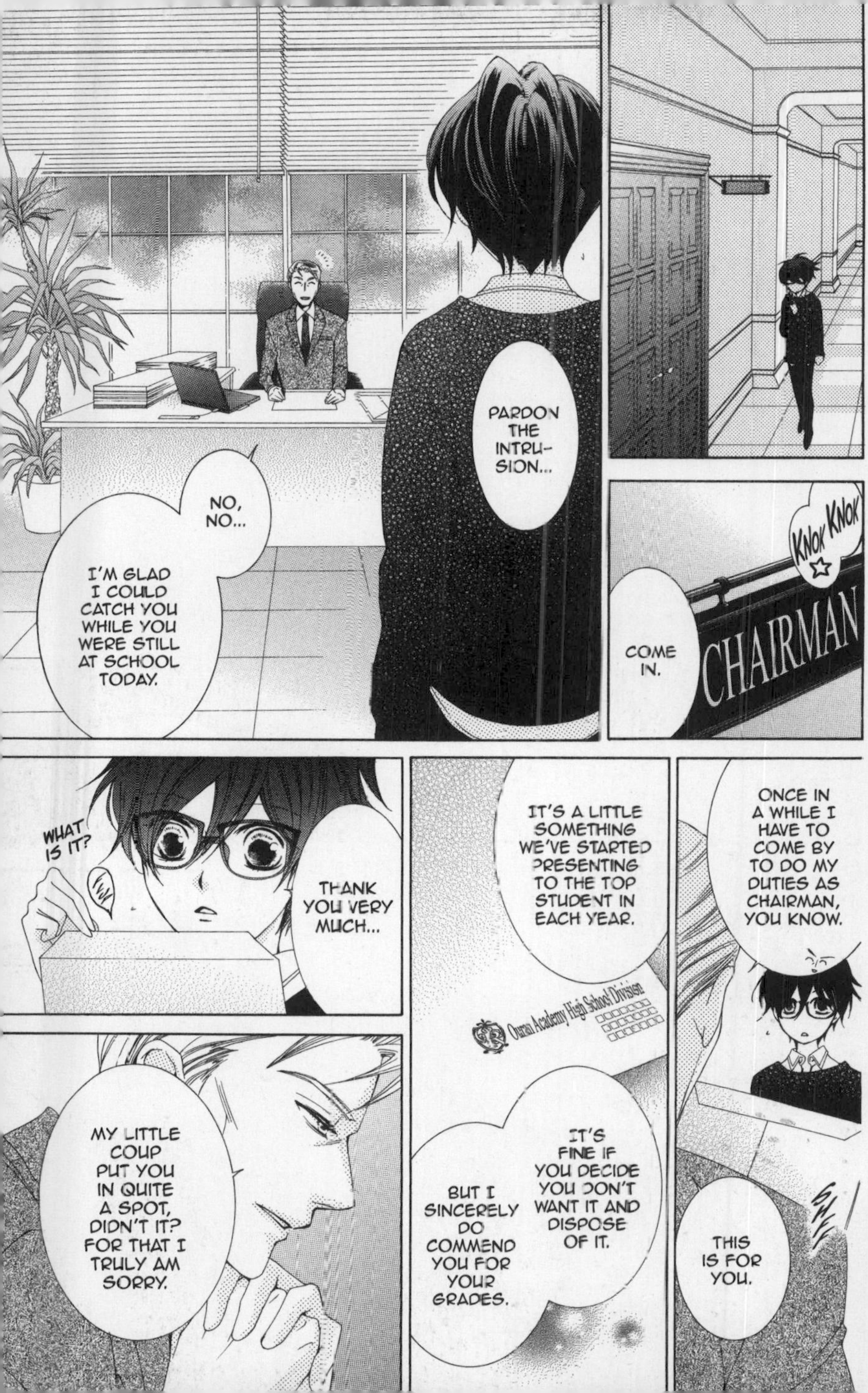
KNOK KNOK
CHAIRMAN
COME IN.
PARDON THE INTRUSION...
NO, NO...
I'M GLAD I COULD CATCH YOU WHILE YOU WERE STILL AT SCHOOL TODAY.
ONCE IN A WHILE I HAVE TO COME BY TO DO MY DUTIES AS CHAIRMAN, YOU KNOW.
THIS IS FOR YOU.
IT'S A LITTLE SOMETHING WE'VE STARTED PRESENTING TO THE TOP STUDENT IN EACH YEAR.
Ouran Academy High School Division
IT'S FINE IF YOU DECIDE YOU DON'T WANT IT AND DISPOSE OF IT.
BUT I SINCERELY DO COMMEND YOU FOR YOUR GRADES.
THANK YOU VERY MUCH...
WHAT IS IT?
MY LITTLE COUP PUT YOU IN QUITE A SPOT, DIDN'T IT? FOR THAT I TRULY AM SORRY.

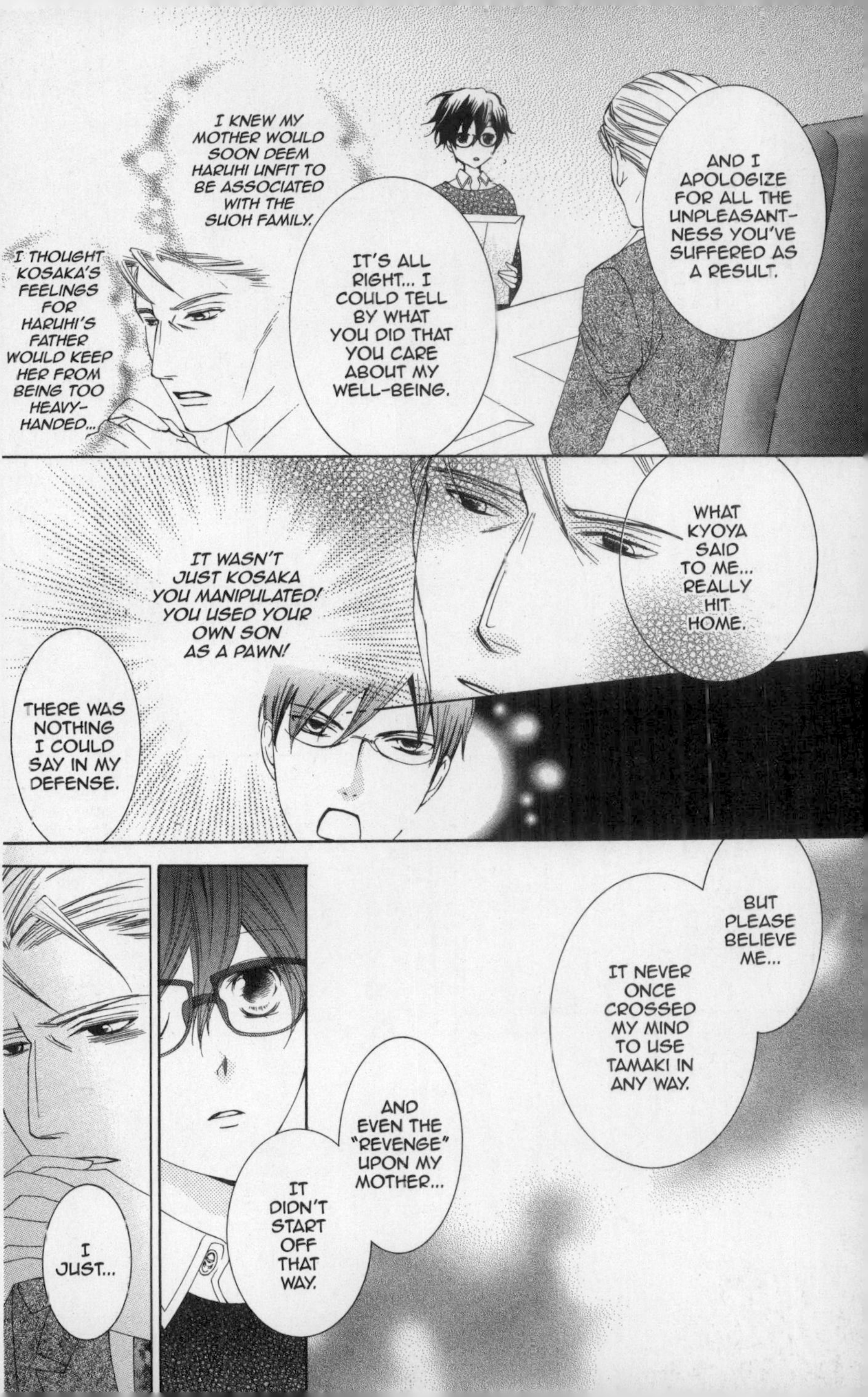
AND I APOLOGIZE FOR ALL THE UNPLEASANTNESS YOU'VE SUFFERED AS A RESULT.
IT'S ALL RIGHT... I COULD TELL BY WHAT YOU DID THAT YOU CARE ABOUT MY WELL-BEING.
I KNEW MY MOTHER WOULD SOON DEEM HARUHI UNFIT TO BE ASSOCIATED WITH THE SUOH FAMILY.
I THOUGHT KOSAKA'S FEELINGS FOR HARUHI'S FATHER WOULD KEEP HER FROM BEING TOO HEAVY-HANDED...
WHAT KYOYA SAID TO ME... REALLY HIT HOME.
IT WASN'T JUST KOSAKA YOU MANIPULATED! YOU USED YOUR OWN SON AS A PAWN!
THERE WAS NOTHING I COULD SAY IN MY DEFENSE.
BUT PLEASE BELIEVE ME...
IT NEVER ONCE CROSSED MY MIND TO USE TAMAKI IN ANY WAY.
AND EVEN THE "REVENGE" UPON MY MOTHER...
IT DIDN'T START OFF THAT WAY.
I JUST...

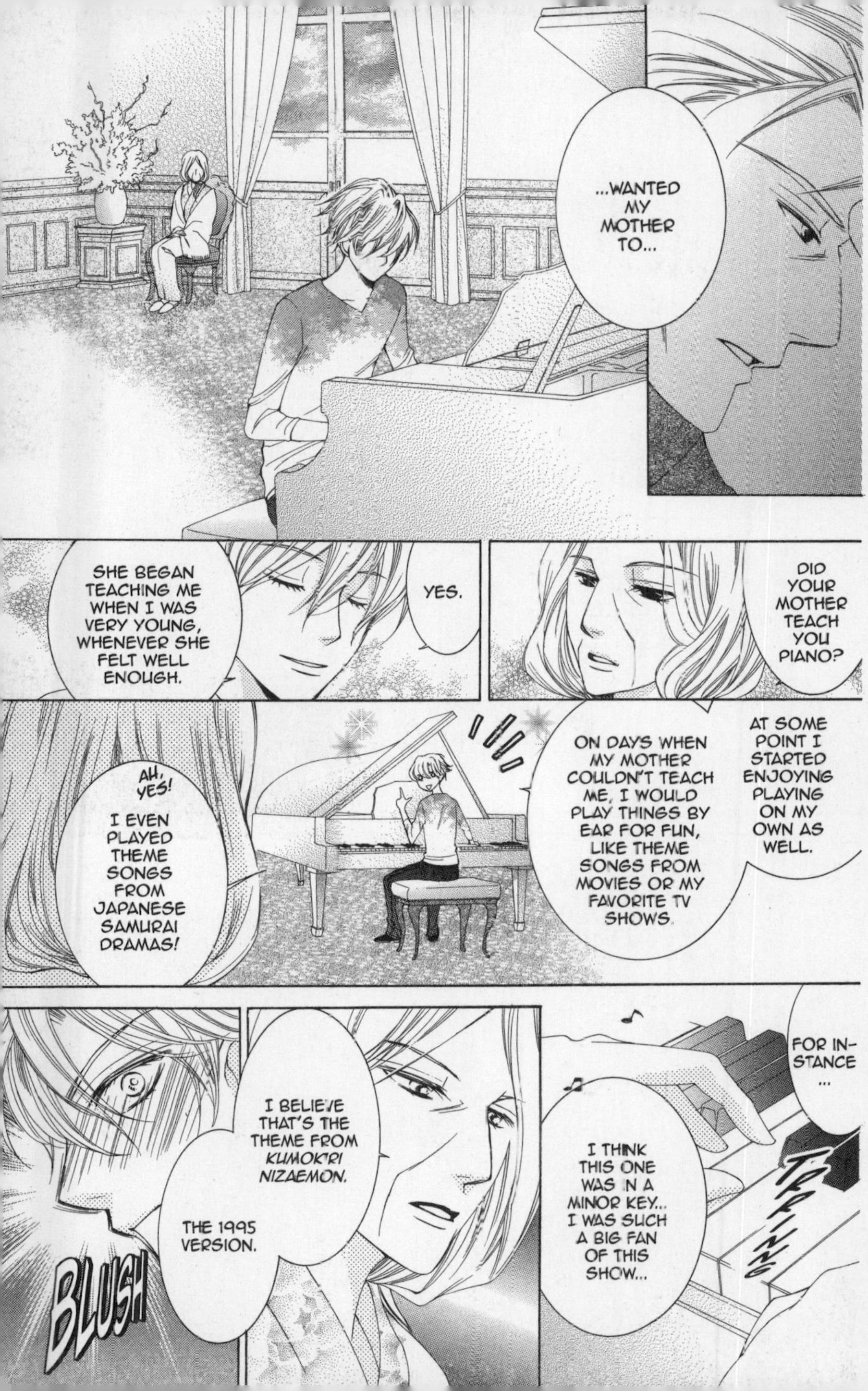
...WANTED MY MOTHER TO...
DID YOUR MOTHER TEACH YOU PIANO?
YES.
SHE BEGAN TEACHING ME WHEN I WAS VERY YOUNG, WHENEVER SHE FELT WELL ENOUGH.
AT SOME POINT I STARTED ENJOYING PLAYING ON MY OWN AS WELL.
ON DAYS WHEN MY MOTHER COULDN'T TEACH ME, I WOULD PLAY THINGS BY EAR FOR FUN, LIKE THEME SONGS FROM MOVIES OR MY FAVORITE TV SHOWS.
AH, YES!
I EVEN PLAYED THEME SONGS FROM JAPANESE SAMURAI DRAMAS!
FOR IN-STANCE ...
TRRIINNG
I THINK THIS ONE WAS IN A MINOR KEY... I WAS SUCH A BIG FAN OF THIS SHOW...
I BELIEVE THAT'S THE THEME FROM *KUMOKIRI NIZAEMON.*
THE 1995 VERSION.
BLUSH

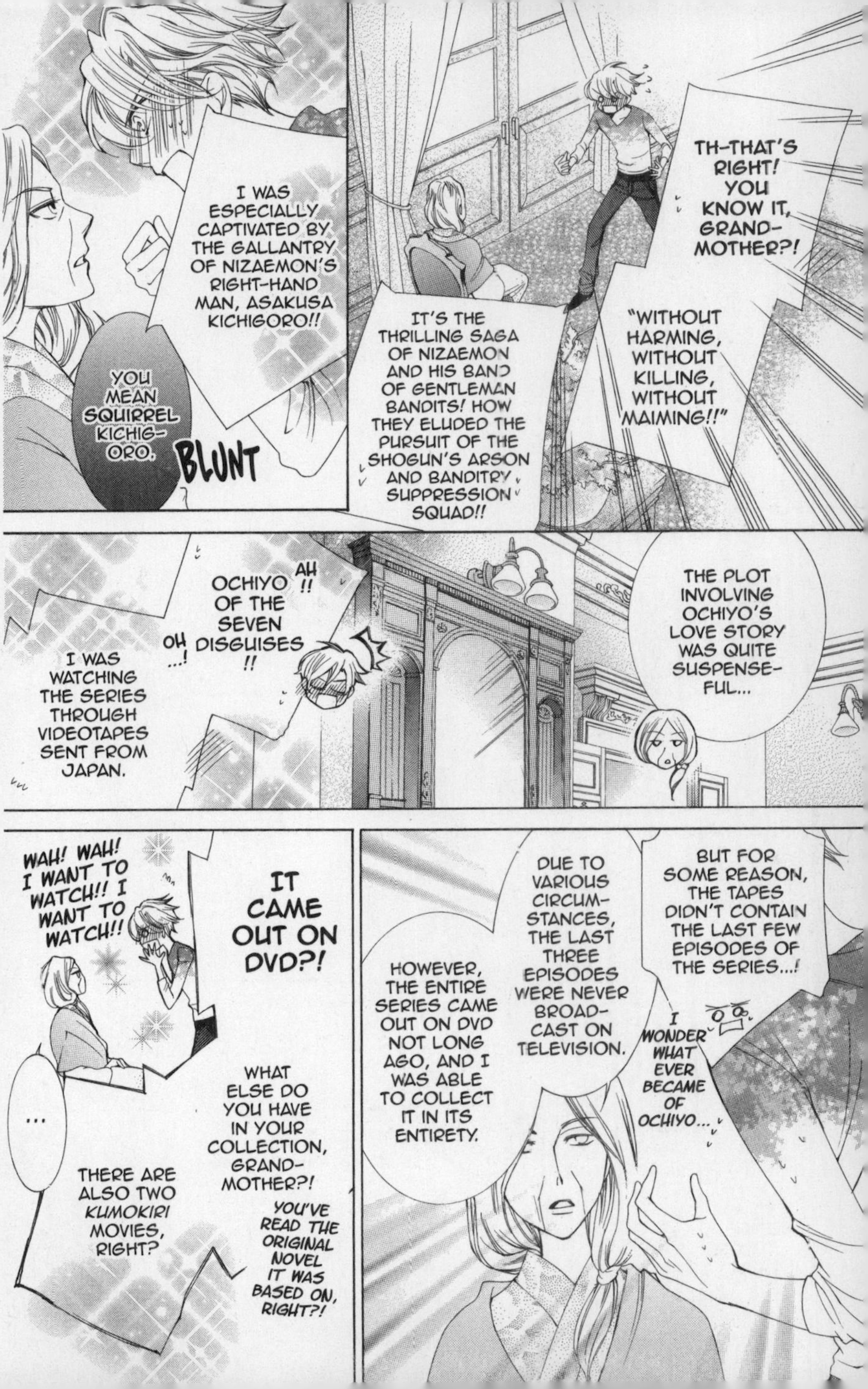

TH-THAT'S RIGHT! YOU KNOW IT, GRAND-MOTHER?!
"WITHOUT HARMING, WITHOUT KILLING, WITHOUT MAIMING!!"
IT'S THE THRILLING SAGA OF NIZAEMON AND HIS BAND OF GENTLEMAN BANDITS! HOW THEY ELUDED THE PURSUIT OF THE SHOGUN'S ARSON AND BANDITRY SUPPRESSION SQUAD!!
I WAS ESPECIALLY CAPTIVATED BY THE GALLANTRY OF NIZAEMON'S RIGHT-HAND MAN, ASAKUSA KICHIGORO!!
YOU MEAN SQUIRREL KICHIG-ORO.
BLUNT
THE PLOT INVOLVING OCHIYO'S LOVE STORY WAS QUITE SUSPENSE-FUL...
AH !!
OCHIYO OF THE SEVEN DISGUISES !!
OH ...!
I WAS WATCHING THE SERIES THROUGH VIDEOTAPES SENT FROM JAPAN.
BUT FOR SOME REASON, THE TAPES DIDN'T CONTAIN THE LAST FEW EPISODES OF THE SERIES...!
I WONDER WHAT EVER BECAME OF OCHIYO...
DUE TO VARIOUS CIRCUM-STANCES, THE LAST THREE EPISODES WERE NEVER BROAD-CAST ON TELEVISION.
HOWEVER, THE ENTIRE SERIES CAME OUT ON DVD NOT LONG AGO, AND I WAS ABLE TO COLLECT IT IN ITS ENTIRETY.
IT CAME OUT ON DVD?!
WAH! WAH! I WANT TO WATCH!! I WANT TO WATCH!!
WHAT ELSE DO YOU HAVE IN YOUR COLLECTION, GRAND-MOTHER?!
...
YOU'VE READ THE ORIGINAL NOVEL IT WAS BASED ON, RIGHT?!
THERE ARE ALSO TWO KUMOKIRI MOVIES, RIGHT?

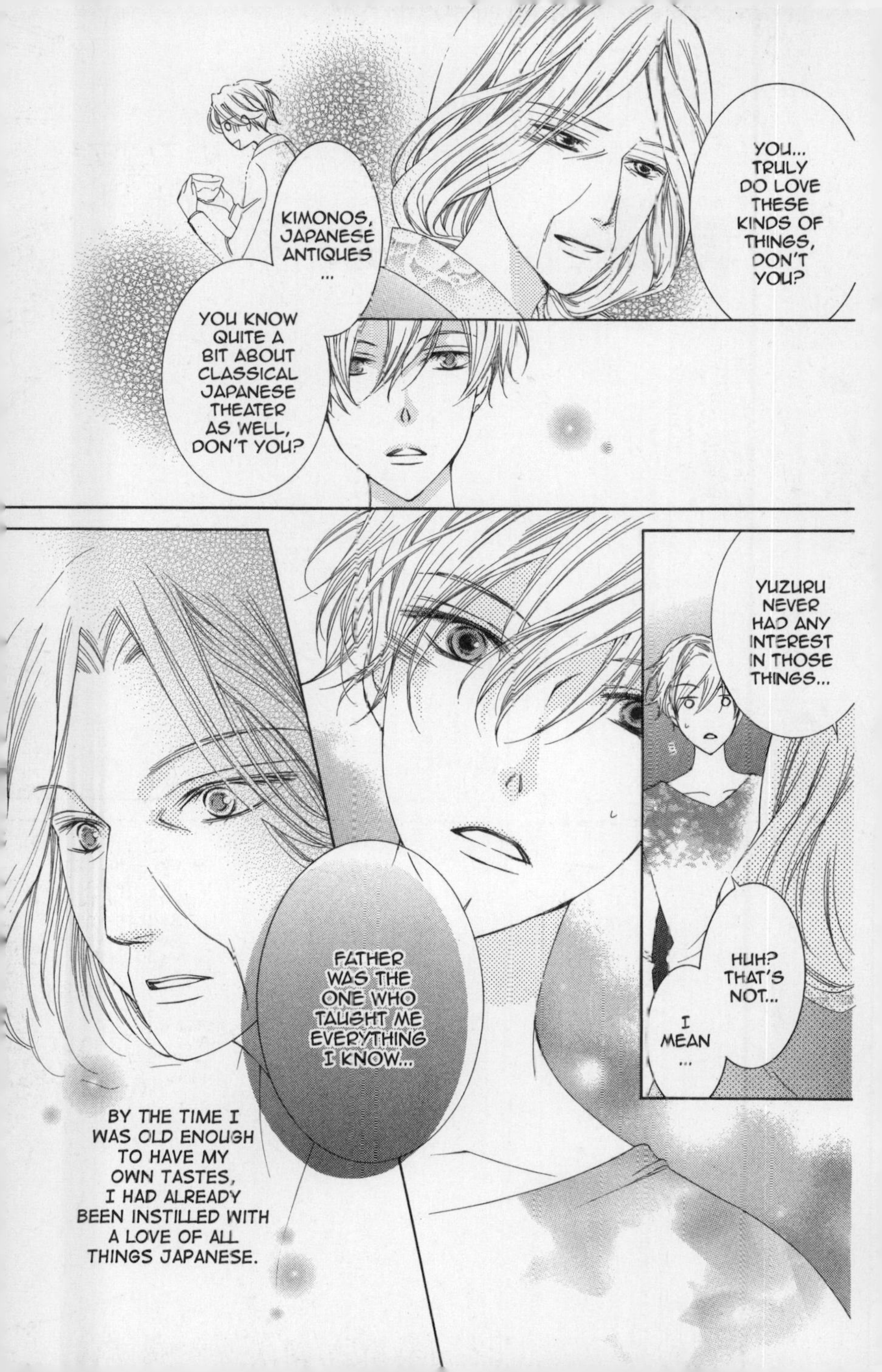
YOU... TRULY DO LOVE THESE KINDS OF THINGS, DON'T YOU?
KIMONOS, JAPANESE ANTIQUES ...
YOU KNOW QUITE A BIT ABOUT CLASSICAL JAPANESE THEATER AS WELL, DON'T YOU?
YUZURU NEVER HAD ANY INTEREST IN THOSE THINGS...
HUH? THAT'S NOT...
I MEAN ...
FATHER WAS THE ONE WHO TAUGHT ME EVERYTHING I KNOW...
BY THE TIME I WAS OLD ENOUGH TO HAVE MY OWN TASTES, I HAD ALREADY BEEN INSTILLED WITH A LOVE OF ALL THINGS JAPANESE.

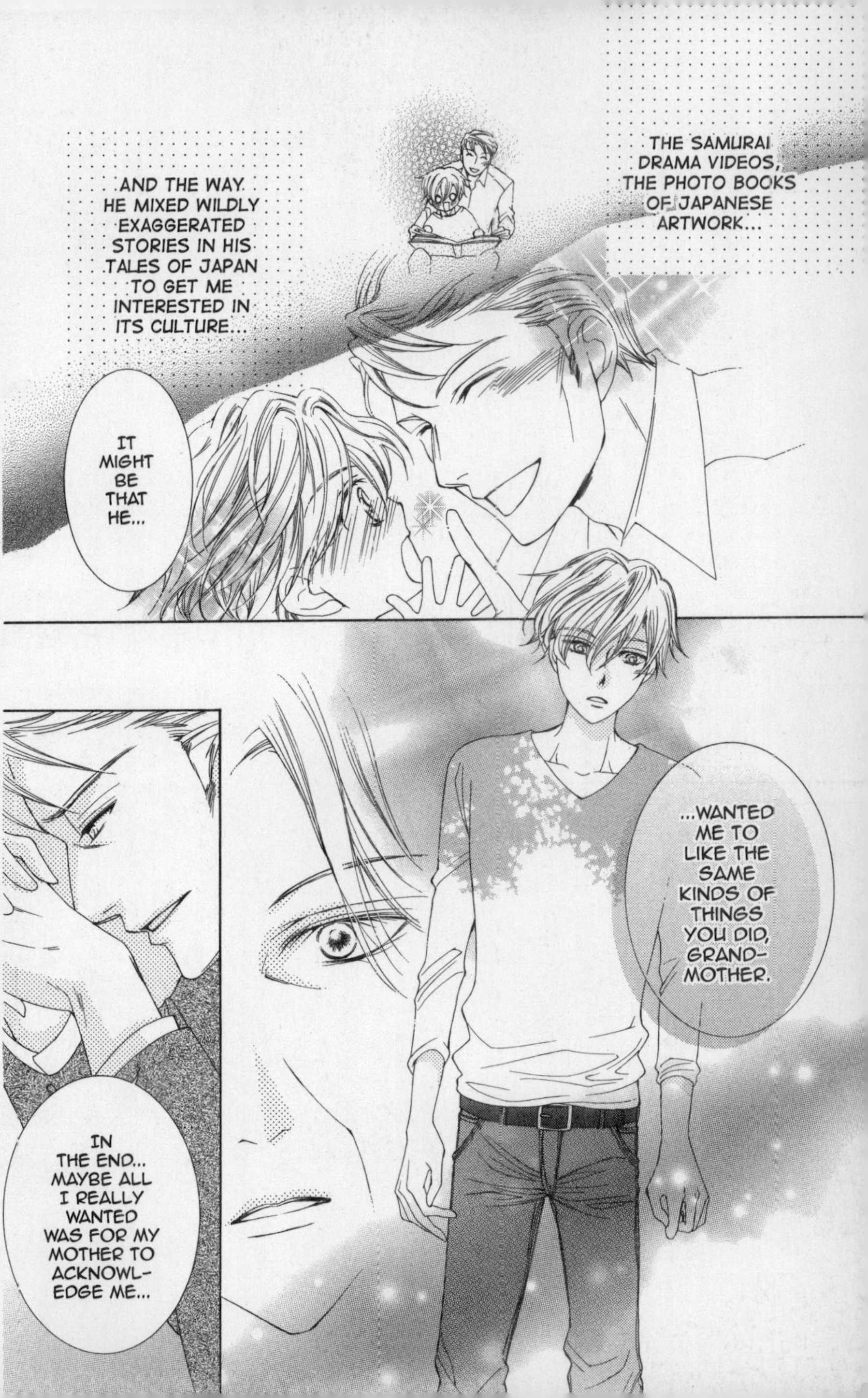
THE SAMURAI DRAMA VIDEOS, THE PHOTO BOOKS OF JAPANESE ARTWORK...
AND THE WAY HE MIXED WILDLY EXAGGERATED STORIES IN HIS TALES OF JAPAN TO GET ME INTERESTED IN ITS CULTURE...
IT MIGHT BE THAT HE...
...WANTED ME TO LIKE THE SAME KINDS OF THINGS YOU DID, GRAND-MOTHER.
IN THE END... MAYBE ALL I REALLY WANTED WAS FOR MY MOTHER TO ACKNOWL-EDGE ME...

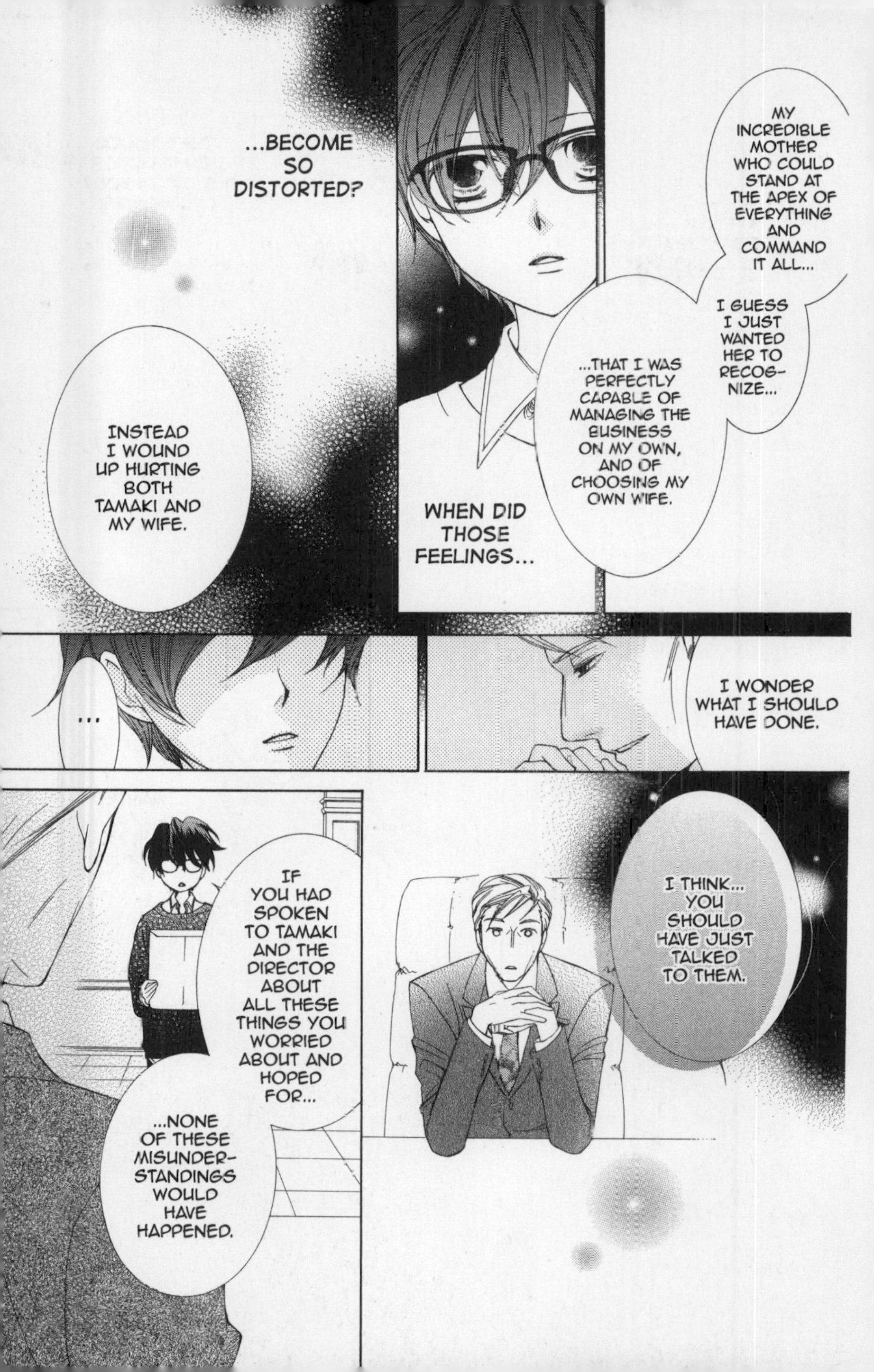
MY INCREDIBLE MOTHER WHO COULD STAND AT THE APEX OF EVERYTHING AND COMMAND IT ALL...
I GUESS I JUST WANTED HER TO RECOGNIZE...
...THAT I WAS PERFECTLY CAPABLE OF MANAGING THE BUSINESS ON MY OWN, AND OF CHOOSING MY OWN WIFE.
WHEN DID THOSE FEELINGS...
...BECOME SO DISTORTED?
INSTEAD I WOUND UP HURTING BOTH TAMAKI AND MY WIFE.
I WONDER WHAT I SHOULD HAVE DONE.
...
I THINK... YOU SHOULD HAVE JUST TALKED TO THEM.
IF YOU HAD SPOKEN TO TAMAKI AND THE DIRECTOR ABOUT ALL THESE THINGS YOU WORRIED ABOUT AND HOPED FOR...
...NONE OF THESE MISUNDER-STANDINGS WOULD HAVE HAPPENED.

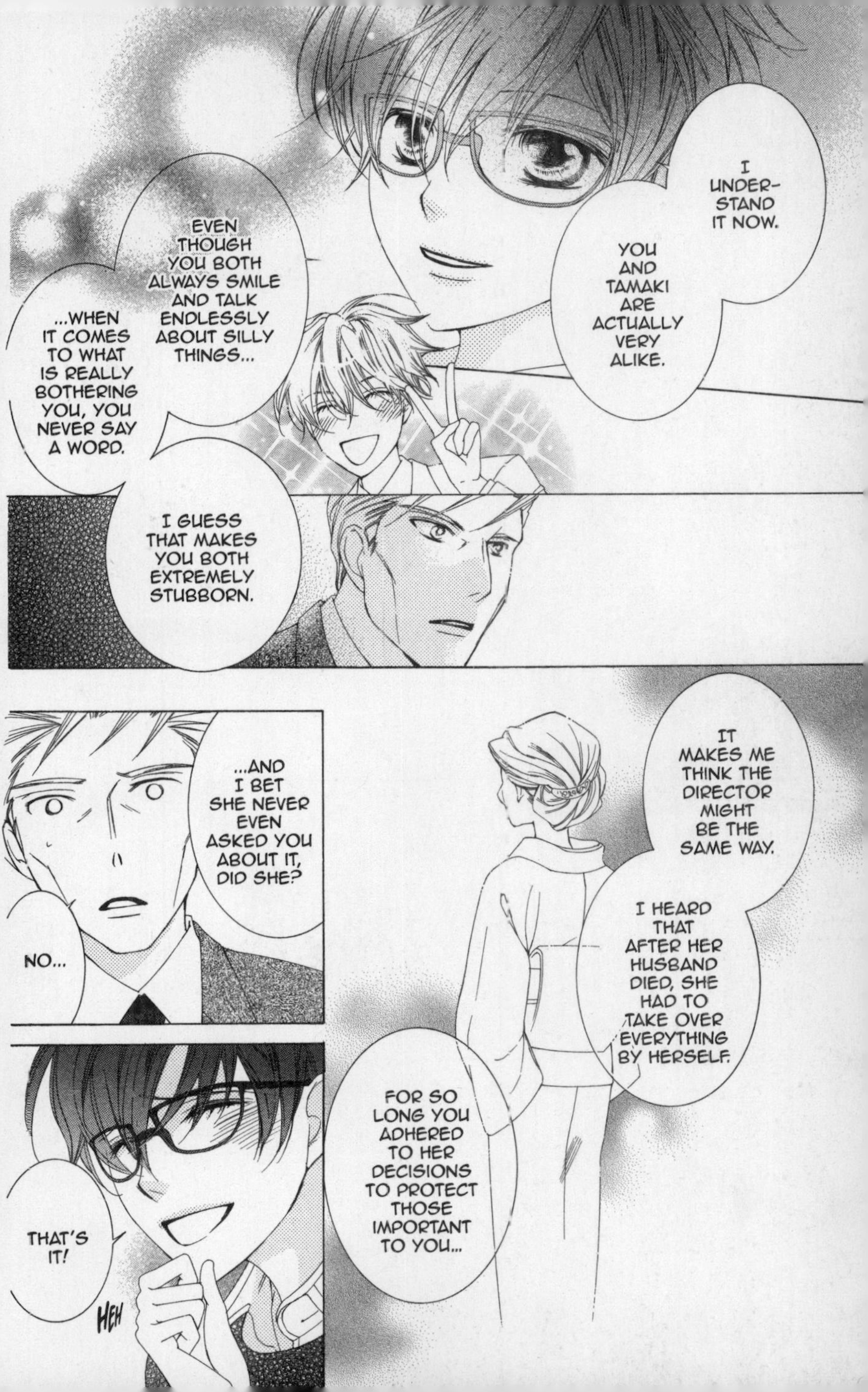
I UNDER-STAND IT NOW.
YOU AND TAMAKI ARE ACTUALLY VERY ALIKE.
EVEN THOUGH YOU BOTH ALWAYS SMILE AND TALK ENDLESSLY ABOUT SILLY THINGS...
...WHEN IT COMES TO WHAT IS REALLY BOTHERING YOU, YOU NEVER SAY A WORD.
I GUESS THAT MAKES YOU BOTH EXTREMELY STUBBORN.
IT MAKES ME THINK THE DIRECTOR MIGHT BE THE SAME WAY.
I HEARD THAT AFTER HER HUSBAND DIED, SHE HAD TO TAKE OVER EVERYTHING BY HERSELF.
FOR SO LONG YOU ADHERED TO HER DECISIONS TO PROTECT THOSE IMPORTANT TO YOU...
...AND I BET SHE NEVER EVEN ASKED YOU ABOUT IT, DID SHE?
NO...
THAT'S IT!
HEH

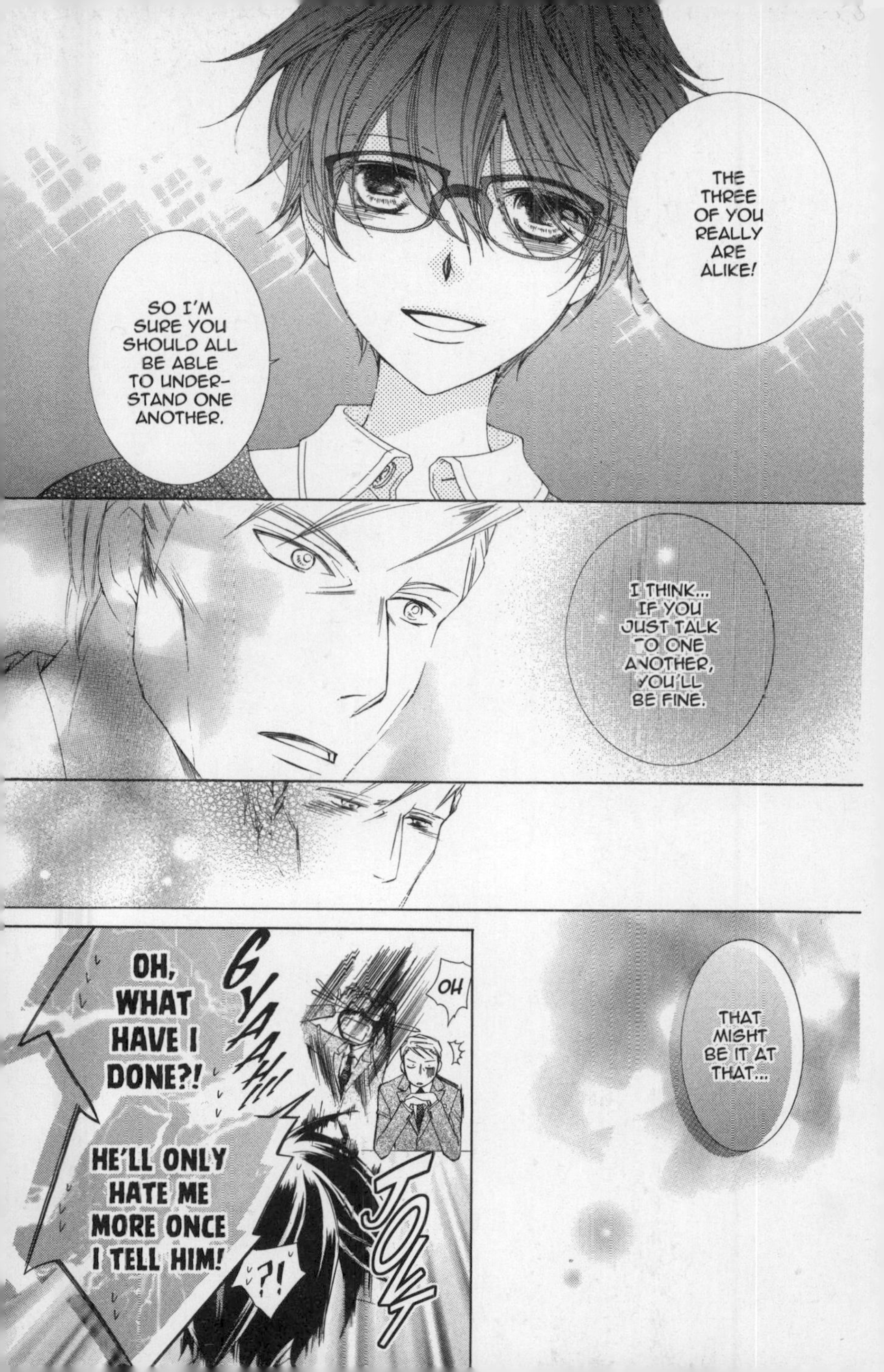
THE THREE OF YOU REALLY ARE ALIKE!
SO I'M SURE YOU SHOULD ALL BE ABLE TO UNDER-STAND ONE ANOTHER.
I THINK... IF YOU JUST TALK TO ONE ANOTHER, YOU'LL BE FINE.
THAT MIGHT BE IT AT THAT...
OH
GYAAH!!
OH, WHAT HAVE I DONE?!
HE'LL ONLY HATE ME MORE ONCE I TELL HIM!
?!
TJONK

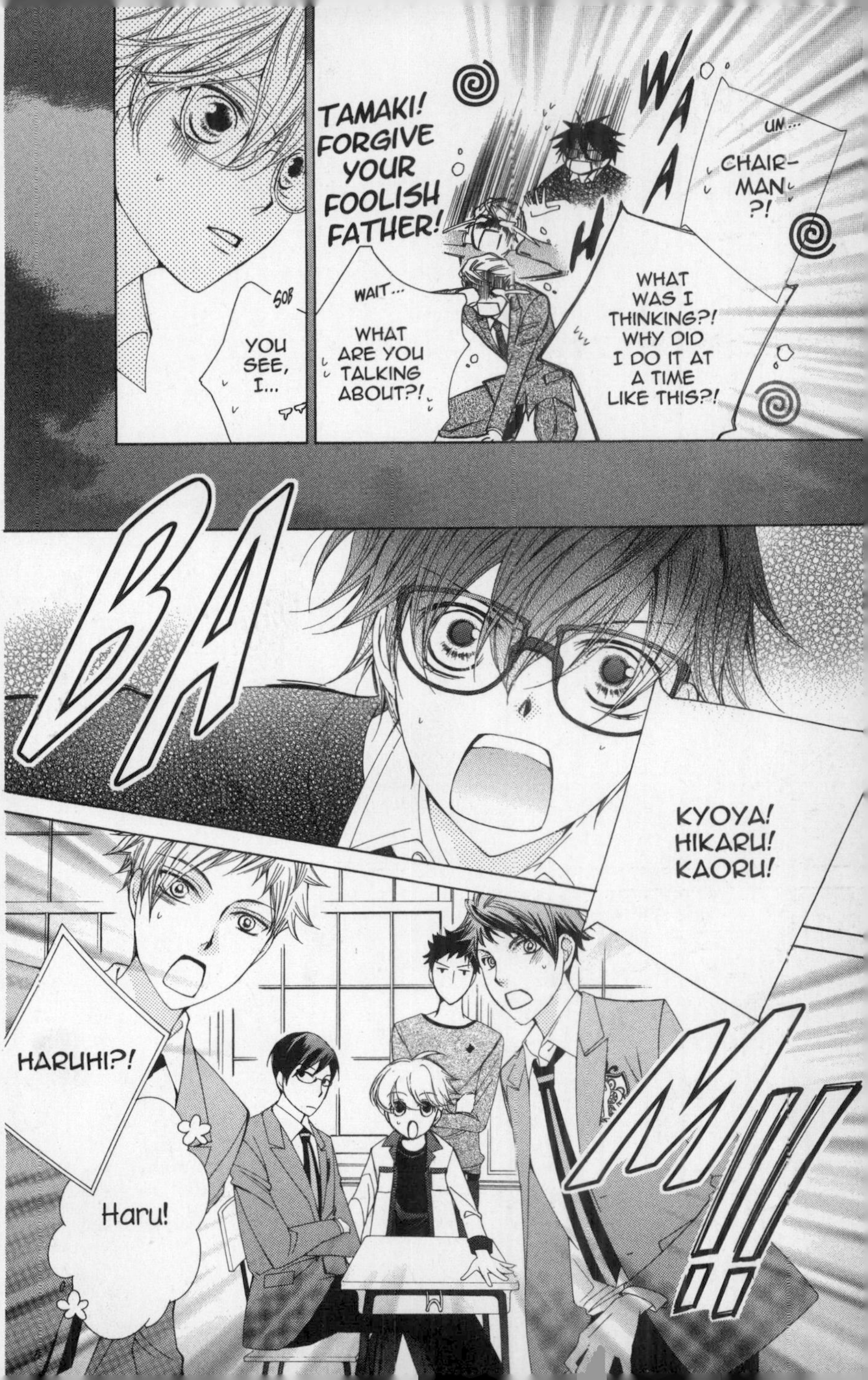
UM... CHAIR-MAN?!
WAAAH
TAMAKI! FORGIVE YOUR FOOLISH FATHER!
WHAT WAS I THINKING?! WHY DID I DO IT AT A TIME LIKE THIS?!
WAIT...
WHAT ARE YOU TALKING ABOUT?!
SOB
YOU SEE, I...
BAM!!
KYOYA! HIKARU! KAORU!
HARUHI?!
Haru!

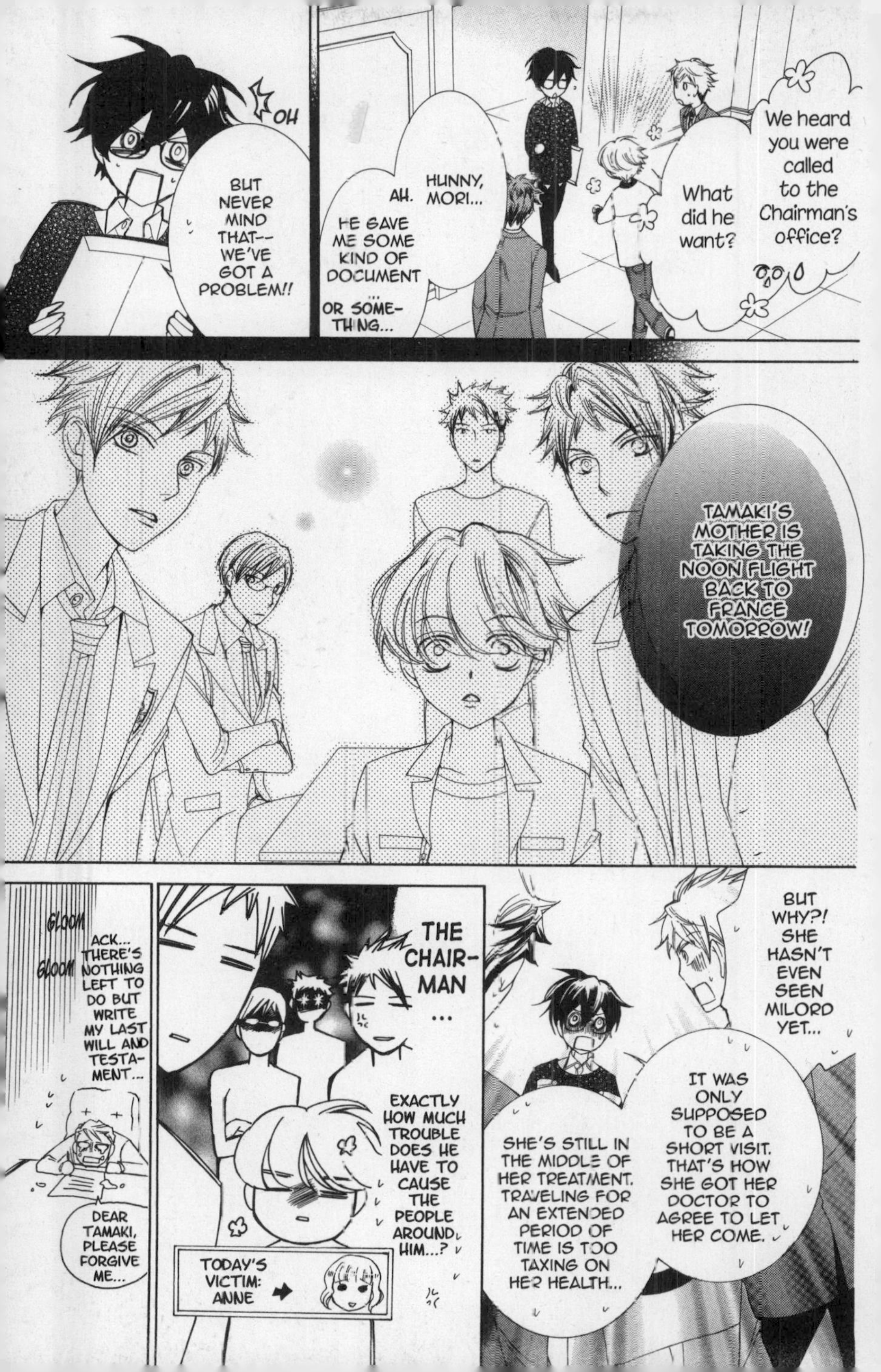
We heard you were called to the Chairman's office?
What did he want?
HUNNY, MORI...
AH.
HE GAVE ME SOME KIND OF DOCUMENT ... OR SOMETHING...
OH
BUT NEVER MIND THAT-- WE'VE GOT A PROBLEM!!
TAMAKI'S MOTHER IS TAKING THE NOON FLIGHT BACK TO FRANCE TOMORROW!
BUT WHY?! SHE HASN'T EVEN SEEN MILORD YET...
IT WAS ONLY SUPPOSED TO BE A SHORT VISIT. THAT'S HOW SHE GOT HER DOCTOR TO AGREE TO LET HER COME.
SHE'S STILL IN THE MIDDLE OF HER TREATMENT. TRAVELING FOR AN EXTENDED PERIOD OF TIME IS TOO TAXING ON HER HEALTH...
THE CHAIRMAN...
EXACTLY HOW MUCH TROUBLE DOES HE HAVE TO CAUSE THE PEOPLE AROUND HIM...?
TODAY'S VICTIM: ANNE
GLOOM
GLOOM
ACK... THERE'S NOTHING LEFT TO DO BUT WRITE MY LAST WILL AND TESTAMENT...
DEAR TAMAKI, PLEASE FORGIVE ME...

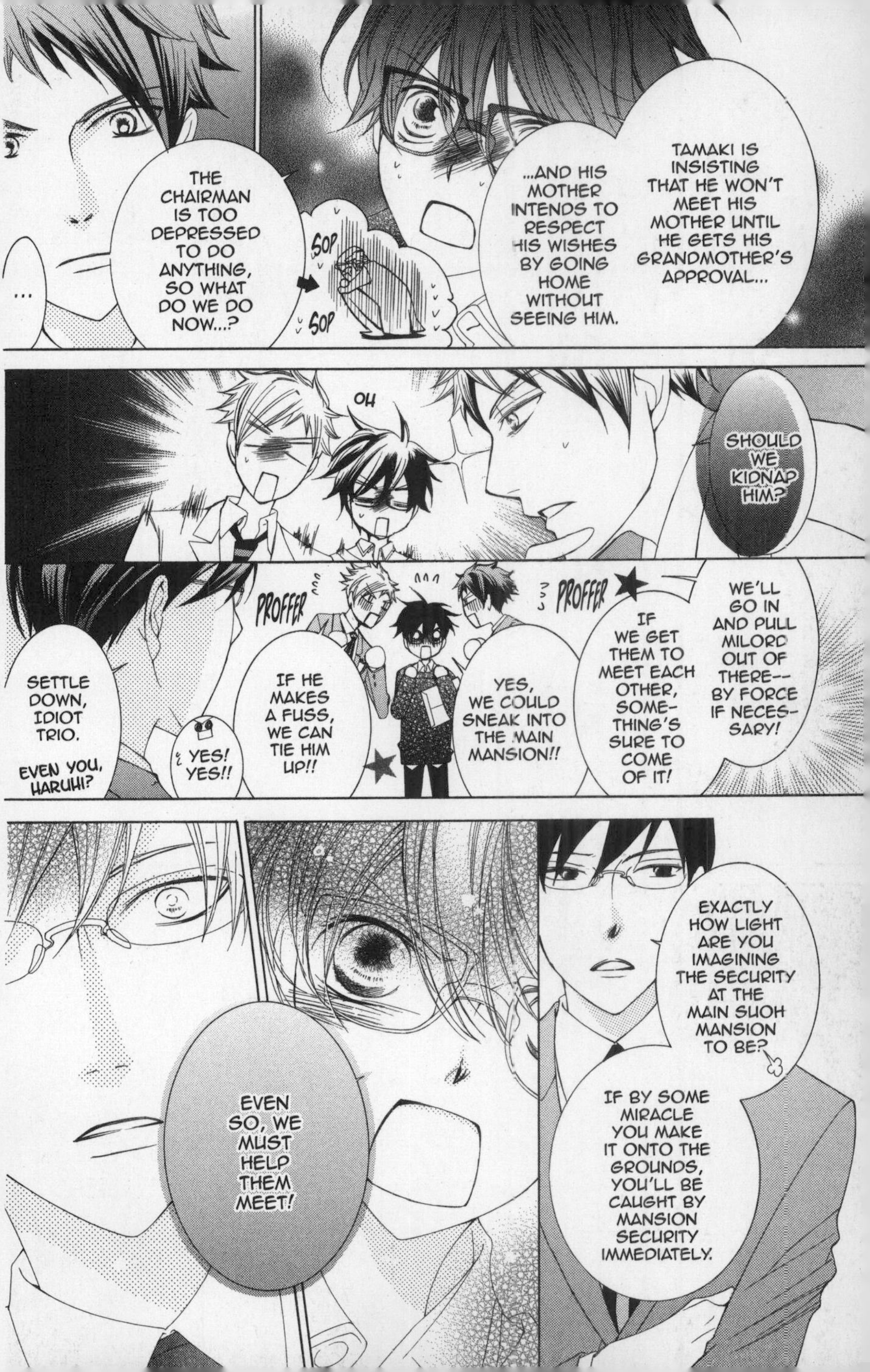
TAMAKI IS INSISTING THAT HE WON'T MEET HIS MOTHER UNTIL HE GETS HIS GRANDMOTHER'S APPROVAL...
...AND HIS MOTHER INTENDS TO RESPECT HIS WISHES BY GOING HOME WITHOUT SEEING HIM.
SOP
SOP
THE CHAIRMAN IS TOO DEPRESSED TO DO ANYTHING, SO WHAT DO WE DO NOW...?
...
SHOULD WE KIDNAP HIM?
OH
WE'LL GO IN AND PULL MILORD OUT OF THERE--BY FORCE IF NECES-SARY!
IF WE GET THEM TO MEET EACH OTHER, SOME-THING'S SURE TO COME OF IT!
PROFFER
YES, WE COULD SNEAK INTO THE MAIN MANSION!!
PROFFER
IF HE MAKES A FUSS, WE CAN TIE HIM UP!!
YES! YES!!
SETTLE DOWN, IDIOT TRIO.
EVEN YOU, HARUHI?
EXACTLY HOW LIGHT ARE YOU IMAGINING THE SECURITY AT THE MAIN SUOH MANSION TO BE?
IF BY SOME MIRACLE YOU MAKE IT ONTO THE GROUNDS, YOU'LL BE CAUGHT BY MANSION SECURITY IMMEDIATELY.
EVEN SO, WE MUST HELP THEM MEET!

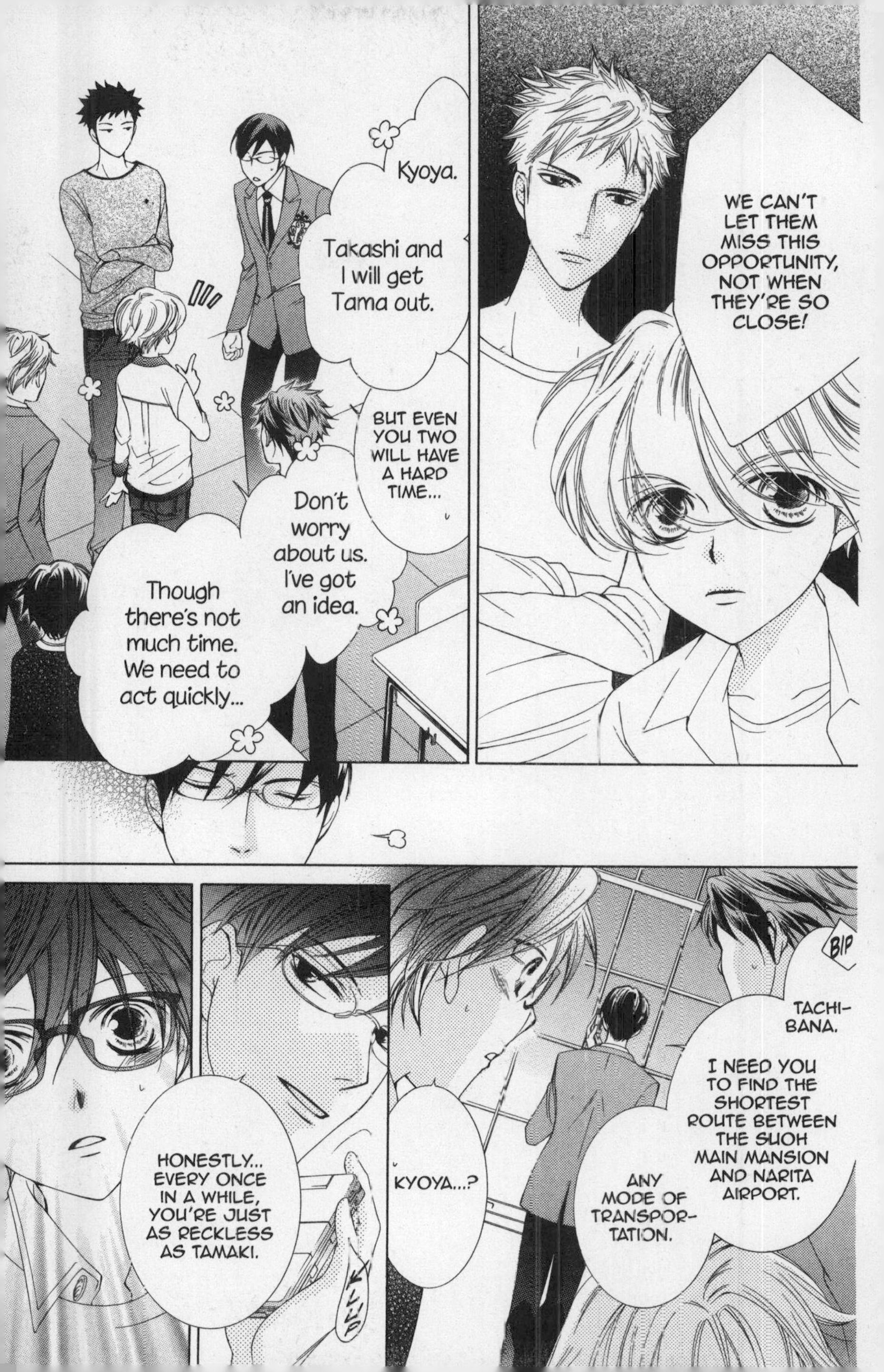
WE CAN'T LET THEM MISS THIS OPPORTUNITY, NOT WHEN THEY'RE SO CLOSE!
Kyoya.
Takashi and I will get Tama out.
BUT EVEN YOU TWO WILL HAVE A HARD TIME...
Don't worry about us. I've got an idea.
Though there's not much time. We need to act quickly...
BIP
TACHIBANA.
I NEED YOU TO FIND THE SHORTEST ROUTE BETWEEN THE SUOH MAIN MANSION AND NARITA AIRPORT.
ANY MODE OF TRANSPORTATION.
KYOYA...?
HONESTLY... EVERY ONCE IN A WHILE, YOU'RE JUST AS RECKLESS AS TAMAKI.

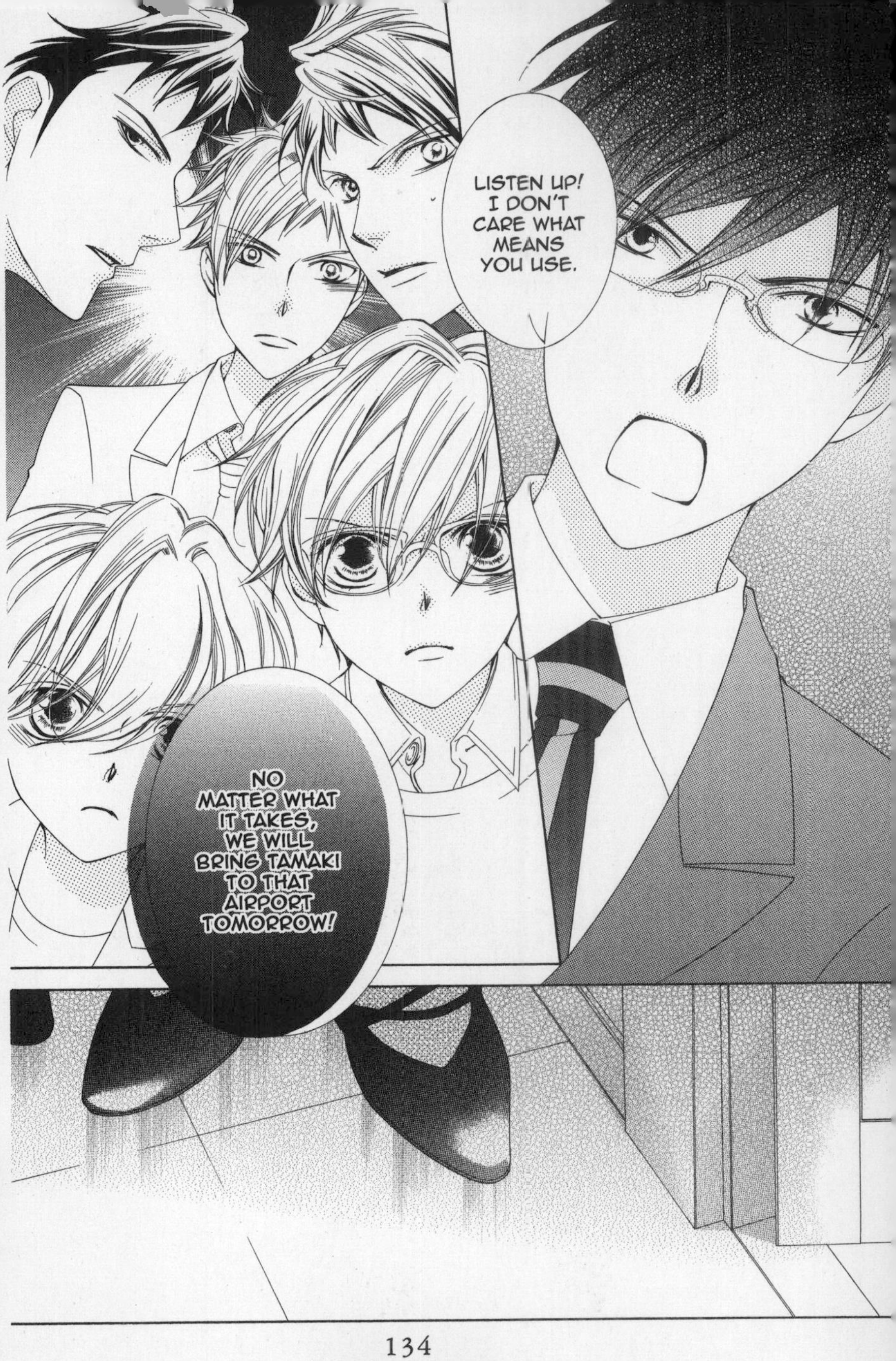
LISTEN UP! I DON'T CARE WHAT MEANS YOU USE.
NO MATTER WHAT IT TAKES, WE WILL BRING TAMAKI TO THAT AIRPORT TOMORROW!

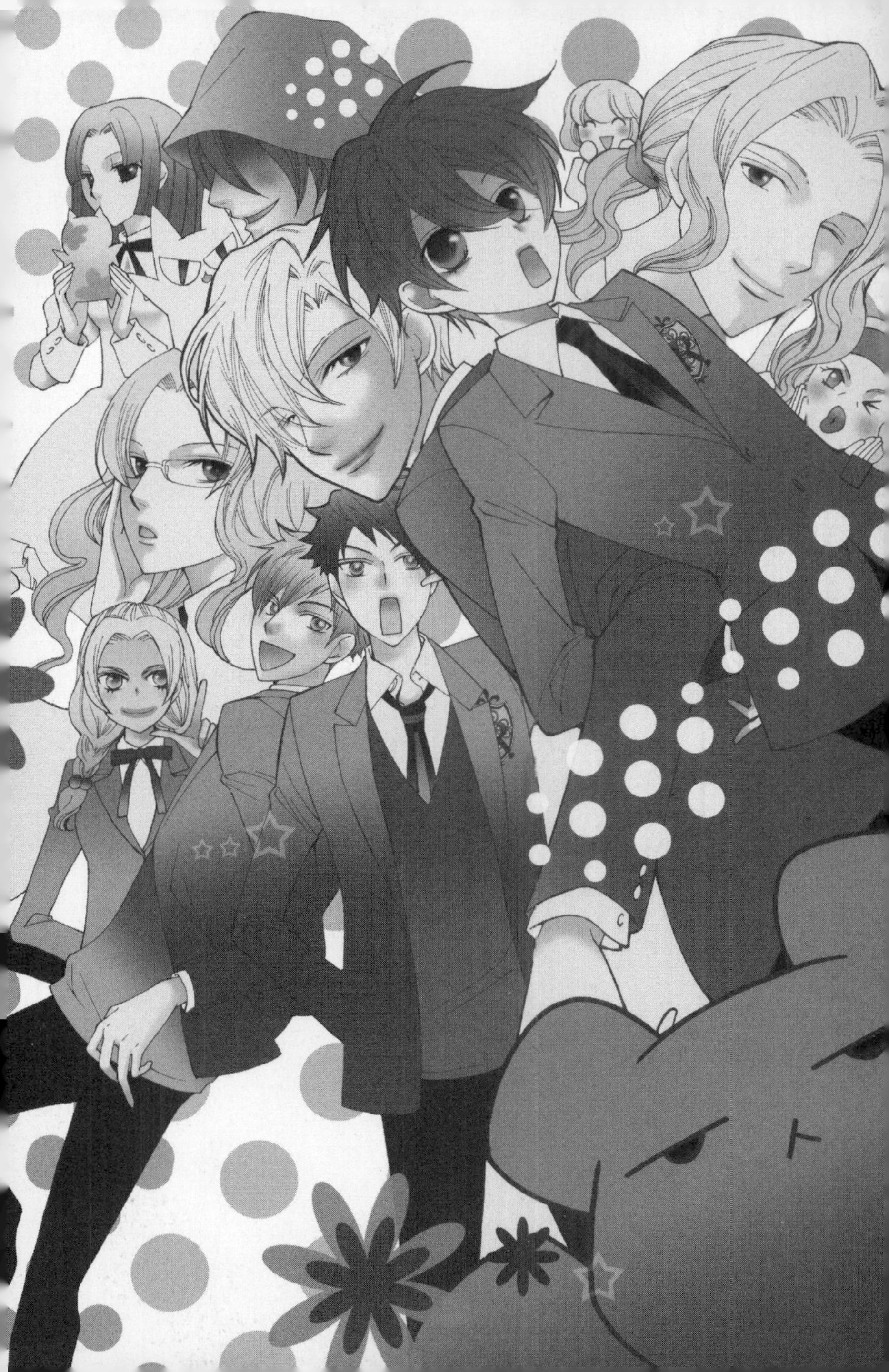

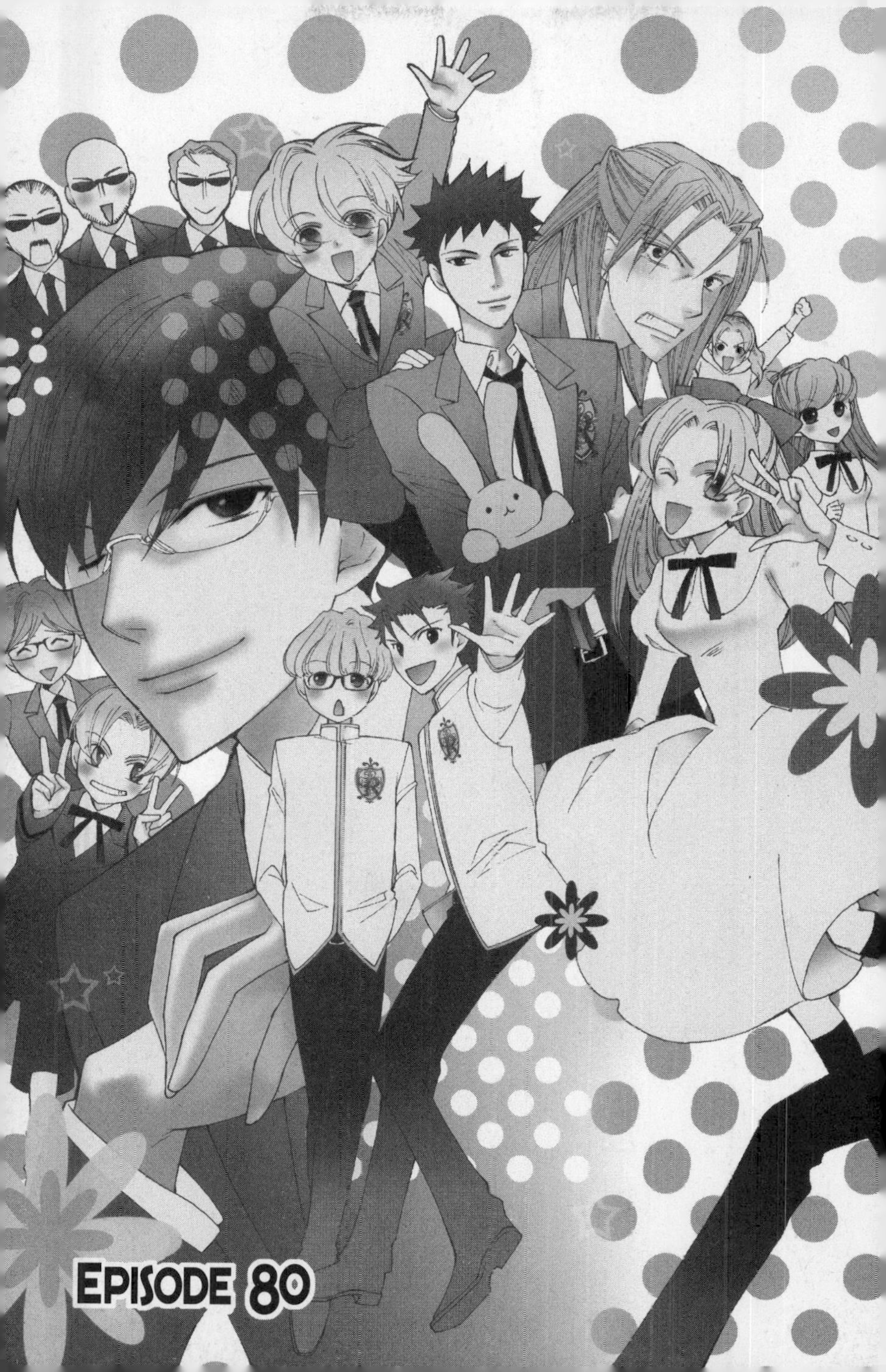
EPISODE 80

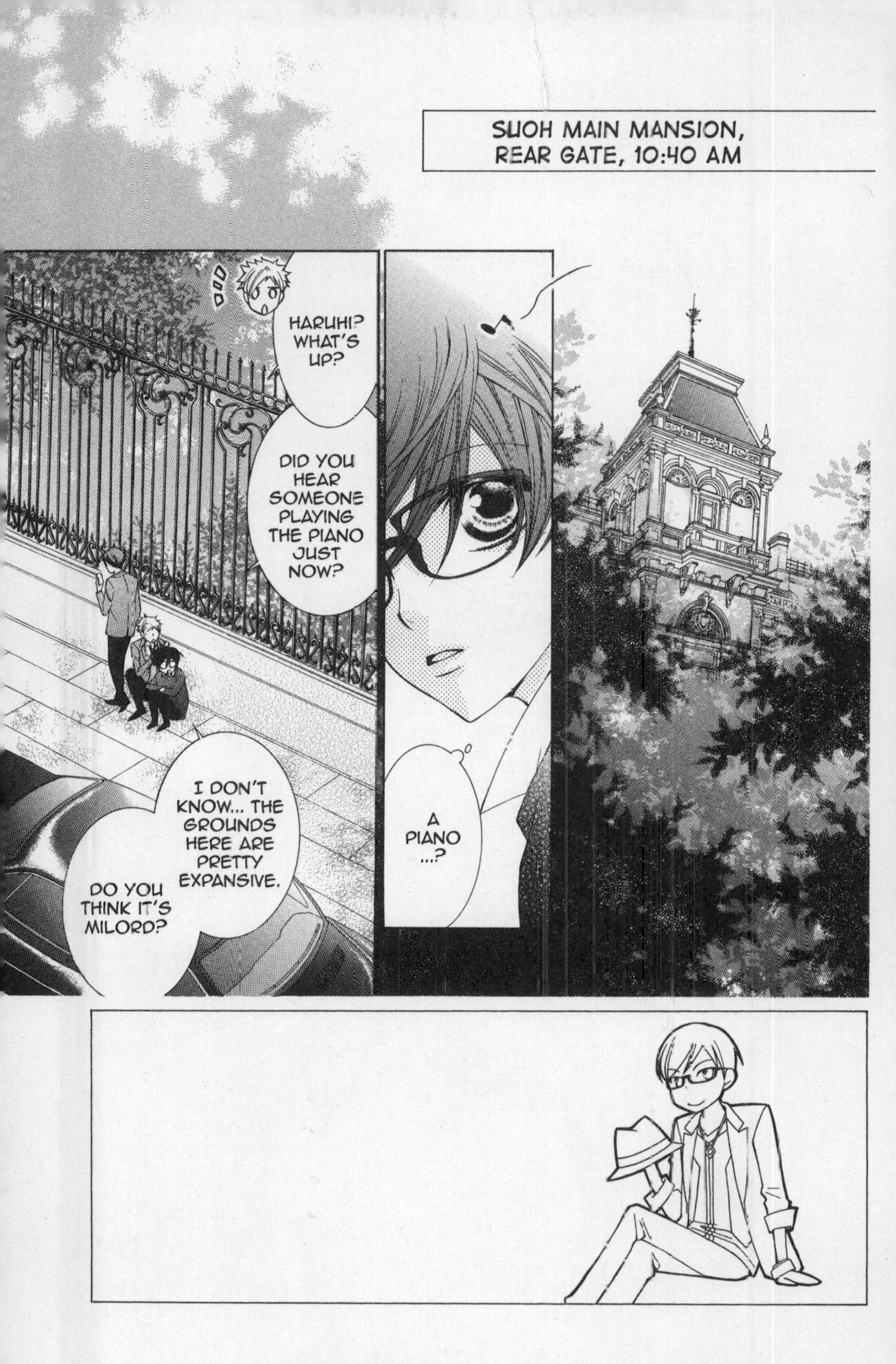
SUOH MAIN MANSION,
REAR GATE, 10:40 AM
A PIANO ...?
HARUHI? WHAT'S UP?
DID YOU HEAR SOMEONE PLAYING THE PIANO JUST NOW?
I DON'T KNOW... THE GROUNDS HERE ARE PRETTY EXPANSIVE.
DO YOU THINK IT'S MILORD?

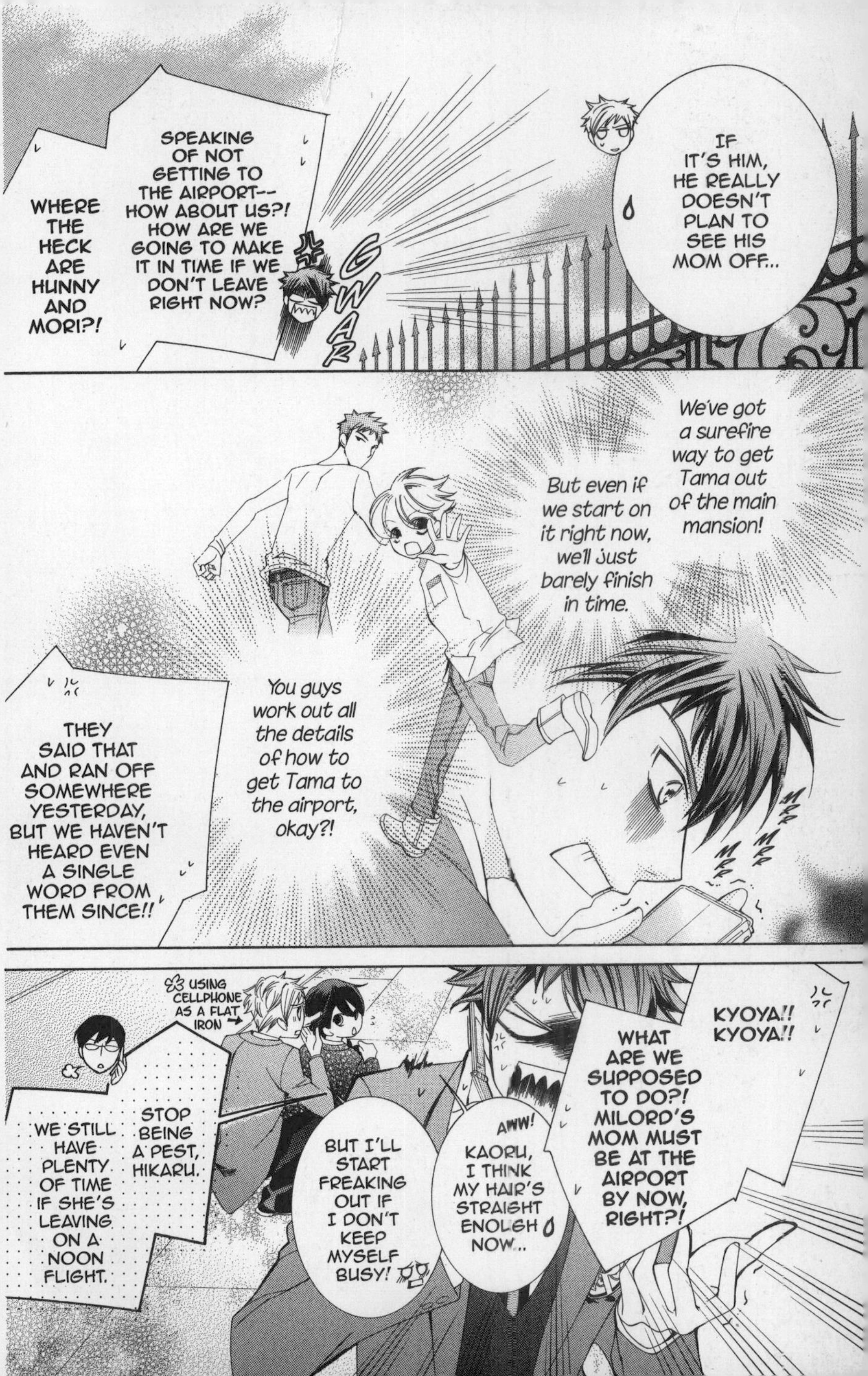
IF IT'S HIM, HE REALLY DOESN'T PLAN TO SEE HIS MOM OFF...
GWAR
SPEAKING OF NOT GETTING TO THE AIRPORT-- HOW ABOUT US?! HOW ARE WE GOING TO MAKE IT IN TIME IF WE DON'T LEAVE RIGHT NOW?
WHERE THE HECK ARE HUNNY AND MORI?!
We've got a surefire way to get Tama out of the main mansion!
But even if we start on it right now, we'll just barely finish in time.
You guys work out all the details of how to get Tama to the airport, okay?!
MRR MRR MRR
THEY SAID THAT AND RAN OFF SOMEWHERE YESTERDAY, BUT WE HAVEN'T HEARD EVEN A SINGLE WORD FROM THEM SINCE!!
KYOYA!! KYOYA!!
WHAT ARE WE SUPPOSED TO DO?! MILORD'S MOM MUST BE AT THE AIRPORT BY NOW, RIGHT?!
AWW!
KAORU, I THINK MY HAIR'S STRAIGHT ENOUGH NOW...
BUT I'LL START FREAKING OUT IF I DON'T KEEP MYSELF BUSY!
USING CELLPHONE AS A FLAT IRON
STOP BEING A PEST, HIKARU.
WE STILL HAVE PLENTY OF TIME IF SHE'S LEAVING ON A NOON FLIGHT.

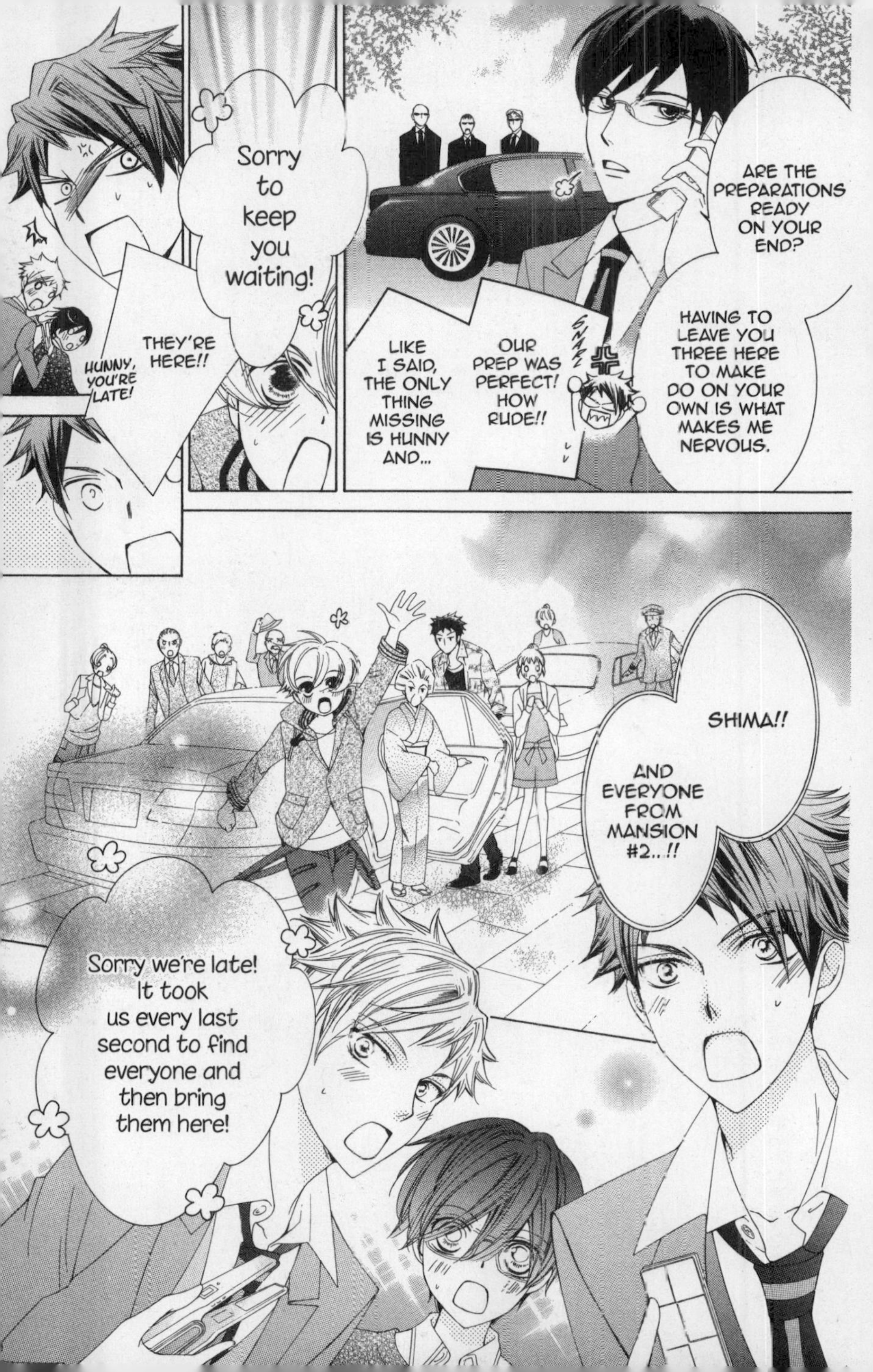
ARE THE PREPARATIONS READY ON YOUR END?
HAVING TO LEAVE YOU THREE HERE TO MAKE DO ON YOUR OWN IS WHAT MAKES ME NERVOUS.
OUR PREP WAS PERFECT! HOW RUDE!!
LIKE I SAID, THE ONLY THING MISSING IS HUNNY AND...
Sorry to keep you waiting!
THEY'RE HERE!!
HUNNY, YOU'RE LATE!
SHIMA!!
AND EVERYONE FROM MANSION #2...!!
Sorry we're late! It took us every last second to find everyone and then bring them here!

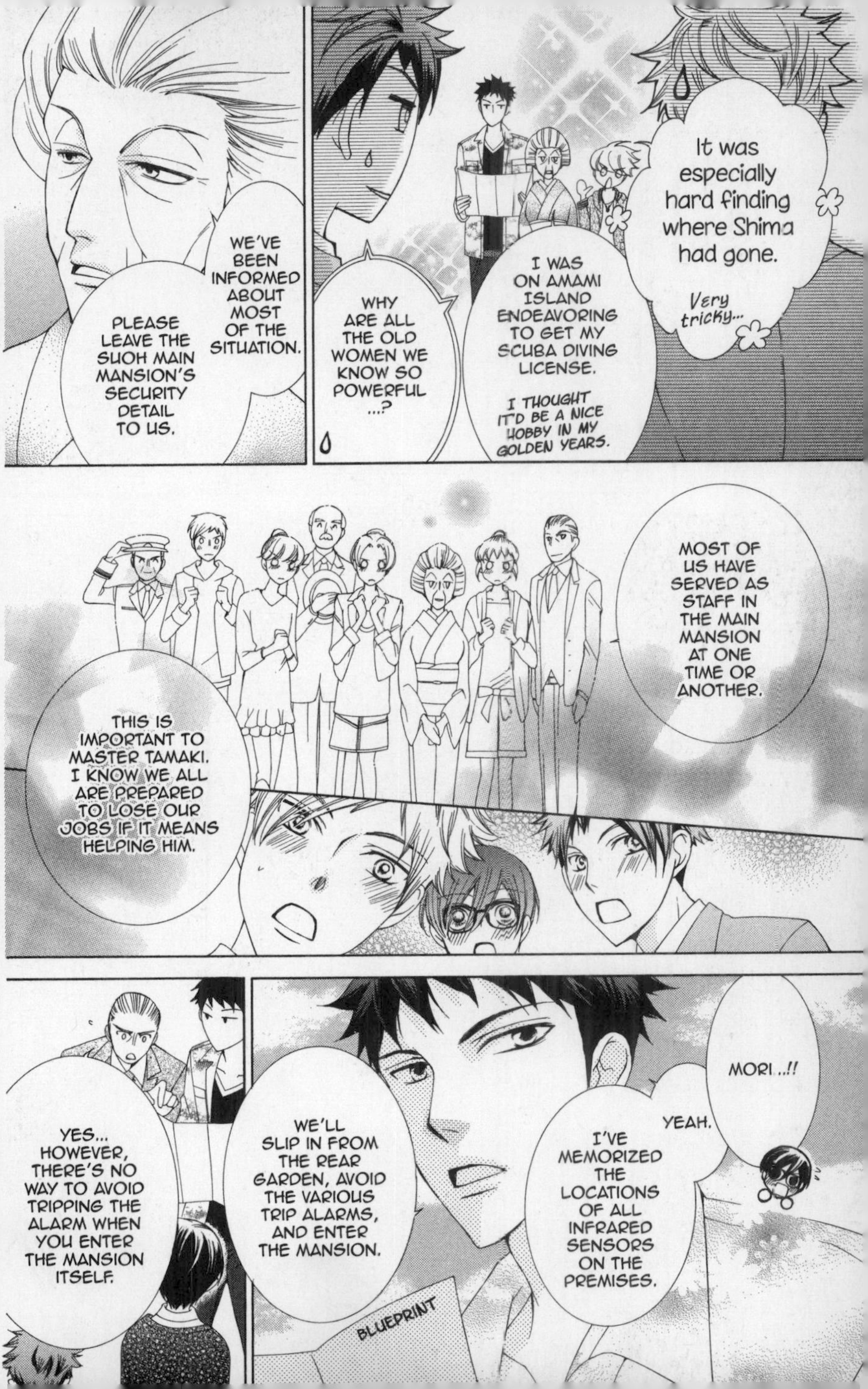
It was especially hard finding where Shima had gone.
Very tricky...
I was on Amami Island endeavoring to get my scuba diving license.
I thought it'd be a nice hobby in my golden years.
Why are all the old women we know so powerful ...?
We've been informed about most of the situation.
Please leave the Suoh main mansion's security detail to us.
Most of us have served as staff in the main mansion at one time or another.
This is important to Master Tamaki. I know we all are prepared to lose our jobs if it means helping him.
Mori...!!
Yeah.
I've memorized the locations of all infrared sensors on the premises.
We'll slip in from the rear garden, avoid the various trip alarms, and enter the mansion.
Blueprint
Yes... however, there's no way to avoid tripping the alarm when you enter the mansion itself.

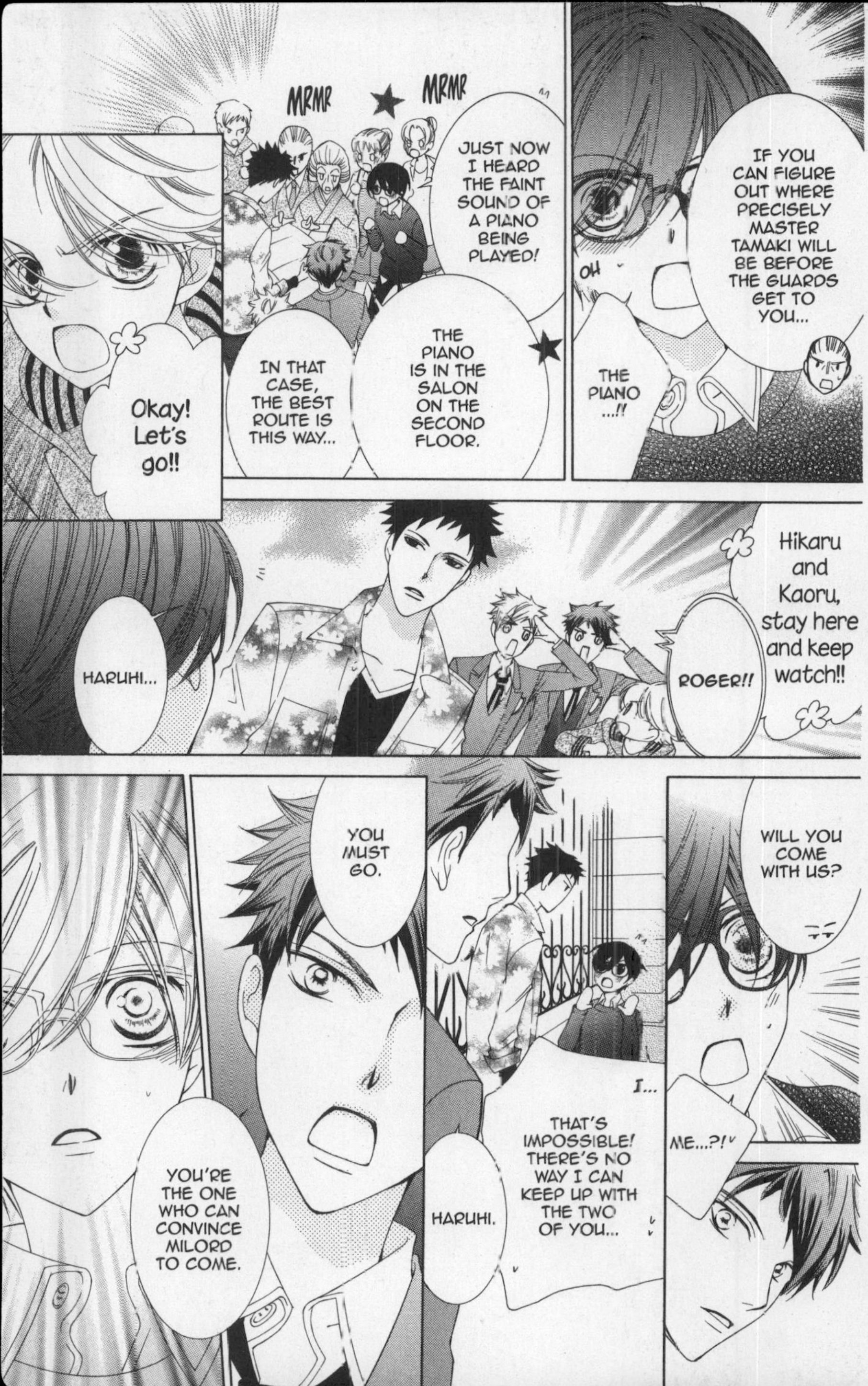
IF YOU CAN FIGURE OUT WHERE PRECISELY MASTER TAMAKI WILL BE BEFORE THE GUARDS GET TO YOU...
OH
THE PIANO ...!!
MRMR ★ MRMR
JUST NOW I HEARD THE FAINT SOUND OF A PIANO BEING PLAYED!
THE PIANO IS IN THE SALON ON THE SECOND FLOOR.
IN THAT CASE, THE BEST ROUTE IS THIS WAY...
Okay! Let's go!!
Hikaru and Kaoru, stay here and keep watch!!
ROGER!!
HARUHI...
WILL YOU COME WITH US?
ME...?!
YOU MUST GO.
I...
THAT'S IMPOSSIBLE! THERE'S NO WAY I CAN KEEP UP WITH THE TWO OF YOU...
HARUHI.
YOU'RE THE ONE WHO CAN CONVINCE MILORD TO COME.

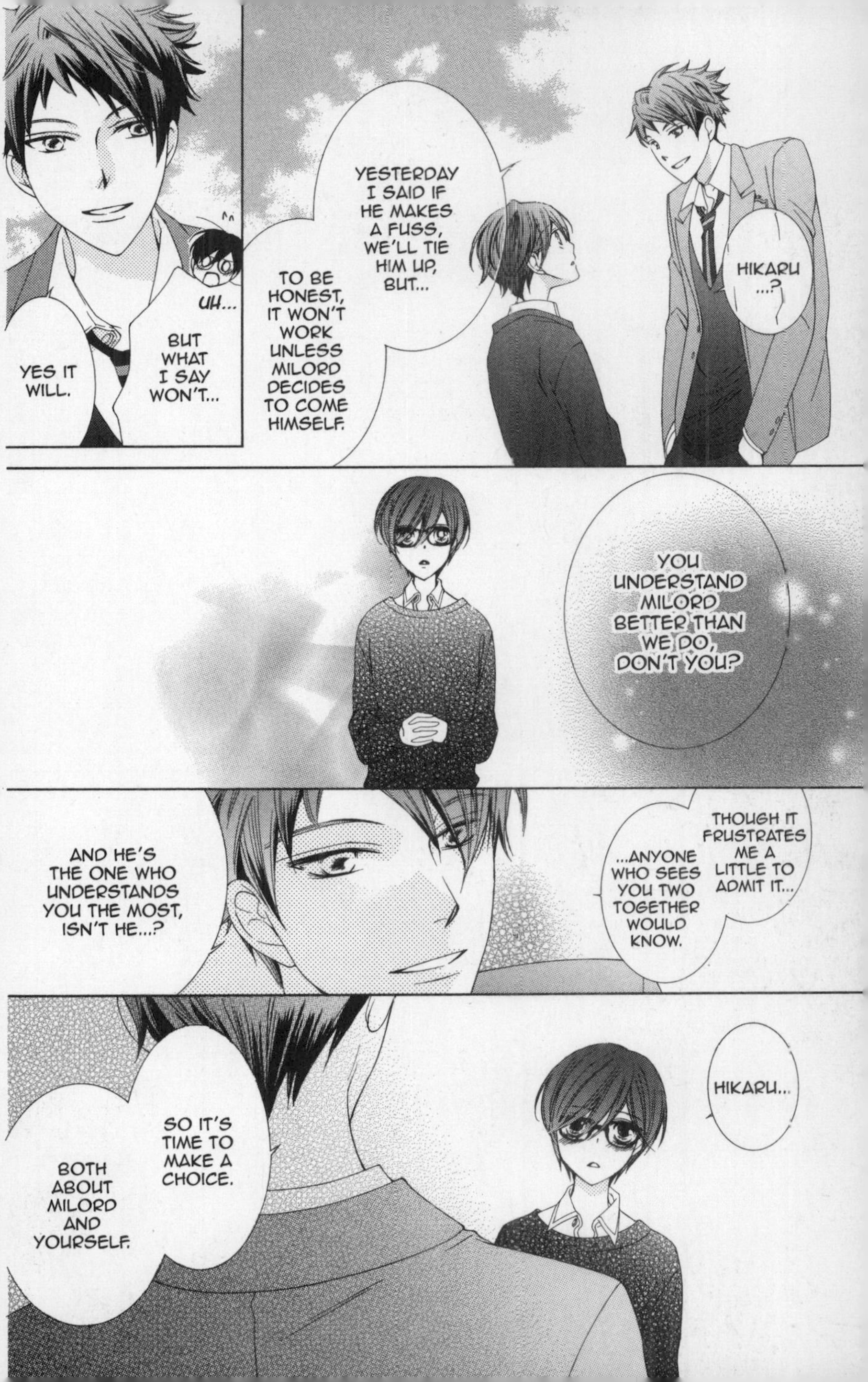
HIKARU ...?
YESTERDAY I SAID IF HE MAKES A FUSS, WE'LL TIE HIM UP, BUT...
TO BE HONEST, IT WON'T WORK UNLESS MILORD DECIDES TO COME HIMSELF.
UH...
BUT WHAT I SAY WON'T...
YES IT WILL.
YOU UNDERSTAND MILORD BETTER THAN WE DO, DON'T YOU?
THOUGH IT FRUSTRATES ME A LITTLE TO ADMIT IT...
...ANYONE WHO SEES YOU TWO TOGETHER WOULD KNOW.
AND HE'S THE ONE WHO UNDERSTANDS YOU THE MOST, ISN'T HE...?
HIKARU...
SO IT'S TIME TO MAKE A CHOICE.
BOTH ABOUT MILORD AND YOURSELF.

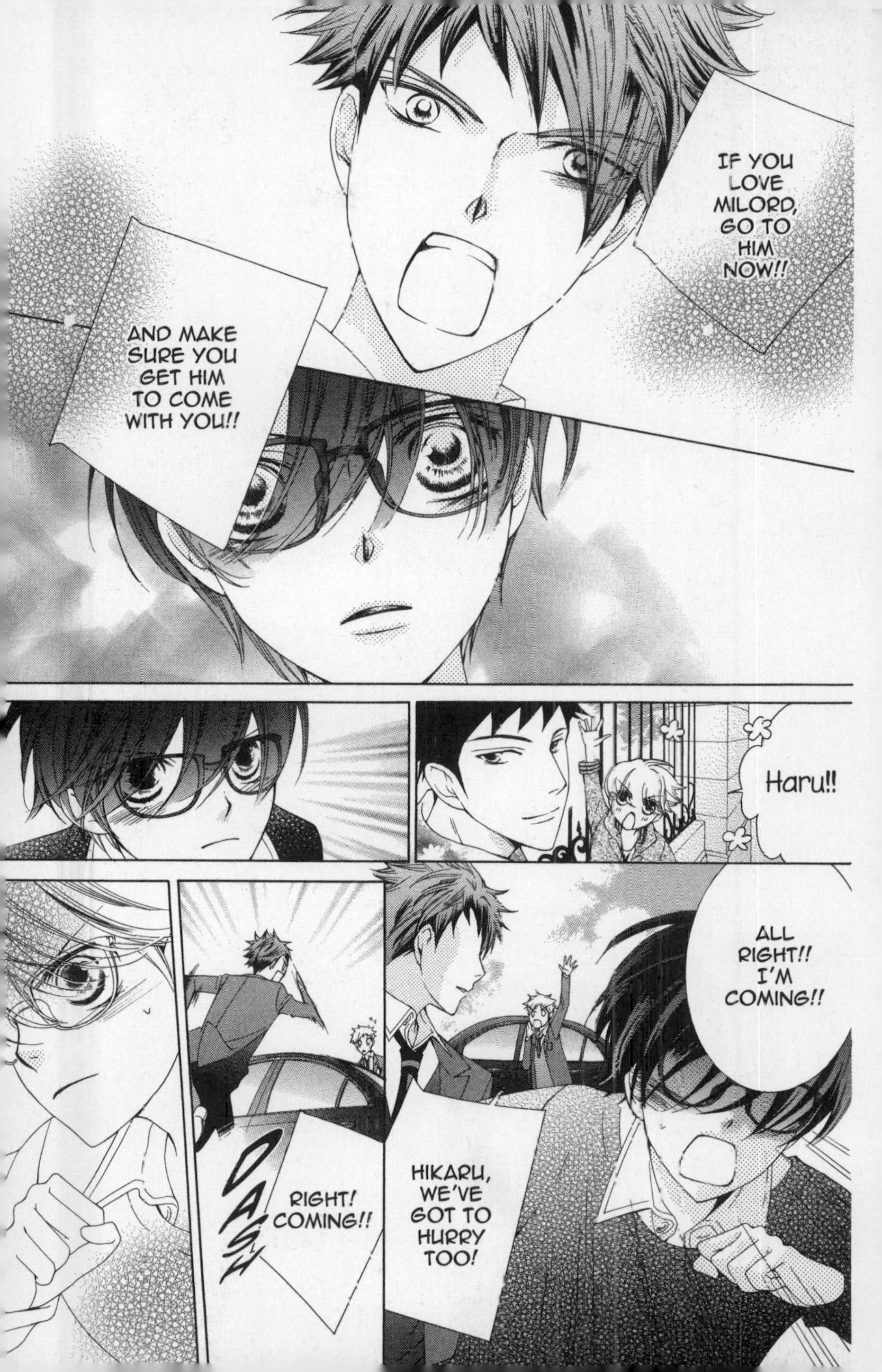
IF YOU LOVE MILORD, GO TO HIM NOW!!
AND MAKE SURE YOU GET HIM TO COME WITH YOU!!
Haru!!
ALL RIGHT!! I'M COMING!!
HIKARU, WE'VE GOT TO HURRY TOO!
RIGHT! COMING!!
DASH

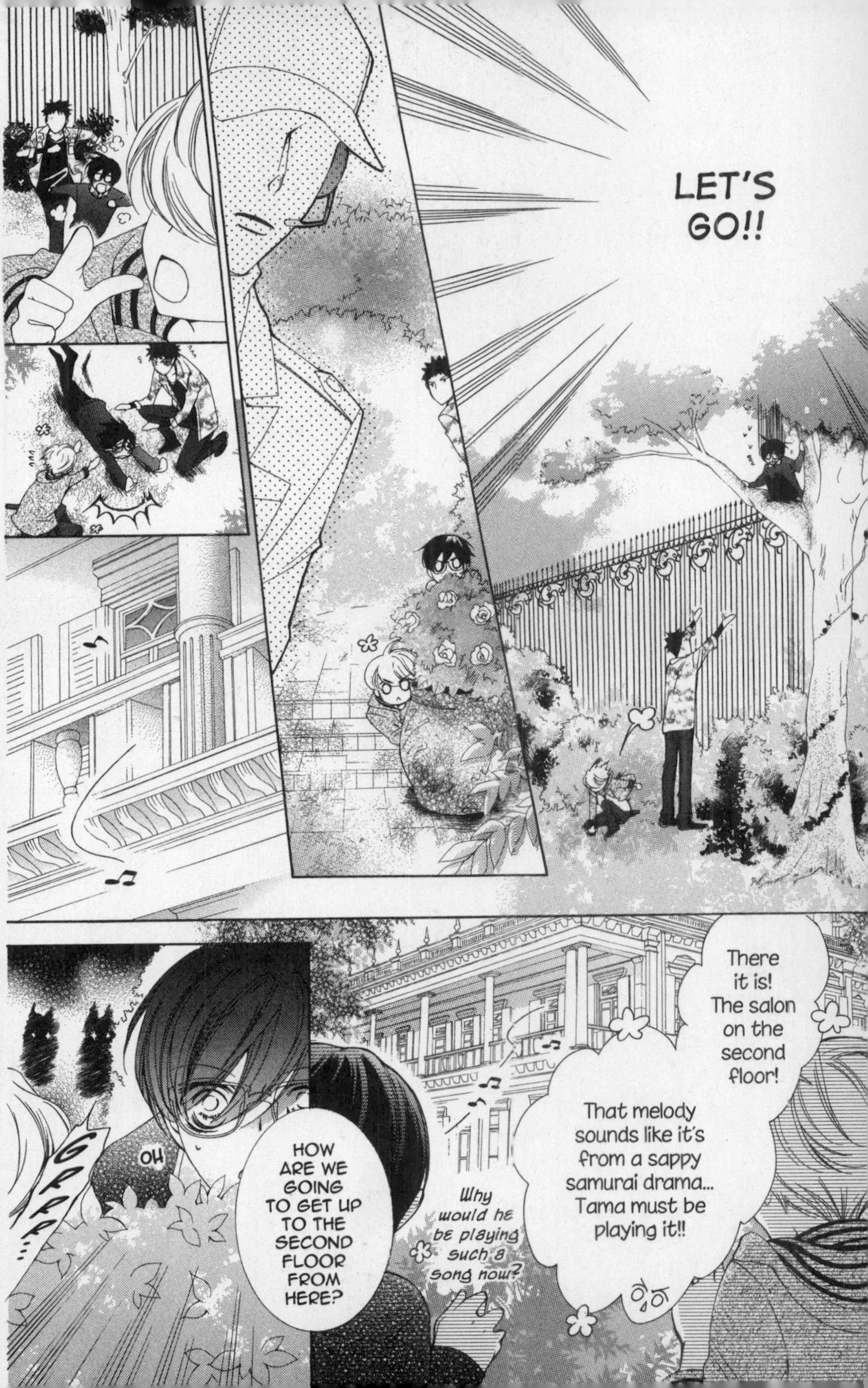
LET'S GO!!
There it is! The salon on the second floor!
That melody sounds like it's from a sappy samurai drama... Tama must be playing it!!
Why would he be playing such a song now!?
HOW ARE WE GOING TO GET UP TO THE SECOND FLOOR FROM HERE?
OH
GRRR...

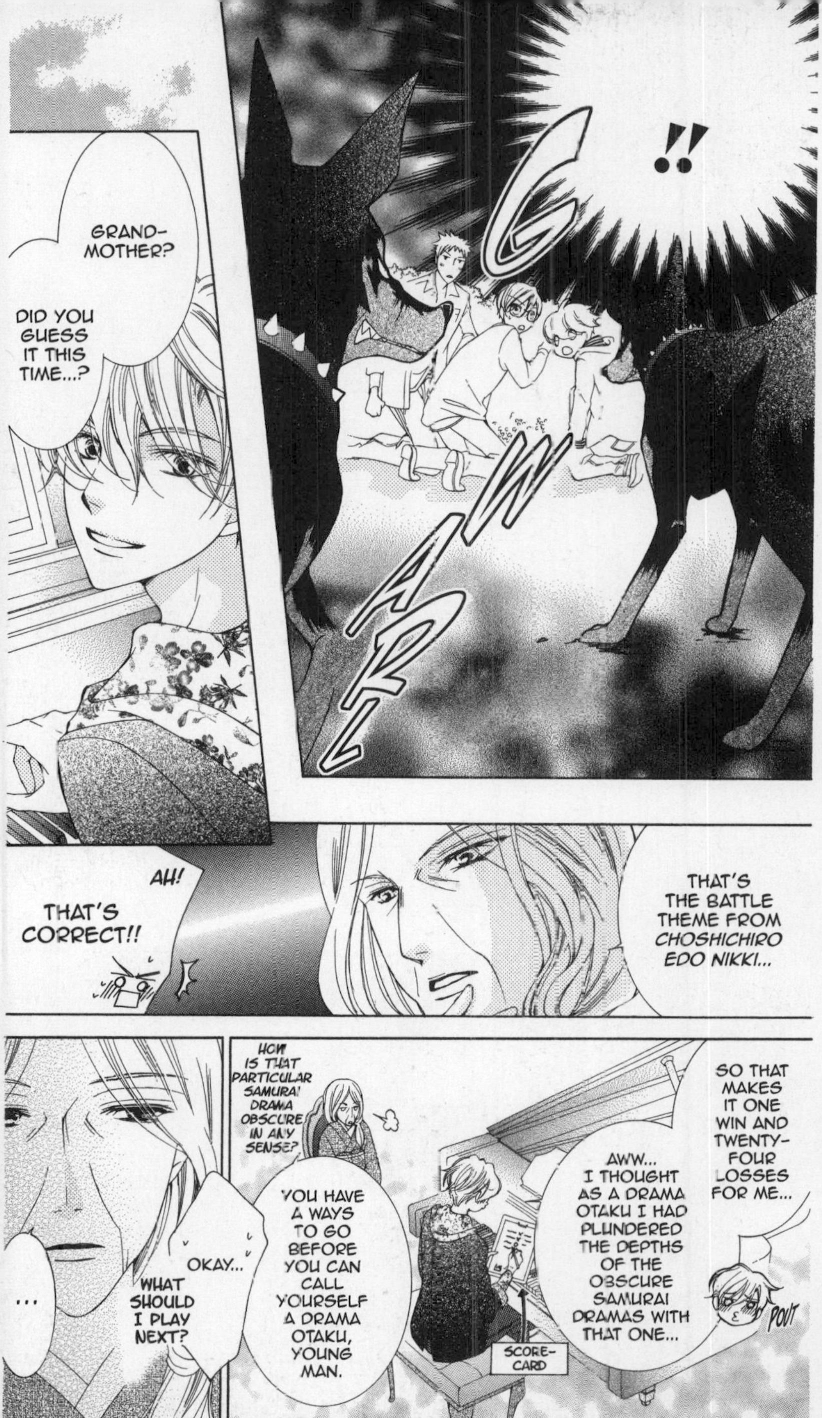
!!
GWARL
GRAND-MOTHER?
DID YOU GUESS IT THIS TIME...?
THAT'S THE BATTLE THEME FROM CHOSHICHIRO EDO NIKKI...
AH!
THAT'S CORRECT!!
SO THAT MAKES IT ONE WIN AND TWENTY-FOUR LOSSES FOR ME...
POUT
AWW... I THOUGHT AS A DRAMA OTAKU I HAD PLUNDERED THE DEPTHS OF THE OBSCURE SAMURAI DRAMAS WITH THAT ONE...
SCORE-CARD
HOW IS THAT PARTICULAR SAMURAI DRAMA OBSCURE IN ANY SENSE?
YOU HAVE A WAYS TO GO BEFORE YOU CAN CALL YOURSELF A DRAMA OTAKU, YOUNG MAN.
OKAY...
WHAT SHOULD I PLAY NEXT?
...

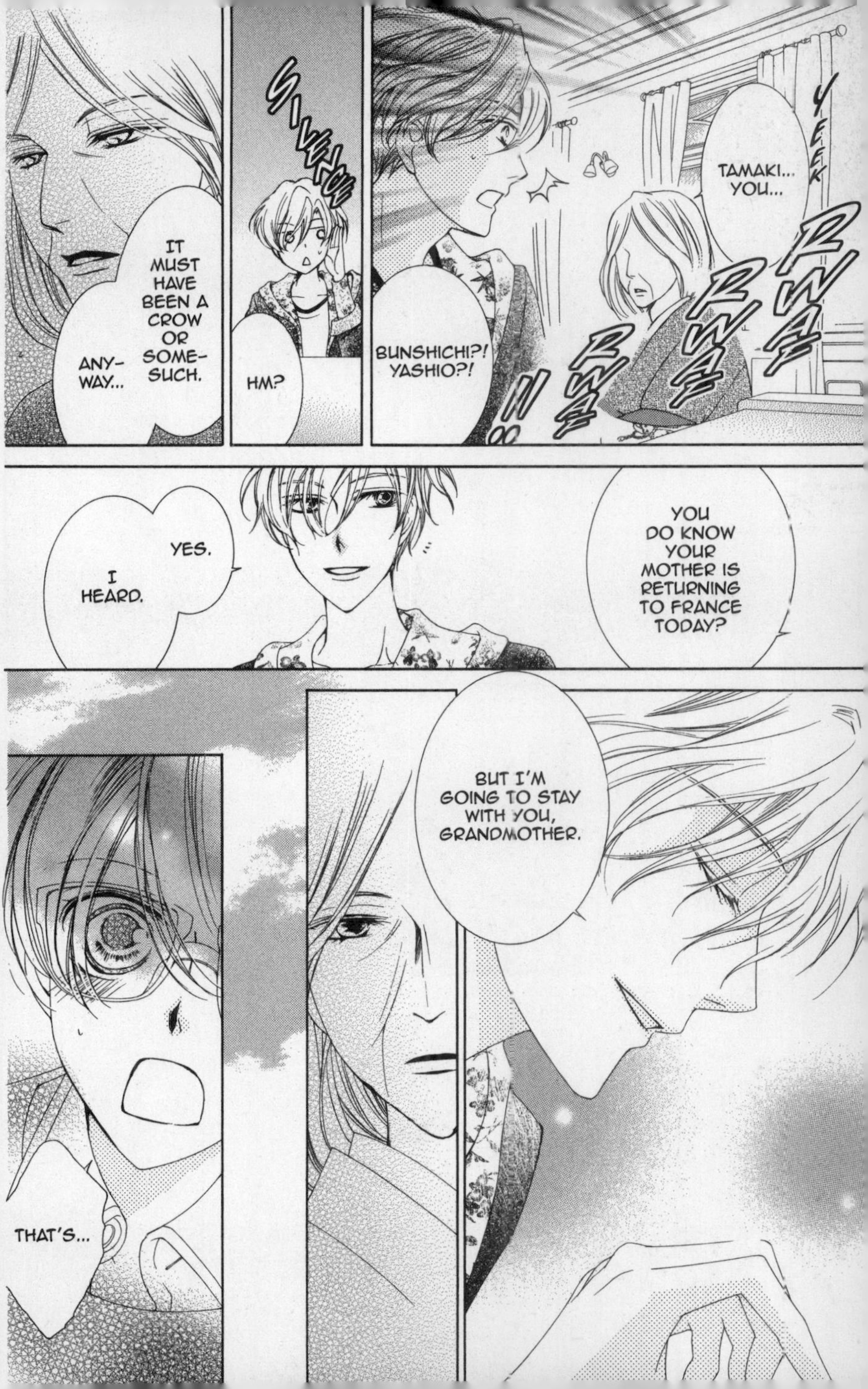
TAMAKI... YOU...
YEEK
RWAA RWAA RWAA!!
BUNSHICHI?! YASHIO?!
HM?
IT MUST HAVE BEEN A CROW OR SOME-SUCH.
ANY-WAY...
YOU DO KNOW YOUR MOTHER IS RETURNING TO FRANCE TODAY?
YES.
I HEARD.
BUT I'M GOING TO STAY WITH YOU, GRANDMOTHER.
THAT'S...

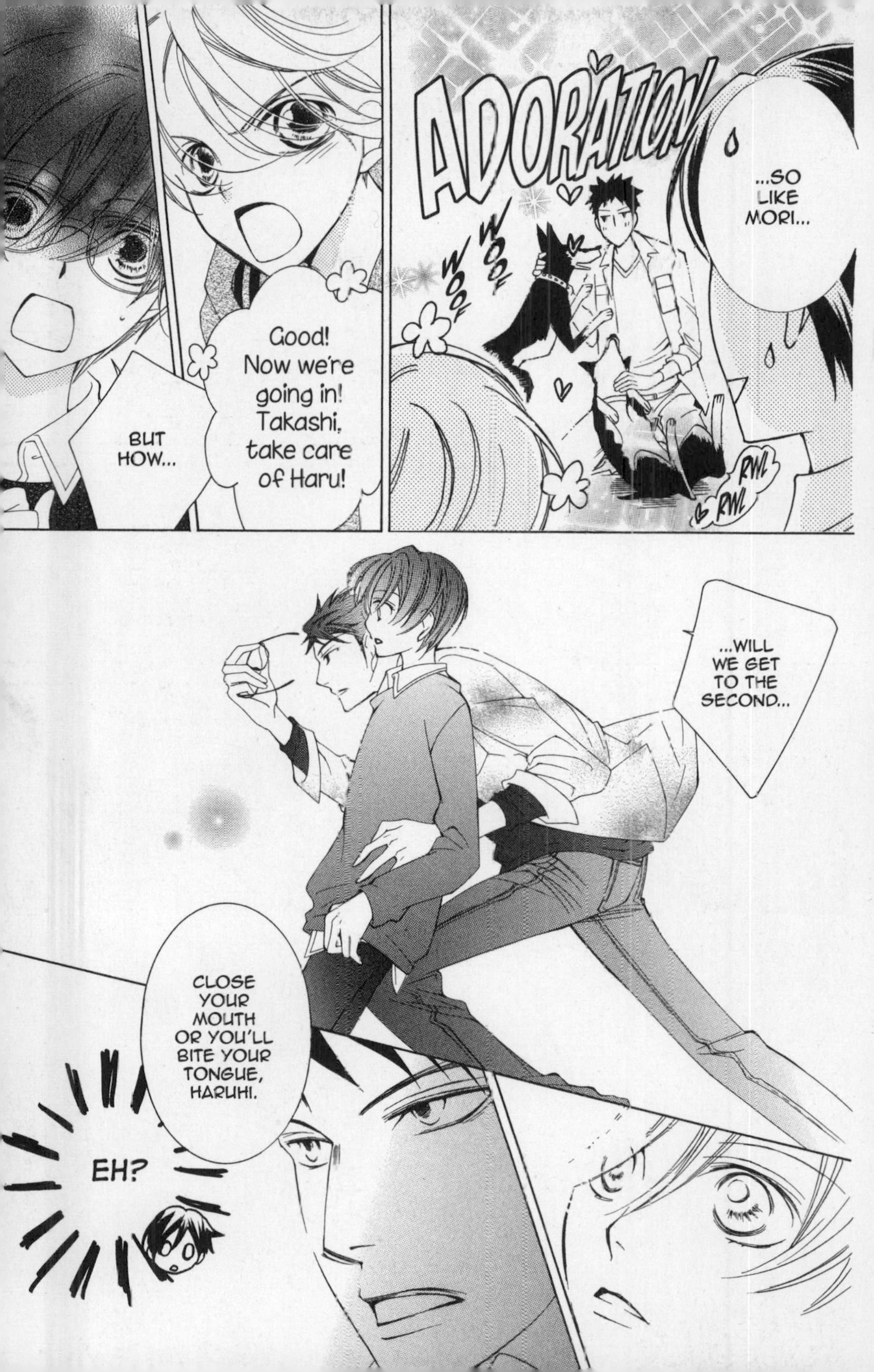
...SO LIKE MORI...
ADORATION
WOOF WOOF
RWL RWL
Good! Now we're going in! Takashi, take care of Haru!
BUT HOW...
...WILL WE GET TO THE SECOND...
CLOSE YOUR MOUTH OR YOU'LL BITE YOUR TONGUE, HARUHI.
EH?

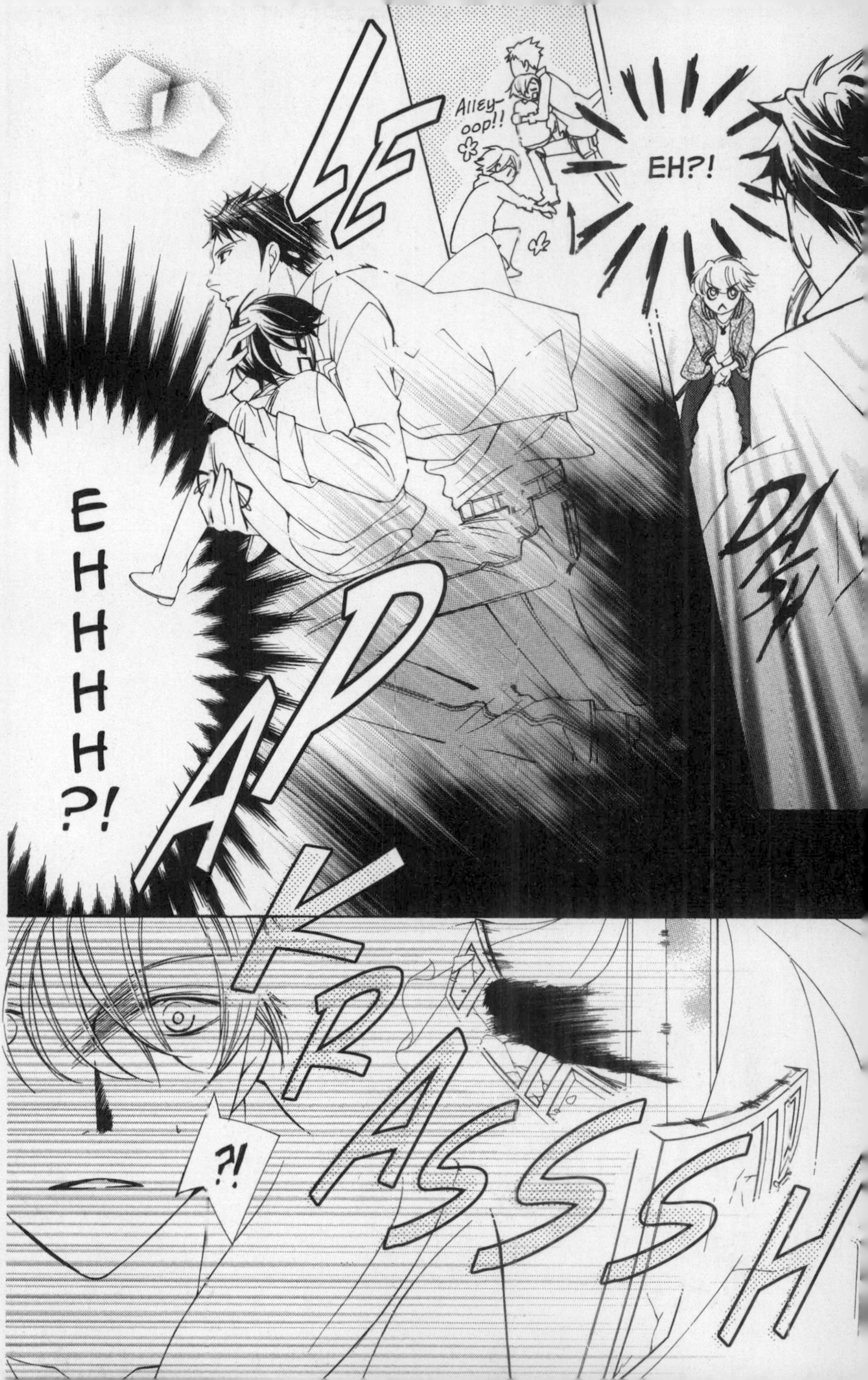
EH?!
Alley-oop!!
LEAP
EHHHHH?!
?!
KRASSSH

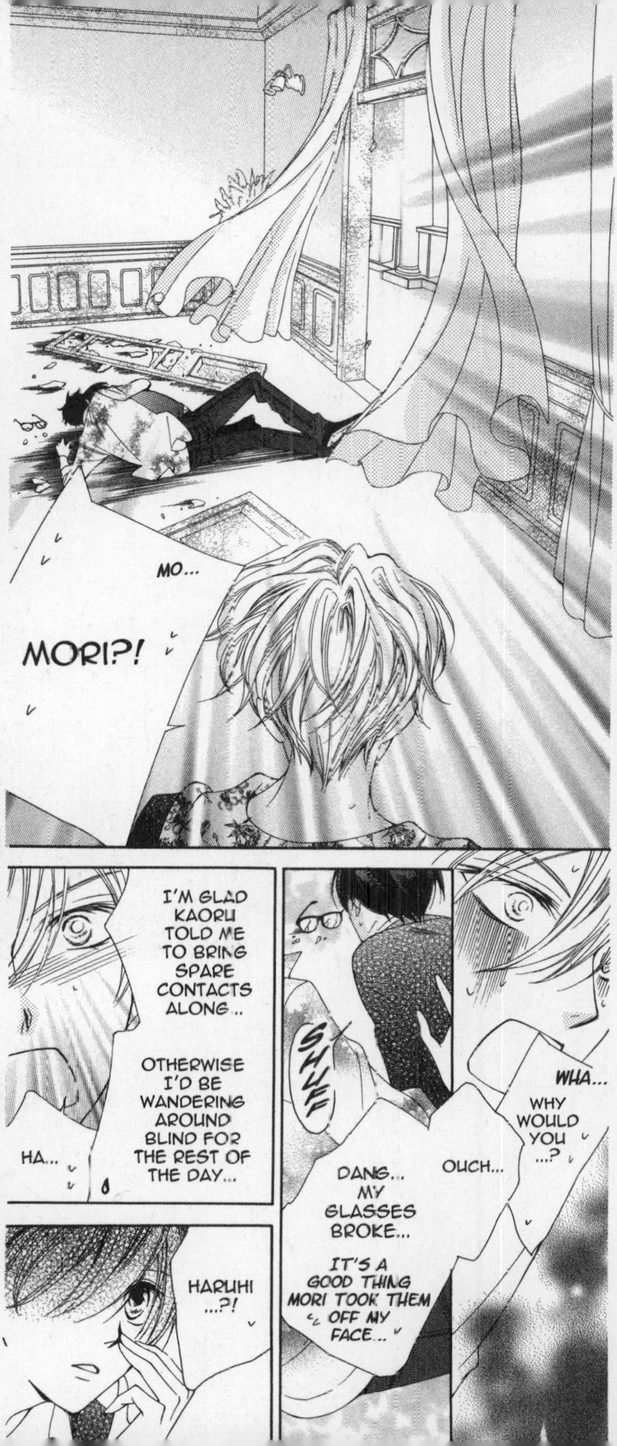
MO...
MORI?!
WHA...
WHY WOULD YOU ...?
OUCH...
SHUFF
DANG... MY GLASSES BROKE...
IT'S A GOOD THING MORI TOOK THEM OFF MY FACE...
I'M GLAD KAORU TOLD ME TO BRING SPARE CONTACTS ALONG...
OTHERWISE I'D BE WANDERING AROUND BLIND FOR THE REST OF THE DAY...
HA...
HARUHI ...?!

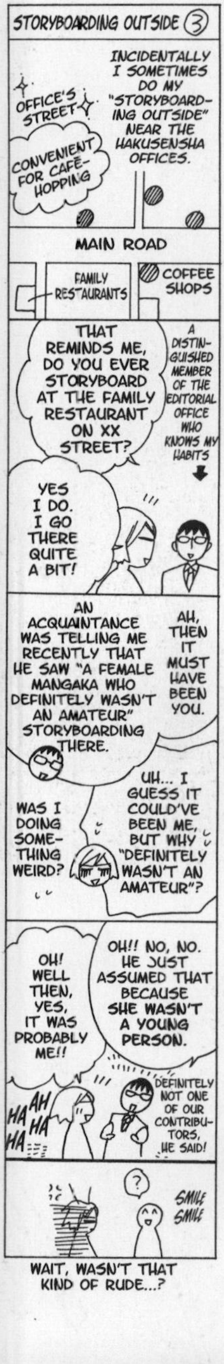
STORYBOARDING OUTSIDE 3
INCIDENTALLY I SOMETIMES DO MY "STORYBOARDING OUTSIDE" NEAR THE HAKUSENSHA OFFICES.
OFFICE'S STREET
CONVENIENT FOR CAFÉ-HOPPING
MAIN ROAD
FAMILY RESTAURANTS
COFFEE SHOPS
THAT REMINDS ME, DO YOU EVER STORYBOARD AT THE FAMILY RESTAURANT ON XX STREET?
A DISTINGUISHED MEMBER OF THE EDITORIAL OFFICE WHO KNOWS MY HABITS
YES I DO. I GO THERE QUITE A BIT!
AN ACQUAINTANCE WAS TELLING ME RECENTLY THAT HE SAW "A FEMALE MANGAKA WHO DEFINITELY WASN'T AN AMATEUR" STORYBOARDING THERE.
AH, THEN IT MUST HAVE BEEN YOU.
UH... I GUESS IT COULD'VE BEEN ME, BUT WHY "DEFINITELY WASN'T AN AMATEUR"?
WAS I DOING SOMETHING WEIRD?
OH!! NO, NO. HE JUST ASSUMED THAT BECAUSE SHE WASN'T A YOUNG PERSON.
OH! WELL THEN, YES, IT WAS PROBABLY ME!!
AH HA HA HA
DEFINITELY NOT ONE OF OUR CONTRIBUTORS, HE SAID!
?
SMILE SMILE
WAIT, WASN'T THAT KIND OF RUDE...?

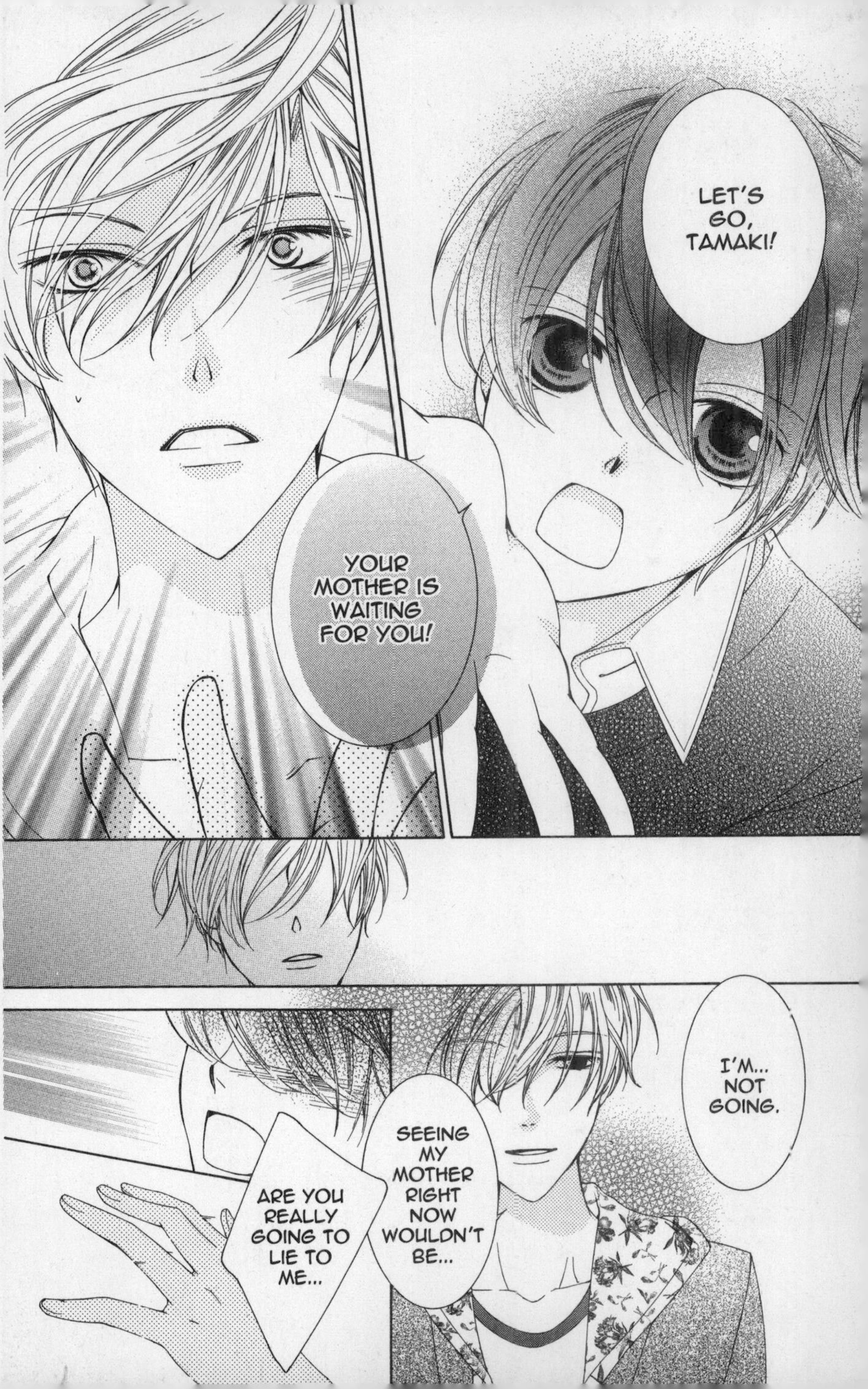
LET'S GO, TAMAKI!
YOUR MOTHER IS WAITING FOR YOU!
I'M... NOT GOING.
SEEING MY MOTHER RIGHT NOW WOULDN'T BE...
ARE YOU REALLY GOING TO LIE TO ME...

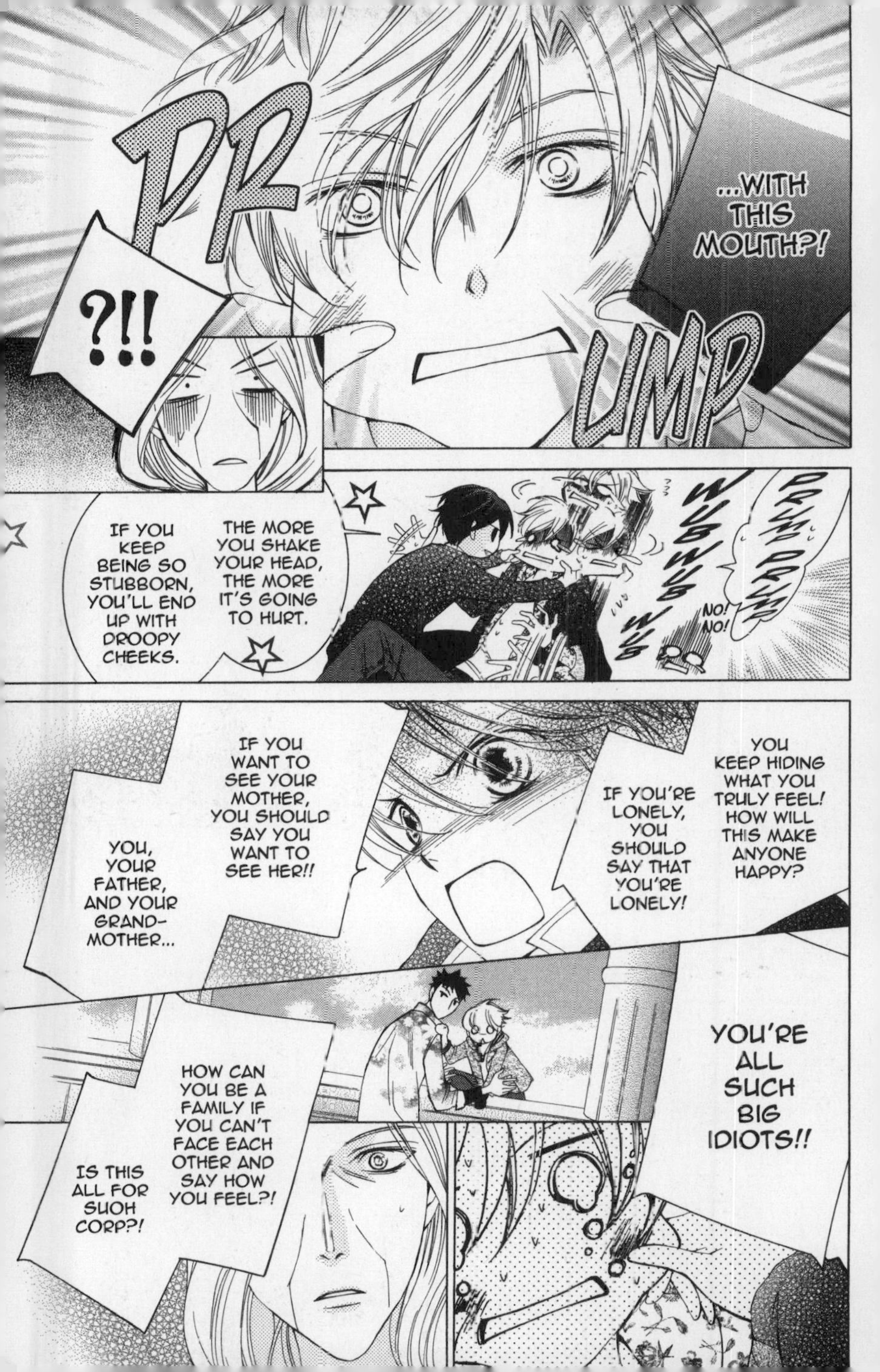

...WITH THIS MOUTH?!
PR
UMP
?!!
DRUM DRUM
WUB WUB WUB
NO! NO!
THE MORE YOU SHAKE YOUR HEAD, THE MORE IT'S GOING TO HURT.
IF YOU KEEP BEING SO STUBBORN, YOU'LL END UP WITH DROOPY CHEEKS.
YOU KEEP HIDING WHAT YOU TRULY FEEL! HOW WILL THIS MAKE ANYONE HAPPY?
IF YOU'RE LONELY, YOU SHOULD SAY THAT YOU'RE LONELY!
IF YOU WANT TO SEE YOUR MOTHER, YOU SHOULD SAY YOU WANT TO SEE HER!!
YOU, YOUR FATHER, AND YOUR GRAND-MOTHER...
YOU'RE ALL SUCH BIG IDIOTS!!
HOW CAN YOU BE A FAMILY IF YOU CAN'T FACE EACH OTHER AND SAY HOW YOU FEEL?!
IS THIS ALL FOR SUOH CORP?!

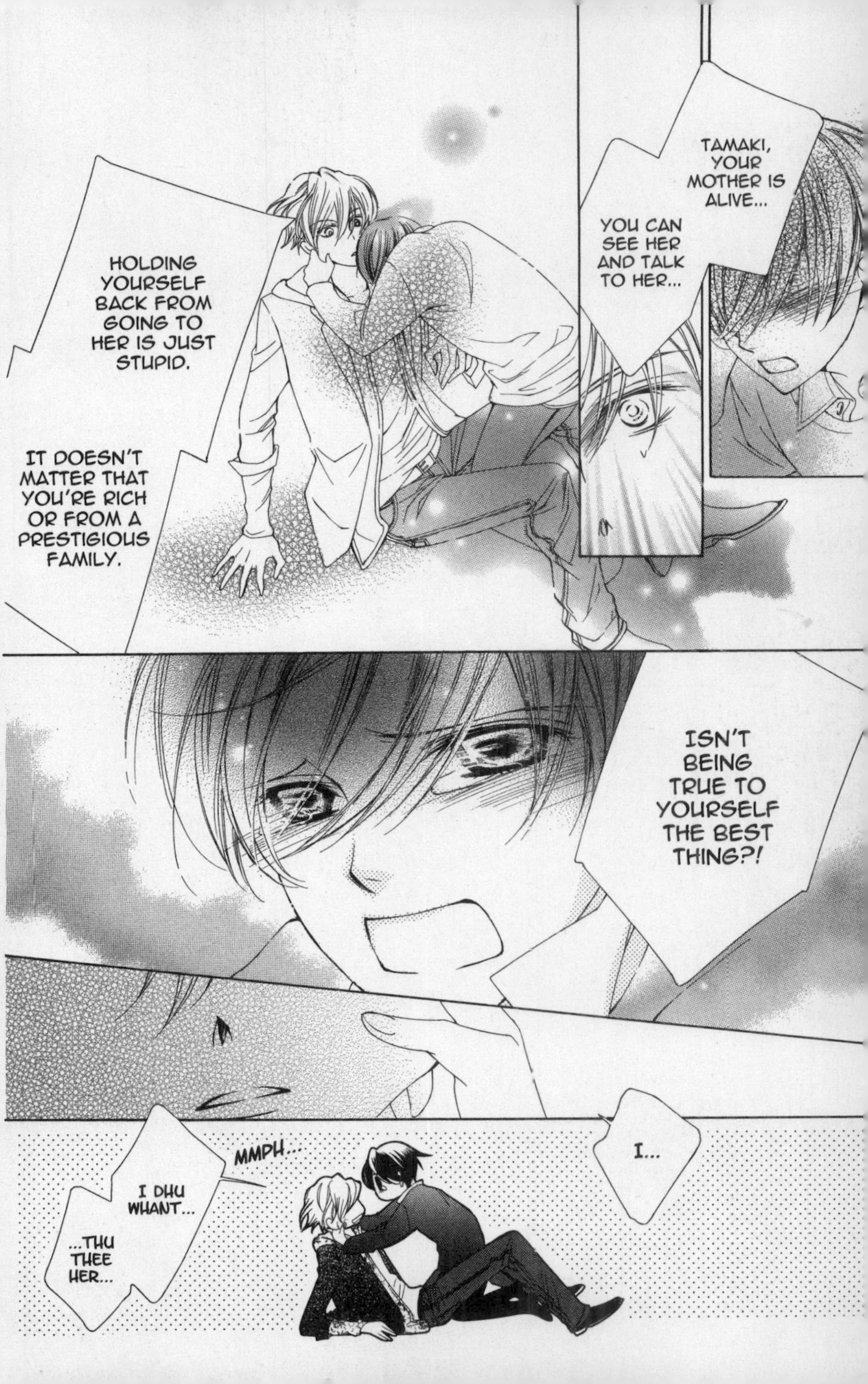
TAMAKI, YOUR MOTHER IS ALIVE...
YOU CAN SEE HER AND TALK TO HER...
HOLDING YOURSELF BACK FROM GOING TO HER IS JUST STUPID.
IT DOESN'T MATTER THAT YOU'RE RICH OR FROM A PRESTIGIOUS FAMILY.
ISN'T BEING TRUE TO YOURSELF THE BEST THING?!
I...
MMPH...
I DHU WHANT...
...THU THEE HER...

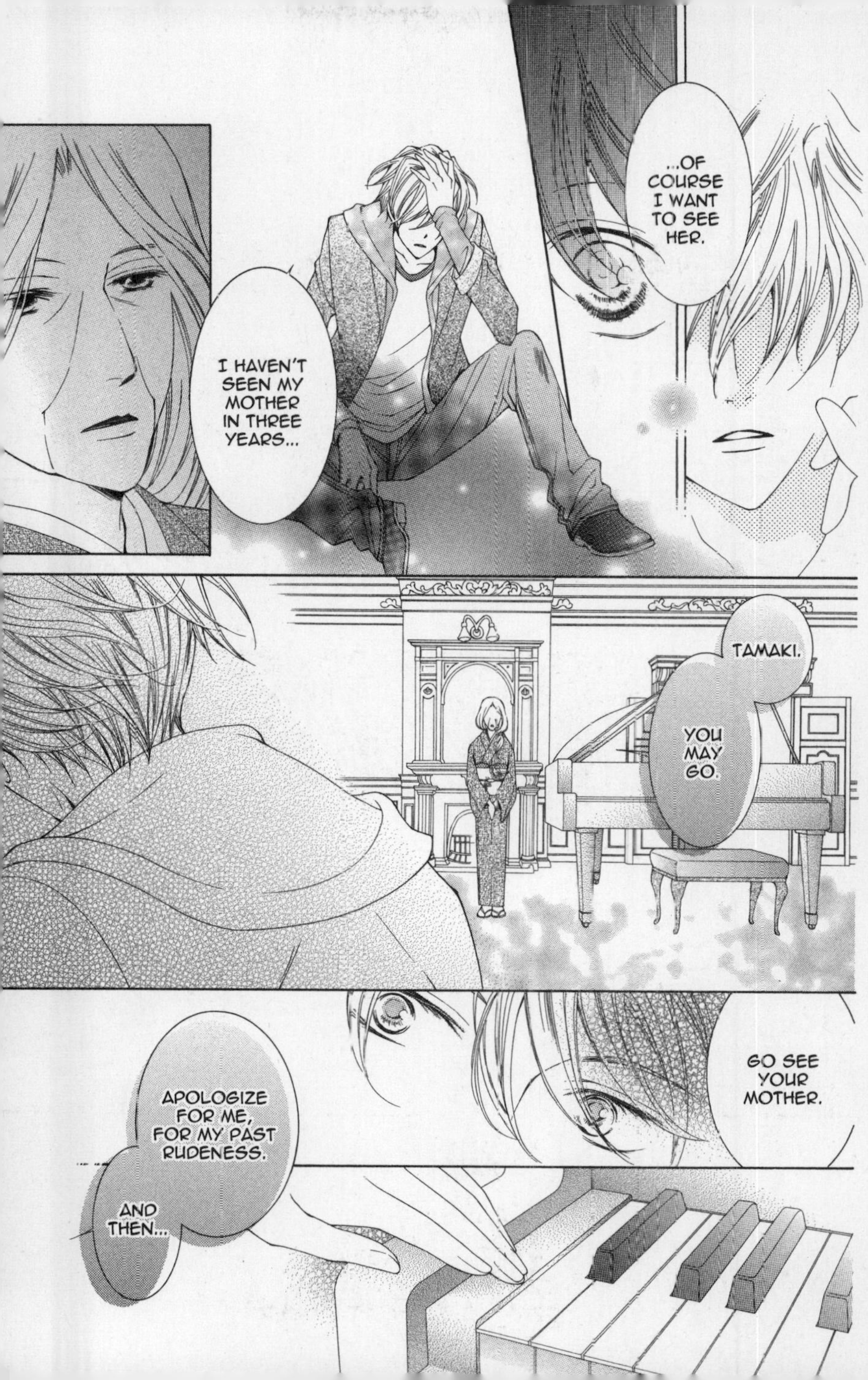
...OF COURSE I WANT TO SEE HER.
I HAVEN'T SEEN MY MOTHER IN THREE YEARS...
TAMAKI.
YOU MAY GO.
GO SEE YOUR MOTHER.
APOLOGIZE FOR ME, FOR MY PAST RUDENESS.
AND THEN...

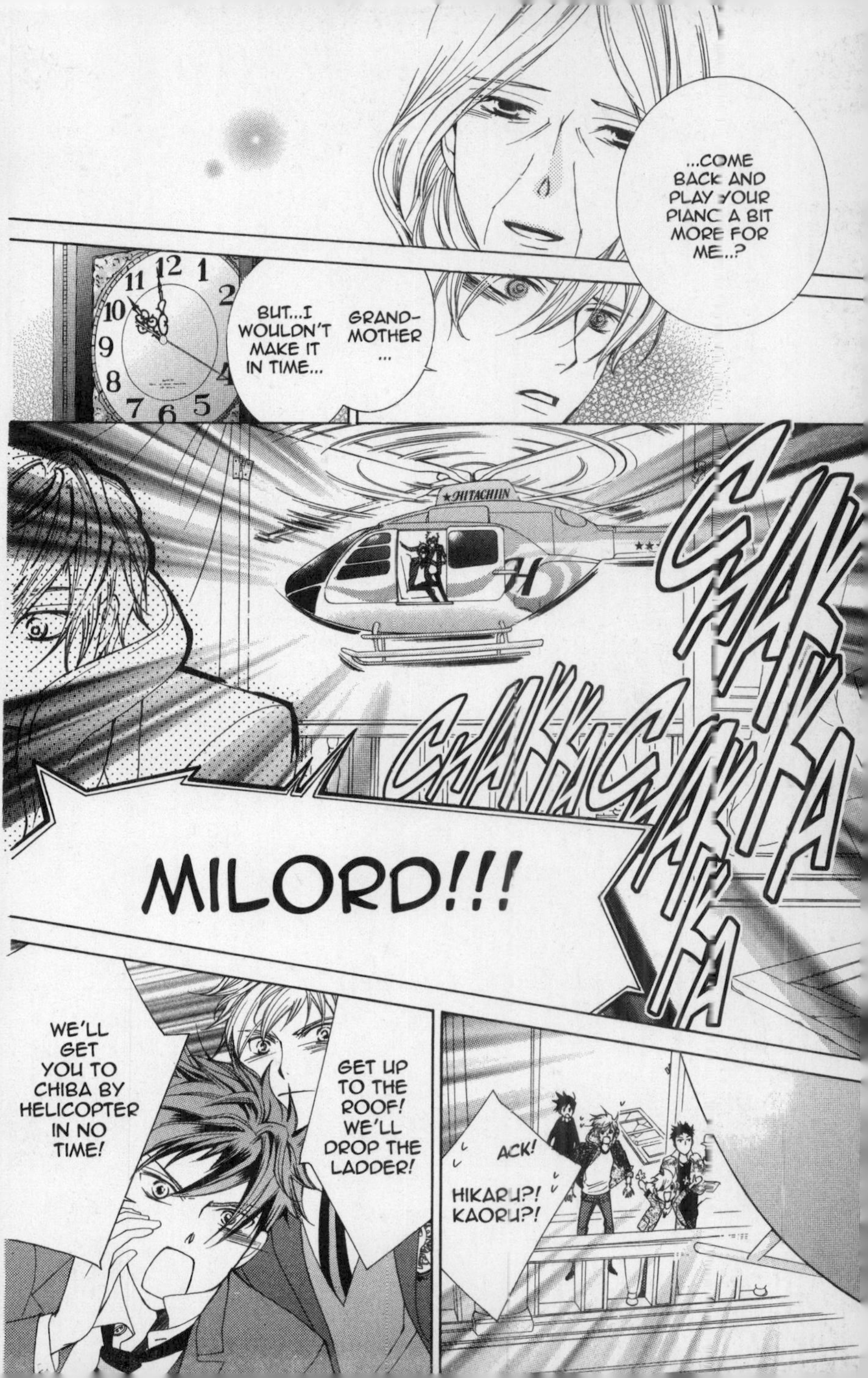
...COME BACK AND PLAY YOUR PIANO A BIT MORE FOR ME...?
GRAND-MOTHER ...
BUT...I WOULDN'T MAKE IT IN TIME...
HITACHIIN
MILORD!!!
ACK!
HIKARU?! KAORU?!
GET UP TO THE ROOF! WE'LL DROP THE LADDER!
WE'LL GET YOU TO CHIBA BY HELICOPTER IN NO TIME!

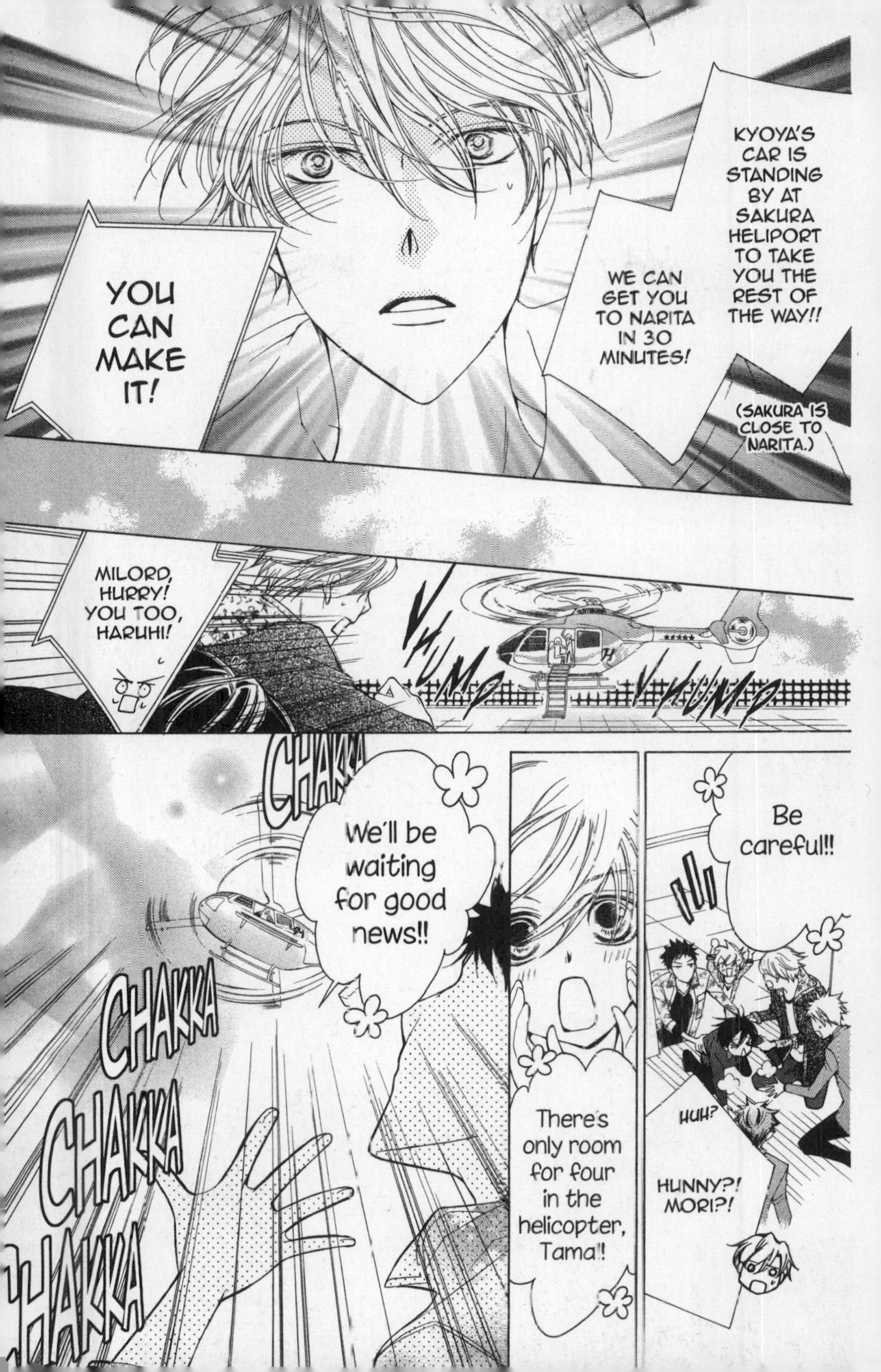
KYOYA'S CAR IS STANDING BY AT SAKURA HELIPORT TO TAKE YOU THE REST OF THE WAY!!
WE CAN GET YOU TO NARITA IN 30 MINUTES!
(SAKURA IS CLOSE TO NARITA.)
YOU CAN MAKE IT!
VHUMP
VHUMP
MILORD, HURRY! YOU TOO, HARUHI!
Be careful!!
HUH?
HUNNY?! MORI?!
There's only room for four in the helicopter, Tama!!
We'll be waiting for good news!!
CHAKKA
CHAKKA
CHAKKA
CHAKKA

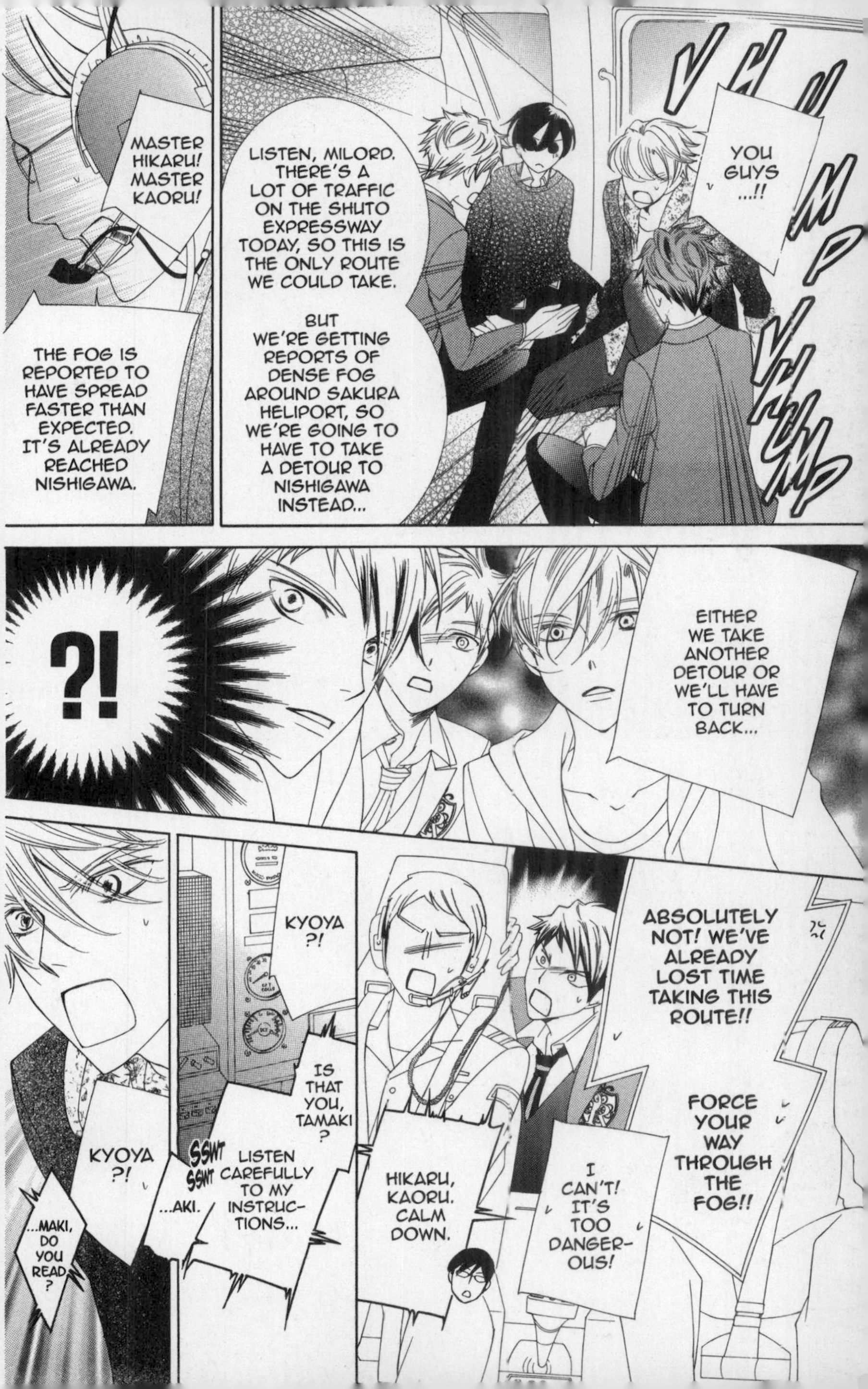
YOU GUYS ...!!
LISTEN, MILORD. THERE'S A LOT OF TRAFFIC ON THE SHUTO EXPRESSWAY TODAY, SO THIS IS THE ONLY ROUTE WE COULD TAKE.
BUT WE'RE GETTING REPORTS OF DENSE FOG AROUND SAKURA HELIPORT, SO WE'RE GOING TO HAVE TO TAKE A DETOUR TO NISHIGAWA INSTEAD...
MASTER HIKARU! MASTER KAORU!
THE FOG IS REPORTED TO HAVE SPREAD FASTER THAN EXPECTED. IT'S ALREADY REACHED NISHIGAWA.
EITHER WE TAKE ANOTHER DETOUR OR WE'LL HAVE TO TURN BACK...
?!
ABSOLUTELY NOT! WE'VE ALREADY LOST TIME TAKING THIS ROUTE!!
FORCE YOUR WAY THROUGH THE FOG!!
I CAN'T! IT'S TOO DANGER-OUS!
HIKARU, KAORU. CALM DOWN.
KYOYA ?!
IS THAT YOU, TAMAKI ?
LISTEN CAREFULLY TO MY INSTRUC-TIONS...
SSWT SSWT
KYOYA ?!
...AKI.
...MAKI, DO YOU READ ?

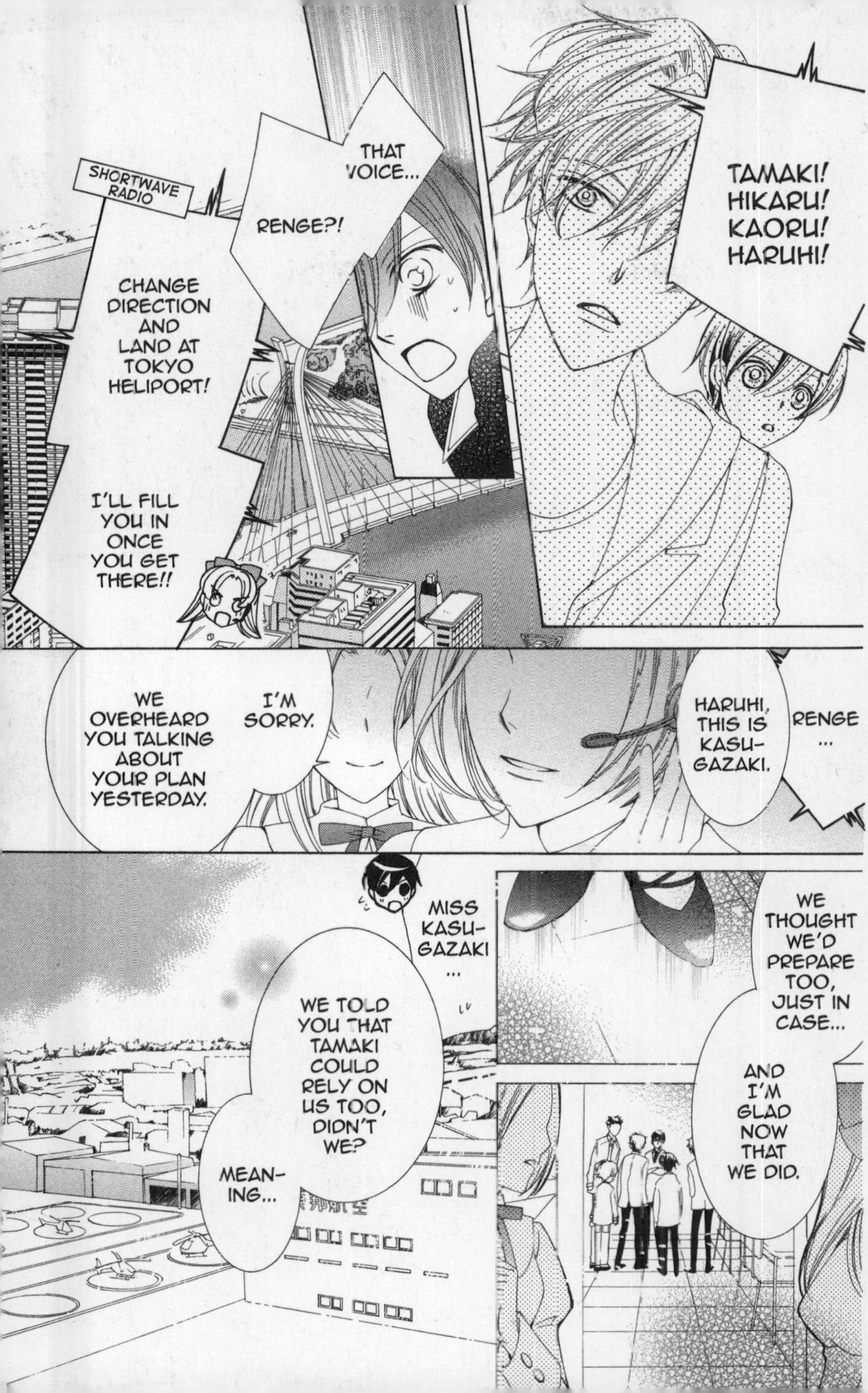
TAMAKI! HIKARU! KAORU! HARUHI!
THAT VOICE...
RENGE?!
SHORTWAVE RADIO
CHANGE DIRECTION AND LAND AT TOKYO HELIPORT!
I'LL FILL YOU IN ONCE YOU GET THERE!!
RENGE ...
HARUHI, THIS IS KASU-GAZAKI.
I'M SORRY.
WE OVERHEARD YOU TALKING ABOUT YOUR PLAN YESTERDAY.
WE THOUGHT WE'D PREPARE TOO, JUST IN CASE...
AND I'M GLAD NOW THAT WE DID.
MISS KASU-GAZAKI ...
WE TOLD YOU THAT TAMAKI COULD RELY ON US TOO, DIDN'T WE?
MEAN-ING...

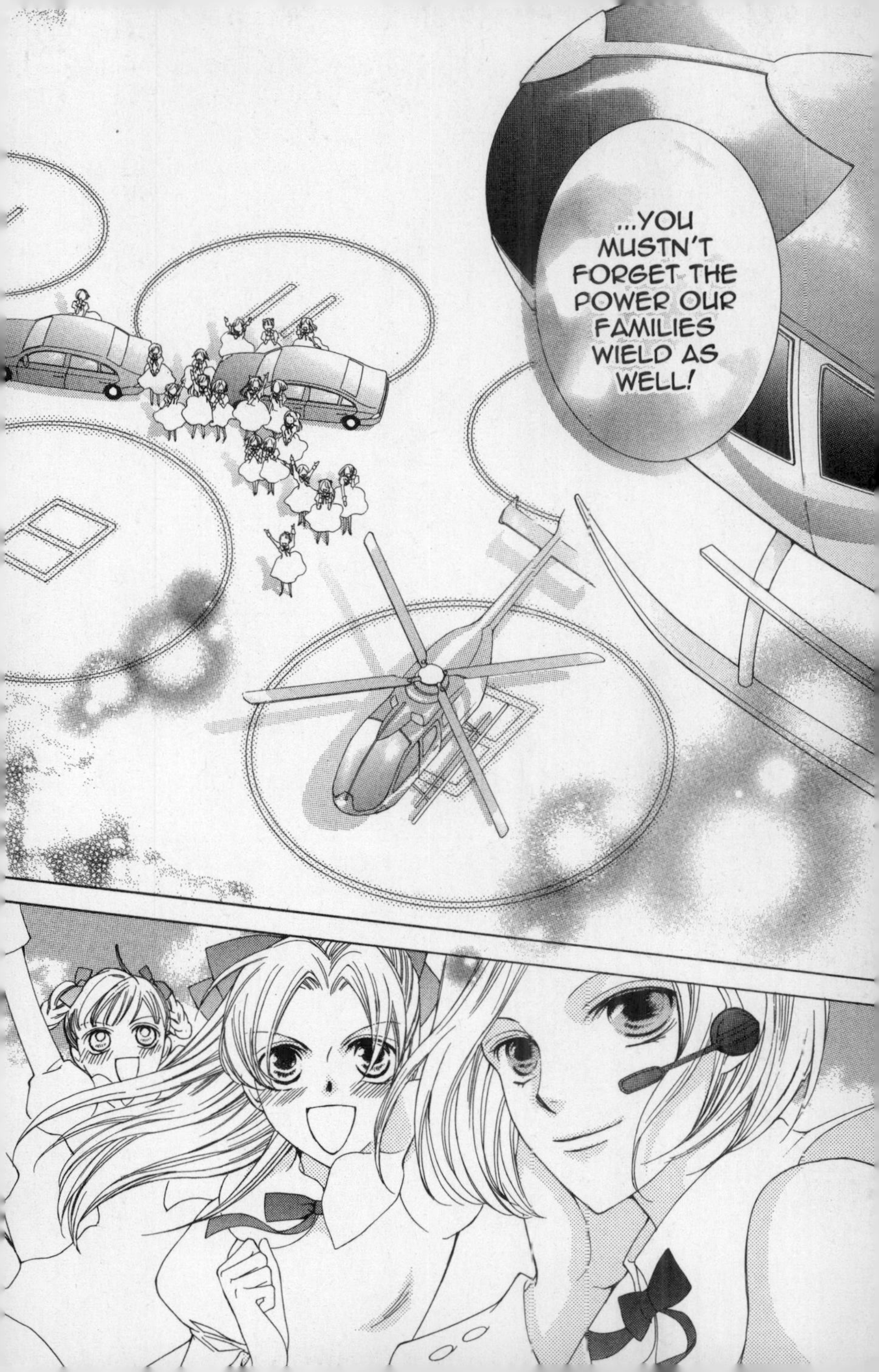
...YOU MUSTN'T FORGET THE POWER OUR FAMILIES WIELD AS WELL!

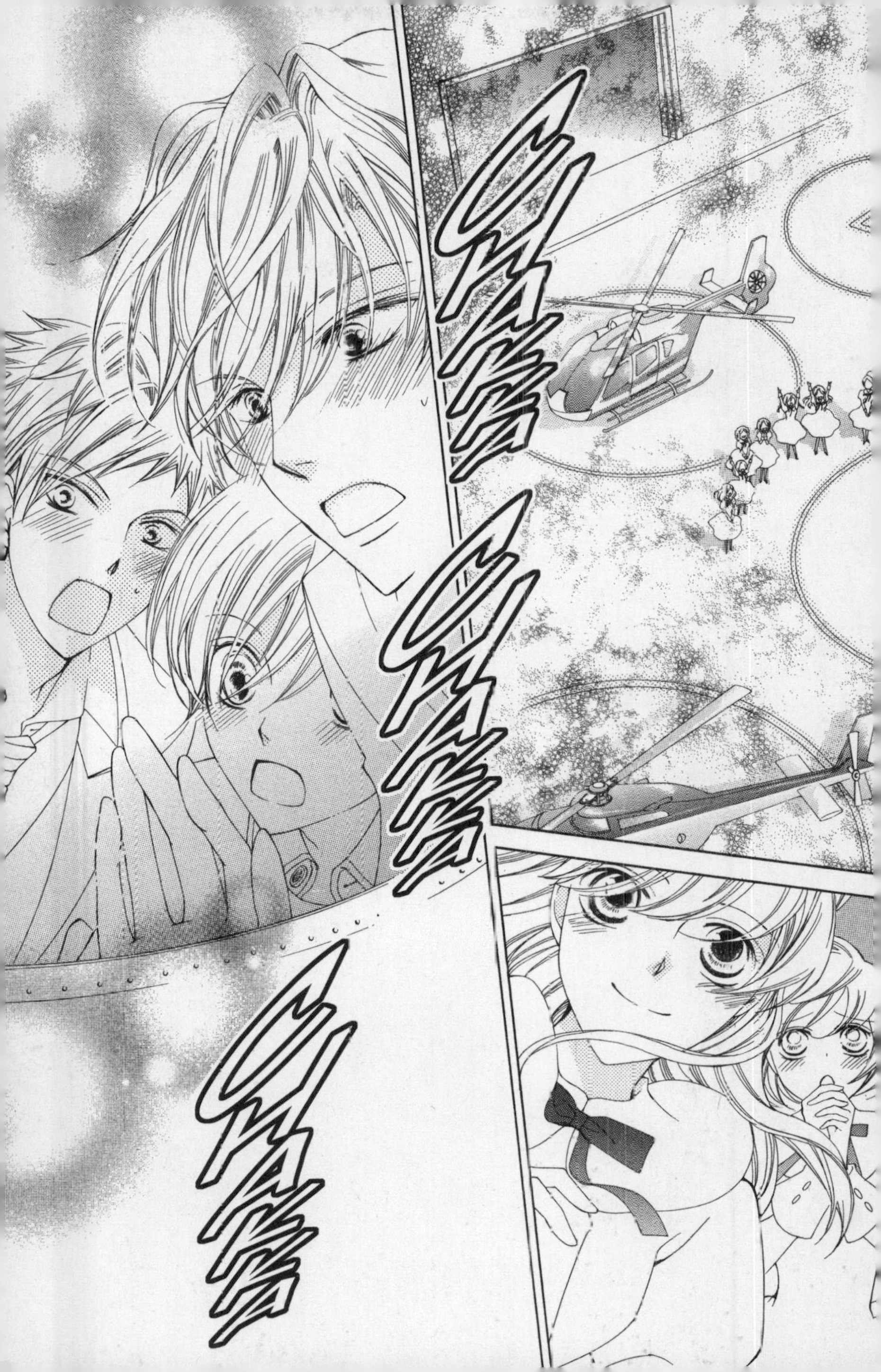

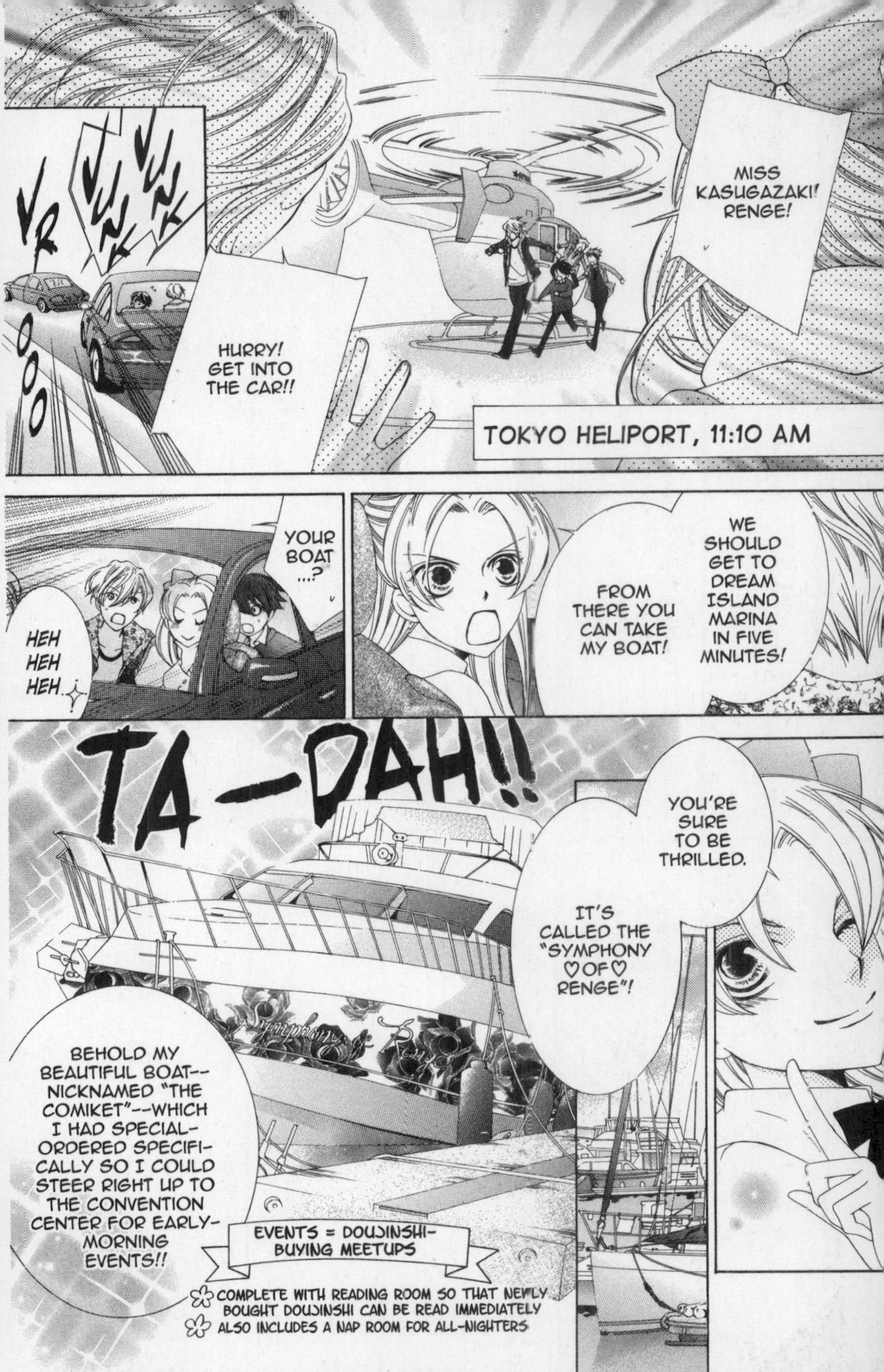
MISS KASUGAZAKI! RENGE!
TOKYO HELIPORT, 11:10 AM
HURRY! GET INTO THE CAR!!
WE SHOULD GET TO DREAM ISLAND MARINA IN FIVE MINUTES!
FROM THERE YOU CAN TAKE MY BOAT!
YOUR BOAT ...?
HEH HEH HEH...
TA-DAH!!
YOU'RE SURE TO BE THRILLED.
IT'S CALLED THE "SYMPHONY ♡OF♡ RENGE"!
BEHOLD MY BEAUTIFUL BOAT--NICKNAMED "THE COMIKET"--WHICH I HAD SPECIAL-ORDERED SPECIFICALLY SO I COULD STEER RIGHT UP TO THE CONVENTION CENTER FOR EARLY-MORNING EVENTS!!
EVENTS = DOUJINSHI-BUYING MEETUPS
COMPLETE WITH READING ROOM SO THAT NEWLY BOUGHT DOUJINSHI CAN BE READ IMMEDIATELY
ALSO INCLUDES A NAP ROOM FOR ALL-NIGHTERS

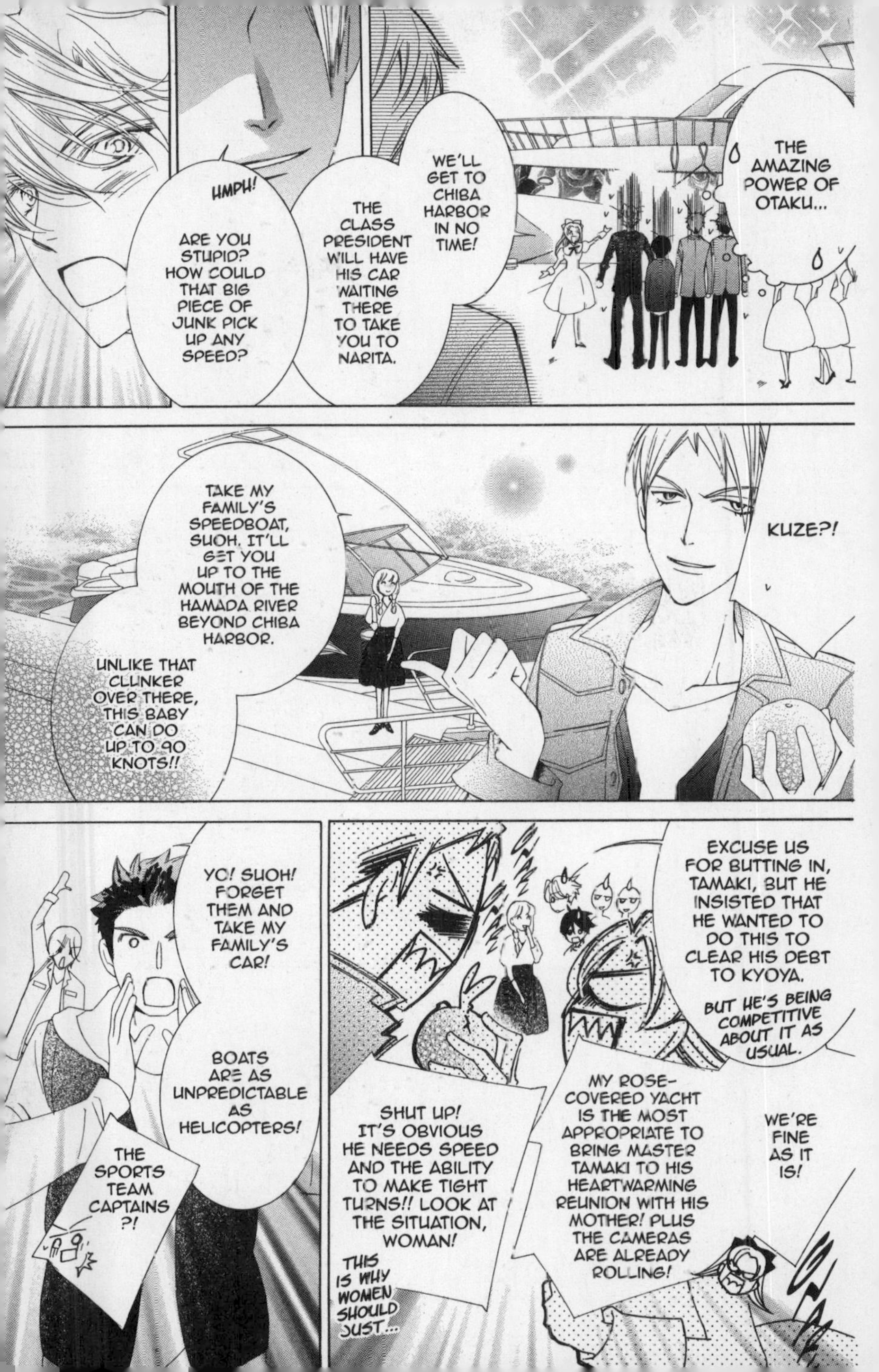
THE AMAZING POWER OF OTAKU...
WE'LL GET TO CHIBA HARBOR IN NO TIME!
THE CLASS PRESIDENT WILL HAVE HIS CAR WAITING THERE TO TAKE YOU TO NARITA.
HMPH!
ARE YOU STUPID? HOW COULD THAT BIG PIECE OF JUNK PICK UP ANY SPEED?
KUZE?!
TAKE MY FAMILY'S SPEEDBOAT, SUOH. IT'LL GET YOU UP TO THE MOUTH OF THE HAMADA RIVER BEYOND CHIBA HARBOR.
UNLIKE THAT CLUNKER OVER THERE, THIS BABY CAN DO UP TO 90 KNOTS!!
EXCUSE US FOR BUTTING IN, TAMAKI, BUT HE INSISTED THAT HE WANTED TO DO THIS TO CLEAR HIS DEBT TO KYOYA.
BUT HE'S BEING COMPETITIVE ABOUT IT AS USUAL.
WE'RE FINE AS IT IS!
MY ROSE-COVERED YACHT IS THE MOST APPROPRIATE TO BRING MASTER TAMAKI TO HIS HEARTWARMING REUNION WITH HIS MOTHER! PLUS THE CAMERAS ARE ALREADY ROLLING!
SHUT UP! IT'S OBVIOUS HE NEEDS SPEED AND THE ABILITY TO MAKE TIGHT TURNS!! LOOK AT THE SITUATION, WOMAN!
THIS IS WHY WOMEN SHOULD JUST...
YO! SUOH! FORGET THEM AND TAKE MY FAMILY'S CAR!
BOATS ARE AS UNPREDICTABLE AS HELICOPTERS!
THE SPORTS TEAM CAPTAINS ?!

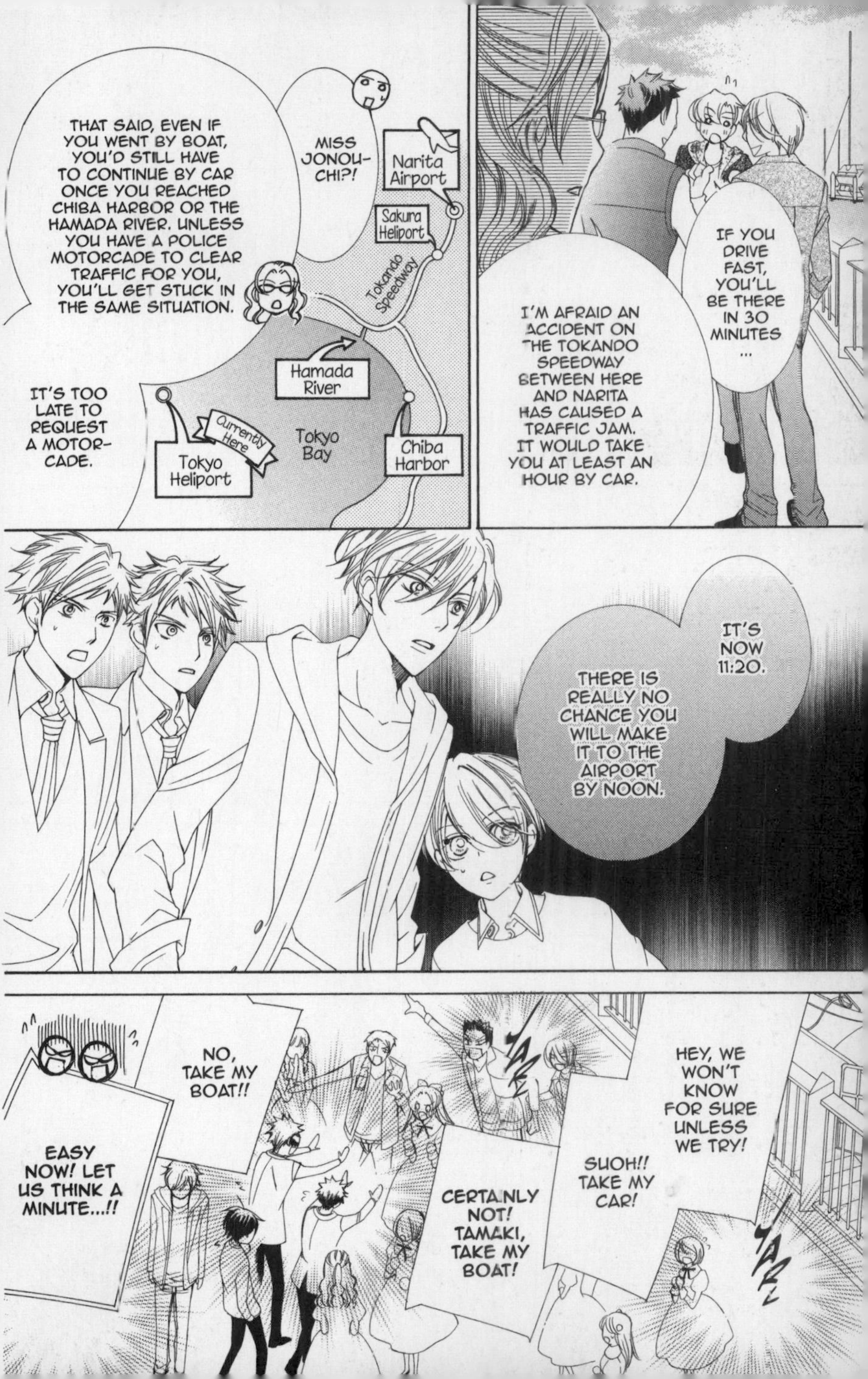
IF YOU DRIVE FAST, YOU'LL BE THERE IN 30 MINUTES ...
I'M AFRAID AN ACCIDENT ON THE TOKANDO SPEEDWAY BETWEEN HERE AND NARITA HAS CAUSED A TRAFFIC JAM. IT WOULD TAKE YOU AT LEAST AN HOUR BY CAR.
MISS JONOUCHI?!
THAT SAID, EVEN IF YOU WENT BY BOAT, YOU'D STILL HAVE TO CONTINUE BY CAR ONCE YOU REACHED CHIBA HARBOR OR THE HAMADA RIVER. UNLESS YOU HAVE A POLICE MOTORCADE TO CLEAR TRAFFIC FOR YOU, YOU'LL GET STUCK IN THE SAME SITUATION.
Narita Airport
Sakura Heliport
Tokando Speedway
Hamada River
Chiba Harbor
Tokyo Bay
Currently Here
Tokyo Heliport
IT'S TOO LATE TO REQUEST A MOTOR-CADE.
IT'S NOW 11:20.
THERE IS REALLY NO CHANCE YOU WILL MAKE IT TO THE AIRPORT BY NOON.
HEY, WE WON'T KNOW FOR SURE UNLESS WE TRY!
SUOH!! TAKE MY CAR!
CERTAINLY NOT! TAMAKI, TAKE MY BOAT!
NO, TAKE MY BOAT!!
EASY NOW! LET US THINK A MINUTE...!!

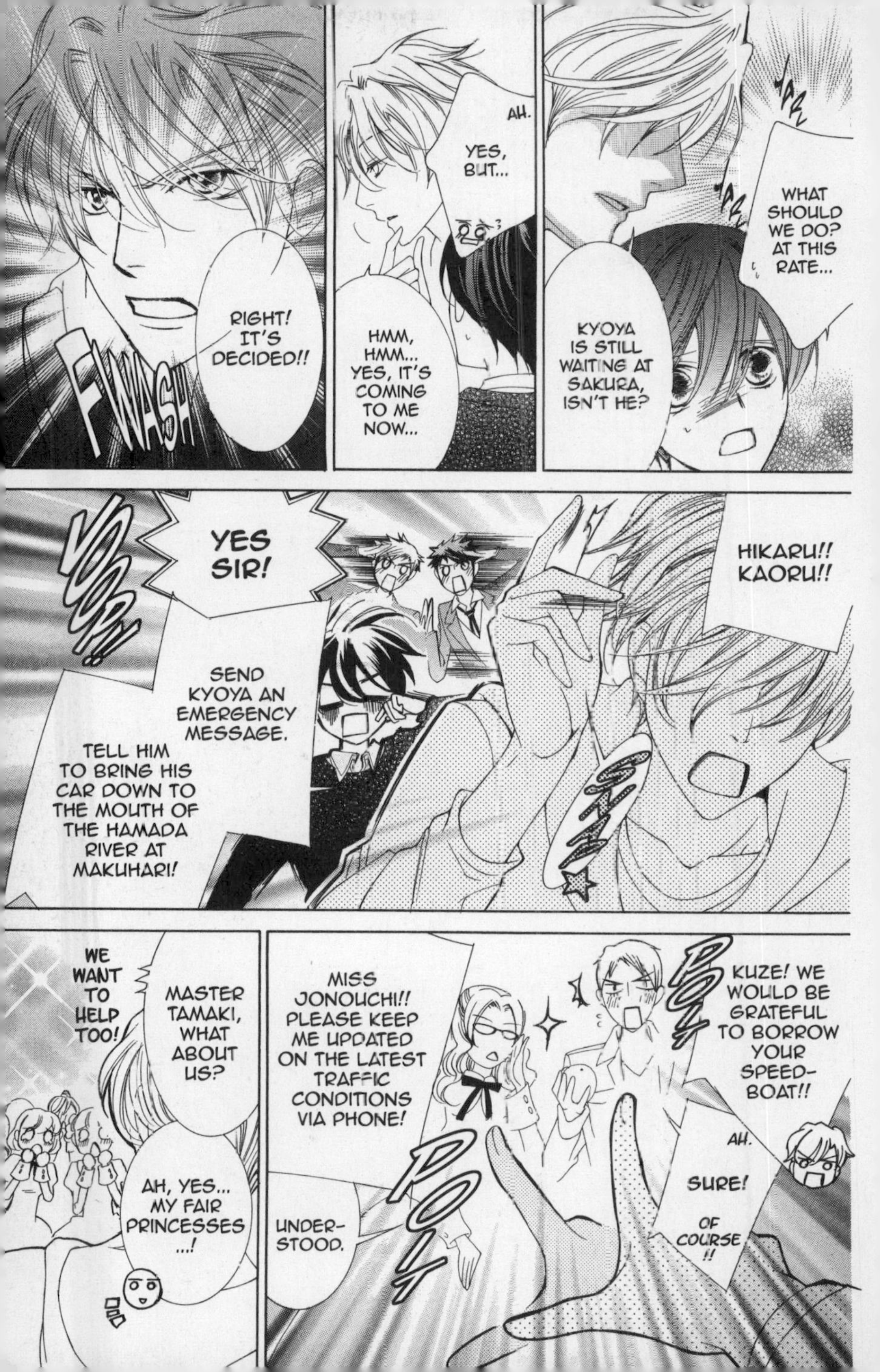
WHAT SHOULD WE DO? AT THIS RATE...
KYOYA IS STILL WAITING AT SAKURA, ISN'T HE?
AH.
YES, BUT...
HMM, HMM... YES, IT'S COMING TO ME NOW...
RIGHT! IT'S DECIDED!!
FWASH
HIKARU!! KAORU!!
YES SIR!
SEND KYOYA AN EMERGENCY MESSAGE.
TELL HIM TO BRING HIS CAR DOWN TO THE MOUTH OF THE HAMADA RIVER AT MAKUHARI!
VOOM!!
KUZE! WE WOULD BE GRATEFUL TO BORROW YOUR SPEED-BOAT!!
AH.
SURE!
OF COURSE!!
MISS JONOUCHI!! PLEASE KEEP ME UPDATED ON THE LATEST TRAFFIC CONDITIONS VIA PHONE!
UNDER-STOOD.
MASTER TAMAKI, WHAT ABOUT US?
WE WANT TO HELP TOO!
AH, YES... MY FAIR PRINCESSES ...!

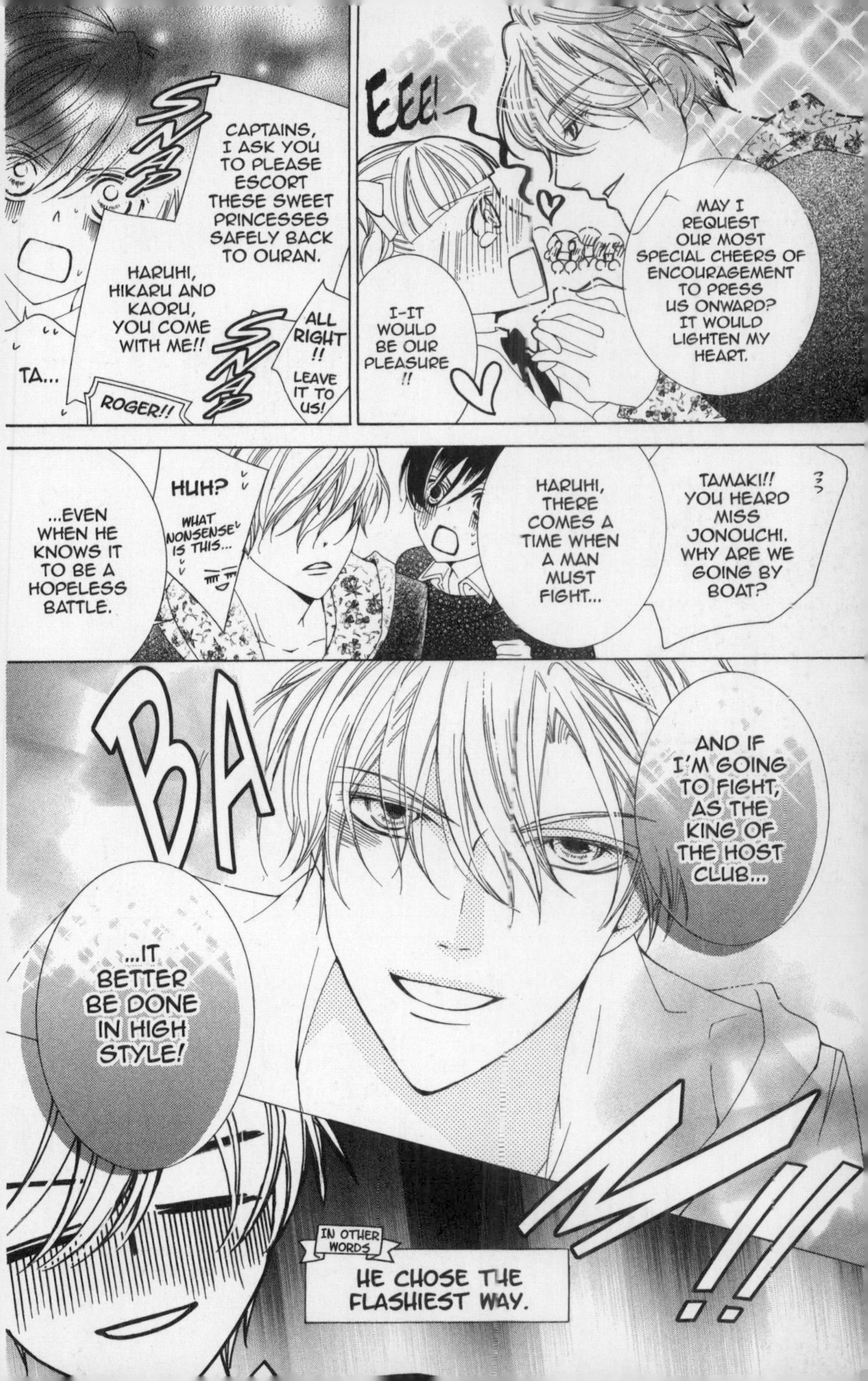
EEE!
MAY I REQUEST OUR MOST SPECIAL CHEERS OF ENCOURAGEMENT TO PRESS US ONWARD? IT WOULD LIGHTEN MY HEART.
I-IT WOULD BE OUR PLEASURE!!
CAPTAINS, I ASK YOU TO PLEASE ESCORT THESE SWEET PRINCESSES SAFELY BACK TO OURAN.
SNAP
ALL RIGHT!! LEAVE IT TO US!
HARUHI, HIKARU AND KAORU, YOU COME WITH ME!!
SNAP
ROGER!!
TA...
TAMAKI!! YOU HEARD MISS JONOUCHI. WHY ARE WE GOING BY BOAT?
HARUHI, THERE COMES A TIME WHEN A MAN MUST FIGHT...
HUH?
WHAT NONSENSE IS THIS...
...EVEN WHEN HE KNOWS IT TO BE A HOPELESS BATTLE.
AND IF I'M GOING TO FIGHT, AS THE KING OF THE HOST CLUB...
BA
...IT BETTER BE DONE IN HIGH STYLE!
M!!
IN OTHER WORDS
HE CHOSE THE FLASHIEST WAY.

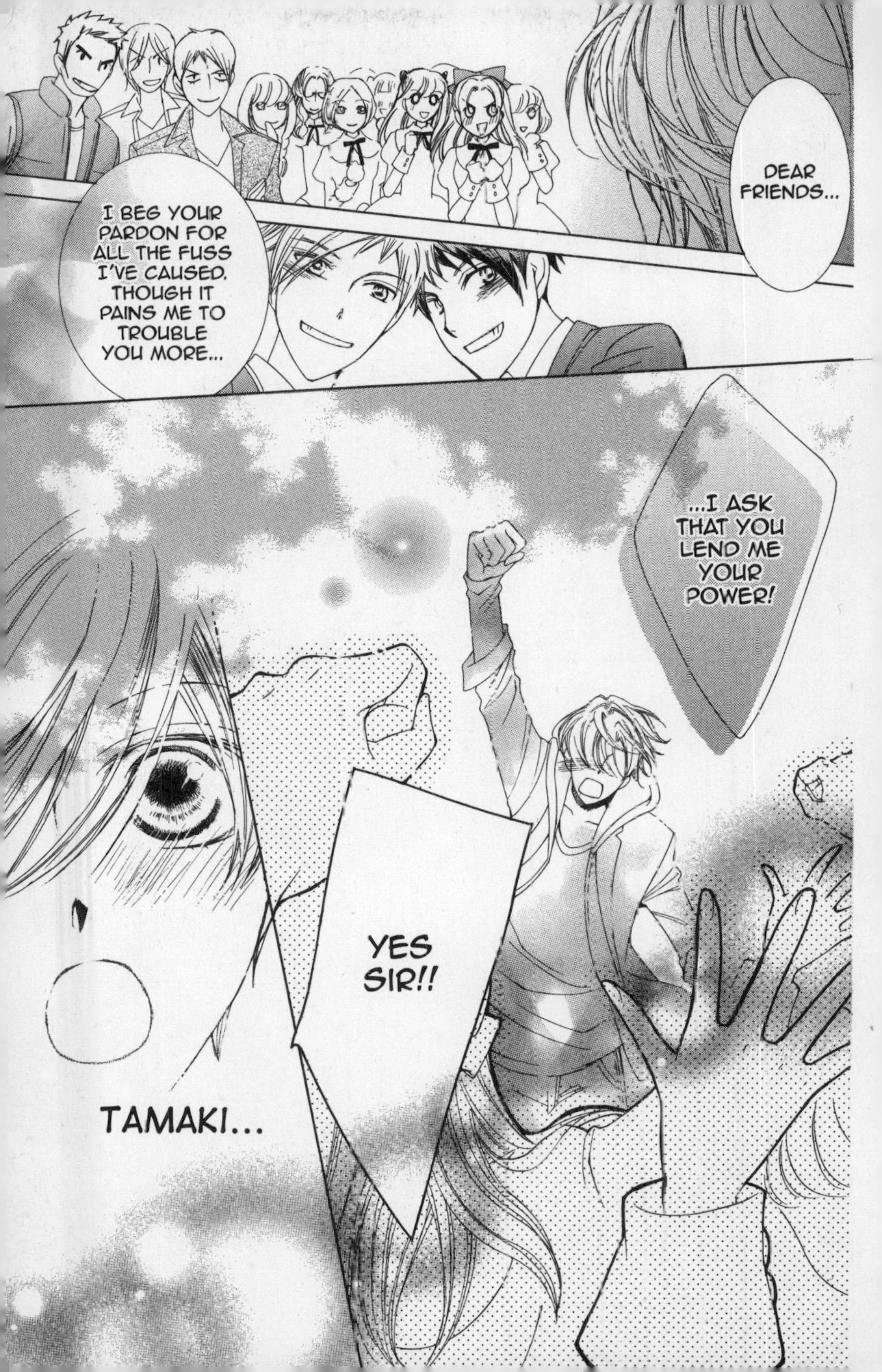
DEAR FRIENDS...
I BEG YOUR PARDON FOR ALL THE FUSS I'VE CAUSED. THOUGH IT PAINS ME TO TROUBLE YOU MORE...
...I ASK THAT YOU LEND ME YOUR POWER!
YES SIR!!
TAMAKI...

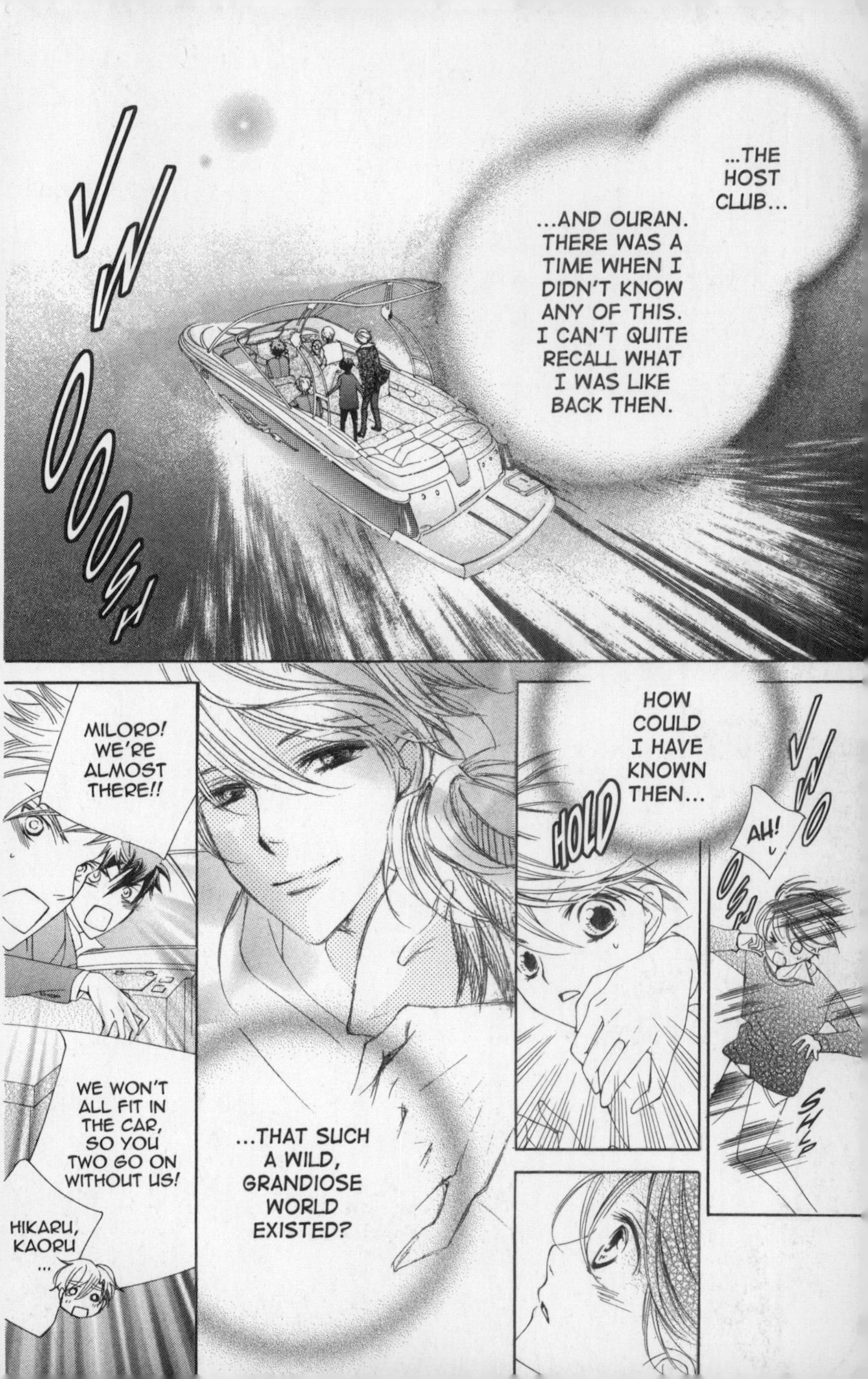
VWOOOOOSH
...THE HOST CLUB...
...AND OURAN. THERE WAS A TIME WHEN I DIDN'T KNOW ANY OF THIS. I CAN'T QUITE RECALL WHAT I WAS LIKE BACK THEN.
AH!
HOW COULD I HAVE KNOWN THEN...
HOLD
...THAT SUCH A WILD, GRANDIOSE WORLD EXISTED?
MILORD! WE'RE ALMOST THERE!!
WE WON'T ALL FIT IN THE CAR, SO YOU TWO GO ON WITHOUT US!
HIKARU, KAORU ...

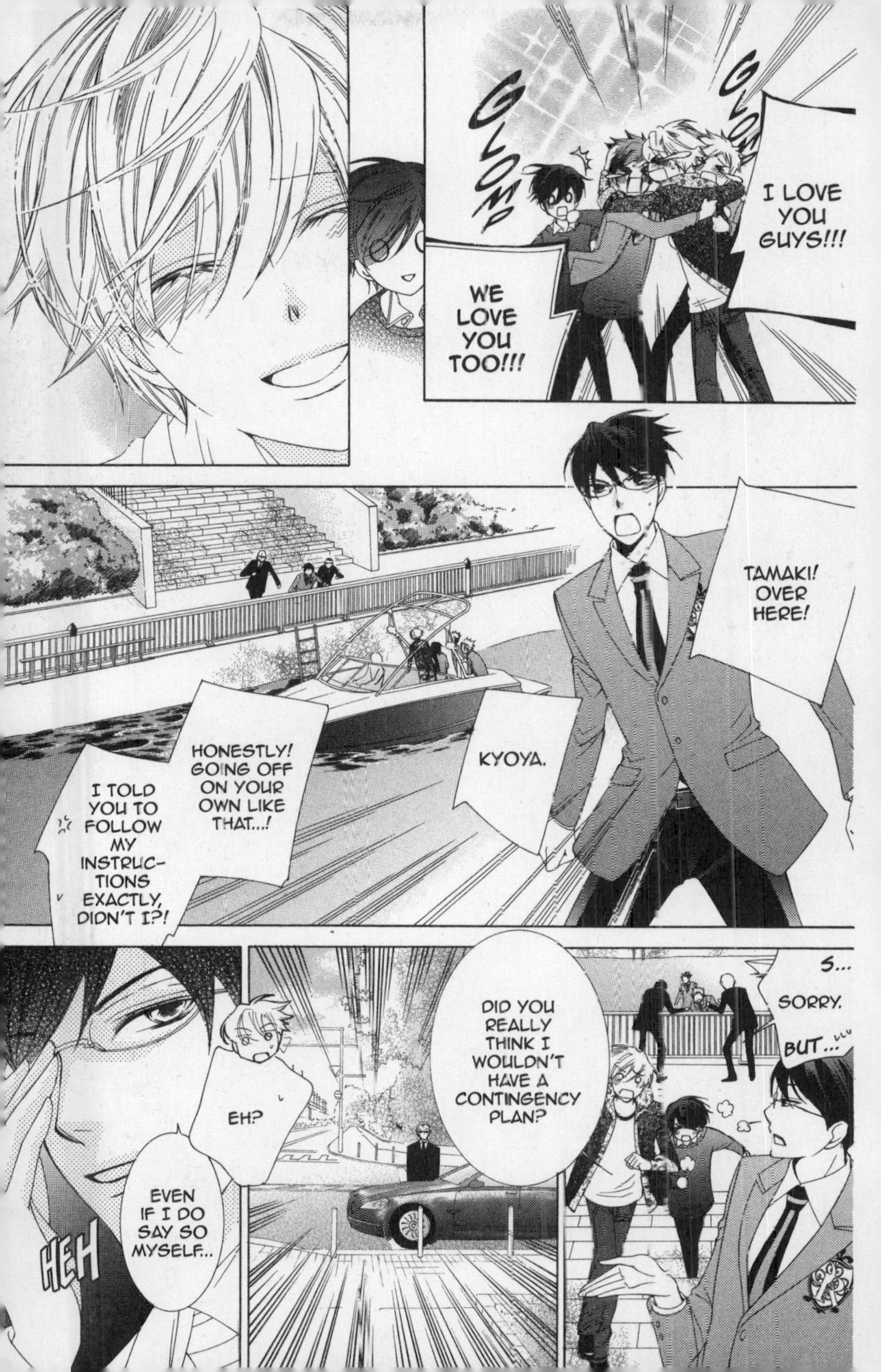
GLOMP
I LOVE YOU GUYS!!!
WE LOVE YOU TOO!!!
TAMAKI! OVER HERE!
KYOYA.
HONESTLY! GOING OFF ON YOUR OWN LIKE THAT...!
I TOLD YOU TO FOLLOW MY INSTRUCTIONS EXACTLY, DIDN'T I?!
S... SORRY.
BUT...
DID YOU REALLY THINK I WOULDN'T HAVE A CONTINGENCY PLAN?
EH?
EVEN IF I DO SAY SO MYSELF...
HEH

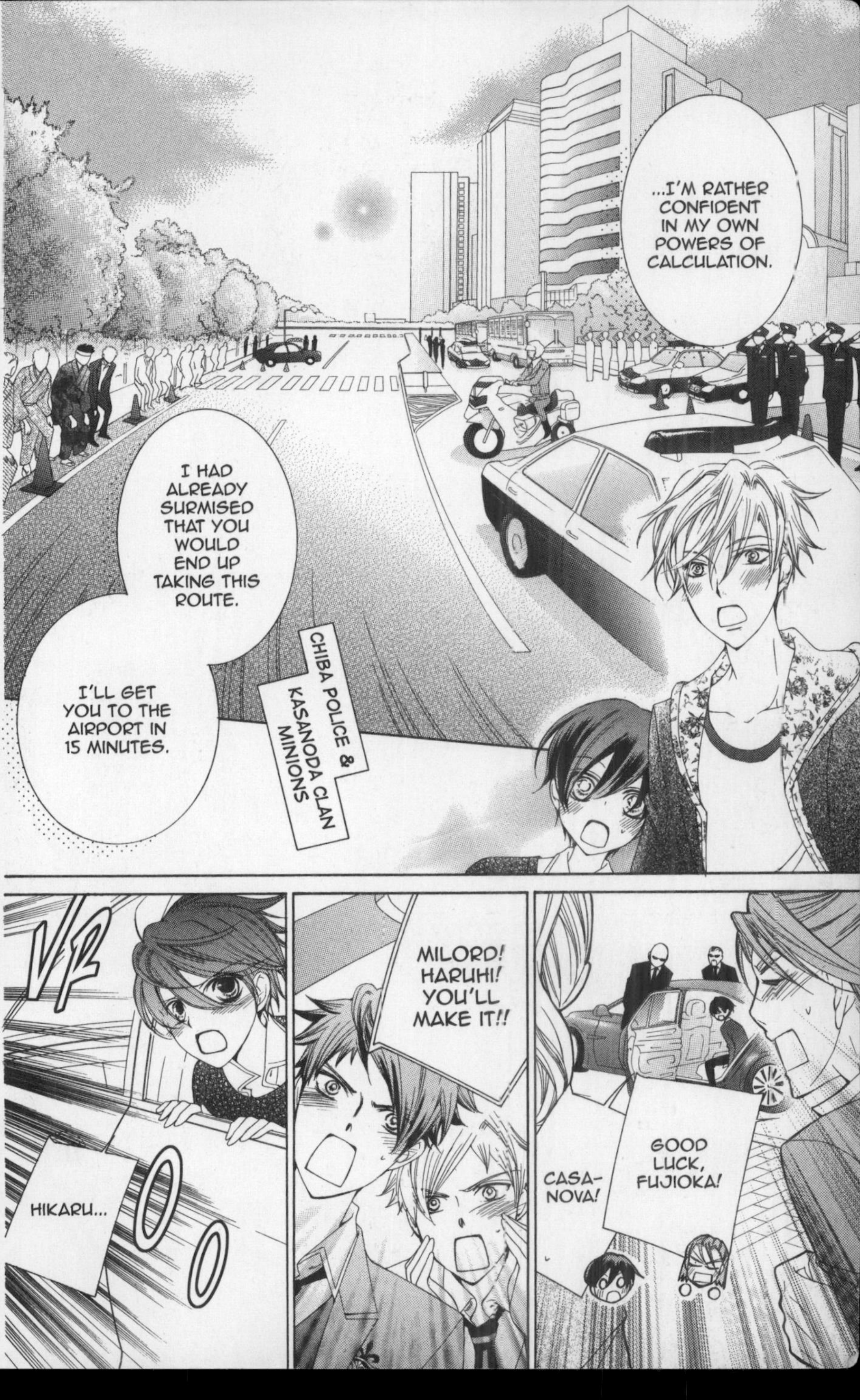
...I'M RATHER CONFIDENT IN MY OWN POWERS OF CALCULATION.
I HAD ALREADY SURMISED THAT YOU WOULD END UP TAKING THIS ROUTE.
CHIBA POLICE & KASANODA CLAN MINIONS
I'LL GET YOU TO THE AIRPORT IN 15 MINUTES.
GOOD LUCK, FUJIOKA!
CASA-NOVA!
MILORD! HARUHI! YOU'LL MAKE IT!!
HIKARU...

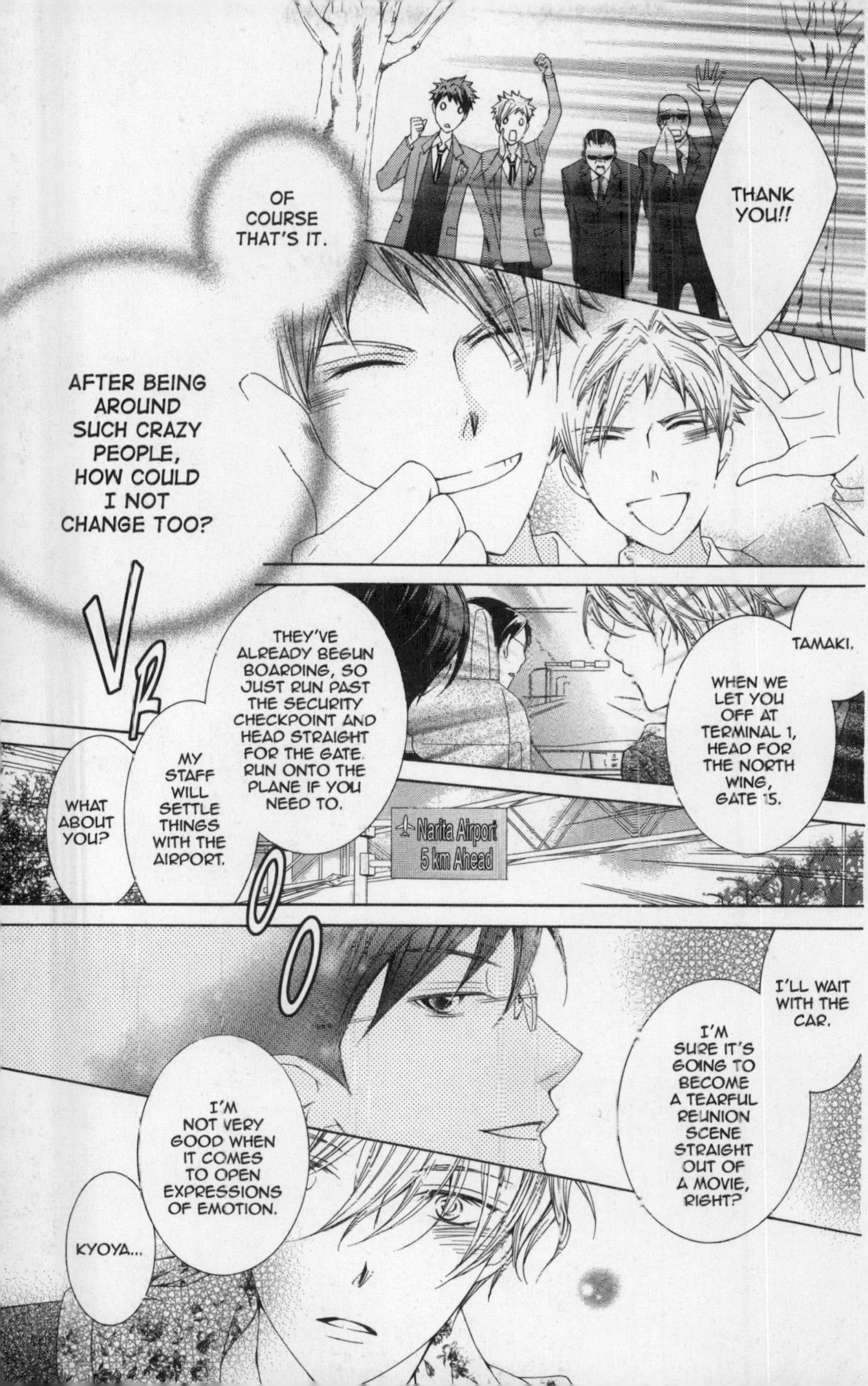
THANK YOU!!
OF COURSE THAT'S IT.
AFTER BEING AROUND SUCH CRAZY PEOPLE, HOW COULD I NOT CHANGE TOO?
TAMAKI.
WHEN WE LET YOU OFF AT TERMINAL 1, HEAD FOR THE NORTH WING, GATE 15.
THEY'VE ALREADY BEGUN BOARDING, SO JUST RUN PAST THE SECURITY CHECKPOINT AND HEAD STRAIGHT FOR THE GATE. RUN ONTO THE PLANE IF YOU NEED TO.
Narita Airport 5 km Ahead
MY STAFF WILL SETTLE THINGS WITH THE AIRPORT.
WHAT ABOUT YOU?
VROO
I'LL WAIT WITH THE CAR.
I'M SURE IT'S GOING TO BECOME A TEARFUL REUNION SCENE STRAIGHT OUT OF A MOVIE, RIGHT?
I'M NOT VERY GOOD WHEN IT COMES TO OPEN EXPRESSIONS OF EMOTION.
KYOYA...

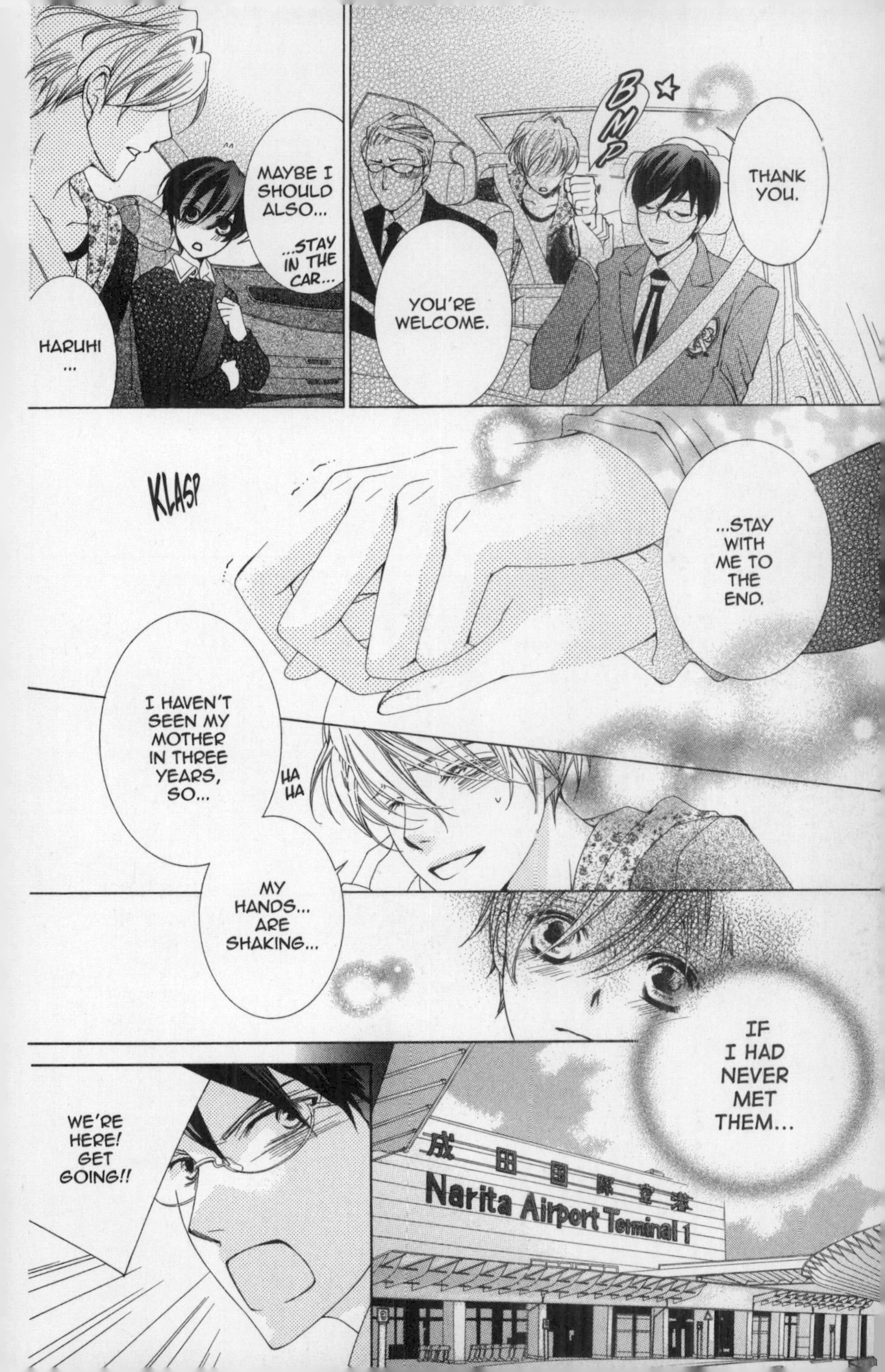
THANK YOU.
BMP
YOU'RE WELCOME.
MAYBE I SHOULD ALSO...
...STAY IN THE CAR...
HARUHI ...
...STAY WITH ME TO THE END.
KLASP
I HAVEN'T SEEN MY MOTHER IN THREE YEARS, SO...
HA HA
MY HANDS... ARE SHAKING...
IF I HAD NEVER MET THEM...
成田国際空港
Narita Airport Terminal 1
WE'RE HERE! GET GOING!!

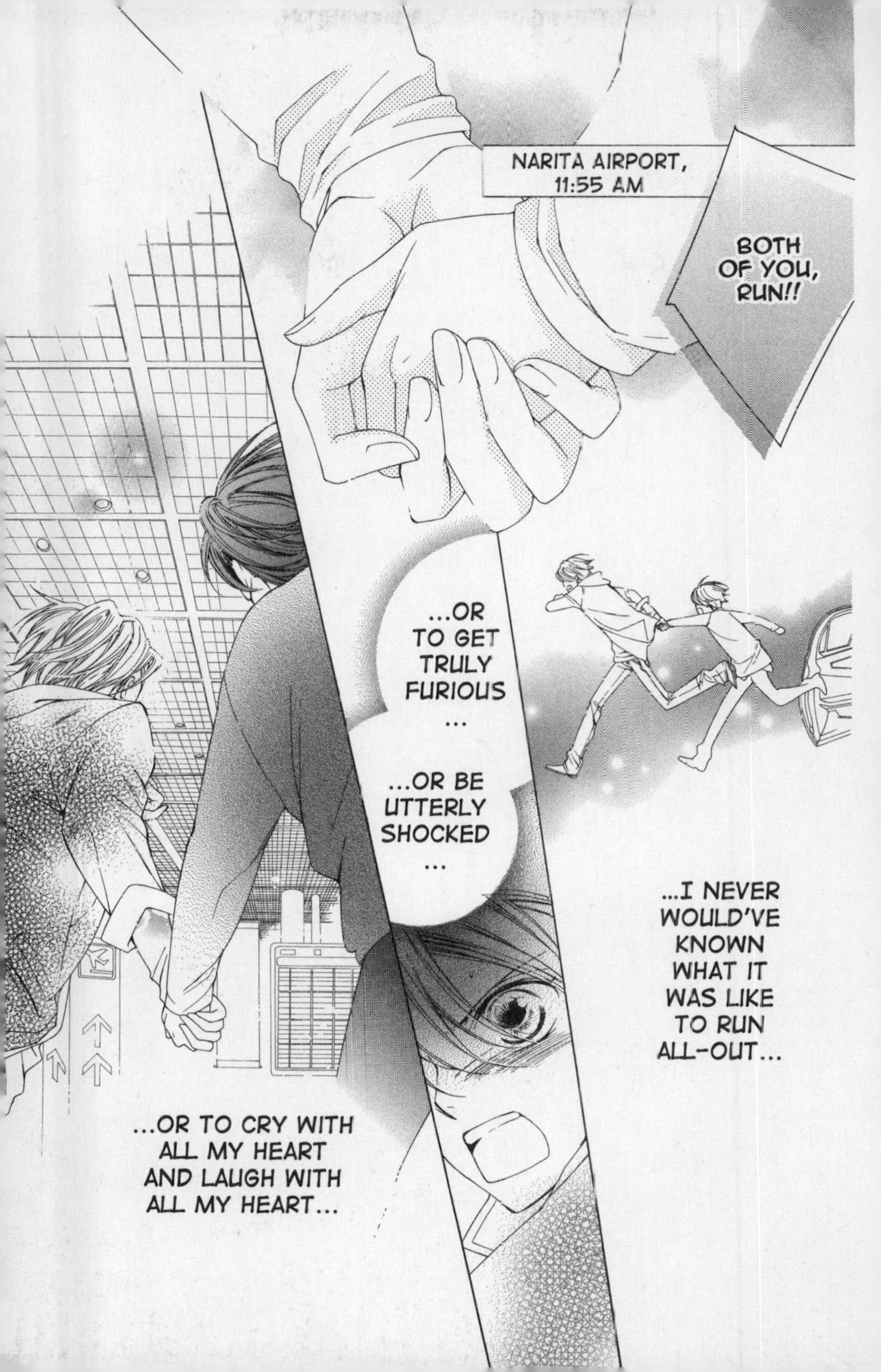
NARITA AIRPORT, 11:55 AM
BOTH OF YOU, RUN!!
...I NEVER WOULD'VE KNOWN WHAT IT WAS LIKE TO RUN ALL-OUT...
...OR TO GET TRULY FURIOUS ...
...OR BE UTTERLY SHOCKED ...
...OR TO CRY WITH ALL MY HEART AND LAUGH WITH ALL MY HEART...

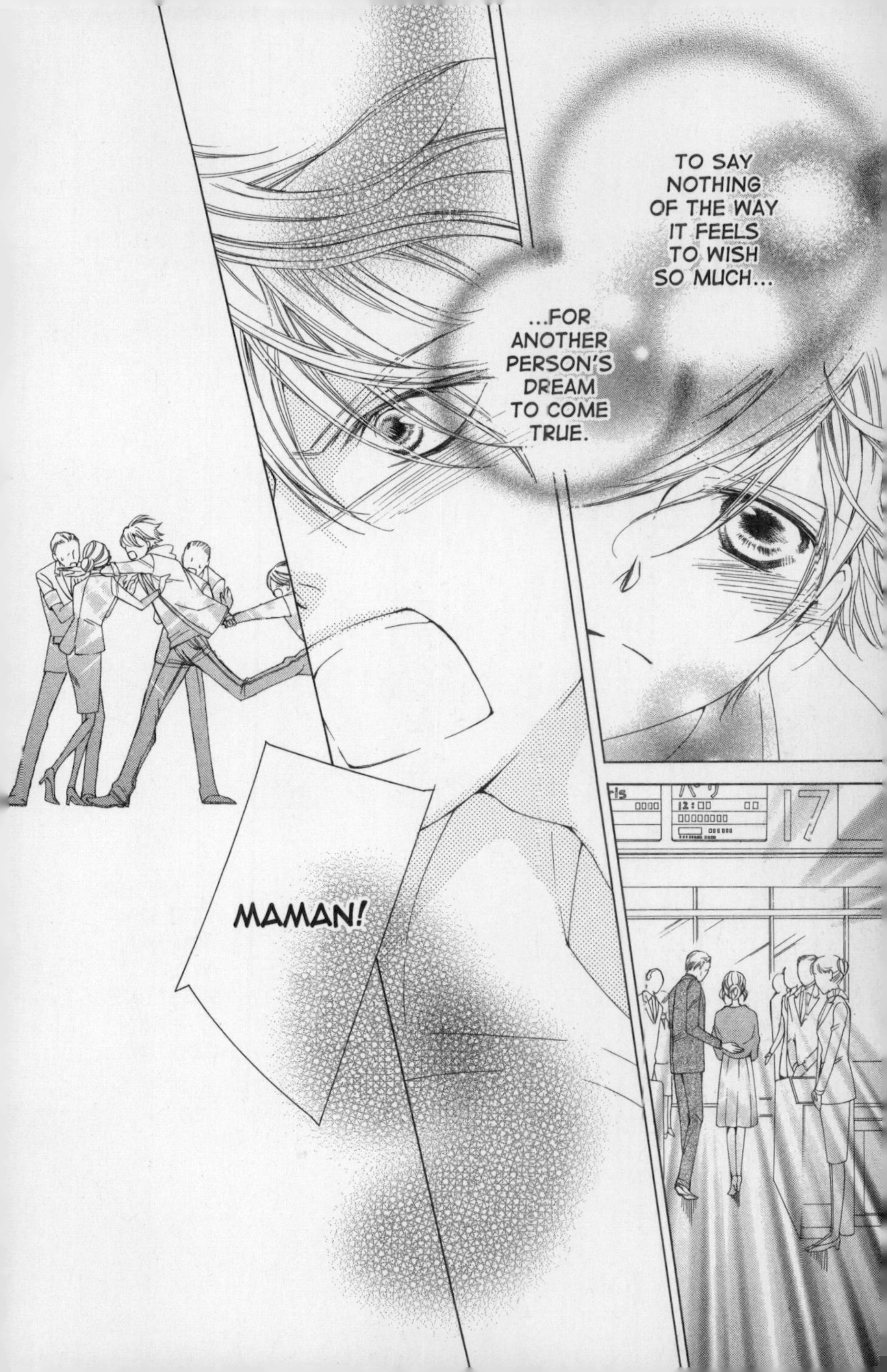
TO SAY NOTHING OF THE WAY IT FEELS TO WISH SO MUCH...
...FOR ANOTHER PERSON'S DREAM TO COME TRUE.
MAMAN!

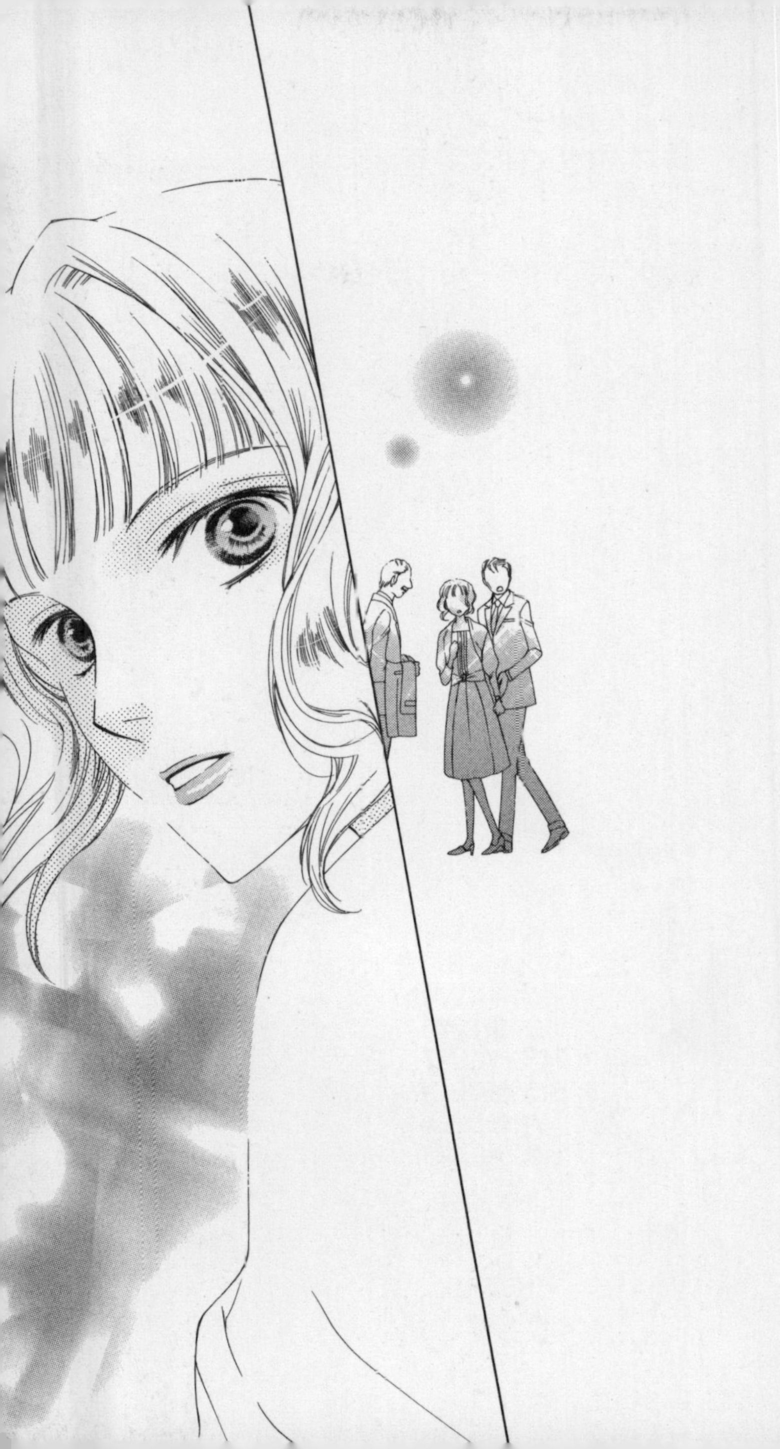

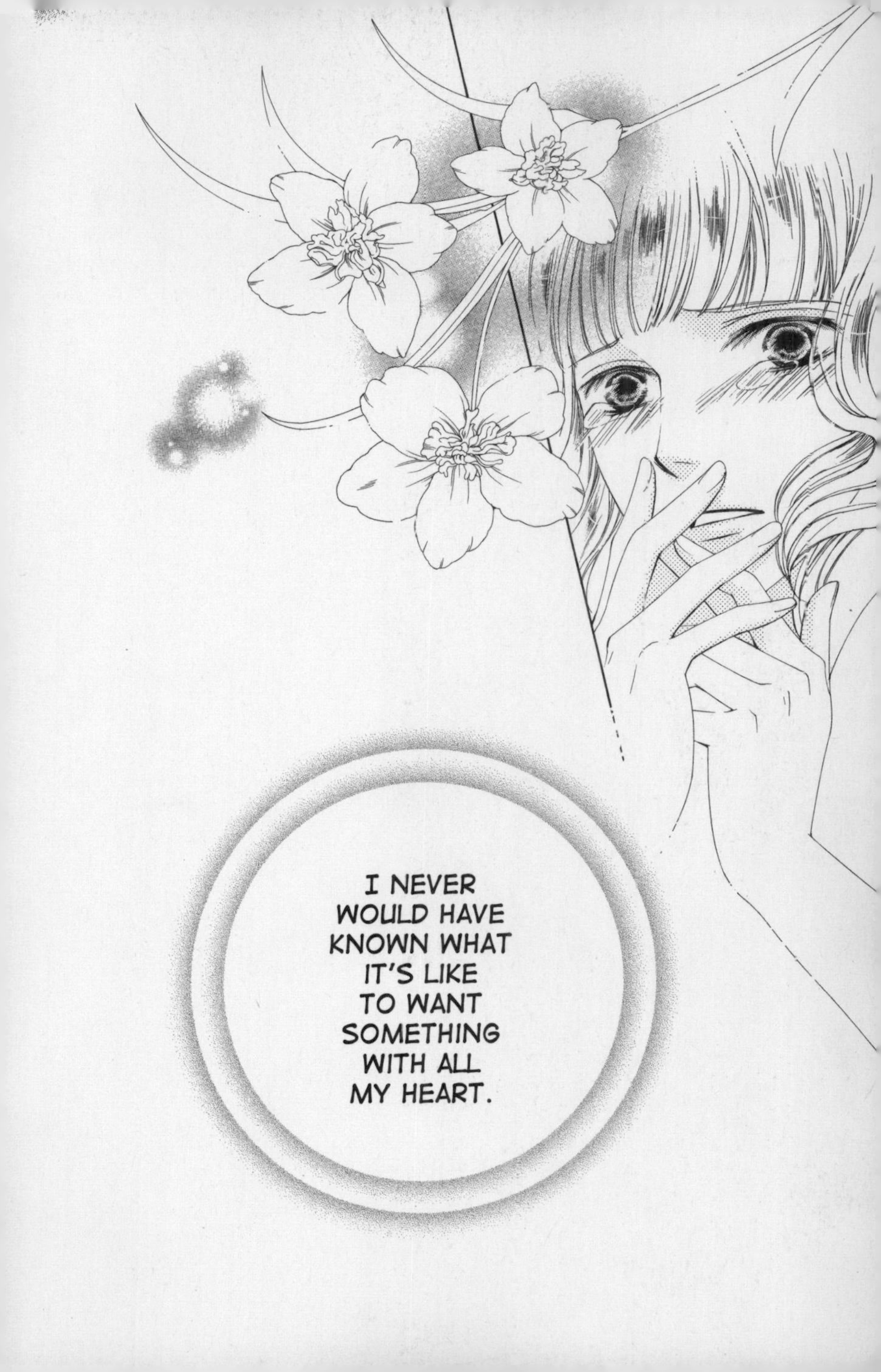
I NEVER WOULD HAVE KNOWN WHAT IT'S LIKE TO WANT SOMETHING WITH ALL MY HEART.

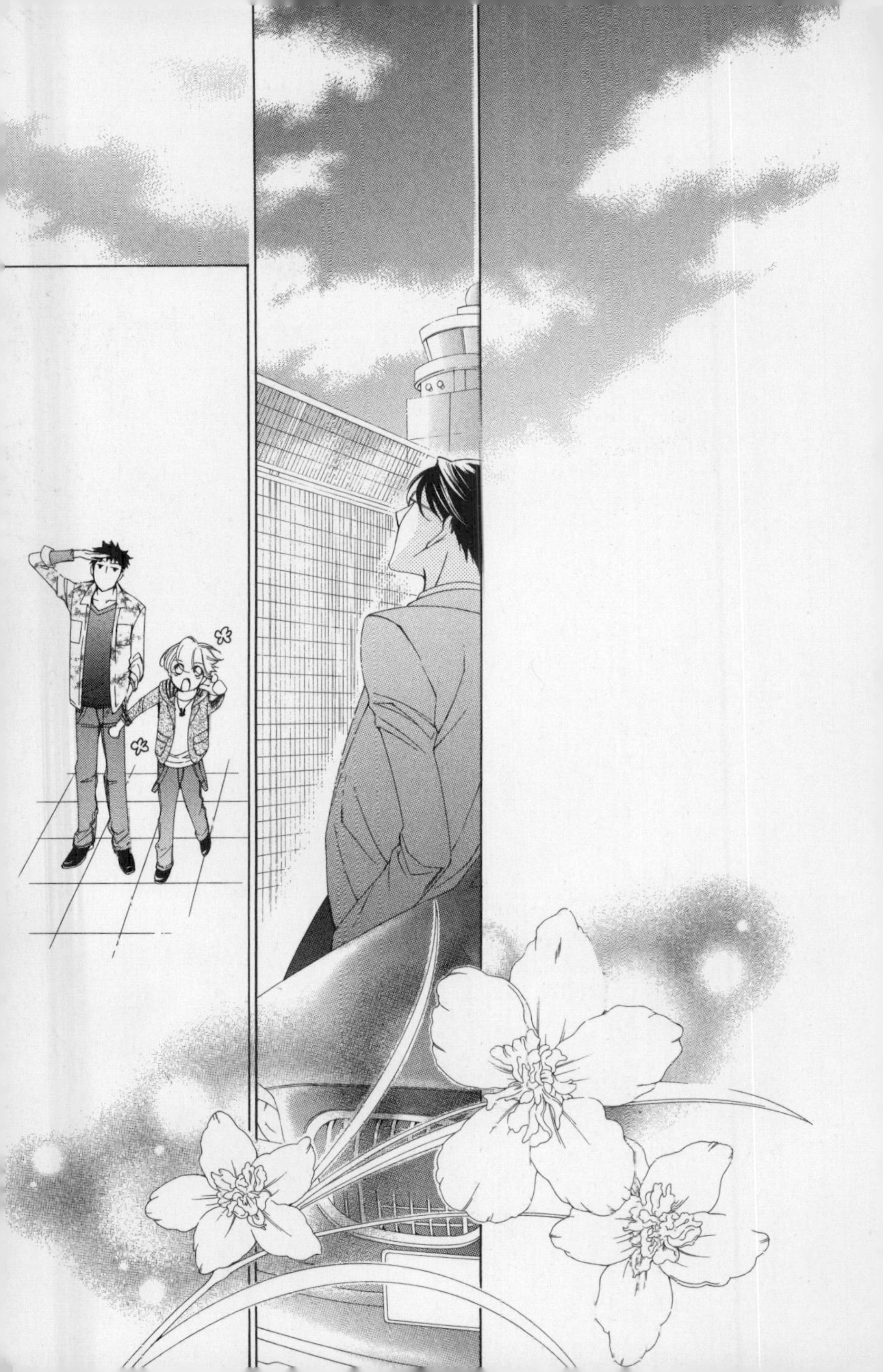

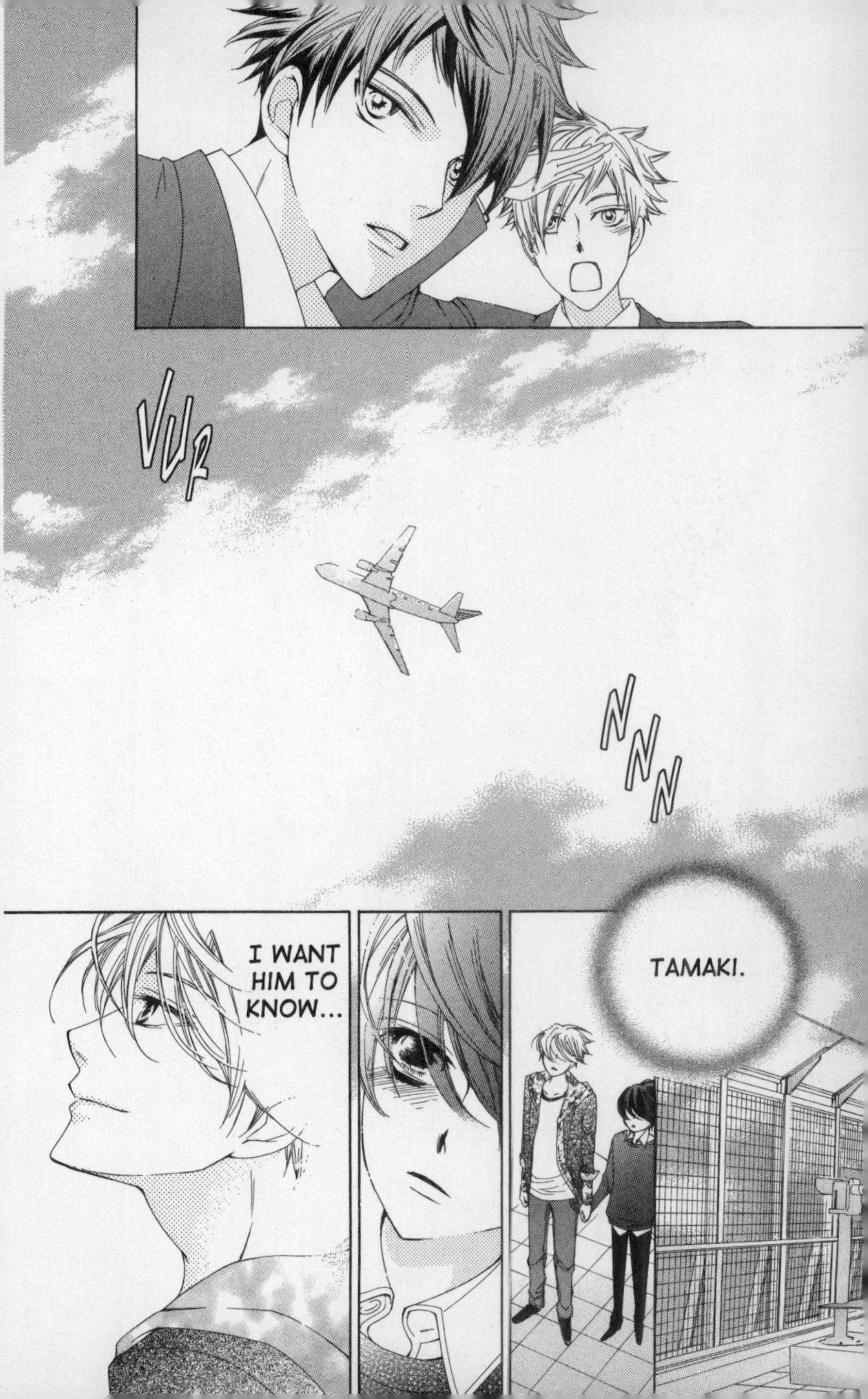
VVR
NNN
TAMAKI.
I WANT HIM TO KNOW...

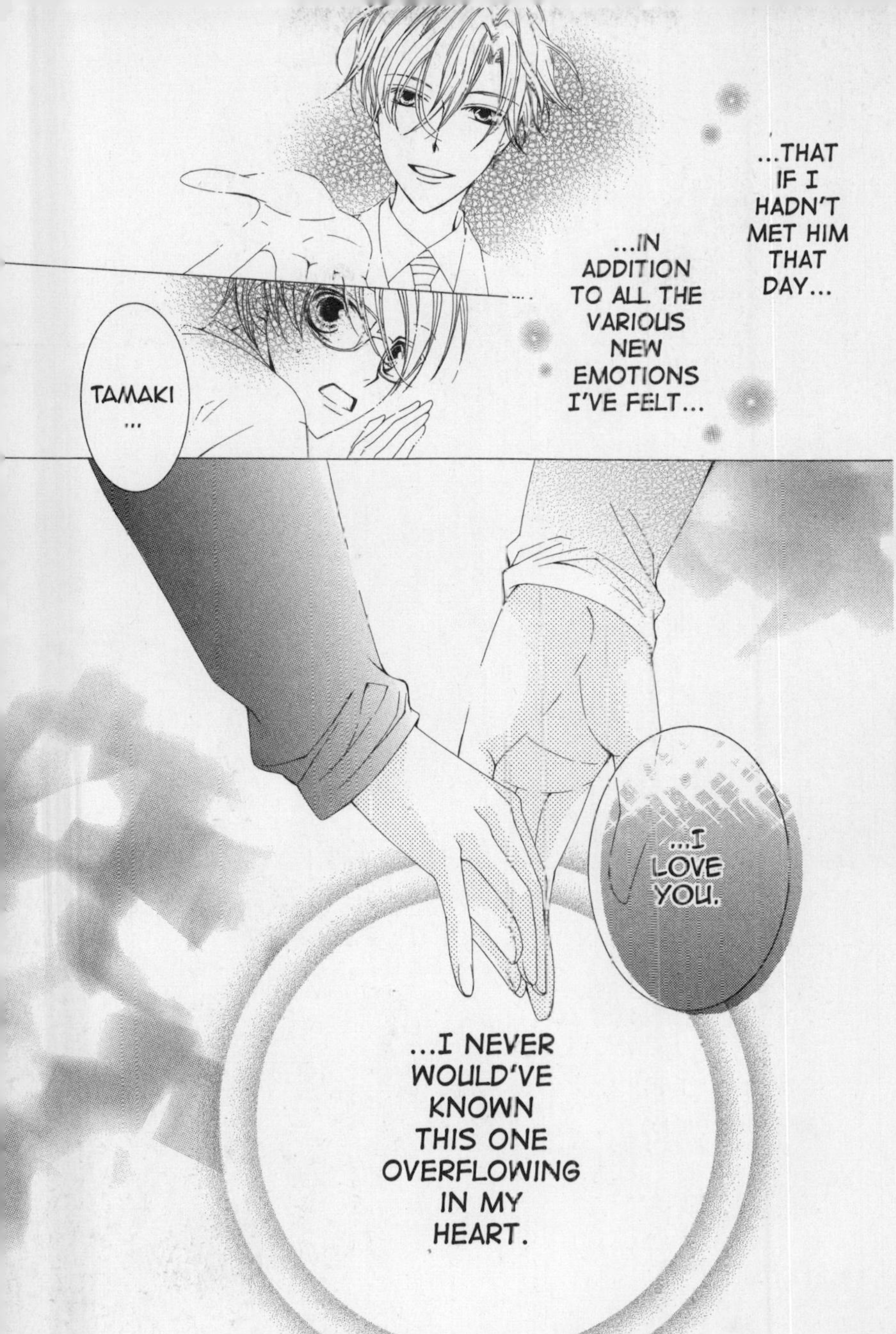
...THAT IF I HADN'T MET HIM THAT DAY...
...IN ADDITION TO ALL THE VARIOUS NEW EMOTIONS I'VE FELT...
TAMAKI ...
...I LOVE YOU.
...I NEVER WOULD'VE KNOWN THIS ONE OVERFLOWING IN MY HEART.

OURAN HIGH SCHOOL HOST CLUB, VOL. 17/THE END

EGOISTIC CLUB

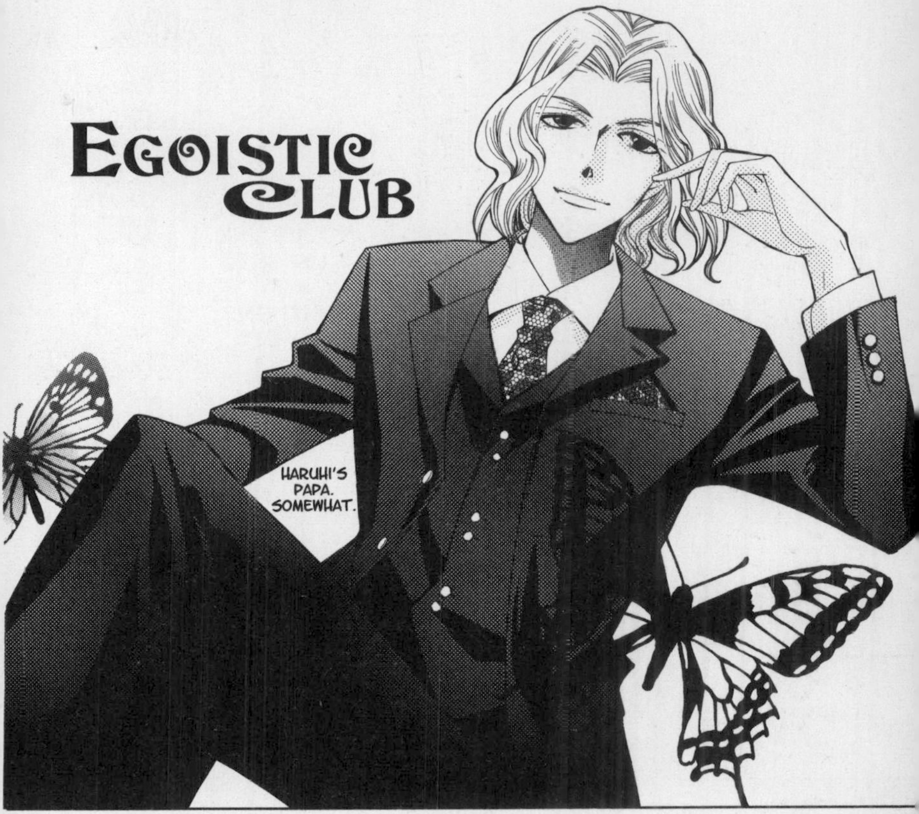
HARUHI'S PAPA. SOMEWHAT.

THANK YOU SO MUCH TO ALL YOU WHO HAVE READ ALONG THIS FAR!! YOU MUST BE WORN OUT!

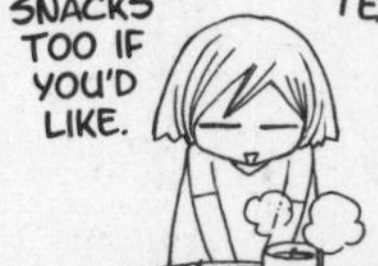
HERE, HAVE SOME TEA...
I HAVE SOME SNACKS TOO IF YOU'D LIKE.

IT SEEMS THAT *HOST CLUB* IS FINALLY REACHING THE BIG "AT LAST! COULD IT REALLY BE?!" AND "IT'S ABOUT TIME!" PARTS IN THE PLOT.

I DO MAKE AS MUCH USE OF THE JAPANESE LANGUAGE'S AMBIGUITY AS POSSIBLE, DON'T I?

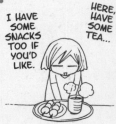

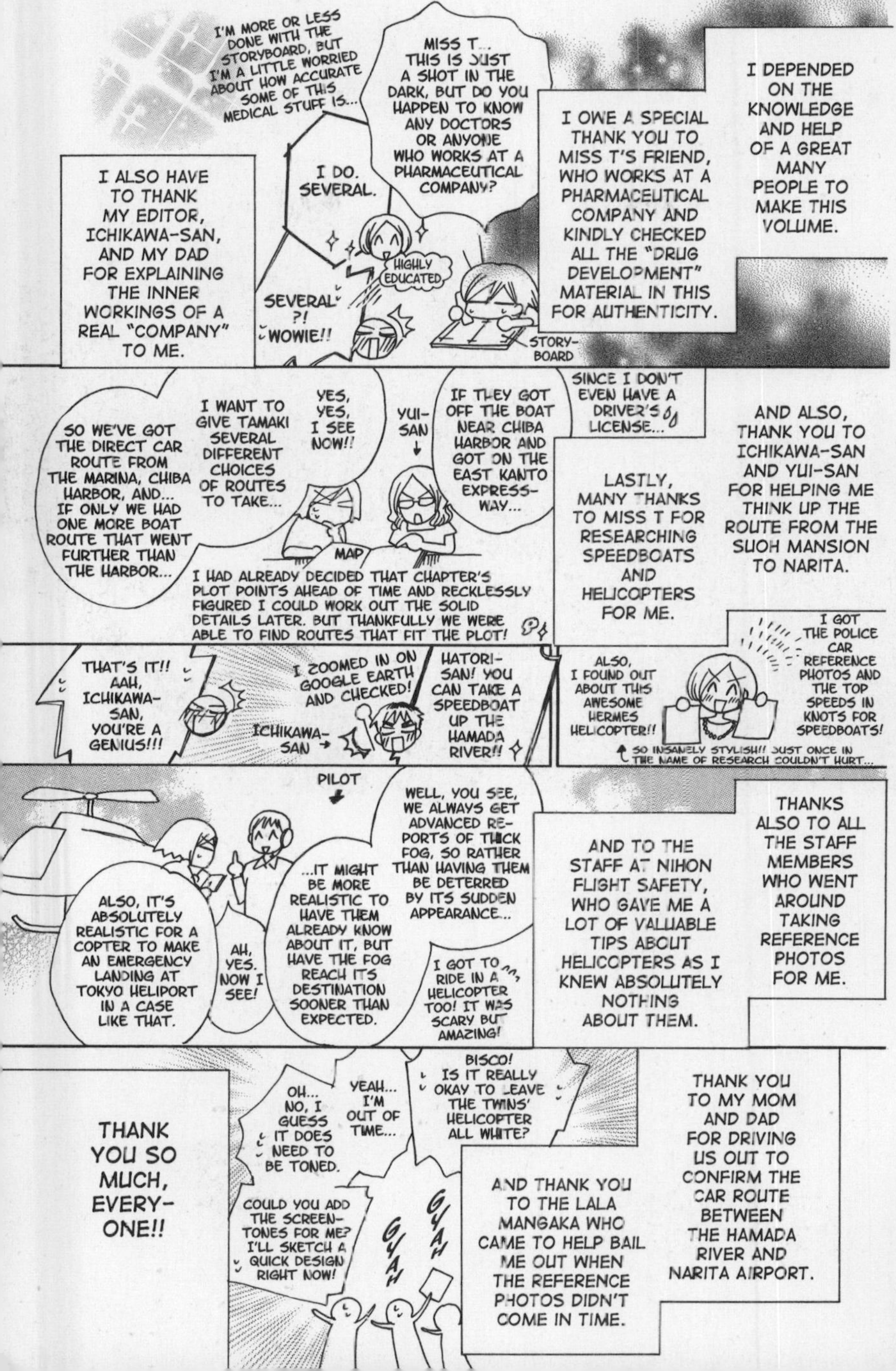
I DEPENDED ON THE KNOWLEDGE AND HELP OF A GREAT MANY PEOPLE TO MAKE THIS VOLUME.
I OWE A SPECIAL THANK YOU TO MISS T'S FRIEND, WHO WORKS AT A PHARMACEUTICAL COMPANY AND KINDLY CHECKED ALL THE "DRUG DEVELOPMENT" MATERIAL IN THIS FOR AUTHENTICITY.
I'M MORE OR LESS DONE WITH THE STORYBOARD, BUT I'M A LITTLE WORRIED ABOUT HOW ACCURATE SOME OF THIS MEDICAL STUFF IS...
MISS T... THIS IS JUST A SHOT IN THE DARK, BUT DO YOU HAPPEN TO KNOW ANY DOCTORS OR ANYONE WHO WORKS AT A PHARMACEUTICAL COMPANY?
I DO. SEVERAL.
HIGHLY EDUCATED
STORY-BOARD
SEVERAL?! WOWIE!!
I ALSO HAVE TO THANK MY EDITOR, ICHIKAWA-SAN, AND MY DAD FOR EXPLAINING THE INNER WORKINGS OF A REAL "COMPANY" TO ME.
AND ALSO, THANK YOU TO ICHIKAWA-SAN AND YUI-SAN FOR HELPING ME THINK UP THE ROUTE FROM THE SUOH MANSION TO NARITA.
SINCE I DON'T EVEN HAVE A DRIVER'S LICENSE...
LASTLY, MANY THANKS TO MISS T FOR RESEARCHING SPEEDBOATS AND HELICOPTERS FOR ME.
IF THEY GOT OFF THE BOAT NEAR CHIBA HARBOR AND GOT ON THE EAST KANTO EXPRESS-WAY...
YUI-SAN
YES, YES, I SEE NOW!!
I WANT TO GIVE TAMAKI SEVERAL DIFFERENT CHOICES OF ROUTES TO TAKE...
SO WE'VE GOT THE DIRECT CAR ROUTE FROM THE MARINA, CHIBA HARBOR, AND... IF ONLY WE HAD ONE MORE BOAT ROUTE THAT WENT FURTHER THAN THE HARBOR...
MAP
I HAD ALREADY DECIDED THAT CHAPTER'S PLOT POINTS AHEAD OF TIME AND RECKLESSLY FIGURED I COULD WORK OUT THE SOLID DETAILS LATER. BUT THANKFULLY WE WERE ABLE TO FIND ROUTES THAT FIT THE PLOT!
I GOT THE POLICE CAR REFERENCE PHOTOS AND THE TOP SPEEDS IN KNOTS FOR SPEEDBOATS!
ALSO, I FOUND OUT ABOUT THIS AWESOME HERMES HELICOPTER!!
SO INSANELY STYLISH!! JUST ONCE IN THE NAME OF RESEARCH COULDN'T HURT...
HATORI-SAN! YOU CAN TAKE A SPEEDBOAT UP THE HAMADA RIVER!!
I ZOOMED IN ON GOOGLE EARTH AND CHECKED!
ICHIKAWA-SAN
THAT'S IT!! AAH, ICHIKAWA-SAN, YOU'RE A GENIUS!!!
THANKS ALSO TO ALL THE STAFF MEMBERS WHO WENT AROUND TAKING REFERENCE PHOTOS FOR ME.
AND TO THE STAFF AT NIHON FLIGHT SAFETY, WHO GAVE ME A LOT OF VALUABLE TIPS ABOUT HELICOPTERS AS I KNEW ABSOLUTELY NOTHING ABOUT THEM.
WELL, YOU SEE, WE ALWAYS GET ADVANCED RE-PORTS OF THICK FOG, SO RATHER THAN HAVING THEM BE DETERRED BY ITS SUDDEN APPEARANCE...
I GOT TO RIDE IN A HELICOPTER TOO! IT WAS SCARY BUT AMAZING!
...IT MIGHT BE MORE REALISTIC TO HAVE THEM ALREADY KNOW ABOUT IT, BUT HAVE THE FOG REACH ITS DESTINATION SOONER THAN EXPECTED.
PILOT
AH, YES. NOW I SEE!
ALSO, IT'S ABSOLUTELY REALISTIC FOR A COPTER TO MAKE AN EMERGENCY LANDING AT TOKYO HELIPORT IN A CASE LIKE THAT.
THANK YOU TO MY MOM AND DAD FOR DRIVING US OUT TO CONFIRM THE CAR ROUTE BETWEEN THE HAMADA RIVER AND NARITA AIRPORT.
BISCO! IS IT REALLY OKAY TO LEAVE THE TWINS' HELICOPTER ALL WHITE?
AND THANK YOU TO THE LALA MANGAKA WHO CAME TO HELP BAIL ME OUT WHEN THE REFERENCE PHOTOS DIDN'T COME IN TIME.
YEAH... I'M OUT OF TIME...
OH... NO, I GUESS IT DOES NEED TO BE TONED.
GYAH GYAH
GYAH GYAH
COULD YOU ADD THE SCREEN-TONES FOR ME? I'LL SKETCH A QUICK DESIGN RIGHT NOW!
THANK YOU SO MUCH, EVERY-ONE!!

ABOUT THE SUOH FAMILY

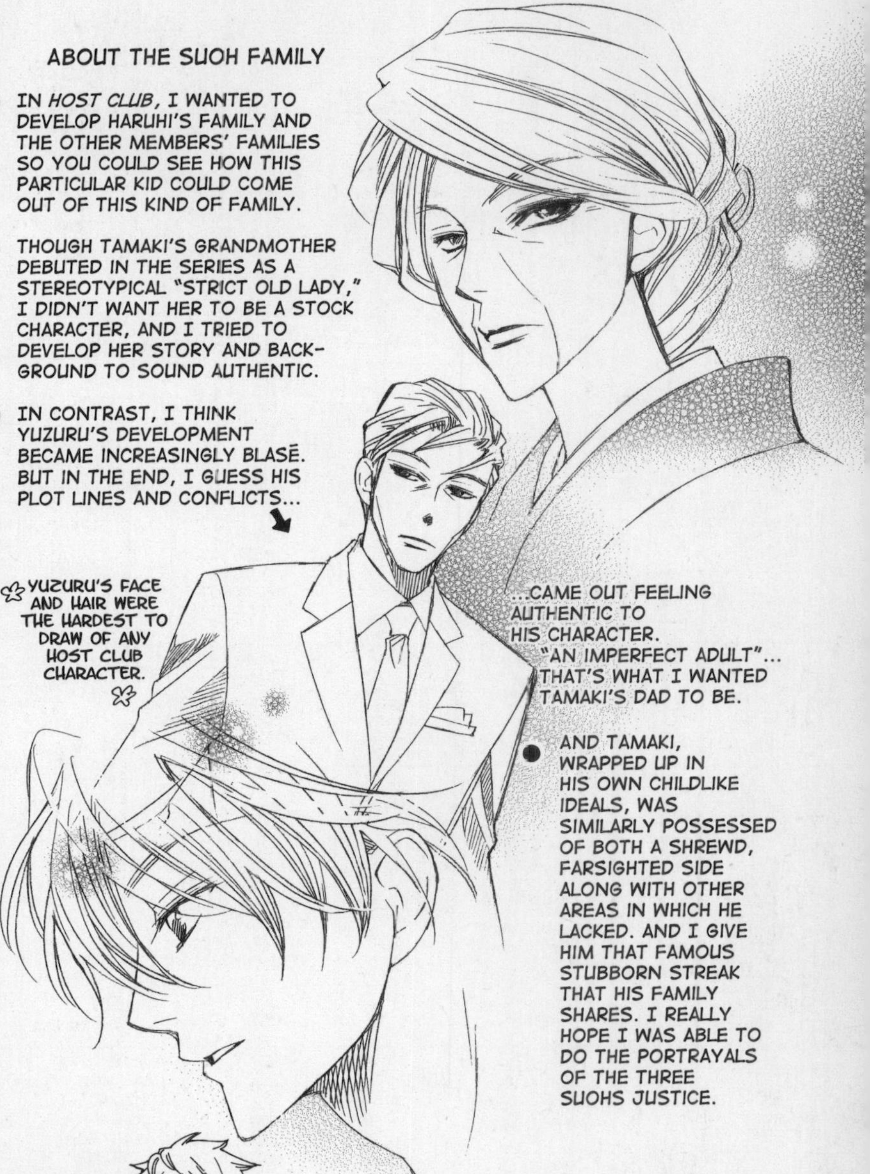

- IN *HOST CLUB*, I WANTED TO DEVELOP HARUHI'S FAMILY AND THE OTHER MEMBERS' FAMILIES SO YOU COULD SEE HOW THIS PARTICULAR KID COULD COME OUT OF THIS KIND OF FAMILY.
- THOUGH TAMAKI'S GRANDMOTHER DEBUTED IN THE SERIES AS A STEREOTYPICAL "STRICT OLD LADY," I DIDN'T WANT HER TO BE A STOCK CHARACTER, AND I TRIED TO DEVELOP HER STORY AND BACKGROUND TO SOUND AUTHENTIC.
- IN CONTRAST, I THINK YUZURU'S DEVELOPMENT BECAME INCREASINGLY BLASÉ. BUT IN THE END, I GUESS HIS PLOT LINES AND CONFLICTS...

...CAME OUT FEELING AUTHENTIC TO HIS CHARACTER.
"AN IMPERFECT ADULT"... THAT'S WHAT I WANTED TAMAKI'S DAD TO BE.

YUZURU'S FACE AND HAIR WERE THE HARDEST TO DRAW OF ANY HOST CLUB CHARACTER.

- AND TAMAKI, WRAPPED UP IN HIS OWN CHILDLIKE IDEALS, WAS SIMILARLY POSSESSED OF BOTH A SHREWD, FARSIGHTED SIDE ALONG WITH OTHER AREAS IN WHICH HE LACKED. AND I GIVE HIM THAT FAMOUS STUBBORN STREAK THAT HIS FAMILY SHARES. I REALLY HOPE I WAS ABLE TO DO THE PORTRAYALS OF THE THREE SUOHS JUSTICE.

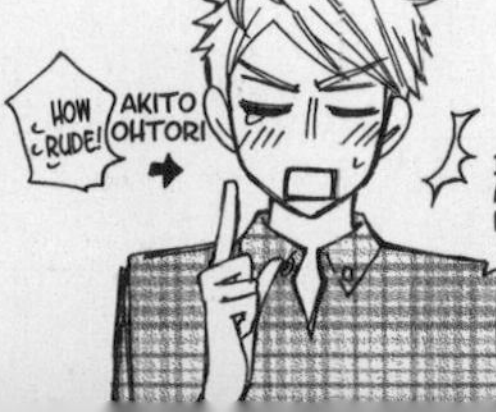
HOW RUDE!
AKITO OHTORI

INCIDENTALLY, THE BIGGEST "STOCK CHARACTER" IN THIS MANGA MUST ABSOLUTELY BE THIS GUY. DESPITE THAT, I (REALLY!) LIKE AKITO. ^^ I KIND OF WANT TO DRAW A 4-KOMA ABOUT HIM.

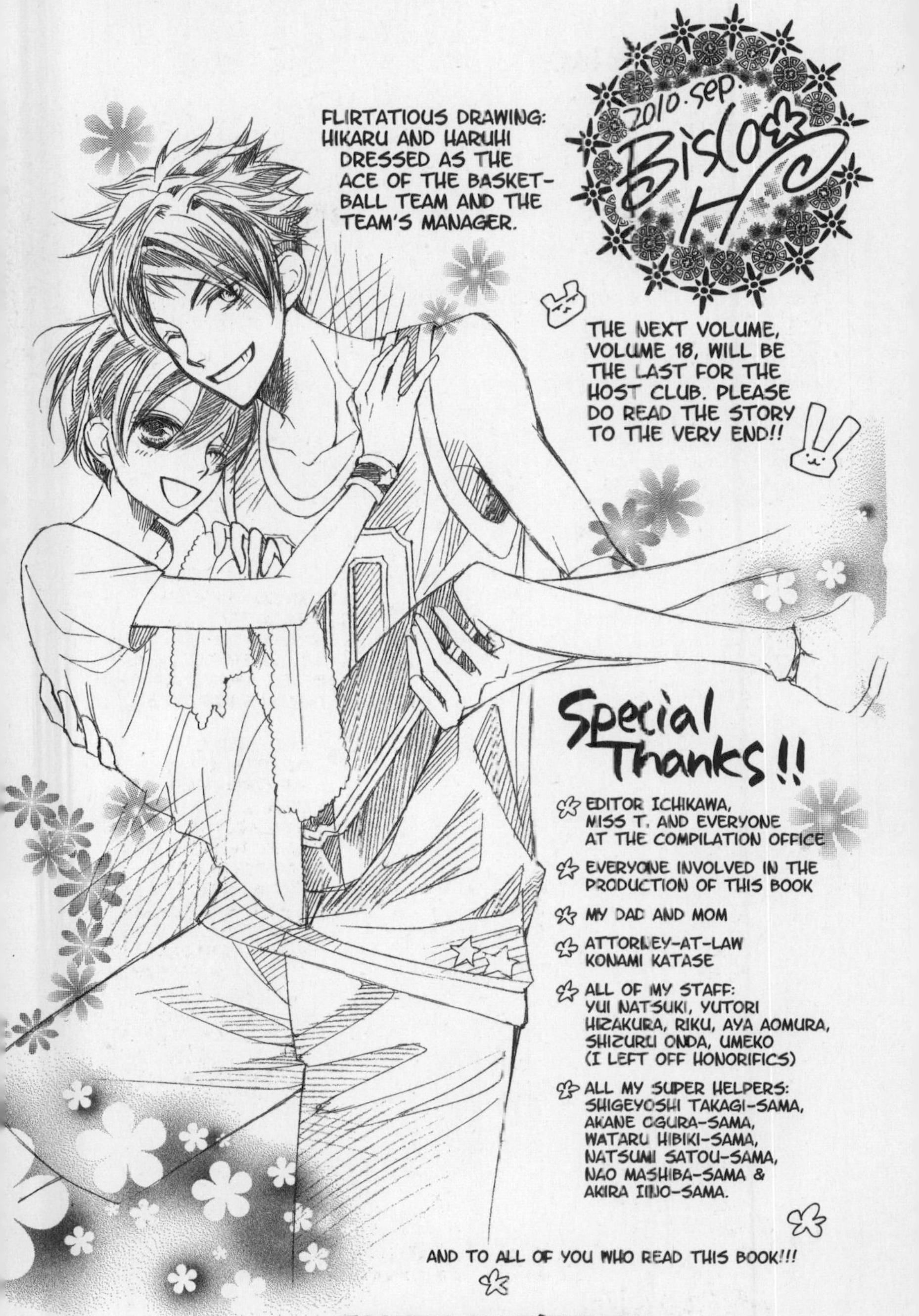
2010.sep.
Bisco Hatori
FLIRTATIOUS DRAWING: HIKARU AND HARUHI DRESSED AS THE ACE OF THE BASKET-BALL TEAM AND THE TEAM'S MANAGER.
THE NEXT VOLUME, VOLUME 18, WILL BE THE LAST FOR THE HOST CLUB. PLEASE DO READ THE STORY TO THE VERY END!!
Special Thanks!!
EDITOR ICHIKAWA, MISS T. AND EVERYONE AT THE COMPILATION OFFICE
EVERYONE INVOLVED IN THE PRODUCTION OF THIS BOOK
MY DAD AND MOM
ATTORNEY-AT-LAW KONAMI KATASE
ALL OF MY STAFF: YUI NATSUKI, YUTORI HIZAKURA, RIKU, AYA AOMURA, SHIZURU ONDA, UMEKO (I LEFT OFF HONORIFICS)
ALL MY SUPER HELPERS: SHIGEYOSHI TAKAGI-SAMA, AKANE OGURA-SAMA, WATARU HIBIKI-SAMA, NATSUMI SATOU-SAMA, NAO MASHIBA-SAMA & AKIRA IIJO-SAMA.
AND TO ALL OF YOU WHO READ THIS BOOK!!!
EGOISTIC CLUB/THE END

EDITOR'S NOTES

EPISODE 76

Page 7: *Bunraku* is a type of traditional Japanese puppetry theatre. The *kashira* are the heads of the puppets. *Bunshichi* is a warrior, and *Yashio* is a female villain.

EPISODE 77

Page 44: An *ikemen* is a handsome, cool guy.

EPISODE 80

Page 162: Comiket is a manga fair held twice a year in Tokyo. Artists sell *doujinshi*, or self-published works.

Author Bio

Bisco Hatori made her manga debut with *Isshun kan no Romance* (**A Moment of Romance**) in *LaLa DX* magazine. The comedy *Ouran High School Host Club* is her breakout hit. When she's stuck thinking up characters' names, she gets inspired by loud, upbeat music (her radio is set to NACK5 FM). She enjoys reading all kinds of manga, but she's especially fond of the sci-fi drama *Please Save My Earth* and *Slam Dunk*, a basketball classic.

OURAN HIGH SCHOOL HOST CLUB
Vol. 17
Shojo Beat Edition

STORY AND ART BY BISCO HATORI

Translation/Su Mon Han
Touch-up Art & Lettering/Gia Cam Luc
Graphic Design/Amy Martin
Editor/Nancy Thistlethwaite

The rights of the author(s) of the work(s) in this publication to be so identified have
been asserted in accordance with the Copyright, Designs and Patents Act 1988. A CIP
catalogue record for this book is available from the British Library.

The stories, characters and incidents mentioned in this publication
are entirely fictional.

Printed in the U.S.A.

Published by VIZ Media, LLC
P.O. Box 77010
San Francisco, CA 94107

10 9 8 7 6 5 4 3 2 1
First printing, December 2011

www.viz.com   www.shojobeat.com

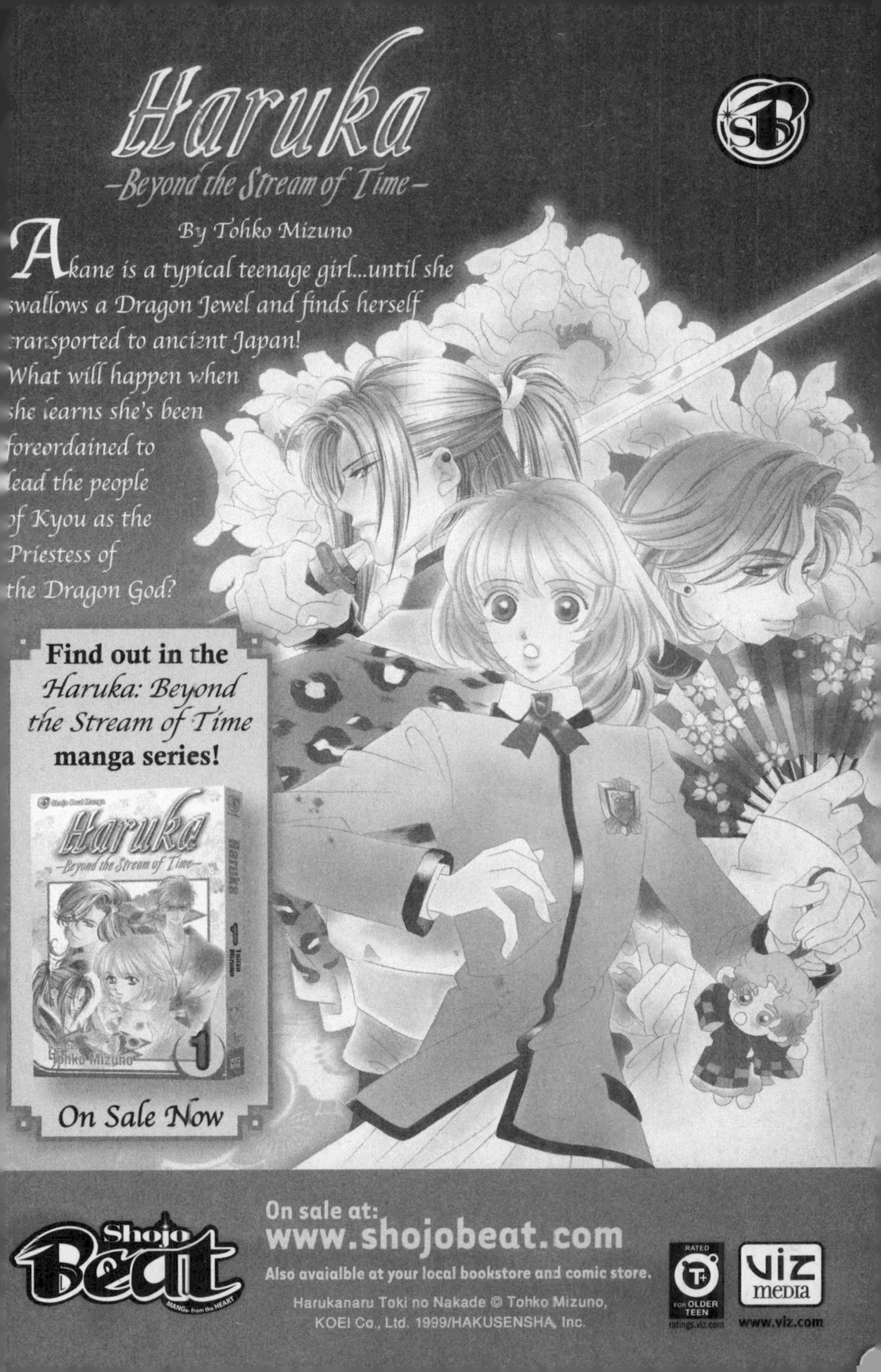
Haruka
-Beyond the Stream of Time-
By Tohko Mizuno
Akane is a typical teenage girl...until she swallows a Dragon Jewel and finds herself transported to ancient Japan! What will happen when she learns she's been foreordained to lead the people of Kyou as the Priestess of the Dragon God?
Find out in the Haruka: Beyond the Stream of Time manga series!
On Sale Now
Shojo Beat
On sale at:
www.shojobeat.com
Also avaialble at your local bookstore and comic store.
Harukanaru Toki no Nakade © Tohko Mizuno, KOEI Co., Ltd. 1999/HAKUSENSHA, Inc.
RATED T+ FOR OLDER TEEN
ratings.viz.com
VIZ media
www.viz.com

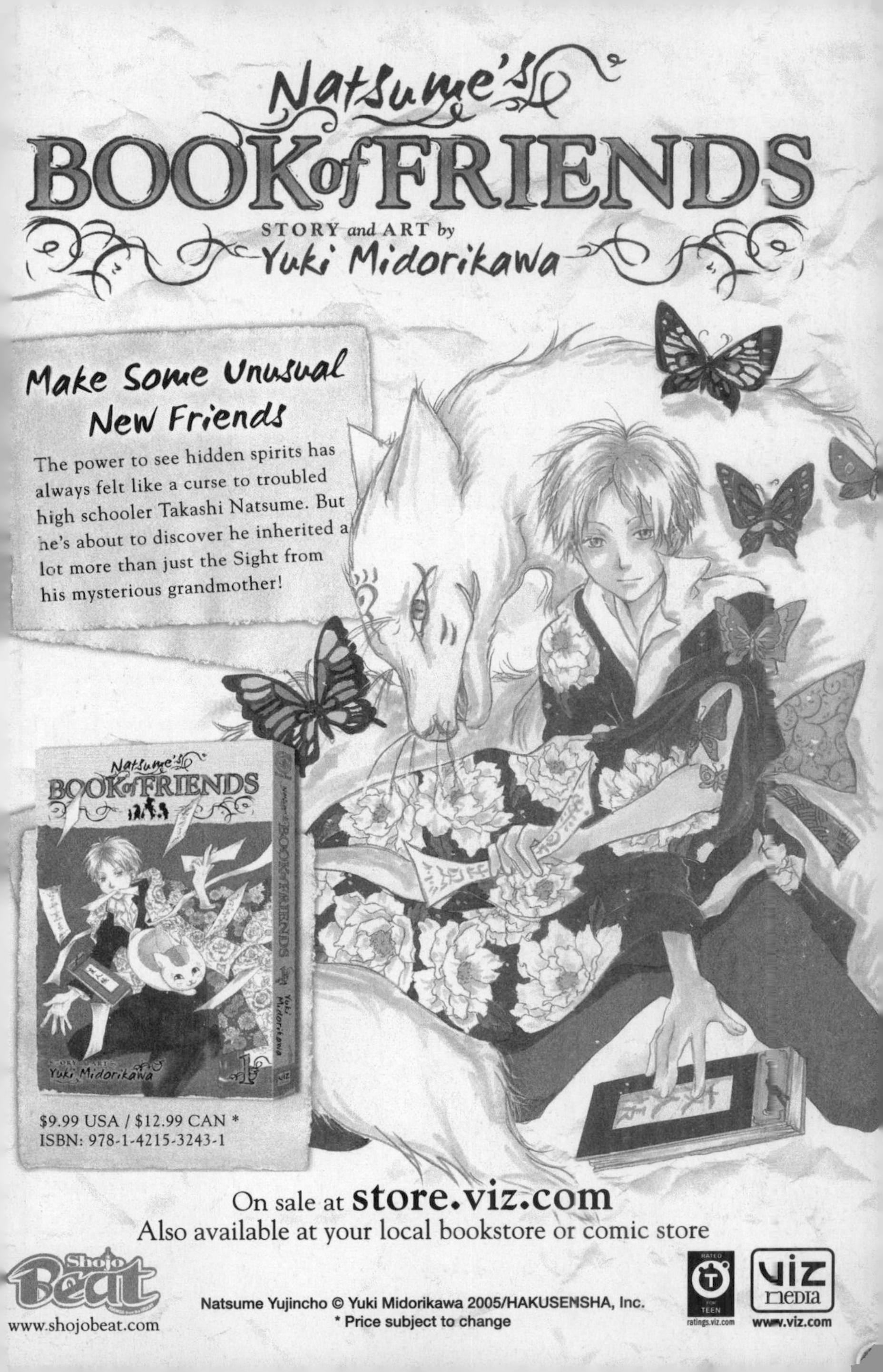
Natsume's BOOK of FRIENDS
STORY and ART by Yuki Midorikawa
Make Some Unusual New Friends
The power to see hidden spirits has always felt like a curse to troubled high schooler Takashi Natsume. But he's about to discover he inherited a lot more than just the Sight from his mysterious grandmother!
Natsume's BOOK of FRIENDS
Yuki Midorikawa
$9.99 USA / $12.99 CAN *
ISBN: 978-1-4215-3243-1
On sale at store.viz.com
Also available at your local bookstore or comic store
Shojo Beat
www.shojobeat.com
Natsume Yujincho © Yuki Midorikawa 2005/HAKUSENSHA, Inc.
* Price subject to change
RATED T FOR TEEN
ratings.viz.com
viz media
www.viz.com